CLASSIC STUDIES IN ABNORMAL PSYCHOLOGY

Classic Studies in Abnormal Psychology

STEVEN SCHWARTZ

University of Queensland, Australia

Mayfield Publishing Company
Mountain View, California
London • Toronto

Library of Congress Cataloging-in-Publication Data

Schwartz, Steven.
    Classic studies in abnormal psychology / Steven Schwartz.
        p.   cm.
    Includes bibliographical references and index.
    ISBN 0-87484-866-0
    1. Psychology, Pathological.   2. Psychiatry.   3. Psychiatry-
-History.   I. Title.
    [DNLM: 1. Mental Disorders.   2. Psychopathology.   WM 100 S399c]
    RC454.S36   1993
    616.89--dc20
    DNLM/DLC
    for Library of Congress   92-49375
                                                                                          CIP

Manufactured in the United States of America
10 9 8 7 6 5 4 3 2 1

Mayfield Publishing Company
1240 Villa Street
Mountain View, California 94041

*Sponsoring editor, Franklin C. Graham; production editor, Lynn Rabin Bauer; manuscript editor,
Margaret Moore; text and cover designer, Joan Greenfield; art editor, Jean Mailander; photo researcher,
Melissa Kreischer; illustrator, Willa Bower; cover art, René Magritte, ''Le Poison,'' (''Poison''), 1939,
gouache, 14 × 16". Giraudon/Art Resource, New York © 1992 C. Herscovici/ARS, New York;
manufacturing manager, Martha Branch. The text was set in 9/11 Palatino by TypeLink, Inc. and
printed on 50# Finch Opaque by Banta Company.*

Acknowledgments and copyrights continue at the back of the book on page 246, which
constitutes an extension of the copyright page.

Once again, for Gregory
As always, for Carolyn

There is properly no history; only biography.
Ralph Waldo Emerson

CONTENTS

PREFACE

This book was born one bitter cold Boston night when Frank Graham, my editor at Mayfield, rang to ask me to write a follow-up to my book, *Classic Studies in Psychology.* The earlier book explored the concepts and methods of scientific psychology by examining 15 classic psychological experiments. The new project would be in the same mold but more specific. It would focus on abnormal psychology. The call came at an exceptionally opportune moment for me. Working at Harvard has its undeniable attractions, but the weather is not one of them. A continuous series of blizzards plagued New England that winter, and an indoor pursuit was just what I needed.

We settled early on a theme—the interaction between the "art" and "science" of psychology. Psychologists are justifiably proud of the progress they have made in the 100 years since their field became an experimental science. In the 1890s, psychologists had barely an inkling of how their profession would develop. Mental hospitals were overcrowded, largely custodial institutions. Neuropsychology barely existed. Psychoanalysis was beginning to emerge, but there were no other psychological treatments, no intelligence tests, no personality tests, no community psychology, and almost nothing was known about psychotropic drugs. Clearly, much has changed in 100 years. Nevertheless, it is overstating the case to attribute our present knowledge about abnormal behavior entirely to controlled research. Clinical observations, especially detailed case studies, have made an equally important contribution. For example, the first descriptions of childhood autism, anorexia nervosa, and Tourette's syndrome were all made by clinicians working with troubled people. Their initial observations were then refined, tested, and extended by scientific research. My goal was to describe and explain this interactive process, to show how clinical art combines with scientific theory and controlled experimentation to advance knowledge.

As in my earlier book, the focus of this book was to be on a small number of landmark studies. Concentrating on relatively few studies was a deliberate departure from the encyclopedic style of abnormal psychology textbooks, which rarely present individual studies in depth. Textbooks tell readers what researchers have done; I wanted to explain why. To do this, I had to include information about the background, rationale, and findings of each research project as well as its place in history and the effect of its findings on subsequent research. To give the reader some idea of what motivates people to devote their lives to scientific research, I also decided to include biographical information about individual researchers. Several criteria were used to select studies for inclusion. At a minimum, they had to be true landmarks that have produced lasting effects on the field. From among these, I chose 20 studies that are entertaining and interesting to all readers—not just psychologists. Some of the studies are experiments, others are case histories, and several are critical literature reviews, but all possess the clarity and insight scientists describe as "elegant." The studies come from all major areas of abnormal psychology and deal with diagnosis, assessment, etiology, and treatment. My desire was to produce an accessible and (with luck) entertaining book, while maintaining scientific accuracy and rigor.

The book begins with an "Introduction" designed to give the reader a sense of how modern ideas about the causes and cures of mental illness evolved over the ages. It also describes the research methods used by scientists and clinicians to reveal the hidden nature of psychopathology. The remainder of the book is divided into four parts: "Assessment and Classification," "Developmental Psychopathology," "Patterns of Psychopathology," and "Psychological Treatment." Each part contains chapters describing relevant classic studies and cases. The chapters are organized historically. That is, the events leading up to each classic study are described first followed by a detailed discussion of the study itself. Each chapter concludes with an "Aftermath" section, which analyzes the effects of the classic study on subsequent research and treatment. Because the chapters were all written to stand alone, instructors can assign them in any order (and even skip some). Sufficient detail has been included to make the book a suitable adjunct to an undergraduate psychopathology course. It may also prove useful to instructors who wish to add a "human" touch to courses on the history of psychology, psychiatry, or nursing. However, because no specific background in psychology is assumed, this volume may appeal not only to students but to anyone interested in psychology in general and psychopathology in particular.

Despite having a detailed plan, a multitude of minor, and a few major, disasters kept popping up to delay the completion of this book. Finally, 1992 brought a rare interval of relative calm and the job was done. It could never have happened without the patience of Frank Graham, the advice of Mandy Little, and the support of many students and colleagues. I am especially grateful for the generous research support provided to me over the years by the Australian Research Council, Australian Academy of Science, British Council, National Health and Medical Research Council, the British Red Cross Society, and the Royal Society. I would also like to acknowledge the helpful advice of my students, colleagues, and the reviewers, Bernardo J. Carducci, Indiana University Southeast; David J. Lutz, Southwest Missouri State University; and Forrest Scogin, University of Alabama, who read earlier drafts of this manuscript. Finally, I must express my appreciation to the devoted scientists and clinicians whose work has done so much to illuminate the nature of abnormal behavior. Without them, there would be no book to write.

CLASSIC STUDIES IN ABNORMAL PSYCHOLOGY

Introduction: Psychopathology and Science

Franz Anton Mesmer was an 18th-century Viennese doctor with celestial interests and astronomical ambitions. He was well known in high society; one of Mozart's operas premiered in the garden of his fashionable home. Unfortunately, Mesmer's thesis, "The Influences of the Planets on the Human Body," was poorly received by the Austrian medical community. (To put it bluntly, the other doctors considered him a quack.) Wounded by the hostile reaction to his work, Mesmer left Vienna for Paris in 1778 where he was an immediate success. The French were particularly taken with his discovery of an invisible magnetic fluid that existed everywhere, even within human bodies. No one, not even Mesmer, could actually see this fluid—after all, it was invisible—but Mesmer justified its existence on theoretical grounds. He argued that planets could not be attracted by gravity if space is a vacuum; there must be some medium or fluid through which forces are transmitted across the universe.

According to Mesmer, human bodies are special types of magnets. Illness occurs when "Universal Magnetic Fluid," the same fluid that holds the planets together, becomes blocked in one of the body's organs. Like water in a clogged pipe, the fluid collects at the blockage causing illness. To restore free circulation, the doctor must force large amounts of magnetic fluid into a patient's body. Once the blockage is cleared, the patient's internal magnetic field is again in harmonious balance with nature and the illness is cured. Mesmer's preferred unclogging technique relied on an invention he called the *baquet*, a tub filled with iron filings and bottles of "mesmerized" water (see Figure I.1). The water bottles were arranged in a circle similar to the spokes of a wheel, and the whole tub was covered with a special lid. The lid contained metal rods that

It is the very error of the moon;
She comes more near the earth than she was wont,
And makes men mad.

—William Shakespeare

FIGURE I.1 Mesmer's patients gathered around the baquet, a tub filled with metal filings, which was designed to concentrate and transmit Universal Magnetic Fluid. Mesmer is pictured at the rear, on the right, holding a wand.

acted as antennae. Mesmer had patients arrange themselves around the baquet to receive the magnetic fluid (which he began to call "animal magnetism") that flowed from the baquet through the antennae and into their bodies. To put patients in the right mood, the baquet was housed in a dimly lit room decorated with astrological symbols. Heavy carpets and drawn curtains were used to silence the external world. Dressed in a lavender cape, Mesmer would circulate among the patients while soft music played in the background. Every so often, he would touch a patient with a special wand. The patient would then fall to the floor writhing and even convulsing. This "crisis" was a sign that the blockage was being cleared.

Mesmer's patients claimed great benefits from their treatment; many were cured of longstanding ailments. The French medical establishment was not so enthusiastic. Like their Viennese colleagues before them, the French doctors began to suspect that Mesmer's methods were nothing but fraud. They convinced the king to establish a royal com-

mission to investigate Mesmer and his methods. The commission contained four doctors. One, the respected Dr. Guillotin, would soon fall victim to his own invention, the guillotine, in the impending revolution. Also included were five members of the Academy of Sciences, one of whom was the American ambassador, the statesman-scientist-philosopher Benjamin Franklin. In addition to listening to expert testimony, the commission decided to conduct a few small experiments. For example, they substituted plain tap water for the mesmerized variety and found that patients still fell into convulsions and still claimed to be cured. Even eliminating the baquet altogether did not affect the cure rate. The commission concluded that Mesmer's Universal Magnetic Fluid existed only in his and his patients' imaginations. The commission admitted that some patients were cured but suggested that they probably had not been physically ill in the first place. Instead, the commission believed that these patients' symptoms were caused by psychological rather than organic factors. Mesmer's treatment was construed as a form of "faith healing," an approach to medicine that pre-dated the baquet and one that remains popular today.

Mesmer was crushed by the commission's findings and quickly disappeared into obscurity, but at least part of his legacy survived. His followers discarded the baquet, emphasizing instead the altered state of consciousness (*mesmeric somnambulism*) their techniques produced in some patients. For example, one of Mesmer's disciples, the Marquis de Puységur, reported putting a shepherd into a trance. The boy then followed any instructions he was given. In the United States, Mary Baker Eddy, the founder of Christian Science, was also put into a trance by one of Mesmer's disciples and cured of a painful condition by suggestion: "When I snap my fingers you will wake up and your pain will be gone." Patients cured this way were said to have been "mesmerized." Mesmerism continued to be practiced for decades after Mesmer's death. It eventually became known as hypnotism, a routine tool in clinical practice.

Mesmerism, at least in its original form, was discredited by the royal commission's scientific studies. It is important to note, however, that the conflict between Mesmer and the royal commission was not about his success in curing patients but whether animal magnetism was the underlying curative mechanism. The commission used scientific methods to assess Mesmer's *theory*, not his results. They found his explanations inadequate and suggested an alternative that was better able to account for all the known facts: Namely, patients were suffering from a psychological illness curable by suggestion. The Mesmer affair was an early illustration of how empirical observations can be used to choose between competing theories — a process that has been repeated many times since. But the royal commission's report was more than just another interesting investigation; it marked a turning point in the history of abnormal psychology. Before the report, it was taken for granted that symptoms always have a physiological cause. The royal commission gave respectability to the notion that at least some illnesses have psychological origins. This important idea was Mesmer's legacy to the field of abnormal psychology. In his own misguided way, Mesmer set the stage for the scientific study of abnormal behavior.

Most modern psychologists believe that the study of abnormal psychology is (or should be) a scientific enterprise. But science does not take place in a vacuum; investigations are carried out in a particular social and scientific environment. The cultural milieu can influence scientific work as much or even more than the scientific theories of the day. Consequently, the landmark studies described in this book are all placed in their historical context. The events and ideas that gave rise to each research program are described in detail. In addition, the aftermath of each study — its impact on subsequent research — is reviewed and evaluated. Because the studies come from many different areas of abnormal psychology, their diversity makes it difficult to see the field in a unified light. The purpose of this introduction is to assist unification by providing a general framework into which the later, more specific, discussions may be incorporated. The introduction begins by explaining why the historical approach is important. This is followed by a brief summary of major historical trends. It is instructive to note how each era approaches abnormal psychology according to the social and cultural values prevalent at the time. The introduction concludes by examining common research techniques and defining important terms.

WHY STUDY THE HISTORY OF PSYCHOPATHOLOGY?

Historical studies of the suffering (pathology) of the mind (psyche), or psychopathology, have always been more interesting to historians than clinicians. There are at least two reasons for this. The first is the abstract nature of historical knowledge. Clinicians tend to be practical people, and most historical knowledge is of little everyday use. No one would claim that a thorough understanding of medieval attitudes toward the mentally ill makes it any easier for a clinician to help a patient overcome a severe depressive episode. A second reason for ignoring the history of psychopathology is that it is so unpleasant. According to physician and essayist Lewis Thomas, "For century after century, all the way to the remote millennia of its origins, medicine got along by sheer guess work and the crudest form of empiricism. It is hard to conceive of a less scientific enterprise among human endeavors."[1] Although

Thomas's judgment applies equally well to abnormal psychology, it does not mean that scientists and clinicians should confine their curiosity solely to present-day knowledge. An ignorance of history guarantees that mistakes made in the past will be repeated in the future.

All psychopathology textbooks—and there are dozens—contain at least one "historical" chapter. Typically, the history of abnormal psychology is portrayed as a reasonably steady progression (albeit with the occasional stumble) from ignorance, superstition, and cruelty to rationality and more humane values. Outmoded, dangerous, and useless treatments are inevitably replaced by newer, more effective, ones so that current practices reflect the cumulative wisdom of the centuries. According to British historian Patricia Allderidge, the received version of psychopathology's history

> runs roughly as follows, give or take a century or two here or there (which is about the accepted level of precision): from the dawn of history, or just before, or just after, until about the middle of the nineteenth century, nothing happened at all: or (depending on *where* you received your version) the mentally disordered were indiscriminately exorcised, or burnt, or left to wander at will, or chained up and beaten, or all four. From the middle of the nineteenth century they were all rounded up and driven into enormous asylums (where, according to a subtle sociological variation, mental illness was invented) and were left to vegetate until the 1950's. Around 1960 dawned the enlightenment, and it was suddenly revealed that everything that had ever happened before—whatever it was—was completely wrong, and probably intentionally malicious too; and over the years following there were gradually also revealed a number of brand new ways of putting it right.[2]

An alternative to the received view is to look on the history of abnormal psychology as a series of attempts to solve essentially the same problems (What is "mental illness"? Is this treatment effective? and so on). These problems represent enduring issues for students of psychopathology; they are present in all eras no matter how dramatically superficial characteristics may change. Each generation of researchers and practitioners attempts to solve these problems using the tools and resources available to them. Often their solutions seem satisfactory for a time, but new problems inevitably develop. For example, during the 19th century, providing large hospitals for patients who could not cope in the community was viewed as a progressive step. Today's concern with individual liberty has led to the closing of large hospitals and the return of patients back to the community. The history of psychopathology appears to proceed in such cycles—ideas appear, fade away, and then reappear—but the basic issues remain unchanged. This is what makes historical study worthwhile. When it comes to psychopathology, there are very few ideas that have not been around at least once before.

PSYCHOPATHOLOGY BEFORE MESMER

References to what is known today as "mental illness" can be found even among prehistoric artifacts. It is likely, however, that early civilizations did not make a great distinction between physical and mental illness. All illness was thought to be caused by demons; mental illness occurred when these evil spirits happened to get into the brain. The belief in demonology and other mystical forces was challenged as early as 400 B.C. by Hippocrates and his contemporaries. During a time of great advances under the Greek and Roman civilizations, they suggested that mental illness (defined relatively narrowly by today's usage) was caused by diseases of the brain and should be treated no differently from other diseases. Comforting and relaxing treatments were favored *for those who could afford them.* This point is well worth emphasizing; only the important citizens of classical Greece and Rome were the recipients of humanitarian treatment. The poor, foreigners, and most minorities were not so lucky. They were likely to find themselves shunned, banished, or even forced into slavery. Throughout history, including the present, people from different social classes have received different types and quality of care. Providing humane treatment for all who require help is a perennial problem for those working in abnormal psychology.

The Hippocratic approach, especially the notion of the four humors, was elaborated by the great classical physician, Galen. The basic idea was that health requires a balance of four types of bodily fluids called the humors. Blood, choler, melancholer, and phlegm were all present in the body; the

FIGURE I.2 Each of the four humors produced a different personality. From left: sanguine, melancholic, choleric, and phlegmatic.

relative proportions of each determined an individual's personality (see Figure I.2). Thus, a "phlegmatic" (calm) person had too much phlegm and a melancholic (depressed) person had too much melancholer. Clearly, the theory of humors was partly designed to explain individual differences in behavior. Our modern approach would be to attribute behavioral differences to psychological traits. For example, we interpret a lively, outgoing person's behavior as a sign of *extroversion.* Explaining personality differences is another enduring issue in the history of abnormal psychology.

According to Galen, psychological illness resulted from an excessively abnormal imbalance of humors. Excess phlegm produced fatigue and apathy. Depression resulted when the brain filled with melancholer. Galen recommended special diets and purges to reduce or increase one or more of the humors thereby restoring balance. His ideas, and the treatments derived from them, lasted for centuries. As recently as 1795, the famous American doctor Benjamin Rush still advised bleeding "excited" patients to rid their brains of excess blood.

Just to prove that there are few new ideas in psychopathology, Galen believed that at least some conditions were not the result of humor imbalance but of psychological conflicts and desires. These conditions could be identified by careful, controlled observation. Consider, for example, Galen's approach to a woman who came to him complaining of sleeplessness, fatigue, and generally feeling unwell:

> After I had diagnosed that there was no bodily trouble, and that the woman was suffering from some mental uneasiness . . . somebody came from the theater and said he had seen Pylades dancing. Then both her expression and the colour of her face changed. Seeing this, I applied my hand to her wrist, and noticed that her pulse had suddenly become extremely irregular. This kind of pulse indicates that the mind is disturbed; thus it occurs also in people who are disputing over any subject. So on the next day I said to one of my followers that, when I paid my visit to the woman, he was to come a little later and announce to me, "Morphus is dancing today." When he said this, I found that the pulse was unaffected. . . . On the fourth evening I kept very careful watch when it was announced that Pylades was dancing, and I noticed that the pulse was very much disturbed. Thus I found out that the woman was in love with Pylades, and by careful watch on the succeeding days my discovery was confirmed.[3]

Galen's enlightened approach to psychological distress remained dominant among the Arabian civilizations even after the Fall of Rome. In Europe, however, the Middle Ages saw the return to demonology. The destruction of the economic system, the decline in commerce and trade, and a loss of belief in the established social order all produced a sense of helplessness in medieval Europe, a climate that breeds superstition. Anything that could be construed as "different" was suspect. For example, even a hint of a lack of faith in the religious orthodoxy of the time or any objection to the rulers of the community could be interpreted as a sign of mental derangement. Those judged deranged were turned over to the clergy who, in collusion with the secular authorities, contrived to punish the agents of the devil by burning them at the stake or otherwise disposing of them. The practice of burning "witches" continued for 1,000 years and did not completely die out until the 18th century. Of course, not all mentally disturbed persons were dealt with in this manner nor were all of those punished suffering from psychopathology. Accusations of mental illness or demonic possession were often used by the authorities to suppress their enemies and retain power. Labeling those who disagree as "mentally deranged" is still a popular approach to controlling dissent in totalitarian countries, and it is not unheard of in Western democracies, either.

The many dangers of medieval life and the uncertainties of existence led to aberrations of behavior appropriate to that precarious time. For example, the curious phenomenon Saint Vitus' Dance would engulf the entire population of a village. The inhabitants would throw off their clothing, roll on the ground, bang their heads, and scream incessantly — a form of mass hysteria unlikely to be seen on such a scale today. On the other hand, it is likely that many of the aberrations seen by modern psychologists were unheard of in the Middle Ages. Whatever psychopathology might be, it is definitely not culture-free.

Cultural influences also affected our medieval ancestors' attitudes toward psychological problems in childhood. Put simply, these problems were largely ignored. The entire notion of childhood as a separate developmental stage, different from adulthood, was foreign to them. Paintings and sculptures portrayed children as little adults differing from their parents only in size and strength. There were no special children's games or literature; children were mainly a labor resource to be exploited by

stronger adults. It is possible that high infant mortality (as late as 1750 the odds were still three to one against a newborn living past age 5) may have kept parents from becoming too attached to their children. Still, even when economic conditions improved, attitudes toward child welfare were slow to change. It was not until the 19th century that the Society for the Prevention of Cruelty to Children was founded — an offshoot of the older Society for the Prevention of Cruelty to Animals. As recently as 1959, the United Nations found it necessary to pass a resolution confirming that human rights belong to children as well as adults.

Demonology went into decline in the 17th century, but many disturbed individuals, especially the poor, were still abused, locked in cellars, and kept in chains. In psychopathology, treatment is very much a creature of the social milieu. Treatments changed slowly in the 17th and 18th centuries because cultures changed slowly. The greatest progress occurred in those countries whose cultures, marked by revolution, changed most rapidly: America and France. Both countries revolted against elitist monarchies; democracy and social egalitarianism were widely espoused. The introduction of hospitals and asylums for the mentally ill was not the result of new psychological discoveries but of changed political attitudes, especially the belief that the state had a responsibility for the welfare of its citizens.

The state's responsibility to its citizens did not extend to making them comfortable. State hospitals were squalid, degrading, and terribly overcrowded (see Figure I.3). Students, and even curious visitors, could examine patients at will; those who complained were immediately discharged. When a patient died — an all too frequent occurrence — his or her family were obliged to pay for the burial. If they could not afford this, the body would be used for dissection. Private care was better but too expensive for all but the wealthiest class.

By the end of the 18th century, the pace of scientific progress began to accelerate. The germ theory of disease was still a way off, but physical etiologies were discovered for many derangements of behavior — alcoholic psychosis, senile psychosis, and general paresis (the final stage of syphilis). Even the notorious "mad hatters" of *Alice in Wonderland* fame were found to be suffering from nervous system damage caused by the mercury used to treat the felt

FIGURE I.3 A scene in the hospital known as Bedlam taken from Hogarth's "The Rake's Progress." Note the two women in the background are upper-class visitors on a sightseeing excursion.

from which hats were manufactured. Eighteenth-century medicine was a major success story, but there were some holdovers from the past. Weird theories, such as the belief that the moon drives people mad (the word *lunatic* is derived from *luna*, the Latin word for "moon"), and even stranger treatments (cupping, bleeding, purging) were still accepted as if they had some basis in fact (see Figure I.4). Anything that could be dreamed up was given a try (Mesmer's baquet, for example); it did not seem to matter that practically all treatments were demonstrably worthless and that some were worse than the conditions they were designed to cure.

By the turn of the century, it became apparent that many patients were not responding to treatment. Moreover, some patients who were clearly in distress did not appear to be suffering from any physical disease. Despite valiant attempts and numerous autopsies of the brains of deranged patients, scientists failed to find a physical cause for most psychological problems. Yet clinicians and scientists could think of little to do but keep looking. It

took Mesmer's odd treatments, and the royal commission's report, to draw attention back to what Galen knew 1,600 years earlier: Some apparently physical ailments may have a psychological origin.

FROM MESMERISM TO PSYCHOGENESIS

Doctors in ancient Greece were intrigued. Patients were appearing with mysterious aches and pains, voice loss, headaches, sleeplessness, deafness, blindness, lameness, paralysis, and depression, yet there appeared to be no clear-cut physical cause for their afflictions. Most of these patients were unmarried or widowed women; the doctors were men. In what was to become almost a tradition in medicine, the Greek doctors blamed the illness on gender. The reason women were ill was because they were women. They suffered from a malady from which men were immune: a roaming *hystera*, or womb. Greek doctors believed that the uterus could detach itself from its usual site and go searching for

FIGURE I.4 Any bizarre treatment that could be dreamed up was given a try—for example, treating depression by spinning the patient in a rotating chair.

oped. By 1807 there were 37,000 hospital beds in Paris alone. In comparison, in the same year, *all* of Britain contained a total of only 5,000 beds. By the middle of the 19th century, Paris became the undisputed medical center of Europe attracting visitors and students from all over the world. Jean Charcot directed the neurology service at one of the largest French hospitals, La Salpêtrière. Six thousand female patients resided in the hospital; about 10% were considered to be ''mental'' patients. Many of these suffered from hysteria.

Charcot was puzzled by the peculiar symptoms displayed by hysterical patients. For example, some of his patients complained that they had no feeling in one or both hands (*glove anesthesia*) but had perfectly normal feeling from the wrist up into the arm. Because the nerves that detect pain in the hands also extend to the arms, it is anatomically impossible to lose feeling only from the wrist down. Nevertheless, Charcot was convinced that hysteria had to be a form of neurological illness. The problem, Charcot argued, was clearly not in the lower nerves but in the brains of hysterical patients. Their brains had somehow lost the ability to interpret signals from the sensory nerves. Not all of his students and colleagues were convinced, but Charcot was a fierce and impatient teacher and not easily swayed in his beliefs. Perhaps this is why his students decided to fool him by hypnotizing a female patient and having her mimic neurological symptoms. Charcot examined the patient but was unable to tell that she was not really a hysteric. He was shocked when he learned how easily hysterical symptoms could be produced and removed by suggestion. Many similar demonstrations eventually led Charcot to abandon his earlier view in favor of the royal commission's idea that hysteria is not a physical illness at all but a psychological condition. His prestige ensured that *psychogenesis* (the theory that at least some behavioral problems have a psychological etiology) would be taken seriously by the medical establishment.

One of Charcot's students, Pierre Janet, made a career of studying hysteria, which he also construed as a psychological disorder. According to Janet, the hysteric seeks to drive unacceptable thoughts from consciousness by transforming them into symptoms. Another of Charcot's students, Sigmund Freud, was impressed with Janet's ideas but did not get a chance to put them into practice until many

nourishment. If it came to rest in the liver, it would affect that organ; if it stopped at the heart, other symptoms would be produced. The Greeks called the illness *hysteria* because of its supposedly gynecological origin. Over the years, doctors slowly discarded the literal notion of a traveling womb focusing instead on the organ's function. Hysteria, they believed, was the result of a malfunctioning or inadequate sexual organ (or, later, an inadequate or malfunctioning sex life).

Hysteria remained a background preoccupation of doctors for the next 1,800 years. It took on a more important role in medical thinking after the royal commission investigating mesmerism suggested that at least some hysterics were suffering from a psychological illness that could be cured by psychological means. Mesmerism, later called hypnosis, became a semirespectable method of medical treatment. It did not become fully respectable, however, until it was used to deceive the leading French neurologist, Jean Martin Charcot.

The French Revolution and subsequent wars produced a need for new hospitals to treat and rehabilitate the wounded. These were rapidly devel-

years later when he returned to Vienna to work with the well-known Austrian doctor Josef Breuer. Breuer was treating a young woman who had presented with an array of hysterical symptoms. Her legs and one arm were paralyzed, and she would periodically lose her sight and hearing. Breuer hypnotized the woman and encouraged her to speak freely of her past and feelings. Her symptoms receded. Breuer concluded that reliving past events allowed patients to release bottled-up psychic tension, a process called *catharsis*. In 1895 Breuer and Freud published several case histories under the title *Studies in Hysteria*. This book marked the beginning of Freud's long and productive career. One hundred years after the Mesmer royal commission issued its findings, the radical idea that illnesses can have a psychological origin was on the threshold of acceptance.

As might be expected, psychologists were quick to embrace the psychogenesis concept. But, in contrast to Freud and his colleagues, many questioned the importance of unconscious conflicts and the value of catharsis. Instead, they viewed abnormal behavior as faulty habits that had somehow been learned and that could be "unlearned" given the right conditions. This view reached its apotheosis in the early part of the 20th century when the American behaviorist John Watson showed how procedures derived from Ivan Pavlov's studies of the conditioned reflex could produce neurotic behavior in an otherwise normal child. Later, Watson's most famous disciple, Harvard psychologist B. F. Skinner, entered Watson's approach by demonstrating how other, more flexible types of learning could modify undesirable behavior. Watson, Skinner, and their followers view most forms of psychopathology not as the work of mysterious demons or as manifestations of nervous disease but as the result of experience. Treatment does not require exorcism, torture, or surgery; what is required are new, carefully controlled experiences.

Although psychogenesis is now firmly established, late-20th-century researchers have rediscovered that some psychopathologies can be successfully treated with drugs and other physiological interventions. "Rediscovered" is the correct word because even these treatments are not entirely new. Some "modern" drugs (*reserpine*, for example) have been around for years in herbal form (*rau-*

wolfia). Convulsions, sleep treatments, and physiological treatments also have a long Nevertheless, it is fair to say that we are now witnessing a revival of *biogenesis* (the theory that behavior disorders have biological etiologies). The swing back to biogenesis is consistent with the historical pattern. Biogenesis gives way to psychogenesis, which is replaced by biogenesis, and so on. At present, the cycle appears to be a point midway between the two extreme positions. Drug researchers are developing safer, more effective medications than those previously available. At the same time, psychological researchers are producing efficient and specific psychotherapies. The neurophysiological causes of serious disorders such as schizophrenia and infantile autism are beginning to be revealed while the effects of psychological stress on emotional and physical well-being are also widely acknowledged. Many psychopathology researchers have adopted an explicitly "bio-psychological" position that recognizes both biological and psychological factors as essential to any explanation of psychopathology.

Abnormal psychology is not yet a fully matured science; no single theoretical view is dominant. Instead, the field is characterized by a variety of paradigms all vying for acceptance. The result is markedly divergent interpretations of the same set of facts. The current eclecticism may appear confusing to those outside the field, but competition among rival scientific viewpoints does not cause scientists much concern. They take it as a sign that psychopathology remains an intellectually challenging research field. This does not mean that all theories of psychopathology are equally valid. Science progresses by exchanging outmoded theories for more useful ones. The remainder of this chapter is concerned with the process by which this occurs.

PARADIGMS IN ABNORMAL PSYCHOLOGY

Scientists, whatever their field, share a basic set of values about how knowledge should be gained and verified. All researchers believe that theories should make testable predictions and that findings should be repeatable. Most also acknowledge the need to ensure that their observations are carefully controlled. Interestingly, these common values do not ensure that scientists will all agree about what research results mean.

Science develops through an evolutionary (some might say revolutionary) process. At various periods in the development of a discipline, a particular method or theory is dominant. Research techniques associated with this theory become "standard," and scientists become quite conformist in their behavior. Such periods last until a major change occurs and a widely held theory is replaced with another, incompatible one. In the physical sciences, pioneers such as Newton and Einstein were responsible for drastic changes of this sort. Thomas Kuhn, a well-known philosopher and historian of science, refers to the drastic changes in outlook that characterize the history of science as "paradigm shifts."

A paradigm is a conceptual framework within which a scientist works. It consists of a set of basic assumptions that specify which questions are worth studying, what types of explanation are legitimate, and which methods should be used to collect data. Clearly, a shared paradigm aids progress by facilitating communication among scientists; it ensures that those working in a field "speak the same language." But paradigms can also retard progress by restricting scientists' thinking to the currently dominant view. Consider, for example, the clash between the earth-centered and sun-centered paradigms in astronomy.

Like most classical astronomers, Claudius Ptolemaeus, or Ptolemy, was also an astrologer. Notions such as planets "ascendant" in some lunar "house" and the "Age of Aquarius" come from Ptolemy, who believed that not only human behavior but also physical appearance and national character are determined by the stars. To further his astrological work, Ptolemy named the visible stars, worked out how to predict eclipses, and set out a reasonably detailed proof that the earth was round (1,300 years before Columbus). While watching the skies each night, Ptolemy struggled to develop a conceptual model that would explain planetary motions. Because the Earth seemed to be immobile, Ptolemy believed that the Earth is the center of the universe. He was certain that the stars, moon, and planets all go around a stationary Earth. But he noted that some planets moved in mysterious ways, wandering from one constellation to another and, in the case of Mars, sometimes even reversing direction. To explain this erratic movement, Ptolemy de-

vised a model of the universe that had each planet rotating around invisible spheres. The spheres had other spheres attached to them, and each rotated at a different speed. One sphere would turn, the attached sphere would rotate, and from Earth, planets could appear to sometimes be going backward.

Ptolemy's model of the universe permitted astronomers to predict planetary motions so well that, for centuries, those working in the Ptolemaic "paradigm" never considered that the same data could be better explained by assuming that the planets orbit around the sun. Instead, astronomers just kept adding spheres within spheres to make the Ptolemaic paradigm fit their observations. This went on for 1,400 years until the medieval Polish astronomer Nicholas Copernicus proposed an alternative, sun-centered theory. Copernicus did not have access to any new facts, nor was his original theory better able to predict what was then known about planetary movements than the classical model of the solar system. His reason for rejecting the Ptolemaic paradigm was that the traditional model of the solar system was more complicated than one which had the sun at the center. In other words, Copernicus preferred his sun-centered theory not because it was better able to explain the available data but because its explanation seemed subjectively more plausible than Ptolemy's alternative. Copernicus's theory, which reduced the Earth to just one more planet orbiting the sun, annoyed the Catholic church, which put his works on their list of forbidden books until 1835. The clash between these two paradigms caused deep rifts in science and religion that would not be healed for many years.

This astronomical example demonstrates how paradigms can bias the way facts are interpreted. Pre-Copernican astronomers interpreted their observations to fit the theory that the planets revolve around the Earth. Post-Copernican astronomers interpreted the same facts in a different way. In psychopathology, a variety of paradigms exist simultaneously. The result: many different ways of viewing the same problem. Consider, for example, the common childhood problem of bed-wetting, or enuresis. Very young children all wet their beds. When this behavior persists beyond early childhood, parents often seek advice from professionals. If the person they consult is a follower of Freud, they are likely to be told that the bed-wetting is a symbolic symptom of a deep-seated psychological conflict. For example, according to Otto Fenichel, a well-known Freudian, enuresis "represents a substitute and equivalent of suppressed masturbation." That is, the child wishes to masturbate but represses this desire out of guilt and wets the bed instead.

Because they see enuresis as a symptom, Freudian psychologists seek to treat the underlying disturbance rather than the bed-wetting itself. Using a medical analogy, they argue that treating the actual bed-wetting is like bathing a feverish patient in ice water. The patient's fever will diminish, but whatever is causing the fever will remain unaffected. The patient is still sick, so we can expect other symptoms to develop until the underlying illness is cured. Freudians contend that treating bed-wetting directly is similarly futile because the symptom's cause — the underlying sexual conflict — remains unaffected. They argue that successful treatment requires uncovering and resolving the child's unconscious guilt feelings about sex and masturbation. If the underlying conflict is not resolved, other symptoms are sure to develop. This prediction is known as the *symptom-substitution* hypothesis.

In contrast to the Freudian view, behavioral psychologists look on enuresis not as a symptom of some underlying conflict but as a failure to learn. They argue that toilet training requires a child to learn to respond to bladder stimulation not with the reflexive response of elimination but with a series of steps that lead to the toilet. If, for some reason, this series of steps is not learned, enuresis is the result. Because they see enuresis as faulty habit-learning, behaviorists reject the idea that bed-wetting is a symbolic symptom of an underlying conflict. Their preferred mode of treatment ignores unconscious feelings. Instead, treatment is designed to inculcate proper elimination habits. For many children, a simple device consisting of a rubber sheet and bell that rings with the first drop of urine has proven to be a fast method for the elimination of nocturnal bed-wetting.

The Freudian and behavioral paradigms construe the same problem very differently. One sees the etiology of enuresis as an unconscious conflict, the other blames faulty learning. One recommends psychotherapy to resolve the underlying disturbance, the other views conditioning as the treatment of choice. Is there a way to choose between the two? The answer is yes. We can study children treated behaviorally and find out whether they develop new symptoms as the Freudians predict. Such studies have been conducted by several psychologists. All failed to confirm the symptom-substitution hypothesis. On the contrary, the elimination of bed-wetting was found to produce unexpected positive effects. Brothers and sisters ceased their ridicule, mothers were no longer angry about having to change the sheets. Instead of symptom substitution, treating bed-wetting alone resulted in an improvement in overall psychological adjustment. Thus, data collected from behaviorally treated children failed to support the symptom-substitution hypothesis. Empirical tests of hypotheses are the engine of scientific progress. As data accumulate, theories are modified and, eventually, paradigms fall. Testing theories and hypotheses is the main work of scientists. Some of the methods they use are described in the next section.

RESEARCH METHODS IN PSYCHOPATHOLOGY

In its most basic sense, the term *science* simply means knowledge. Given such a broad definition, any organized body of knowledge is technically a science. But most lay persons, and many scientists, have adopted a more restrictive definition. For them, scientific knowledge comes from laboratory-based experiments, as in chemistry and the other physical sciences. They find it difficult to think of abnormal psychology as scientific because psychology laboratories bear little resemblance to those depicted in science fiction films. There are no mysterious white liquids bubbling in glass beakers and, often, no technicians in white coats. Nevertheless, modern abnormal psychology is a scientific enterprise with its own theories and research techniques. These range from careful case descriptions to full-scale experiments. Some of the most commonly used research methods are described in this section.

Naturalistic observation — observing phenomena as they occur in nature — is the most prevalent scientific method. In some sciences (astronomy, for example), it is the only method. A special type of naturalistic observation with a long history in clinical psychology is the case study. A complete case study includes information on a person's family history, early development as well as specific details about the current problem. Intensive studies of individual cases have played a central role in clinical research. The first mention of many important disorders (early infantile autism, for instance) occurred in case studies. Several landmark case studies are described in this book.

Although they have given rise to important research programs, as research tools, case studies have serious shortcomings. The main problem is one of limited generality. Because case studies, by definition, involve only one patient, it is impossible to know whether a case study's findings apply to other patients or whether the particular case is unique. To illustrate the problem, imagine that you are a psychologist interviewing a woman who has been accused of abusing her child. During the interview, you discover that the woman herself was abused as a child. It is possible that a history of having been abused predisposes people to become abusers themselves. On the other hand, this woman's history may be unique. It is not possible, from the case history alone, to decide which of these two possibilities is correct. Case studies are invaluable sources of hypotheses about the causes and treatment of psychopathology, but other types of research are required to generalize these hypotheses beyond the specific case.

The most common approach to generalizing hypotheses is to study more than one individual. To continue with our earlier example, you could examine the histories of a large number of people accused of child abuse. If many report having been abused children themselves, you would be more certain that the case study was not unique. The data show that there is a relationship (known as a *correlation*) between two *variables*: child abuse and a reported history of having been abused. It would be tempting to conclude that abuse received as a child causes people to become child abusers; unfortunately, such a conclusion would not be warranted. The problem is that a correlation between two variables does not mean that one causes the other. Guilt about their behavior may have led child abusers to exaggerate the abuse they received as children thereby producing a spurious relationship. Alternatively, their reports of early abuse may be accurate, but some third factor may be responsible for the apparent relationship with later child abuse. For example, a psychologically disturbed, excessively violent child may elicit strong physical punishment from his or her parents. The same child may grow up to be an equally violent adult who abuses children. In such cases, abuse as a child is not the cause of the adult behavior; the individual's psychological disturbance is responsible for both.

Although correlations cannot be used to infer that one variable causes another, they may be of value in predicting one variable from knowledge of another, correlated variable. For example, within broad limits, school performance may be predicted from a child's IQ score. Children with high scores should, in general, get better school grades than children with low IQ scores. Such predictions are clearly useful, but predictions based solely on correlational relationships can sometimes be misleading. For example, just because we have found a relationship between child abuse and a history of abuse does not mean that abused children will grow up to be child abusers themselves. The relationship was established by studying only accused child abusers. We do not know how many nonabusing adults were abused as children nor do we know whether those abusers who have not been caught were abused as children. Without this information, we cannot make confident predictions about whether abused children will grow up to become child abusers.

The best way to be certain that one variable causes another is to perform a controlled experiment. In an experiment, psychologists manipulate one variable and observe any changes produced in the other. Experimenters call the variable they manipulate the *independent variable*; the one they observe is known as the *dependent variable*. For example, it has been suggested that "hyperactivity" (a childhood syndrome characterized by a high level of motor activity and a short attention span) is the result of eating certain foods. An experimenter who wishes to study the effect of diet on children's behavior can assign children to different diets (independent variable) and observe the effect of each diet on the children's activity level (dependent variable). To be certain that diet alone is responsible for any observed changes in behavior, the experimenter must ensure that any extraneous factors that could affect activity level are *controlled*.

At the very minimum, the children must all have had comparable activity levels before the experiment started. If the children were different at the outset, then the experimenter would be unable to claim that the diets were responsible for any ob-

WHEN CORRELATION DOES NOT IMPLY CAUSATION

All psychologists are taught that a correlation between two variables does not imply that one causes the other. But what happens when two variables are not correlated? Is it safe to assume that no causal relationship exists? The answer, unfortunately, is no. Psychologists Robin Hogarth and the late Hillel Einhorn provide the following example.

Suppose some prehistoric cave dwellers have somehow generated the hypothesis that intercourse causes pregnancy. To test this hypothesis, the cave dwellers design an experiment in which 100 females are randomly assigned to an intercourse condition and another 100 are kept celibate. With the passage of time, 20 women in the intercourse condition

become pregnant and 80 do not. Of the 100 females in the celibacy condition, 5 females become pregnant and 95 do not. (These five women represent mistakes in data recording, faulty memory, and biased reporting—all inevitable when doing research with human beings.) Thus, at the end of the experiment, the cave dwellers find only a modest correlation between intercourse and pregnancy. They conclude that the two are practically unrelated.

This example, although meant to be facetious, reminds us that we must take great care when drawing conclusions from correlational data. High correlations do not imply causation nor does causation imply a high correlation.

---

served differences in activity level. Comparability can be ensured by "matching" children in the diet groups or, more commonly, by randomly assigning children to diets. The experimenter must also make certain the diets are equally nutritious and palatable. If one tastes better than the other, this factor alone may produce changes in children's behavior. These are only minimum requirements for a valid experiment. To further ensure the integrity of the experiment, the expected outcome must be kept secret from the children and their parents. If the experimenter lets parents know which diet is expected to reduce hyperactive behavior, they may unwittingly demand better behavior from children. In such a case, parental demands, not the diet, may be responsible for behavioral improvements. (Expectations are not just a problem for psychological research. To rule out the effect of patient expectations, pharmaceutical researchers often compare new drugs to *placebos*—chemically inactive substances designed to look like the real drugs.) An experiment's value is directly proportional to how thoroughly extraneous variables are controlled. Because there are so many extraneous factors that can affect behavior, psychologists must be even more concerned with controls than other scientists. Failure to control an important factor can lead to the misinterpretation of experimental results.

Experiments can be performed in the laboratory or in naturalistic settings. Often the same phenomena can be studied in both ways. For example, we can study the odd language used by some schizophrenic patients by inviting patients (and control subjects) to the laboratory, administering a set of language tests, and noting their relative performance. Alternatively, we can observe the way patients and control subjects use language in the hospital and other "natural" settings. Each approach has its advantages and disadvantages. Knowledge gained in artificial laboratory settings may not apply when other influences, such as those present in the hospital, are permitted to operate. On the other hand, the uncontrolled variables of the natural environment may make naturalistic observations difficult to interpret. When planning their research, scientists must decide whether the increased control provided by a laboratory experiment outweighs the greater generality gained from naturalistic investigations. Research always involves a trade-off between control and generalizability.

Carefully controlled experiments are the best test of a scientific hypothesis, but they are not always feasible. No one would suggest, for example, that randomly chosen children be subjected to child abuse to see whether they grow up to be child abusers. "Analogue" experiments using animals are sometimes possible, but designing an appropriate animal analogue for human psychopathology research is often impossible. Moreover, research ethics forbid subjecting animals to unnecessarily harmful procedures. Thus, for many problems in psychopathology, the correlational approach is the only practical one. In some cases, however, a *longitudinal* study may offer a useful alternative. Longitudinal studies examine a group of individuals over an extended period of time. Because the same people are observed at each stage, longitudinal studies provide information about the development of psychopathology that is not available any other way. For example, it has been observed that children with schizophrenic mothers are more likely to develop schizophrenia themselves than children with nonschizophrenic mothers. By following children born to both types of mothers, we can not only learn how strong the relationship between maternal and child schizophrenia is, but we can also shed light on the mechanism by which schizophrenia is transmitted from mother to child. (Do schizophrenic mothers engage in unusual child-rearing practices? for example.) Longitudinal studies also permit researchers to test programs designed to prevent psychopathology from developing. By comparing children exposed to the program with those not exposed, we can determine whether the program reduces the likelihood that a child with a schizophrenic mother will develop schizophrenia. Because it requires subjects to be studied over many years, longitudinal research is very expensive. A common cost-saving ploy is to perform the research retrospectively. That is, individuals with a specific problem are identified and their pasts explored to see whether they had certain experiences in their youth. As already noted in the child abuse example discussed earlier, however, memories can be selective and biased. For these reasons, retrospective studies are a poor substitute for longitudinal research.

Researchers are primarily motivated by curiosity and a search for scientific knowledge, but they must also consider the social context in which they live and work before planning their studies. Whether an experiment is concerned with animals or people, there are ethical obligations to which all scientists must adhere. Professional organizations such as the American Psychological Association have formulated ethical standards for their members. Probably the most important ethical issue in psychopathol-

ogy research is the problem of informed consent. A basic tenet of ethical research is that subjects voluntarily consent to participate. To do this, they must be informed of all potential risks and benefits and must have the capacity to make a mature judgment. Voluntary consent means more than simply asking someone to participate. Children asked by their teachers, prisoners asked by their wardens, and soldiers asked by their commanding officers may agree to participate because they are asked to do so by someone in authority. In such cases, special care must be taken to ensure that participation is really voluntary. It is usually best if recruitment is conducted by the scientist rather than a person in authority who may be seen to pressure someone to volunteer. Informed consent requires not only that potential volunteers are informed of the relative risks and benefits of participation but also that they are informed in a way that they can understand. They also have a right to learn about the outcomes of the research. The requirement for informed consent is particularly difficult with special populations such as children, the mentally retarded, and the severely disturbed. Members of these groups may lack the capacity to decide for themselves; those given responsibility for the care of these people must consent on their behalf. Even when informed consent is obtained, it is still up to scientists to be certain that their research is really worth doing. Morally, the best decision rule is one that compares a study's risks and benefits. Research in which the risks to the populations to be studied outweigh the study's expected benefits is difficult to justify. Finally, all research participants deserve anonymity. Participants should never be identified without their consent.

This brief review of research methodology is meant to do no more than provide a feel for how researchers attempt to answer questions about psychopathology. Not all research techniques have been mentioned; several additional methods will be described in later chapters. In addition, many of the topics discussed in this introduction—research paradigms, historical cycles, the interaction between theory and research findings—will be dealt with in greater detail as they apply to the landmark studies described in succeeding chapters. When reading these later chapters, keep in mind the important issues raised in this introduction. Ask yourself which scientific paradigm influenced each researcher and whether social factors may have influenced how their research findings were interpreted. Note also whether their interpretations were justified on scientific grounds. Were control groups adequate? Are correlational relationships being interpreted as causal? Albert Einstein once said that "the whole of science is nothing more than the refinement of everyday thinking." When reading about the landmark studies, note especially how each researcher and clinician went about "refining" the everyday thinking of the time.

This book is divided into four parts. The first part, "Assessment and Classification," describes classic studies concerned with the definition, measurement, and identification of psychopathology. The second part, "Developmental Psychopathology," deals with the psychological problems of children and adolescents. Part III, "Patterns of Psychopathology," discusses how different types of psychopathology have come to be identified and understood while the fourth part, "Treatment," is concerned with how individuals suffering from psychological disturbances can be helped to lead more fulfilling lives.

Further Reading

Hearnshaw, L. S. (1987). *The shaping of modern psychology.* London: Routledge and Kegan Paul.

Peterson, D. (Ed.) (1982). *A mad people's history of madness.* Pittsburgh: University of Pittsburgh Press.

Roback, A. A. (1961). *History of psychology and psychiatry.* New York: Citadel Press.

Notes

1. Thomas, L. (1979). *The Medusa and the Snail.* New York: Viking Press. P. 131.
2. Allderidge, P. (1979). Hospitals, madhouses and asylums: Cycles in the care of the insane. *British Journal of Psychiatry, 134,* 321.
3. Sarton, G. A. L. (1954). *Galen of Pergamon.* Lawrence: University of Kansas Press. P. 112.

PART I

Assessment and Classification

Science, like most important human endeavors, thrives on precise description and measurement. Psychopathology is no exception. Mental health, however, is a completely different type of trait from, say, height or weight. Height and weight can be measured objectively. Ten people, using the same ruler and scale, will all come up with much the same values. Their measurements will not be affected by cultural or social factors. (A person may change religion, politics, and career without affecting his or her height or weight.) Mental health, or psychological functioning, is another matter entirely. Experts frequently disagree about whether an individual is mentally healthy. One reason disagreements arise is the nature of the available measurement instruments. Psychological tests are not nearly as reliable or as easy to use as rulers or scales. A second, and even more important, reason for conflict among experts is that mental health is "relative." Whether or not a particular behavior indicates psychological disturbance depends on the context in which it occurs.

Consider suicide, for example. Taking one's own life is normally a sign of severe psychological disturbance. We find it hard to accept that any well-adjusted person would wish to die. But what if the person were terminally ill and in intractable pain? Would suicide still be interpreted as a sign of psychological disturbance? Probably not. Thus, a specific behavior may be interpreted as either abnormal or "normal" depending on the context. There are even times when *not* committing suicide might be considered abnormal. For centuries, the Indian ritual called *suttee* required a widow to jump on to her husband's funeral pyre. Such suicides were a form of religious observance. To refuse would have been considered a sign of "abnormality." In the right circumstances, suicide may even be construed as praiseworthy and laudable. For example, Japanese kamikaze pilots, who committed suicide by piloting their planes into enemy ships, were honored for their actions. These examples illustrate that "abnormality" cannot be assessed solely by observing a specific behavior. Even the most self-destructive behaviors may be considered "normal" in some situations.

Defining and measuring abnormal behavior have always been controversial issues in the history of psychopathology. The chapters in this section are concerned with three particularly thorny questions: How should abnormal behavior be measured? Does psychopathology exist independent of social context? What are the costs and benefits of classifying someone as "mentally ill"?

CHAPTER 1

Examining the Mind

When we describe a friend who attends many parties and hates to spend a night at home as *sociable* or when we describe an air force pilot as *heroic* or an embezzler as *greedy*, we are implying that the causes of their behavior lie within these individuals. That is, we attribute their behavior to certain personality *traits*. At one time or another, we have all come across greedy, heroic, sociable, shy, honest, rigid, and many other types of people. This is one of the great attractions of *trait theory* — it fits with our everyday observation that people have different personalities. But to psychologists interested in personality differences, traits are more than simply a handy way to describe another person. They are meant to reflect general behavioral dispositions. In theory, it should be possible to develop personality tests to identify a person's enduring personality traits. Once we know these traits, we should be able to predict that person's behavior in a variety of different situations. Heroes should typically act courageously, shy people should avoid social contact, greedy people should refuse requests for charity. In practice, it turns out that people are not nearly as consistent as trait theory would suggest. "Greedy" financiers have been known to donate millions to philanthropic foundations, heroes lose their nerve, and even sociable people sometimes prefer to spend a night alone. This does not mean that people are totally unpredictable. There are regularities to behavior, but how people behave *at any particular moment* depends not just on their character traits but also on the context — the social situation in which they are operating.

Because most personality tests ignore social context, they are imperfect predictors of behavior. An obvious conclusion, you might think. Yet it took psychologists a long time to recognize the limitations of

HAMLET: Do you see yonder cloud that's almost in the shape of a camel?

POLONIUS: By the mass, and 'tis like a camel, indeed.

HAMLET: Methinks it is like a weasel.

POLONIUS: It is backed like a weasel.

HAMLET: Or like a whale?

POLONIUS: Very like a whale.

—William Shakespeare

their personality tests. On the surface at least, tests appear to yield useful information. A good example is Hermann Rorschach's famous inkblot test. It rose from nowhere to become the most famous of all psychological tests. It remained popular for decades before psychologists began to question its validity. This chapter chronicles the history of Rorschach's test. While interesting in its own right, the history of the inkblot test is also a miniature study of the conflict between clinical "art" and psychological "science." This conflict, which may never be completely resolved, was made explicit by the American psychologist Paul Meehl, whose classic study of "clinical versus statistical" prediction is also discussed in this chapter. Although their methods were vastly different, both Rorschach and Meehl were concerned with two of psychopathology's most fundamental problems—the assessment and prediction of human behavior.

ORIGINS OF PSYCHOLOGICAL ASSESSMENT

For many centuries, psychological assessment relied on physiological and anatomical indicators of character and ability. A pioneer in applying physiology to psychological assessment was the Spanish physician Juan Huarte, whose book, *Probe of Minds*, was published in 1575 and soon became a publishing sensation. It went through dozens of editions and was translated into many languages. The content of the book is aptly summarized in the title to the English edition: *The Tryal of Wits, Discovering the Great Differences of Wits Among Men and What Sort of Learning Suits Best With Each Genius*. Huarte recommended that the king of Spain appoint special examiners to assess the personality of the country's youth and guide them to the careers for which they were most suited. These vocational assessments involved reworkings of the classical four humors adding distinctions such as "hot and cold" or "moist and dry" personality types. For example, Huarte claimed that memory requires great moisture. Germans, he believed, have good memories because they consume considerable volumes of liquid. However, because Germans are "cold" in temperament, they lack the "hot" Spaniard's power of imagination. (Germans are also bigger than Spaniards because all of that moisture swells their bodies.)

Huarte was clearly deluded on several points; nevertheless, he played an important role in the development of personality testing. His writings influenced many others to study individual differences in personality, and he identified one of the major values of psychological testing: measuring vocational aptitude.

The next major development in personality assessment occurred 200 years later when the Viennese doctor Franz Joseph Gall set out to relate personality to brain anatomy. Gall believed that the brain is composed of dozens of separate organs each associated with a specific psychological process. His reasoning went something like this: People have imaginations, so there must be an organ devoted to imagination; people also have memories, so there must be an organ devoted to memory, and so on. According to Gall, individuals with good memories have larger brain memory organs than do those with poor memories. The same goes for imagination and all other psychological traits. (For Gall, bigger almost always meant better.) Gall assumed that the skull is a visible mirror of the underlying brain. So, by examining the shapes and contours of the skull, it should be possible to discern the size of the underlying brain organs. Gall's approach, which became known as *phrenology*, developed into a pseudoscientific social movement whose adherents claimed that such matters as career choice, mate selection, and psychological well-being could all be determined by examining the bumps on people's skulls (see Figure 1.1). It did not seem to bother anyone that all phrenological statements were completely circular. Saying that someone has a good memory because they have a large memory organ is little different from Molière's famous physician who explained that a sleeping potion induces sleep because it has a "soporific" quality.

The phrenologists were soon faced with anomalous cases. Some people with extraordinary talents were found to have small bumps in the skull areas where large bumps were expected; other individuals with large bumps had no special talents. The phrenologists were forced to introduce ad hoc explanations to explain each deviant case. These new explanations made phrenology increasingly complicated. Eventually, all the special cases proved too heavy a load and the whole system collapsed. From today's perspective, it is clear that the phrenologists

TREMORS IN THE BLOOD

Given human nature, personality traits are not the only psychological disposition worth measuring. Being able to tell when someone is lying also has no end of practical uses. Perhaps this is why so much energy has been devoted to lie detection.

The first recorded lie-detection method appears in a 1,000-year-old Egyptian papyrus.* According to its author, a liar reveals deception when he "rubs the big toe along the ground, shivers, and rubs the roots of his hair with his fingers." During the Middle Ages, the emphasis in lie detection switched from overt behavior to the body's internal physiological processes. Noting that fear produces a dry mouth and assuming that liars are, by definition, afraid of being caught, medieval priests had suspects lick a hot iron. Those whose tongues escaped unscathed were believed to be truthful. Chinese judges developed their own variation of this technique. They required witnesses to chew a mouthful of dry rice and spit it into a sacred leaf. Those who could produce a moist rice ball were believed to be telling the truth.

Of course, a dry mouth is not the only sign of fear; there is often a marked increase in heart rate as well. The first person to suggest that heart rate rather than salivation be used as an index of lying was Daniel Defoe, author of *Rob-*

*History of lie detection from: Lykken, D. T. (1981). *A tremor in the blood: Uses and abuses of the lie detector.* New York: McGraw-Hill.

inson Crusoe. Writing in 1730, Defoe claimed that "guilt carries fear always about with it; there is a tremor in the blood of a thief . . . a fluttering heart, an unequal pulse." It took a while, but in the late 1800s the Italian criminologist Cesare Lombroso tested Defoe's idea. He measured the pulse of suspected criminals while they were being interrogated and reported that liars indeed had faster pulses. Lombroso's work was followed up by the father of modern lie detection, William Moulton Marston. It was Marston, a lawyer and the creator of the Wonder Woman cartoon character, who first popularized the term *lie detector* early in the 20th century. Marston's lie detector measured mainly changes in blood pressure; his successors have added measures of respiration (breathing rate) and perspiration. The lie detector does not actually detect lies—it records the physiological responses that are supposed to signal lies.

Years of research on lie detectors has failed to provide much evidence that they actually work. As a result, many American states and foreign countries have placed strong restrictions on their use. But technology marches forward, and we now have a machine that is claimed to detect lies from the tremors in a speaker's voice. Investigations of this machine have been uniformly negative. Nevertheless, it is still being used by practitioners anxious to find a physiological equivalent of Pinocchio's nose, which grew longer every time he lied. Unfortunately, there never was a machine that could detect lies, and it is unlikely that there ever will be.

had the germ of a good idea—the brain does consist of specialized organs—but these specializations are at a completely different level from those proposed by Gall. The brain has regions specialized for elementary psychological processes such as vision, touch, and hearing and not for character traits such as generosity, envy, and heroism.

Phrenology's demise was not the end of craniometry (the estimation of psychological competence from measurement of heads). Skull bumps lost their appeal, but skull size remained a matter of great scientific interest. American scientists such as Samuel Morton used craniometric measures to argue that blacks and American Indians have smaller brains and are therefore intellectually and morally inferior to Europeans. Similarly, Paul Broca, the pioneer French neurologist who identified the part of the brain concerned with expressive language, argued

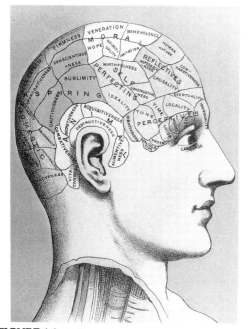

FIGURE 1.1 A phrenological map showing the skull sites for 37 different psychological processes.

that women are inherently inferior to men because they have smaller brains. Because women are generally smaller than men, they also have smaller hearts, lungs, and kidneys, but this was not considered relevant.

A few investigators, not content with simply measuring heads, turned to physiognomy, the study of personality based on facial and bodily appearance. Physiognomy originated with the classical philosopher Aristotle, who held that human beings have the character traits of the animals they most closely resemble. Cesare Lombroso, a 19th-century Italian physician, went a step further claiming that "deviant" personality types including criminals and the insane can be differentiated from good citizens on the basis of their physical appearance alone. His argument was that personality traits, including a tendency toward criminality, are hereditary. According to Lombroso, criminals are evolutionary throwbacks who can be identified by certain physical "stigmata" such as a big jaw, narrow forehead, long arms, and a preference for tattoos.

Lombroso's stigmata became important in criminal trials where his testimony about the relationship between physical appearance and criminality was often admitted in evidence.

Although their influence was great while it lasted, craniometrists and physiognomists both fell out of favor in the early part of the 20th century with the development of modern "mental" tests. Instead of physiological and anatomical measurements, these new tests used a standardized set of materials and procedures that required overt behavioral response. Performance on the tests was used to infer mental functioning. Over the years, psychological tests have produced heated controversies, false claims, blind alleys, and gross exaggeration. Nevertheless, not even their severest critics can deny the major role tests have played in the evolution of the science of psychopathology.

ASSESSING PERSONALITY USING PSYCHOLOGICAL TESTS

The first mental testers were concerned with intelligence. Foremost among them was the brilliant 19th-century British scientist Francis Galton. Galton, who was Charles Darwin's cousin, was an advocate of *eugenics,* a term he coined to cover his ideas about improving the "genetic endowment" of the population by the control of marriage and family size. The idea was that only those with the "best" genes would be allowed to marry and have children. Galton saw eugenics as a natural extension of Darwin's notion of "survival of the fittest." Convinced that intelligence is inherited and influenced by the philosophical position that all information comes from the senses, Galton concluded that the most intellectually able people are those who have inherited especially acute senses. Based on this theory, Galton designed measures of sensory function (visual acuity, tone discrimination), but he failed to find any real difference between intellectually able people and those of average intelligence.

Interest in mental testing waned for a while, but it was revived at the end of the century by Alfred Binet. Binet, the most prominent psychologist of his time, began his research by using methods similar to Galton's but changed course when he was commissioned by the French government to study mental deficiency in the Paris school system. Binet abandoned Galton's theoretical approach and set out to develop a purely empirical test that could predict school performance. The result was the first modern intelligence, or IQ, test.

Binet's test was developed in response to a practical issue, the need to identify and provide remedial help for certain school children. Many of the first personality tests were also developed in response to practical needs. For example, General Pershing, commander of American Expeditionary Forces in France in World War I, was alarmed at the mental casualties being caused by trench warfare. He called on psychologist Robert Woodworth, chair of the Committee on Emotional Fitness, to help design a psychiatric screening method for new recruits so that those with a high level of emotional instability could be excused from military service. Using expert opinion as a guide, Woodworth formulated a set of test items that described fears, anxieties, emotional complaints, variations in mood, self-confidence, and bizarre experiences. Each item consisted of a simple statement, such as "I often feel depressed." Individuals were asked to check those items that described their own feelings. The total set of items was given to psychiatric patients, college students, military personnel, and medical patients in military hospitals. Counts were made of the number of items that the various groups acknowledged as self-descriptive. Items that could not be used to discriminate among the various groups were eliminated. Woodworth called the remaining 116 items, the "Psychoneurotic Inventory." (The version administered to military recruits actually bore the title "Personal Data Sheet" so as not to alert them to the real purpose of the test.) The inventory represented a major departure from traditional psychiatric practice. Instead of prompting patients to discuss specific problems, the content of specific items was considered less important than the total *number* that a person endorsed.

Woodworth's inventory continued to be used after the war for employee selection and other purposes. Although it showed that personality can be assessed quantitatively (by adding up the number of endorsed items), psychologists soon began to express some uneasiness about its validity—whether it was really measuring what it purported to measure. Critics pointed out that Woodworth assumed everyone would understand what each item meant.

However, in some instances, more than one interpretation was possible. For example, the word *often* in the item "I often feel depressed" could mean once a year, once a month, or once a week. The word *depressed* could mean anything from sad to suicidal. The real meaning of an inventory score cannot be determined unless the examiner knows how the various items are being interpreted. Woodworth also assumed that people always respond honestly and accurately. Critics challenged this assumption claiming that deception, whether conscious or unconscious, could invalidate a result. Considerations such as these spurred some psychologists to develop increasingly sophisticated inventories. Others spurned such tests entirely. They put their faith, instead, in another type of assessment device, which they believed to be less prone to misinterpretation and deception. These tests became known as "projective" techniques. Foremost among them was Hermann Rorschach's inkblot test.

HERMANN RORSCHACH: FATHER OF PROJECTIVE TESTING

Hermann Rorschach was born in Zurich in 1884 and grew up in a nearby village. His father, Ulrich Rorschach, was a rather undistinguished painter who supported himself as a drawing teacher in the local school. Rorschach's mother died when he was 12, and he was looked after by housekeepers until his father remarried, taking as his bride his wife's younger sister. Young Hermann resented his aunt-stepmother, with whom he was never able to form a close relationship. Their estrangement became permanent when his father died a few years later.

Rorschach's family problems did not affect his school performance or his social life. He was elected to a school social club whose other members gave him the nickname Klex, a variant on the German word *klecks*, which, believe it or not, means "inkblot." Although it is possible that this was an instance of extrasensory perception, or precognition, a more likely explanation is that the word *klecks* was used colloquially to describe a mediocre painting. ("That painting looks like an inkblot.") Rorschach's friends may have been teasing him by suggesting that he would grow up to be an undistinguished painter like his father. Of course, it is possible that Rorschach's nickname influenced his future life's

FIGURE 1.2 Hermann Rorschach as a young academic.

work. It is amusing to think what would have happened if Rorschach's friends had nicknamed him "squeaky." Perhaps he would have devised his test using sounds instead of inkblots. In any event, throughout his life, Rorschach remained keenly in-

terested in art and took a great interest in galleries and museums.

After high school, Rorschach decided to study medicine. Following the custom of the time, he studied at several universities in Switzerland and

Germany, but the bulk of his education was received at the University of Zurich, which was becoming well known as a major psychiatric training center. Its clinic director, Eugen Bleuler, was later to be credited with coining the word *schizophrenia*. The university was also one of the first to accept Freud's ideas that unconscious feelings and conflicts lie at the bottom of many psychiatric disturbances.

While at Zurich, Rorschach conceived the idea of studying children's responses to inkblots. *Klecksography* was a popular childhood game at the time. It consisted of putting inkblots on paper, folding the paper, and seeing what shapes are formed. Rorschach's hypothesis was that more gifted students would "see" more in the resulting inkblots than less gifted students would. Rorschach did not conduct these experiments systematically, nor did he publish the results. Indeed, he seems to have quickly lost interest and pursued studies in psychoanalysis instead. It was not until several years later, when he learned of the work of the Polish doctor Szymon Hens that Rorschach once again became interested in inkblots.

Hens had published an inkblot test in his doctoral dissertation in 1917. Following the lead of several earlier researchers who claimed that inkblots could be used to assess personality, Hens administered his test to 1,200 people. While he failed to find any real differences between the *content* of the responses produced by psychiatric patients and those produced by normal adults, he did note a tendency for some people to interpret the whole inkblot whereas others responded mainly to details. Rorschach was taken with Hens's work, particularly the possibility that personality may be characterized not by what people actually see in an inkblot but by the characteristics of the inkblot (the location, the color, and so on) that elicit perceptions from different people. From that moment on, Rorschach devoted himself to inkblots whenever he could steal time from his clinical duties. Within 3 years, he had produced and tested his own inkblot-based personality test.

Although he certainly owed an intellectual debt to Hens (and to Alfred Binet, who studied reactions to inkblots using his own daughters as experimental subjects), Rorschach's approach differed because, unlike his predecessors, he was steeped in psychoanalytic theory. Psychoanalysis emphasizes unconscious motivation as the cause of psychological problems. Treatment requires bringing these unconscious conflicts out into the open, but this is difficult to do because people develop "defenses" that censor unconscious material and keep it from reaching awareness.

The need to bypass protective defenses led the Swiss psychoanalyst Carl Jung to devise his famous "word association" method. In what has become almost a trademark of cinema psychoanalysts, the word association technique requires patients to respond to a stimulus word with the first word that comes to mind. In Jung's original studies, the time taken to respond to each word was measured with a stopwatch while changes in breathing and skin moisture were monitored using suitable physiological equipment. The reaction time and physiological measures were used to measure the emotional reactions triggered by certain words. A long delay before responding to a word, plus labored breathing and sweaty palms, meant that the word had important psychological implications. It is important to emphasize that Jung was primarily concerned with the physiological response to target words; the word associations, themselves, were secondary. Cinema psychoanalysts, on the other hand, typically dispense with Jung's physiological and reaction-time refinements. Instead, they concentrate on the content of word associations, which is presumed to be a direct representation of psychological problems. For example, patients who have a repressed hatred of their mother may be shown responding to the word *mother* with the word *murder*.

Rorschach, like Jung, did not believe that patients reveal their unconscious conflicts so easily. Because defense mechanisms are always on the alert, personality measures must be indirect. Rorschach's artistic interests and his observations of both patients and nonpatients led him to believe that people reveal their unconscious desires and motives in the way they respond to pictures. Initially, Rorschach was unsure whether unstructured, relatively ambiguous materials such as inkblots are better ways to measure personality traits than are more meaningful pictures. He experimented by showing patients pictures of a green cat, a red frog, and a woodcutter cutting down a tree and noting their reactions. He was eventually persuaded to use ambiguous pictures by a patient who used to look at the humidity spots on the ceiling of his bedroom and imagine that they reminded him of a nude woman or a certain Swiss lake.

Like Jung, Rorschach set out to develop measures that did not depend solely on response content (the focus of all previous inkblot research) but also on the underlying processes that give rise to a response. Instead of Jung's physiological measures, Rorschach used behavioral methods to assess the cognitive processes that people use to interpret ambiguous stimuli such as inkblots. Hens had noted that people respond to different aspects of the inkblots. Rorschach hypothesized that responses to different inkblot characteristics (color, form, movement, and location) signify different aspects of personality. His research was originally conceived as an empirical test of this hypothesis.

CLASSIC STUDY 1
The "Projective" Test

In his book *Psychodiagnostics,* published in 1921, Rorschach described an "experiment" on "the interpretation of accidental [nonspecific] forms." These "forms," of course, were inkblots. Ten of the 15 inkblots Rorschach used in his research were published along with the book as separate plates. Six were black with varying shades of grey; the remaining four also contained colored parts. The plates were symmetrical so that the left side of each inkblot was the mirror image of the right. Each inkblot took up about half the space on its respective plate, and each plate was presented horizontally (long side down).

To test the hypothesis that responses to inkblots reveal important aspects of personality, Rorschach presented his inkblots to 405 experimental subjects. Most were psychiatric patients with a variety of different diagnoses, but nonpatients were assessed as well. He described the procedure as follows:

> The subject is given one plate after another and asked, "What might this be?" He holds the plate in his hand and may turn it about as much as he likes. The subject is free to hold the plate near his eyes or far away as he chooses. . . . An attempt is made to get at least one answer to every plate, though suggestion in any form is, of course, avoided. Answers are taken down as long as they are produced by the subject.[1]

If subjects were not sufficiently forthcoming, Rorschach queried them about the inkblot attributes that triggered each of their responses. Rorschach summarized his data statistically. Each subject's protocol yielded eight separate scores: the number of responses, reaction time (the time between the presentation of an inkblot and a subject's response), the number of times the subject failed to produce any response to an inkblot, responses determined by form (the actual shape of the inkblot), responses determined by a color other than black or grey, responses in which the subject perceived "movement" in the blot (people dancing, for example), the number of responses to the whole inkblot, and responses to only parts of an inkblot (and the location of the inkblot part that produced the response).

Within each scoring category, Rorschach also made finer distinctions. Thus, responses determined by form or movement were scored "+" or "−" (good or bad) depending on whether Rorschach himself could see whatever the subject claimed to see in the inkblot. True to his original position, response content was relegated to a minor position in Rorschach's scoring system. Nevertheless, content was not totally without interest. For summary purposes, Rorschach assigned response content to six categories: humans, parts of humans, animals, parts of animals, inanimate objects, and landscapes. He also kept a count of "original" perceptions (those appearing no more than once in every 100 protocols). An example of Rorschach scoring is shown in Figure 1.3.

Each subject's scores constituted the data of the experiment. As expected, there were considerable differences among individuals. According to Rorschach, imaginative people respond to perceived movement, emotional people respond to color, and so on. He devoted considerable space in his book to discussing the relationship between personality and different types of responses. For example, Rorschach wrote that "the more C's [color responses], the greater the tendency to impulsive actions." Although these conclusions were supposed to be based on the data he collected, the relationship between Rorschach's research results and his conclusions were often rather tenuous. Rorschach's final step was to aggregate the various scores achieved by persons suffering from schizophrenia, manic-depressive psychosis, and other conditions. He presented these group scores in a se-

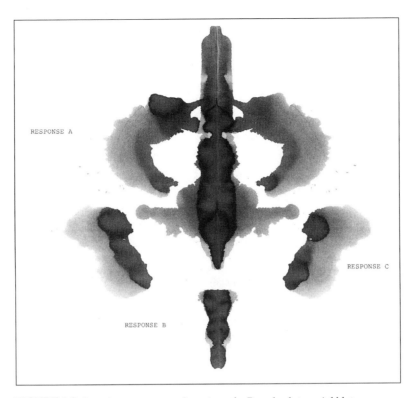

FIGURE 1.3 Sample responses and scoring of a Rorschach-type inkblot.
Response A: "Two kids jumping on either side of a large pogo stick." *Where are
they?* "Here are the kids, here is the pogo stick." *What makes it look like that?* "Their
shape, here, you can see their hands holding on to the stick, and they seem to be
bouncing in the air." Scoring: Location—large detail (everything except the three
unconnected parts of the inkblot). Determinants—form, human movement.
Response B: "A ballerina." Scoring: Location—large detail. Determinants—form,
human movement. Response C: "Storm clouds." Location—large details.
Determinants—form, shading.

ries of tables. An example is shown in Table 1.1,
which summarizes the number of "movement" responses perceived by various groups and includes
some of Rorschach's comments about the people
who fall into the various categories.

As may be seen in the table, there was no simple
relationship between the perception of movement
and diagnostic category. Intelligent normal subjects, paranoid schizophrenics, manics, epileptics,
and patients suffering from Korsakoff's dementia
(brain damage produced by chronic alcoholism) all
perceived a reasonably high level of movement in
the inkblots. Rorschach acknowledged that move-

ment responses are difficult to interpret on their
own and suggested that they be considered together with form and color responses. For example,
among normals, movement and form responses
went together. As "good" (that is, "+") form responses increased so did good movement responses. Among individuals with mood disturbances, however, the relationship was reversed. An
increase in good form responses was related to a decrease in movement responses. Rorschach called a
person's overall pattern of scores a *psychogram.* He
insisted that individual scores were not interpreta-
ble on their own. Personality assessment requires

TABLE 1.1   Movement Responses

	Normal	Feeble-minded	Schizo-phrenic	Manic-Depressive	Epileptic	Organic
More than 5 M	Good, productive intel-ligence.	—	Most in-hibited catatonics. Most pro-ductive paranoids.	Manic	Epileptics with early dementia.	Korsakoff
3–5 M	Average intel-ligence.	—	Inhibited catatonics. Productive paranoids.	Manic	Epileptics with slow dementia.	—
1–2 M	Intel-ligence predomi-nantly re-produc-tive.	Elated mood.	Unproduc-tive cata-tonics + hebe-phrenics.	—	Epileptics with later dementia.	Paretics
0 M	Unintel-ligent. Pedantic.	Morons, imbeciles.	Simple Dementia. Stereo-typed.	Depressed	—	Arterio-sclerotic and Senile Dementia.

Source: Adapted from Rorschach (1942).

that a person's entire configuration of scores be interpreted as an integrated whole. Rorschach admitted that this was difficult to do, but he believed the effort to be worthwhile because psychograms are valuable diagnostic tools. Rorschach considered the discovery that psychograms have diagnostic value to be fortuitous. Toward the end of *Psychodiagnostics*, he describes how he began his experiment solely to test the theoretical notion that personality influences the process of perception, "the discovery that the results could be used in making diagnoses was an empirical finding that had not been looked for."

Although he was vice-president of the Swiss Psychoanalytic Society, Rorschach had considerable difficulty getting *Psychodiagnostics* published. Eventually, he found a publisher who was willing to take a chance on 1,200 copies, but the book was hardly an overnight success. There were several factors working against it. It was difficult to read, psychoanalysis was not yet fashionable, and its author did not have the prestige of a university position behind

him. Rorschach, himself, considered the book something of a failure. He was disappointed that, in a bid to save on overheads, the publisher had reproduced only 10 of the 15 inkblots he used in his research. To make matters worse, even the 10 inkblots were not well presented. Rorschach's original inkblots were of uniform saturation; in the published version, the clear black areas were reproduced as grainy and shady. The printer also altered the original colors. For these reasons, Rorschach began thinking about a revision almost from the moment his book was published. Among other refinements, he planned to produce a parallel set of inkblots that could be used to check the reliability of interpretations made from the original set. Unfortunately, these plans were never realized. Nine months after the publication of *Psychodiagnostics*, Rorschach developed severe abdominal pain. Within days, he was dead of a perforated appendix. He was just 37 years old. Rorschach's total income from his book was less than five American dollars.

AFTERMATH

Hermann Rorschach, a doctor who never studied psychology, never attended international congresses, and had little official recognition, died without knowing the impact that his "experiment" would exert on a generation of psychologists. In the years following his death, interest in the inkblot test grew slowly in psychoanalytic circles. Following a suggestion made by Rorschach in his book, clinicians produced personality descriptions and diagnoses based on the test protocols alone — without any information about the patient's "age, sex, state of health, presence of neurosis or psychosis." These "blind" interpretations became a kind of psychoanalytic parlor game. Practitioners would compare their blind personality descriptions to documented case histories to see how close they could get. Reports began to circulate about the uncannily accurate personality descriptions produced by those skilled in Rorschach interpretation. As interest developed, the "experimental" nature of the inkblot test was completely forgotten. Rorschach's planned revisions were also put aside. Indeed, the growing band of test devotees refused to change the original inkblots in any way. They continued to use the 10 grainy, miscolored plates published in *Psychodiagnostics* capitalizing on the printer's errors by adding chiaroscuro (shading and light) to color, shape, form, and location as another perceptual determinant. The original 10 inkblots are still used today. It is ironic that a test used by a generation of psychologists is, in several important ways, the product of sloppy printing.

The inkblot test gained many new adherents in the years leading up to World War II. The test became especially popular in the United States, the country in which psychoanalysis made its greatest impact. American psychologists gave the inkblot test a new theoretical rationale that they called the *projective hypothesis.* This hypothesis, which is drawn from psychoanalytic thinking, states that people interpret ambiguous stimuli by "projecting" their own unconscious drives and motives into their perceptions. In other words, inkblots, or other ambiguous materials, are a "screen" on to which subjects project their feelings, wishes, and conflicts. Tests using ambiguous stimuli soon became known as *projective techniques;* they were hailed as "x-rays of

the personality." It is doubtful whether Rorschach would have agreed. In *Psychodiagnostics,* he wrote that "the test cannot be considered as a means for delving into the unconscious. At best, it is far inferior to the other more profound psychological methods such as dream interpretation and [word] association experiments."

In any event, Rorschach was not around to complain, and projective tests began to proliferate. The most famous, after the Rorschach, was the Thematic Apperception Test (or TAT, for short). The brainchild of Henry Murray, a surgeon who turned to psychology as a second career, the TAT requires subjects to make up stories to rather vague pictures (see Figure 1.4). Although TAT scoring systems have been developed over the years, most clinicians use the test as a structured interview looking for important themes and making overall impressionistic judgments about mood. During the "golden age" of projective techniques (the 1930s and 1940s) many new tests appeared. Perhaps the most bizarre was the Szondi personality scale (see Figure 1.5). In this test, subjects are shown a set of photographs and asked to choose the most appealing faces. The photographs are of persons with diagnosed psychiatric disorders. Subjects are expected to project their own disorders on to the faces, choosing those patients who share their own psychiatric problems. (In essence, the test is based on the theory that "it takes one to know one.")

Projective tests were widely used during World War II. The war-inspired migration of European psychoanalysts to America provided a population of qualified and enthusiastic teachers. Before long, American and British clinical psychologists were routinely learning to use projective tests as part of their training. Following the war, academic psychology began a period of rapid growth. Because psychology training emphasized controlled experimentation and rigorous research, it was inevitable that psychologists would turn their attention to projective tests. Because of its popularity, the inkblot test was the obvious target. The typical experiment was concerned with the Rorschach's *validity.* That is, does the test really measure what it purports to? Researchers compared predictions made from Rorschach protocols with detailed case histories and behavioral observations. The higher the level of agreement between Rorschach

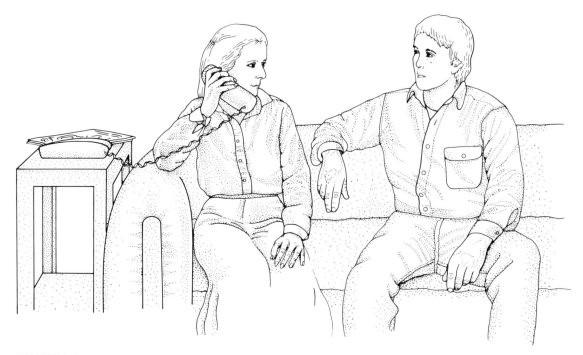

FIGURE 1.4 A picture similar to those used in the TAT.

predictions and objective criteria, the more valid the test.

Some experiments were fairly simple. For example, Rorschach claimed that, among nonpsychiatric patients, human-movement responses signify imagination and creativity. To test this belief, psychologists administered the inkblot test to a sample of well-known artists and to a group of nonartistic control subjects. They found no difference; the artists did not produce more human-movement responses than did the nonartists. Because the prediction made by the inkblot test was not upheld by the research, this finding suggests that human-movement responses are not a valid sign of creativity. Such negative findings were all too common. To take another example, Rorschach claimed that people who see objects in the white areas of inkblots (rather than forms produced by the ink) are rebellious individuals who have difficulty cooperating with those in authority. Psychologists tested this prediction by comparing the inkblot protocols of criminals and juvenile delinquents with those pro-

duced by a control group of law-abiding citizens. Once again, Rorschach's prediction was not upheld. Criminals and juvenile delinquents were no more likely to see forms in the white spaces of the inkblots than were subjects in the control group. By 1959 more than 2,000 of these "validity" studies had been reported in the psychology literature; almost none were able to substantiate Rorschach's predictions.

Had Rorschach been alive, he would have certainly objected to the way these studies were conducted. In *Psychodiagnostics,* he explicitly noted that individual test scores cannot be used in isolation; interpretations must be based on the entire psychogram. Acknowledging this point, psychologists designed studies of interpretations based on complete psychograms. Eminent Rorschach experts were asked to produce personality assessments, and make diagnoses, on the basis of Rorschach protocols. These were precisely the type of "blind" interpretations that helped to make the test popular in the first place. The experts' assessments were compared with those produced by clinicians who had

FIGURE 1.5 Perhaps the strangest psychological test ever developed, the Szondi requires subjects to choose from among pictures of psychiatric patients those they find most appealing.

firsthand knowledge of the individuals involved. The result: almost no overlap. Like judgments based on individual Rorschach signs, those based on complete psychograms were not found to be valid predictors of behavior.

Although overwhelmingly negative research findings have continued to accumulate (over 7,000 studies so far), some clinicians still cling to the inkblot test. They find the research evidence difficult to reconcile with their clinical impression that the test gives valid information. Unfortunately, clinical intuitions are not reliable measures of the test's value. For example, when homosexuality was considered a psychiatric syndrome, clinicians were often interested in making the "diagnosis" in the absence of overt evidence. Often they relied on the Rorschach. Their faith was almost always misplaced. Consider, for example, the following reactions produced by two different male subjects to the same inkblot:

SUBJECT A: This bit here, it's frightening. It looks like some sort of monster. See, here, this part looks like a man, but this looks like an animal. It's a half-man, half-animal monster.

SUBJECT B: It looks like a man bending over. Here are his buttocks and his anus. You can see, he is wearing female underwear and he has, sort of, breasts.

Which of the two is more likely to be homosexual, Subject A or Subject B? If your answer is B, you are in good company. In a study conducted by psychologists Loren Chapman and Jean Chapman of the University of Wisconsin, clinicians (as well as lay persons) overwhelmingly chose responses such as those made by Subject B as indicating homosexuality. In reality, the response produced by Subject B is not a valid predictor of homosexuality. Images of sexual organs, cross dressing, and the like are not common in the responses of homosexuals. Instead, studies have found monsters, part-animal and part-human figures, the type of response produced by Subject A. So, Subject A is more likely to be homosexual than Subject B. Why, then, did most clinicians choose responses similar to Subject B's? The answer is obvious. Subject B's responses sound like what a stereotyped male homosexual might see in an inkblot. Clinicians believed so strongly that certain responses are related to homosexuality, they did not bother to check. Instead, they assumed the existence of an *illusory correlation* between certain responses and homosexuality. Illusory correlations are probably responsible for the persistence of many unwarranted clinical beliefs including a belief in the validity of the Rorschach.

Although many clinicians resisted, others were profoundly affected by the mountain of evidence showing that the inkblot test is not a valid measure of personality. Some turned their efforts to devising more valid, "standardized" scoring schemes (ironically, the best of these rely on the content rather than the perceptual determinants of perceptions). Other psychologists turned back to personality inventories and questionnaires. In the 1940s, they began to develop "objective" personality tests — tests whose validity could be demonstrated by reference to some objective external criterion. Many of these objective tests turned out to be questionnaire inventories. The most famous is the Minnesota Multiphasic Personality Inventory (or, simply, the MMPI). The test was the work of two University of Minnesota researchers, a psychologist, Starke Hathaway, and a psychiatrist, J. Charnley McKinley. It was called "multiphasic" because it was developed to assess several personality dimensions simultaneously.

Hathaway and McKinley did not begin with a theory about how personality should be measured. Instead, they gathered together descriptive statements about personality. These statements came from traditional sources such as psychology textbooks as well as from folk stories, hobbies, anecdotes, and clinical intuition. Each statement was phrased so that subjects could respond *true* or *false*. Examples include: "I like mechanics magazines," "I sometimes keep on a thing until others lose their patience with me," "Bad words, often terrible words, come into my mind and I cannot get rid of them," "I often feel as if things are not real," and "Someone has it in for me."

All statements were presented to carefully selected groups of psychiatric patients, medical patients, and nonpatient adults. The next step was to eliminate those statements that failed to discriminate between psychiatric patients and others. Thus, if psychiatric patients and normal controls both replied *true* to the statement "I sometimes keep on a thing until others lose patience with me," that statement would be eliminated. On the other hand, if patients and controls differed in their response to the item "I like mechanics magazines," it was retained even though no one had any idea why the two groups responded differently. This purely empirical approach (try anything and keep only what works) was a major departure from the past. Woodworth, whose work on the Psychoneurotic Inventory has already been described, chose items by asking expert clinicians to supply plausible questions they believed might discriminate among various groups. Plausibility was not a factor in the MMPI; any item, no matter how strange, could be used. The only requirement was that it be able to discriminate among groups. As might be expected, the vagaries of the empirical approach resulted in a motley conglomeration of odd items that provided a fertile field for satirists. Art Buchwald's parody of test items includes: "Spinach makes me feel alone," "I salivate at the sight of mittens," and "I am never startled by a fish."

The result of Hathaway and McKinley's labors was an inventory of around 500 items that yields scores on numerous subscales. The original subscale scores were tied to traditional psychiatric diagnoses (depression, schizophrenia, paranoia). Over the years, additional subscales have been developed to measure alcoholism, suicide potential, and other clinically important problems. A major innovation of the MMPI was the introduction of special "validity" scales. These were designed to overcome the traditional problem of questionnaire inventories: unreliable responding. Like the rest of the MMPI, the validity scales were developed empirically. For example, the "lie" scale contains items such as "I gossip a little at times" and "Once in a while I laugh at a dirty joke." Because these statements describe almost everyone, those who deny them are either perfect human beings or lying. Another validity scale contains bizarre statements such as "My soul sometimes leaves my body" and "There are persons trying to steal my thoughts and ideas." Even seriously disturbed patients endorse only a small number of these items. Those who admit to many are either not reading the questions or trying to fake a psychiatric illness. A high score on one or more of the validity scales constitutes a warning to the examiner that the test protocol should not be accepted at face value.

Although clinicians initially concentrated on individual scale scores, it was soon realized that the logic of the MMPI demanded that clinicians attend to the entire pattern of scores. This is accomplished by plotting a person's subscale scores on a graph to produce a profile, or *psychograph*. Rorschach, it will be recalled, also insisted that his various scores should not be interpreted in isolation—it was the complete pattern that was important. He called his summary of scores a *psychogram*. These similarities, while largely superficial, are probably not completely accidental. From the outset, the MMPI was seen as an alternative to projective tests such as the Rorschach.

Since its appearance almost 50 years ago, the MMPI has become the most widely used personality test in the world. It can be found in psychiatric institutions, psychology clinics, personnel offices, and military bases. The MMPI has also been a major stimulus to research spawning thousands of published studies. On the whole, these studies have found reasonable evidence for the predictive ability of the test, especially when the overall pattern of subscale scores is considered. Another reason for the MMPI's popularity is the ease with which test profiles can be produced. Practically anyone can administer and score an MMPI. Test interpretation is more difficult. Clinicians have great difficulty considering more than a few statistical relationships simultaneously. Computers, on the other hand, can do this with ease. Thus, it is not surprising that computers have been enlisted to score and interpret the MMPI and other personality tests. To decide what a particular profile means, computer programs must have access to years of accumulated clinical wisdom. To make this information available to computers in a form that they can use, programmers have distilled clinical experience into a set of statistical formulas. Test-interpretation programs apply these general formulas to specific profiles. With the arrival of inexpensive microcomputers, automated testing has become increasingly popular. Yet many clinicians remain uncomfortable with both computers and statistical formulas. They believe that personality assessments should be based on expert clinical evaluations of each individual case, not on statistical formulas derived from many different cases. This conflict between clinical judgment and statistical formulas predates the introduction of computerized testing. It was first brought out into the open by Paul Meehl, whose landmark work is discussed next.

PAUL MEEHL: SCIENTIST-CLINICIAN

Paul Meehl was born in Minneapolis in 1920. As a teenager he had plans to study law, but he changed his career goal to psychotherapist after reading a book on psychoanalysis by Karl Menninger, founder of the famous institution that bears his name. Drawn to psychology by a fascination with psychoanalysis, Meehl entered the University of Minnesota only to find that its staff had little sympathy for the Freudian viewpoint. The famous behaviorist B. F. Skinner was at Minnesota at the time, and the behavioral approach was paramount. Although Meehl maintained his interest in psychoanalysis while earning his B.A. and then his Ph.D. at Minnesota, he also learned a great deal about statistical methods and scientific rigor. His doctoral supervisor was Starke Hathaway, inventor of the MMPI. After receiving his Ph.D., Meehl joined the faculty at Minnesota where he has taught for more than 40 years.

Meehl has had a research career that includes studies of behavior genetics and animal learning as well as pioneering work on the MMPI. He has been involved in research on measurement and on the application of psychology to legal issues. Although a rigorous experimentalist and empiricist, Meehl has also remained true to his first interest by engaging in private psychoanalytic practice throughout his career.

While still in his twenties, Meehl had already begun to experience the inevitable tension produced by trying to pursue careers in both research and clinical work. Problems arise because clinical practice, although supposedly derived from scientific psychology, is also something of an "art." For many psychologists, the term *art* is almost an antonym for science. It connotes a kind of mysterious intuition which is diametrically opposed to the objective laws that constitute scientific knowledge. Interestingly, it

FIGURE 1.6 Paul Meehl (1920–)

shown superior to alternatives, then clinicians should continue to rely on it. Otherwise, it should be abandoned in favor of more reliable judgment methods. By the time he was finished setting out the various arguments, Meehl found that his paper had grown into a book. Like Rorschach, Meehl had great difficulty finding a publisher because no one believed his book would sell. Finally, in 1954, the University of Minnesota Press published Meehl's manuscript under the title *Clinical versus Statistical Prediction*. The controversy that ensued continued for decades.

Meehl's achievements have brought him wide recognition. He received the American Psychological Association's Distinguished Scientific Contribution Award in 1958 (the same year as B. F. Skinner received the award) for his "incisive investigations ranging over the fields of learning theory, clinical psychology, personality theory, psychometric theory, and the philosophy of science." Meehl has also received the Distinguished Scientific Award of the Clinical Psychology Division of the American Psychological Association and the Klopfer Distinguished Contribution Prize, and he was elected president of the American Psychological Association in 1962. He is a fellow of the American Academy of Arts and Sciences, a member of the National Academy of Sciences, a diplomate of the American Board of Examiners in Professional Psychology, and he has been Regents' Professor of Psychology at Minnesota since 1968. In 1989 the American Psychological Foundation awarded Meehl a Gold Medal for Life Achievement in the Application of Psychology.

is not just scientists who feel this way; many clinicians share the same view. They believe that knowledge derived from clinical experience is special and that the controlled experiments which impress researchers are often irrelevant to clinical practice.

Meehl was stimulated to write a paper on clinical versus statistical (scientific) prediction after reading several articles published by psychologist and psychotherapist Theodore Sarbin in the early 1940s. Sarbin showed that clinicians' predictions of academic success were no better than those made by clerks using a simple statistical formula. Sarbin suggested that clinical predictions would be improved if clinicians deliberately adopted statistical methods. Meehl was not so sure. The scientist in him agreed with Sarbin, but the clinician rebelled. As in most things, Meehl took an empirical approach. Clinical intuition should be put to the test. If it is

CLASSIC STUDY 2
Clinical Versus Statistical Decision Making

Under one name or another, the clinical versus statistical debate has been going on for centuries. The Renaissance artist Raphael captured the spirit of the dispute in his famous portrait of the ancient Greek philosophers, the *School of Athens*. Depicted on the right side of the painting are those philosophers who valued logic, science, and mathematics while on the left are those who appealed to intuition.

Some 400 years after Raphael died, Meehl organized the psychological literature along similar lines. That is, he characterized clinical judgment as based on either intuitive or statistical reasoning.

Intuitive reasoning involves making subjective judgments from a case history, clinical observations, and psychological tests. Consider, for example, a clinical psychologist who must decide whether a depressed patient is a suicide risk. Patients likely to attempt suicide require close monitoring and special precautions. Because special precautions are expensive and highly intrusive, they are ordered only when the costs are justified — that is, when the patient is likely to attempt suicide. To gauge the risk, the psychologist conducts a clinical interview. At that time, the patient's sad demeanor, tearfulness, and feelings of hopelessness are noted. From the patient's history, the psychologist learns of at least one previous suicide attempt. In addition, the patient's MMPI suggests severe depression and a tendency to act aggressively. After considering all available information, the psychologist concludes that there is a high probability that the patient will attempt suicide and recommends that precautions be instituted.

The alternative to the clinical approach, the statistical procedure, requires that judgments be made using formal mathematical techniques. The process begins by translating clinical experience and research into a set of numeric relationships. For example, data collected over the years reveal that the greater the number of previous suicide attempts, the more likely it is that another attempt will be made. It has also been noted that the fewer plans a patient has for the future, the greater the probability of a suicide attempt. These, and other, statistical relationships are aggregated to produce a formula that can be used to predict the likelihood that any patient will attempt suicide. To judge a particular patient's suicide risk, he or she is given a score on each predictive attribute (number of previous attempts, plans for the future, and so on). These scores are entered into the formula which yields an overall probability that suicide will be attempted. The higher the probability, the greater the risk. Note that the statistical formula is derived from clinical experience and research, not from the characteristics of the specific case currently under evaluation. This procedure is called "actuarial" because, just as an insurance company actuary predicts life expectancy from population longevity figures, clinical actuarial decision makers base their judgments on the statistical likelihood of various outcomes, not on the characteristics of any specific case.

It is important to note that the intuitive and actuarial approaches both rely on the same information (test scores, history, and so on). Where they differ is in how various items of information should be combined and evaluated. Psychologists in the intuitive camp believe that expert judgment applied on a case-by-case basis — taking into consideration any unique aspects of the individual — will lead to the most sensitive decision making. Those favoring the statistical approach prefer to rely on general mathematical formulas. As both a clinician and a researcher, Meehl approached the clinical versus statistical decision judgment debate from an ambivalent position. He saw advantages and disadvantages to both but, at the outset at least, was neutral about which approach is best. He stated his aim as follows:

> There is no convincing reason to assume that explicitly formalized mathematical rules and the clinician's creativity are equally suited for any given kind of task, or that their comparative effectiveness is the same for different tasks. Current clinical practice should be much more critically examined with this in mind than it has been.[2]

Meehl marshaled arguments in favor of both approaches. Formulas, he admitted, are easy to apply and their predictions are consistent. Given the same set of data, they always make the same prediction. Consistency, however, is not always a virtue. Sometimes, "special circumstances" must be considered. To use Meehl's example, suppose you are trying to predict whether a given professor will attend the movies on a particular night. On the basis of the professor's past behavior and other factors, a statistical formula estimates the probability to be 90%. Normally, the formula is quite reliable. But the clinician knows that, just that day, the professor sustained a broken leg. This fact alone is enough to reduce the probability that the professor will attend the movies to just about zero. The actuarial formula fails because it does not take account of this unique aspect of the case. The intuitive decision maker, who handles each case individually, has no difficulty reaching the correct judgment.

Those favoring the actuarial approach admit that unexpected factors can render a general formula inappropriate for a particular case, but they claim that the opposite is even more likely to be true. That is, clinical judgment may easily be led astray by focusing too much attention on the unique aspects of a single case. For example, consider the case of T. D., provided by Robin Dawes in his book *Rational Choice in an Uncertain World*:

> T. D. had been a good student until eighth grade, when he suddenly failed several courses. He was sent to a school psychologist, who interviewed him, gave him a W.I.S.C. [the standard intelligence test for children], a Rorschach, and a sentence-completion test. The school psychologist concluded that T. D. had an IQ of 125, was basically stable, but had been having social problems with peers and family — from whom he was somewhat distant. He had withdrawn into such pursuits as stamp collecting and reading, at which he spent an inordinate amount of time. The psychologist speculated that this withdrawal would be temporary, because there was no strong evidence of schizoid characteristics [lack of interest in other people and social interaction] or of gross pathology. The school psychologist concluded that T. D. nevertheless had little sympathy or feelings for other people. In fact, T. D. did well in high school, went on to college to graduate cum laude with a major in history and minors in computer science and sociology and entered a master's program in graduate school.[3]

Dawes asked psychologists to judge, from this case history, whether T. D. entered graduate school in library science or in education. Most psychologists (and, I imagine, most readers) chose library science. T. D. sounds like a person who would prefer a technical, bookish career to one that requires constant social interaction. This judgment is clearly based on the unique aspects of the case. Is it reliable? Almost certainly not. After all, it is very difficult to assess personality characteristics from psychological tests. And even if the assessment made when T. D. was in eighth grade was accurate, how do we know that he did not change as he grew older? Most important, the number of education students far exceeds the number enrolled in library science. Thus, on statistical grounds alone, education is a more likely prediction than library science. By concentrating on the unique aspects of the case, psychologists were led to make a highly unlikely prediction.

In what Meehl considered a minor chapter of his book (but which was to become the major focus of both his critics and his supporters), he summarized approximately 20 studies that compared intuitive decision making with the statistical method. A study published in 1953 by psychologist Frank Barron was typical. Barron had eight clinicians predict how well new patients would respond to psychotherapy based only on their MMPI profiles. The clinicians' predictions were compared to those made using a statistical formula that simply weighted the various MMPI subscale scores and used the weighted total to predict response to therapy. Predictions were evaluated by expert assessments. The outcome was clear: The statistical formula made more accurate predictions than did the eight clinicians. Meehl found this pattern repeated over and over again. In every study that he reviewed, clinical judgments (Is this patient schizophrenic? Does this patient have brain damage?) made by following formal statistical rules were at least as accurate, and often more accurate, than judgments arrived at intuitively. He found no instances in which clinicians outperformed a statistical formula.

Meehl was restrained in his conclusions. On the evidence available to him, statistical methods were superior for predictions, but more research was required to determine the generality of this finding. Nevertheless, Meehl left no doubt about his own feelings: "It is my personal hunch, not proved by the presented data or strongly argued in the text, that a very considerable fraction of clinical time is being irrationally expended in the attempt to do . . . jobs that could be done more efficiently, in a small fraction of the clinical time, and by less skilled and lower paid personnel through the systematic and persistent cultivation of complex (but still clerical) statistical methods."

AFTERMATH

Although research psychologists were largely convinced of the superiority of the statistical approach, clinicians were dubious. Some argued that the studies summarized by Meehl were unfair. Formulas may be better at making predictions from MMPIs, but clinicians are better at intuitive judgments.

STEREOTYPED THINKING

Focusing on the unique aspects of a single case almost always results in poor predictions. Sometimes, it can even result in illogical thinking. This was shown most clearly by Amos Tversky and Daniel Kahneman,* who asked college students the following question:

Linda is 31 years old, single, outspoken, and very bright. She majored in philosophy. As a student, she was deeply concerned with issues of discrimination and social justice and also participated in antinuclear demonstrations. How likely is it that:
- Linda is a teacher in an elementary school.
- Linda works in a bookstore and takes yoga classes.
- Linda is active in the feminist movement.
- Linda is a psychiatric social worker.
- Linda is a member of the League of Women Voters.

*Tversky, A., & Kahneman, D. (1983). Extensional versus intuitive reasoning: The conjunction fallacy in probability judgment. *Psychological Bulletin, 90,* 293–315.

- Linda is a bank teller.
- Linda is a bank teller and active in the feminist movement.

Although feminism was not mentioned in Linda's description, she fits the stereotype of a person who might become active in the feminist movement. For this reason, the vast majority of those questioned believed it more likely that Linda is a bank teller and active in the feminist movement than that Linda is just a bank teller. Unfortunately, this response is completely illogical. To see why, imagine that, instead of Linda's future, you were asked to predict the outcome of two coin tosses. Would you predict that a head followed by a tail is more likely than a head alone? Of course not. Yet most respondents believed that Linda's becoming a bank teller *and* an active feminist is more likely than her becoming a bank teller alone. By focusing on the stereotyped aspects of the case, intuitive decision making results in an illogical conclusion.

(Meehl, himself, held this view.) The tasks for which intuitive decision making is superior varied from critic to critic (treatment planning, dream interpretation, and so on), but there was a common thread. None of these skills had yet been put to empirical test. In other words, until research demonstrated otherwise, intuitive judgment was to be considered superior to statistical methods by default. As research evidence accumulated, the number of activities for which the clinician could claim superiority gradually declined. A more insidious criticism was aimed at the research enterprise itself. According to some critics, studies such as those summarized by Meehl are unnecessary because clinical techniques should be evaluated by their perceived usefulness to the clinician. These critics justify ignoring the scientific literature by appealing to expert judgment which, they believe, should take precedence over "artificial" research findings. ("Sure, research studies have failed to find evidence

to support Rorschach predictions, but my experience is that the test is useful when combined with my clinical judgment.")

Meehl anticipated this line of argument in his book. In a chapter called "Unavoidability of Statistics," Meehl challenged those who champion the intuitive approach to prove their case. After all, clinical experience is easily quantified. All clinicians need to do is keep a running tally of their predictions—both successful and unsuccessful. If intuition is clinically useful, then it should lead to more successes than failures. As Meehl wrote: "If the clinical utility is really established and not merely proclaimed, it will have been established by procedures that have all the earmarks of an acceptable validation study. If not, it [clinical utility] is a weasel phrase and we ought not to get by with it."

Many psychologists took Meehl's advice. Ten years after *Clinical versus Statistical Prediction* was published, Jack Sawyer reviewed 45 studies comparing

ASSESSING PREDICTIONS

It is not very difficult to ensure the accuracy of clinical predictions. For example, to ensure that all potentially suicidal patients are prevented from following through on their intentions, all one need do is predict that all depressed patients will attempt suicide and order special precautions for everyone. No suicides will be missed, but many nonsuicidal patients will be restricted unnecessarily. Such an approach is said to have a high *false-positive* rate. (Many people are falsely labeled suicide risks.)

High false-positive rates are tolerated when their costs are relatively low. For example, not only infected individuals but also many healthy people show a "positive" response to the tuberculosis screening test (the one which requires that a fluid be injected under the skin). In other words, the test is good at identifying individuals who have the disease but some "positives" are not really infected. These false-positives are eliminated by follow-up tests such as chest x-rays. Because the costs involved are small (a temporary rash and an unnecessary x-ray) and

because the test identifies practically all of the true-positives, a high false-positive rate is tolerated. There are times, however, when false-positives must be minimized. To return to the suicide example, the cost in money, staff time, and restriction of individual freedom involved in ordering special precautions for all depressed patients is simply too high for most clinics and hospitals to sustain.

Neither clinical or statistical prediction is ever 100% perfect. Both produce true- and false-positive outcomes. To assess whether one method is superior to the other, we need to consider the relative costs and benefits of the various outcomes. An approach to prediction that leads to many correct outcomes, but also produces many false-positives, may not be as useful or practical as an approach which has fewer correct "hits" but does not lead to many "false-positives." Looked at from this perspective, judging whether statistical or clinical prediction is superior becomes a complicated task indeed.

---

clinical and statistical prediction. Again, there was not a single one that showed clinical predictions to be superior. Studies performed in succeeding decades have reinforced these early reviews establishing beyond much doubt the superiority of statistical prediction. Even nonactuarial statistical methods have proven superior to clinical intuition. Nonactuarial formulas are not derived from the research literature, nor are they based on the experience of a large number of clinicians. They are designed to mimic a single clinician's behavior. For example, we can create a formula for the prediction of suicide by asking an expert clinician to "think aloud" while evaluating cases. By noting the questions that the expert asks, and how various items of data are used, we can devise a formula that mimics this specific clinician's approach to the task. We can then test the formula by comparing its predictions with those of the expert. What do we find? Frequently, the formula *outperforms* the expert it was designed to

mimic! This phenomenon is known as *bootstrapping* after the colloquial expression "to pull yourself up by your own bootstraps." According to psychologist Lewis Goldberg, bootstrapping occurs because

> the clinician is not a machine. While he possesses his full share of human learning and hypothesis-generating skills, he lacks a machine's reliability. He "has his days." Boredom, fatigue, illness, situational and interpersonal distractions all plague him, with the result that his repeated judgments of exactly the same stimulus configurations are not identical. . . . If we could remove some of this human unreliability by eliminating the random error in his judgments, we should thereby increase the value of the resulting predictions.[4]

Thirty years after his book was published, Meehl looked back on the ensuing research. He wrote that "there is no controversy in social science which shows such a large body of qualitatively diverse studies coming out so uniformly in the same direction as this one."[5] Nevertheless, despite the impressive research results, intuition remains the dominant mode of professional judgment. One reason is the lack of appropriate performance feedback. We know how well, or poorly, statistical formulas predict because the relevant records are readily available. In contrast, feedback on intuitive judgments is often incomplete. Clinical psychologists never find out whether patients placed on special precautions would really have attempted suicide if left alone. In the absence of any evidence to the contrary, they assume that their predictions were accurate but they may just as well have been wrong. Sometimes, experts ensure the validity of their own predictions. The prototype situation is the piano teacher who predicts that a student will perform exceptionally well. This judgment leads the teacher to give the student extra attention which, in turn, results in exceptional performance — proving, in the teacher's mind at least, that she is a good judge of talent.

An even more important reason for the persistence of clinical intuition is professional pride. States license psychologists certifying their "clinical" expertise. Courts routinely admit intuitive testimony ("In my expert opinion . . .") as evidence in legal proceedings. Experts are well paid and respected. It is difficult for them to acknowledge that their intuitive judgments may be flawed. Yet, not to acknowledge their fallibility may be ethically irresponsible. In his 1986 article, Meehl puts it this way: "If I try to forecast something important about a college student, or a criminal, or a depressed patient by inefficient rather than efficient means, meanwhile charging him or the taxpayer 10 times as much money as I would need to achieve greater predictive accuracy, this is not a sound ethical practice. That it feels good, more warm and cuddly to me as the predictor is a shabby excuse indeed" (p. 375).

Meehl's book produced considerable controversy, and the last word has yet to be heard. The book's success is itself another illustration of the fallibility of intuitive decision making. As previously noted, commercial publishers rejected Meehl's book predicting that it would never sell. It has now been reprinted seven times and is one of the most widely cited books in the field of judgment and decision making. Perhaps publishers should consider replacing acquisition editors with statistical formulas.

Further Reading

Meehl, P. E. (1954). *Clinical versus statistical prediction.* Minneapolis: University of Minnesota Press.

Rorschach, H. (1942). *Psychodiagnostics.* (P. Lemkau & B. Kroneberg, Trans.). New York: Grune and Stratton.

Notes

1. Quotations from Rorschach in this chapter are taken from: Rorschach, H. (1942). *Psychodiagnostics* (P. Lemkau & B. Kroneberg, Trans.). New York: Grune and Stratton. (Original work published 1921)
2. Unless otherwise noted, all quotations are from: Meehl, P. E. (1954). *Clinical versus statistical prediction.* Minneapolis: University of Minnesota Press.
3. Dawes, R. (1988). *Rational choice in an uncertain world.* Orlando, FL: Harcourt, Brace, Jovanovich. Pp. 66–67.
4. Goldberg, L. R. (1970). Man versus model of man: A rationale, plus some evidence, for a method of improving on clinical inferences. *Psychological Bulletin, 73,* 423.
5. Meehl, P. E. (1986). Causes and effects of my disturbing little book. *Journal of Personality Assessment, 50,* 371.

CHAPTER 2

What's in a Name?

Several times each month, Mr. M. has "visions" that he claims are sent to him directly from God. These holy messages contain recommendations about how people should live their lives. Mr. M. feels compelled to convey this advice to anyone who will listen. His speech is normally intelligible, but he occasionally produces a strange babble that he believes to be the voice of a spirit which sometimes occupies his body. He can tell when the spirit departs because, exhausted by its heavenly labors, Mr. M. faints dead away.

Is Mr. M.'s behavior abnormal? Is he mentally ill? There are no easy answers to these questions. Although *abnormal behavior* and *mental illness* are terms that appear frequently in the writings of psychologists, psychiatrists, and sociologists, they have no universally agreed-upon definitions. Precisely the same behavior may sometimes be considered "normal" and at other times "abnormal" depending on the circumstances in which it occurs. For example, Mr. M.'s behavior is common among charismatic evangelists who experience visions, speak in "tongues," and fall into trances. Those attending a fundamentalist prayer meeting would not consider Mr. M. to be abnormal. Indeed, they probably would judge his behavior to be exemplary. In contrast, Mr. M.'s visions and babbling would be viewed as exceedingly strange if they occurred during the annual IBM stockholders' meeting — perhaps strange enough to have him committed to a mental hospital. Because the same behavior can be judged normal (if Mr. M. is an evangelist) or abnormal (if he is chairman of IBM), you can see why it is difficult to define what is meant by the term *abnormal behavior*.

Mental illness is equally contentious. The incoherent speech, rapid changes in mood, hallucinations,

To define true madness,
What is't but to be nothing else but mad?

—William Shakespeare

and bizarre behavior that characterize severe "mental illness" are universally recognized as serious disturbances. Practically all societies—modern and primitive, Eastern and Western, socialist and capitalist—provide special care for those who exhibit severely "disturbed" behavior. To those who work with such people, the existence of mental illness appears self-evident and the controversy surrounding the term seems puzzling. Yet there are important differences between mental and physical illnesses. We have already mentioned one: Mental illnesses are context dependent while physical illnesses are not. If someone has a cough, a cloudy chest x-ray, and a bacterial infection, then he or she has pneumonia. Whether the person is an evangelist or a businessperson is irrelevant.

A second difference between physical and mental illness is that changing social values affect the latter more than the former. For example, until relatively recently, homosexuality was considered to be a *personality disorder* (a medical diagnosis sanctioned by the psychiatric profession). At its 1973 annual meeting, the American Psychiatric Association voted to remove homosexuality from its list of recognized diagnoses. From that day forward, homosexuality was no longer a personality disorder; indeed, it was no longer an illness at all. The American Psychiatric Association's action acknowledged changes in society's views, especially an increased tolerance for alternative sexual preferences. But their vote also underscored an important difference between mental and physical illness. It is ludicrous to imagine a meeting of doctors voting to declare that pneumonia (or diabetes or heart disease) is no longer to be an illness. In the field of abnormal behavior, such events are not only possible, they occur all too frequently. As noted in the Introduction, the history of psychopathology is characterized by constantly changing definitions of abnormal behavior.

The social nature of psychopathology is not always recognized, even by professionals working in the field. Many prefer to think of abnormal behavior as the manifestation of some type of mental illness. This way of thinking is, to a great extent, the legacy of Emil Kraepelin, whose pioneering work on the definition and classification of abnormal behavior is discussed in this chapter. Kraepelin was the great categorizer of psychopathology. He grouped different types of behavior disorders together and gave many their present names. Although most modern psychologists admit that progress in the treatment and prevention of psychopathology requires that behavior be classified into categories, some worry that the classification process itself can prove damaging. For example, people labeled "mentally ill" may face discrimination in employment and housing. Even worse, those who have been diagnosed mentally ill may begin to think differently about themselves. They may, for example, come to believe that they are no longer in control of their own behavior—their "illness" determines how they behave. The power of diagnostic labels was illustrated dramatically by David Rosenhan in a controversial study that is also described in this chapter. By juxtaposing Kraepelin and Rosenhan's work, it is possible to compare the benefits and costs of classifying behavior disorders into categories while highlighting the stark contrast between medical and social views of abnormal behavior. Table 2.1 lists terms that are commonly used to refer to problem behavior.

DEFINING NORMALITY

It is common to read that 10 (or 20 or 50) percent of adults behave abnormally enough to require psychological help at some time in their lives. The source of these figures is often unclear, but one point seems obvious: Before we can say that someone is behaving abnormally, we must first have some conception of what is normal.

Statistical Deviance

A common approach to defining "normality" is to call any behavior that characterizes the majority of people as "normal." This type of definition is called *statistical* because a person is considered to be abnormal when his or her behavior deviates from the statistical average. (This is where the term *deviant* comes from.) Statistical definitions are widely used. A person of normal height is one who is neither much taller nor much shorter than average; a person of normal weight is neither heavier nor lighter than average. Statistical definitions have many virtues: they are intuitively plausible, straightforward, and easy to understand. However, they are inadequate when applied to many human traits. For example, the average intelligence test (IQ) score is 100. A person with a score of 140 deviates as much from the average score as does one with an IQ of 60. Both are equally "abnormal" according to the statistical

TABLE 2.1   Terms Commonly Used to Refer to Problem Behavior

Term	Common Usage
Abnormal behavior	Overt behavior that is either unusual, maladaptive, or a symptom of some mental disorder.
Behavior disorder	Synonymous with "abnormal behavior" but suggests the problem is caused by experience or faulty learning.
Mental illness or emotional disturbance	Supposed underlying cause of abnormal behavior (e.g., "Mr. Smith is afraid of heights because he suffers from acrophobia").
Maladaptive behavior	Behavior that is harmful to an individual or to a group of individuals.
Insanity	A legal term used to refer to people who are unable to manage their lives or to control their actions.
Psychopathology	An umbrella term that includes all the terms given above.

definition, yet we do not think of exceptionally intelligent people as abnormal. Similarly, breathtakingly beautiful and hideously disfigured people are equally rare (or deviant), but we do not consider beautiful people to be abnormal.

Statistical definitions are particularly inappropriate when applied to behavior. As already noted, what might be considered normal behavior at one time and place may be viewed as abnormal in another. The Nazis, who put millions of innocent people to death in Europe, were adhering to social norms within their own subculture. Should their behavior, therefore, have been considered normal? Clearly, the Allies did not think so; they put the Nazis on trial as war criminals. It seems that common behavior can sometimes be considered abnormal. The converse is also true. Relatively uncommon behavior can be viewed as normal. For example, homosexuality was no more common in 1973 (when the American Psychiatric Association voted to remove it from its list of mental disorders) than at other times in history. Whatever abnormal behavior may be, it is clear that it is not simply a deviation from some statistical norm.

Maladaptive Behavior

Most of us like to think of ourselves as nonconformists. We are not slaves to tradition or convention but individualists who control our own destinies. Conformists, on the other hand, are seen as conventional people who stifle their individuality for fear of what others may think. But there is a darker side to nonconformity. For example, criminals are nonconformists, yet few would consider their behavior admirable. They threaten our collective survival, which depends on a certain amount of "team playing." This does not mean that individuals must all think and act alike (new ideas are crucial if society is ever to improve), but we do expect everyone to behave in ways that enhance their own well-being as well as that of the greater society. Alcoholism, suicide, violence, corruption, racial prejudice, wasting natural resources, hallucinations, delusions, anxiety attacks, and depression are all *maladaptive* behaviors because they threaten both individual and collective survival.

Several textbook writers have argued that behavior should be judged abnormal to the extent that it is maladaptive. While this definition solves some of the problems presented by the statistical definition, it is still not entirely satisfactory. The main problem is that it confuses antisocial behavior which may lead to personal gain with irrational behavior. No one would deny that corrupt politicians, industrial polluters, and racial bigots threaten the well-being of society, but it seems inappropriate to lump them together with depressed, anxious, confused, and suicidal people whose maladaptive behavior is not

SUBJECTIVE DISTRESS: AN UNRELIABLE CRITERION OF ABNORMALITY

Although some people are sufficiently distressed by their psychological problems to seek assistance, there are others who are not at all troubled by their maladaptive behavior. Perhaps the most extreme example is those individuals said to be suffering from a *manic* episode. A manic person is neither sad nor troubled. On the contrary, a person experiencing mania is likely to feel good, have a good self-concept, and feel capable of reaching any goal. (In answer to the ritual "How are you today?" one manic patient of my acquaintance replied, "Doc, if I were any better they could sell tickets.") Manic people may spend all of their money (plus money they don't have) on cars and other luxuries, they may go without sleep for days and forget to eat, they may even engage in dangerous, or at least foolish, stunts, yet they are not at all distressed. Their delusions of grandeur protect them from reality. An idea of what it feels like may be gathered from the following excerpt from John Custance's book, *Wisdom, Madness and Folly.** Custance was taken to hospital after entering a church and demanding money to assist a London streetwalker to give up her life of sin for one of righteousness. When he was refused, Custance began to tear apart the building. These words were written while the author was still in the midst of that manic episode:

> I feel so close to God, so inspired by his spirit that in a sense I am God. I see the future, plan the Universe, save mankind; I am utterly and completely immortal; I am even male and female. The whole Universe, animate and inanimate, past, present, and future, is within me. All nature and life, all spirits, are co-operating and connected with me; all things are possible. I am in a sense identical with all spirits from God to Satan. I reconcile Good and Evil and create light, darkness, worlds, universes.

Later, while recovering in hospital, Custance wrote:

> . . . I felt utterly and completely forgiven, relieved from all burden of sin. The whole of infinity seemed to open up before me, and during the weeks and months which followed I passed through experiences which are virtually indescribable. The complete transformation of "reality" transported me as it were into the Kingdom of Heaven. The ordinary beauties of nature, particularly I remember the skies at sunrise and sunset, took on a transcendental loveliness beyond belief. Every morning, quite contrary to my usual sluggish habits, I jumped up to look at them, and when possible went out to drink in, in a sort of ecstasy, the freshness of the morning air. . . . In a way I had fallen in love . . . with the whole Universe. Everything felt akin. I was joined to creation, no longer shut away in my little shell. And my vision of the Power of Love was the key to it all.

Clearly, Custance's subjective perceptions of his mental state could not be relied on as a guide to whether he needed clinical help. He was not subjectively distressed, yet practically everyone who came in contact with him viewed his behavior as seriously abnormal. How such judgments should be made is one of the most important and controversial areas of psychopathology.

---

*Custance, J. (1952). *Wisdom, madness and folly.* N.Y.: Farrar, Straus & Cudahay.

motivated by personal gain. To get around this problem, some mental-health professionals have proposed that maladaptive behavior only be considered pathological if it produces *subjective distress* for the individual involved. To take a common example, many people are frightened of speaking in front of groups. Although this fear is clearly maladaptive in a general sense, it probably will not cause much distress for the average person who is rarely called on to perform. On the other hand, those who are required to speak in public may find their fear distressing enough to seek professional help. People in the latter group have identified their maladaptive behavior as "abnormal" while those who are never called on to speak do not see themselves as having a psychological problem.

Allowing people to decide for themselves whether their behavior is abnormal relieves us of the burden of having to make value judgments about other people. Unfortunately, individuals are not always the best judge of their own behavior. Consider the young woman who decides that she would look better if she lost weight. She diets until she becomes thin, but she still believes that she is too fat. She continues to diet and becomes emaciated, yet she desires to lose even more weight claiming that she would look better if she were even thinner. Continued dieting will put her life at risk, but she refuses to eat. At this point, clinicians would justify force-feeding her because her behavior is life-threatening. They consider such excessive dieting abnormal even though the young woman does not. Clinicians defend their ability to make such judgments by pointing to the irrational nature of this woman's behavior. Emaciated people are not beautiful, and continued starvation will lead to death. Surely, they argue, no normal person would behave this way; therefore, this person must be abnormal.

Clinicians who reason this way are not using a *statistical* or a *subjective distress* definition of abnormality. While the young woman's behavior is clearly maladaptive, their judgment is not based solely on this fact either. (As already mentioned, many types of maladaptive behavior are not considered pathological.) Clinicians who make such judgments rely on a rather different approach to defining abnormality: the *pathology* definition. They believe that the woman who refuses to eat cannot be a good judge of her own behavior because she is suffering from a mental illness, in this case, *anorexia nervosa*.

Behavior Pathology

As discussed in the Introduction, there have been many different theories about the causes of abnormal behavior. At one time or another, demonic possession, imbalanced humors, lunar cycles, unconscious conflicts, brain damage, and microbial infections have all been implicated. Toward the end of the 19th century, these various causes coalesced into two main theories: *somatogenic* and *psychogenic*. Somatogenic causes of psychopathology originate in the body's tissues (the term comes from the

Greek word *soma*, which means "body"). Psychogenic causes are those which originate from the mind or, more accurately, from past experiences that have left their mark on the *psyche* (Greek for "mind"). The 19th century was the golden age of somatogenesis. Somatic causes of abnormal behavior were sought and sometimes found. Toward the end of the century, however, potential psychogenic causes of abnormal behavior (for hysteria, for example) were also identified.

Over the succeeding decades, clinicians have hotly debated whether one or another form of abnormal behavior is psychogenic or somatogenic. But virtually all agree that—no matter what their origin—many behavioral aberrations can be considered illnesses. They are called "mental illnesses" because their symptoms are mainly psychological, but they are illnesses just the same. Given this view, it follows that clinicians should attack the problems of abnormal behavior using the general approach that has worked so well for physical illnesses. Specifically, doctors are taught to observe symptoms and signs and infer their underlying cause (the illness). Treatment is then directed toward eliminating the underlying illness. Once this is accomplished, the symptoms will usually disappear. For example, say that the previously mentioned patient with a cough, fever, and cloudy chest x-ray is diagnosed as having pneumonia. Antibiotic treatment is directed toward removing the underlying respiratory infection, which in turn eliminates the symptoms. The fever could have been reduced by bathing the patient in ice and the cough suppressed by medication, but such *symptomatic* treatment is futile because, underneath, the patient would still be sick. Applying the same general approach to behavioral problems, overt behavioral "symptoms" are believed to result from some underlying (usually unconscious) cause. The example used in the Introduction was enuresis (the symptom), which, according to the pathology definition of behavior disorders, is really the result of unconscious conflict (the illness). To cure the enuresis, the clinicians must eliminate the underlying conflict. Attacking bed-wetting directly is as futile as packing the feverish pneumonia patient in ice because, until the unconscious conflict is resolved, the patient remains "sick."

The widespread adoption of the pathology definition of abnormal behavior was encouraged, at least in part, by clinical training methods. For most of this and the previous century, most clinicians were psychiatrists, trained in medicine and not, as is commonly supposed, in psychology. It is only natural that they would apply their medical training to abnormal behavior. Because individual illnesses typically produce characteristic sets of symptoms, 19th-century doctors devoted themselves to grouping symptoms into *syndromes* (groups of symptoms that tend to occur together). Their goal was to create a reliable set of diagnoses—a classification system for medicine.

CLASSIFICATION AND DIAGNOSIS

An important characteristic of the life sciences (e.g., botany, physiology, and microbiology) that distinguishes them from the physical sciences (physics, chemistry) is the amazing diversity of living things. Plants, insects, birds, mammals, all types of organisms come in a multitude of different forms. Scientific study would be impossibly tedious if every bird, insect, and plant turned out to be unique. It would be far easier if related organisms could somehow be grouped together. Thus, it is not surprising that modern biology began with 18th- and 19th-century *naturalists*.

The naturalists were mainly English and almost entirely amateurs. They supported themselves by collecting unusual specimens (both plant and animal) and selling them to museums. They included among their number, bird watchers, country squires, doctors, surveyors, and anyone else who enjoyed the outdoors. The naturalists were concerned with three interrelated matters. The first was discovering new organisms and giving them names. To think, talk, and write about organisms, to communicate their knowledge to other people, scientists must be able to assign each organism a unique name. Because an organism's name becomes part of our language, there was much competition among naturalists to discover and name new organisms. This competition continues today. The second major interest of naturalists was in classifying organisms into groups. This required the careful study of similarities and differences in both the physical appearance and the functioning of different species. The final matter that occupied the naturalists was explaining the diversity of nature. That is, they wished to know not only what forms organisms can take but also how these forms developed. This inter-

est culminated in the work of Charles Darwin and Alfred Russel Wallace, two Englishmen who independently put forward the theory of evolution by natural selection.

Nineteenth-century doctors and medical scientists became attracted to the work being done by naturalists. According to medical writer and physician Lewis Thomas, the main reason for their interest was a profound loss of faith in the orthodoxies of their own profession. Better medical record keeping, and a more skeptical attitude, showed them that the complicated treatments then in use did not really work. Indeed, some treatments did more harm than good. At the same time, it was noted that when left alone many diseases appeared to be self-limited—patients recovered without medical intervention. These diseases followed a characteristic "natural history" in which patients passed through a series of stages eventually returning to their original state of health. This was a major discovery that had an overwhelming effect on medicine. For centuries, doctors had been in the habit of "treating" every complaint. They believed that without some intervention, patients would never recover. Now it became obvious that they were wrong. Patients could recover by themselves without medical intervention, and they often did better untreated than when they received the bizarre herbs, heavy metals, cupping, bleeding, and poultices that were popular at the time.

In an attempt to put their profession on a scientific basis, 19th-century doctors abandoned their useless treatments and consciously set out to emulate the naturalists. In a parallel of the naturalist's method, medical researchers undertook meticulous observations of the sick. They noted new symptom patterns (syndromes) to which they assigned names. They classified syndromes into groups based on similarities in appearance, disturbances of physiological functioning, and natural history. Finally, they attempted to explain how and why syndromes develop by inferring underlying disease states. Textbook writers of the time pointed out the similarity between medical diagnosis and the scientific classification methods used in botany and other branches of biology. For example, in a text published in 1864, students were told:

> The detection of disease is the product of the close observation of symptoms, and the correct deduction from these symptoms. . . . When . . . the

FIGURE 2.1 Woodcut showing patients suffering from general paresis with varying degrees of deterioration.

symptoms of the malady have been discovered, the next step toward a diagnosis is a proper appreciation of their significance and of their relation toward each other. Knowledge, and above all, the exercise of the reasoning faculties are now indispensable.[1]

In modern terms, 19th-century medical students were advised to make observations, listen to patients describe their symptoms, and consider these to be signs of some underlying disease. The course of the postulated disease could then be observed. For example, unraveling the mystery of general paresis (the most widespread "mental illness" of the 19th century) began when the broad category of "mad" patients was divided into two groups: a large, heterogeneous group and a smaller group whose illness led to delusions of grandeur, intellectual decline, and eventually paralysis. Once this preliminary two-group classification was made, those in the smaller group were subjected to intensive study. Their symptoms were precisely described and so too was the course of their illness. It shortly became clear that their symptoms constituted an independent syndrome—a specific type of madness called *general paresis* (see Figure 2.1). Once the syndrome was described, labeled, and separated from others with similar symptoms, medical researchers began to search for its cause and cure.

Eventually one was found. General paresis turned out to be the result of brain deterioration caused by long-term syphilis. Once the etiology was clear, it was only a matter of time before a cure was discovered, first the arsenic compound arsphenamine and later the more effective drug penicillin.

The general-paresis story was repeated many times in the last century. Soon, doctors began to know what to expect from many different illnesses. Patients could be told not just the name of the disease they were unlucky enough to have contracted but also what was likely to become of them. By trying out different treatments and noting their effects, surgical procedures, medicines, and vaccines became available for many illnesses. The discovery of effective treatments and preventive measures added another link to the inferential chain that doctors constructed each time they examined patients. For the first time in history, they could observe symptoms, diagnose patients by classifying them into disease categories, and link these diagnoses to specific treatments. Once medicine embraced this systematic approach, progress was rapid. By the end of the 19th century, scientific medicine had all but replaced the haphazard empiricism of the past. It is not surprising that an approach which proved so successful in solving the mysteries of general paresis would also be applied to other mental illnesses. Before this could happen, however, the various mental illnesses had to be identified. Accurate diagnosis—classifying patients into more-or-less homogeneous categories—became the major preoccupation of many 19th-century psychiatrists. Foremost among these was Emil Kraepelin.

Emil Kraepelin: A Nomenclature for Psychopathology

Emil Kraepelin was born in Germany in 1856. His father was an actor who eked out a precarious living giving prose recitations in small towns. Kraepelin's childhood coincided with the Prussian victory over the French and the establishment of the German empire. As a consequence, he grew up and remained throughout his life an extreme nationalist convinced of the racial superiority of the German people. When he was 18, after a brief stint in the army, Kraepelin entered the University of Leipzig. He intended to study medicine, but he had difficulty gaining admission to the course and turned to psychology instead. His teacher was Wilhelm Wundt, the person generally regarded as the founder of modern experimental psychology. Although Kraepelin did go on to study medicine and ultimately became a psychiatrist, he maintained a lifelong interest in scientific psychology. Experimental psychology was, and still is, an unusual background for a physician, and Kraepelin made the most of it. Over the years, he performed many psychological experiments including studies of sleep, word associations, humor, fatigue, and intoxication. All told, Kraepelin published eight volumes of psychological experiments in the journal he founded, *Psychological Work*. At one time, he hoped to win the Nobel Prize for his psychological research efforts. This expectation was never fulfilled, but in his later work on the classification of the behavior disorders, Kraepelin always maintained his faith in the scientific approach he learned from Wundt.

Kraepelin wrote his first paper on diagnosis while still a medical student. His purpose was to distinguish between internal causes of psychopathology (brain disease, genetics) and external causes such as traumatic experiences. Although he viewed internal and external causes as independent, Kraepelin believed that psychiatric symptoms were almost always the result of their interaction. ("The various stimuli on the one side and the changes of the nervous system on the other side produce the resulting symptom complex.") In this early paper, Kraepelin also made a stab at classifying the serious psychiatric disorders (known as *psychoses*) into two broad categories: agitated and quiet.

This early paper presaged Kraepelin's later work on classification; it appeared when the study of psychological problems was still in its infancy. Only a few decades before, German doctors had defined mental disorders in moral terms. "Insanity" was seen as the result of uncontrolled desire—a kind of punishment meted out to sinners. No attempt was made to differentiate independent types of mental disorders. Instead, doctors wrote about a single disease whose course passed through a series of stages: depression, agitation, confusion, paranoia, and dementia. As medicine became more scientific, this began to change. Several classification schemes were proposed. Unfortunately, progress was slow because there was little commonality among doctors—each had a different list of mental illnesses.

Kraepelin completed his medical studies in 1878 and then held several different positions including

FIGURE 2.2 Emil Kraepelin (1856–1926)

one as an experimental psychologist in Wundt's laboratory. He considered abandoning psychiatry for a career in psychology but was dissuaded by Wundt, who was not convinced that the fledgling science had much of a future. Following Wundt's advice, Kraepelin took up a clinical post in Munich and, when he was just 27 years old, produced his first book, the *Compendium of Psychiatry*. In the *Compendium*, Kraepelin attacked the single disease concept and reiterated the point made in the paper he published while still a student—that behavioral disorders are the result of an interaction of internal and external causes. He noted the need for a common classification system that all psychiatrists could use and argued that mental illnesses would ultimately be shown to be diseases of the brain. However, until these diseases were discovered, Kraepelin advocated the development of a classification of overt "symptom complexes" or syndromes. Later editions of the *Compendium* and its successor, *Psychiatry: A Textbook for Students and Physicians*, were to make Kraepelin world-famous. He took up his first professorial position when he was just 30 years old and, in his career, held positions at several prestigious universities.

While pursuing many lines of research, Kraepelin continued to revise his textbook. With each revision, he further refined his classification system. Each new refinement was based on his careful clinical observations supplemented by statistical compilations of symptoms. His goal was to classify mental "diseases" according to their etiology, symptoms, natural history, and brain pathology (if any). In the fifth edition of his textbook, Kraepelin carefully delineated *dementia praecox*, a syndrome that is now called schizophrenia. In the sixth edition, Kraepelin introduced the concept of *manic-depressive psychosis* combining what were previously thought to be two unrelated conditions.

The ninth edition appeared in 1927, one year after his death. It had grown to 2,500 pages in which everything known about psychiatry to that time was covered. By this time, Kraepelin had classified psychological disturbances into dozens of categories including organic conditions, mental deficiency, and personality disorders as well as dementia praecox and affective disorders such as manic-depressive psychoses. Many of these categories were not entirely new. Even the terms *dementia praecox* and *manic-depressive psychosis* had been used by others before him. However, Kraepelin was able to combine observations made by others, his own observations, and his great knowledge of both psychological and other research to piece together coherent pictures of many behavior disorders.

Kraepelin was clearly a glutton for work (it is not a coincidence that he called the journal he founded *Psychological Work*). He was also a stern man who forbid his staff, even his guests, from drinking alcohol or smoking. His private life was tragic—four of his six children died young—and he had few close friendships. Yet, when he died, he shared with Sigmund Freud the honor of being one of the two most famous psychiatrists of his time.

CLASSIC STUDY 3
Dementia Praecox

Kraepelin's prodigious work on the classification of mental disorders is too voluminous to be discussed in this book. Nevertheless, it is possible to get a feeling for the flavor of his approach by concentrating on just one of his many accomplishments—the identification and description of *dementia praecox*.

As already noted, until the 19th century, there was no clear notion of separate psychological disorders. The "unitary disease" position was put most forcefully by Heinrich Neumann, a famous 19th-century German psychiatrist who wrote, "There is only one kind of mental disease, we call it insanity." By there were some who objected. One was Benedict Morel, a psychiatrist working in France who became famous for predicting the later madness of Ludwig II of Bavaria. Morel is best known for a case study he published in 1860. He described a teenage boy who started out a star student but who gradually lost interest in school, social activities, and life in general. The boy became silent, withdrawn, and secretive. He spent his time alone and seemed uninterested in any activities. At one time, the boy threatened to murder his father but instead of carrying out his threat he seemed to forget he ever made it. Morel thought that the boy's social and intellectual decline was the irreversible result of some genetic disease. He gave the syndrome the French name *démence précoce* (mental deterioration in youth) to distinguish it from the more common mental deterioration (dementia) of old age.

Some years later, Kraepelin used the Latin version of Morel's term, *dementia praecox,* to group together a variety of superficially dissimilar conditions that he believed constituted a single "symptom-disease complex." Kraepelin first used the term *dementia praecox* in a paper he delivered to a psychiatry convention in 1898, but his major book on the topic, *Dementia Praecox and Paraphrenia*, did not appear until 20 years later. This book was typical of Kraepelin's approach to classification. In 13 chapters, he described the natural history of the syndrome and its physical and mental symptoms. He also discussed problems in differential diagnosis (discriminating dementia praecox from other syndromes) and made suggestions for treatment.

Kraepelin's first step was to differentiate dementia praecox from another serious condition, manic-depressive psychosis. According to Kraepelin, both syndromes were the result of internal causes (that is, their cause could not be found in experience or psychological trauma but could be found in physiology and genetics). But the two conditions had different symptoms and followed different courses. Manic-depressive psychosis followed a cyclic history and was mainly marked by mood changes. Dementia praecox began in youth or young adulthood and almost always followed a progressively deteriorating course. Its primary symptoms were hallucinations, delusions, negativism (uncooperativeness), and an inability to focus attention. According to Kraepelin, disorders that were formerly considered distinct and separate such as *paranoia* (delusions of persecution), *catatonia* (odd movements), and *hebephrenia* (thought disorder evidenced by peculiar language and speech) were actually all forms of dementia praecox. In this way, Kraepelin unified several disparate syndromes and conditions into one classification.

The following excerpts are all taken from *Dementia Praecox and Paraphrenia*.[2] They show the extreme care that characterized Kraepelin's work as well as his ability to use his observations of specific patients to abstract more general principles.

Kraepelin on Dementia Praecox

One of Kraepelin's major strengths was his ability to make symptoms come alive often using his patients' own words. Consider, for example, his discussion of a common symptom of dementia praecox, hallucinations:

> **Hallucinations.** —Sensation is very often profoundly disordered in our patients as is evident by the occurrence of hallucinations. . . . By far the most frequent are *hallucinations of hearing*. At the beginning, these are usually simple noises, rustling, buzzing, ringing in the ears, tolling of bells ("death knell"), knocking, moving of tables, cracking of whips, trumpets, yodel, singing, weeping of children, whistling, blowing, chirping, "shoot-

ing and death-rattle"; the bed echoes with shots. . . . Satan roars under the bed. . . .

> And then there develops gradually or suddenly the symptom peculiarly characteristic of dementia praecox, namely, the *hearing of voices*. Sometimes it is only whispering, "as if it concerned me," as a patient says, a secret language, "taunting the captive"; sometimes the voices are loud or suppressed, as from a ventriloquist, or the call of a telephone, "children's voices"; a person heard "gnats speak." Sometimes they shout as in a chorus or all confusedly; a patient spoke of "drumming in the ear"; another heard "729,000 girls." . . . At other times they do not appear to the patients as sense perceptions at all; they are "voices of conscience," "voices which do not speak with words." . . . A patient said: "It appeared to me in spirit, as though they would find fault, without having heard it." There is an "inner feeling in the soul" and "inward voice in the thoughts." . . .

> . . . For the most part the origin of the voices is sought for in the external world. The patient feels himself influenced by the telephone, is a "living telephone"; "it all came by telephone to the bed" said a patient. . . . A patient heard a bird whistle from a picture, another saw threads from which voices spoke. Often the voices torment the patient the whole day long, and at night also he hears "telephone gossip." . . .

> What the voices say is, as a rule, *unpleasant* and *disturbing*. The patient is everywhere made a fool of and teased, mocked, grossly abused and threatened. People speak about him; everyone is occupied with him. . . . Someone calls out: "Rascal, vagrant, miserable scoundrel, . . . anarchist, rogue, filthy beast . . . whore." . . . The patient is said to have assaulted a child, seduced a girl . . . eaten human flesh. . . .

> Many of the voices make remarks about the thoughts and doings of the patient: "He has good hearing," "Damn it, what ears the fellow has." . . . In a series of cases the voices *give commands* which in certain circumstances are very precisely obeyed. They forbid the patient to eat and to speak, to work, to go to church; he must run barefoot. "Go on, strike him, beat him," it is said, "go on, go on!" "Hands up!" "Jump in!"

> . . . It is quite specially peculiar to dementia praecox that the patients' own *thoughts appear to them to be spoken aloud*. . . . In consequence of this everything is made public. What the patients think . . . is proclaimed to everyone, so that their thoughts are common property. "I have the feel-

ing, as if someone beside me said out loud what I think," said a patient. . . . "Everyone can read my thoughts . . . ," complained a patient. Another said, "A person can have his thoughts traced by another, so that people can learn everything."

Kraepelin not only listened to and observed his patients, he also used his background in experimental psychology to perform "experiments." For example, to measure the "mental efficiency" of dementia praecox patients, Kraepelin had them perform arithmetic calculations for 10 minutes and recorded their performance rate with and without rests. He noted that performance dropped off abruptly because of a rapid build-up of fatigue (see Figure 2.3). Excessive fatigue and a lack of mental alertness became an important sign of dementia praecox that Kraepelin studied in further experiments.

Kraepelin was interested in every aspect of his patients' lives. His book contains samples of his patients' handwriting, transcriptions of their speech, and reproductions of their drawings. Kraepelin also kept careful records of his patients' weight, body temperature, menses, respiration, and blood pressure. He even performed histological studies comparing their nerve cells with those taken from nonpsychiatric patients.

The result of Kraepelin's massive data-collection effort was extraordinarily detailed descriptions of dementia praecox patients. From these descriptions, Kraepelin formulated a set of diagnostic standards as well as some tips for differentiating the syndrome from other, superficially similar mental illnesses. For example:

Hysteria. — Very frequently cases of dementia praecox are regarded as hysteria. . . . What distinguishes hysteria and dementia praecox from each other, is above everything, the *behaviour of the emotions*. In hysteria, we find a heightened susceptibility of the emotional life; in dementia praecox the susceptibility is lowered. In hysterics, therefore, we observe rapid, violent, and often even lasting influence by impressions emphasized by emotion, while the emotional reactions in dementia praecox are mostly shallow or of short duration and essentially independent of external influences. . . . [Dementia praecox] patients remain indifferent toward visits, surprising communications, exciting experiences, which in hysteria immediately find response in lively reactions.

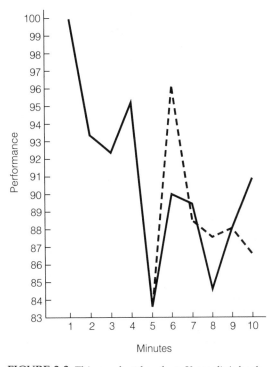

FIGURE 2.3 This graph, taken from Kraepelin's book, shows a rapid decrease in performance over a 10-minute period (solid line) when dementia praecox patients are asked to do continuous arithmetic calculations. The dotted line shows the recovery that occurs when patients are given a rest break after the first 5 minutes. Kraepelin used experiments such as this to gather detailed information about the cognitive abilities of his patients.

Not content with just description and differential diagnosis, Kraepelin also addressed himself to treatment. He politely dismissed the bizarre therapeutic suggestions made by earlier doctors (castration, injections of goat's blood, excision of the thyroid gland), and he was pessimistic about the possibility of total cure ("As we do not know the actual causes of dementia praecox, we shall not be able to . . . combat it"). Instead of cure, Kraepelin concentrated on relieving symptoms. His suggestions provide a good picture of some widely held attitudes of his time. It is interesting to note that Kraepelin argues for the establishment of large institutions on humanitarian grounds. Ironically, the

present-day trend—closing down large institutions—is also justified as humanitarian. This is yet
another reminder of the importance of cultural
values in psychopathology.

> **Treatment of Symptoms.**—Firstly in the cases
> which arise acutely . . . the placing of the patient
> in an institution is necessary to prevent accidents
> and suicide. Rest in bed, supervision, care for
> sleep and food, are here the most important requi-
> sites. In the states of excitement prolonged baths
> are suitable . . . quiet the patient so far by a seda-
> tive . . . that he may remain some hours in the
> bath. . . . If in very severe and lasting excitement
> this procedure is unsuccessful, the best expedient,
> which invariably after a shorter or longer time
> leads to the goal, is the employment of moist
> warm packs. . . . With all our measures we can not
> prevent the great majority of those who are psy-
> chically crippled or half crippled after dementia
> praecox gradually being gathered into large insti-
> tutions and homes for the insane. . . . What is
> necessary for them is occupation . . . *colonies for the
> insane,* with their manifold opportunities for work
> and treatment along general lines, preserving in-
> dependence as much as possible, are a blessing
> which can scarcely be too highly valued.

Near the end of his life, Kraepelin's complete description of dementia praecox had grown to include
36 major symptom categories each consisting of
hundreds of different signs. Although he believed
the signs all reflected dementia and a disintegration
in the normal relationships among thinking, feeling, and behaving, Kraepelin made no serious attempt to move beyond mere description to identify
the central characteristics of the disorder. He left
this for later writers, most notably Eugen Bleuler,
who showed that Kraepelin was wrong about many
aspects of the syndrome. For example, the syndrome does not always begin in adolescence (praecox) and its deteriorating course (dementia) is not
inevitable. Kraepelin's diagnostic terminology was
clearly misleading, so Bleuler proposed his own
name for the disorder, *schizophrenia*. This new name
embodied what Bleuler thought to be the syndrome's essential core problem, the breaking apart
(schizo) of the mind *(phren)*. Schizophrenia, of
course, is the diagnostic label still in use today. This
major form of psychopathology will be discussed in
more detail later in this book. For the present, it is
important to note that, despite his mistakes,
Kraepelin's meticulous observations and his will-

ingness to draw dissimilar conditions together into
a single classification were an essential first step in
the identification of schizophrenia. Many others
have built on his work, and even those who feel un-
easy about psychopathological labels admit that he
turned classification into a legitimate, respectable,
scientific enterprise and has left a legacy that is still
influencing clinical practice today.

AFTERMATH

Kraepelin did not focus solely on dementia praecox. In the final edition of his textbook, he divided
psychopathology into 13 categories: infectious
psychoses (caused by brain disease), exhaustion
psychoses (resulting from stress), intoxication psychoses (such as those caused by extreme alcoholism), thyroigenous psychosis (caused by a malfunctioning thyroid gland), dementia praecox, dementia
paralytica (accompanied by paralysis such as general paresis), organic dementia, involutional psychoses (occurring at menopause), manic-depressive
insanity (cyclic moods), paranoia (delusions of persecution), general neuroses (less serious psychopathology), psychopathy (criminal behaviors), and
mental retardation. Most of these categories contained specific syndromes. Kraepelin believed that
this set of relatively homogeneous diagnoses constituted an essential first step in medical progress. His
analogy was with physical illnesses. Once doctors
spoke of "the fevers" lumping together fever
caused by malaria with fever caused by pneumonia,
infection, and the common cold. Not surprisingly,
the causes of these very different illnesses were not
discovered until the underlying conditions were
recognized as independent. For Kraepelin, mental
illness was no different. Our understanding of
psychopathology must begin with a valid set of
diagnoses.

Most medically trained workers agreed. After a
few early failures, medical groups began to gravitate
toward Kraepelin's classification scheme. Perhaps
the first major group to adopt his diagnostic system
was the Association of Medical Superintendents of
American Institutions for the Insane, a group that
was later merged into the American Psychiatric Association. In Europe, the World Health Organization (WHO) added psychological disorders to its list
of medical illnesses eventually publishing the *International Statistical Classification of Diseases, Injuries*

TABLE 2.2   Axis I. Major Diagnostic Categories

Disorders usually first evident in infancy, childhood, or adolescence (e.g., anorexia nervosa)	Dissociative disorders (e.g., multiple personality)
Organic mental disorders (e.g., senile dementia)	Sexual disorders (e.g., exhibitionism)
Psychoactive substance abuse disorders (e.g., alcohol abuse)	Sleep disorders (e.g., insomnia)
Schizophrenia	Factitious disorder (e.g., feigning illness)
Delusional (paranoid) disorder	Impulse control disorder (e.g., kleptomania)
Mood disorders	Adjustment disorder (e.g., failure to adjust to stress such as excessive grieving)
Anxiety disorders (e.g., phobias)	Psychological factors affecting physical condition (e.g., obesity, migraine headaches)
Somatoform disorders (e.g., hypochondriasis)	Conditions not attributable to a mental disorder that still require treatment (e.g., marital problems)

TABLE 2.3   Axis II. Personality and Developmental Disorders

Specific developmental disorders (e.g., reading disorder)

Personality disorders (e.g., antisocial personality)

and Causes of Death. As Kraepelin had hoped, this classification system has gone through many revisions, but it has always been rather different from the system used in America and described in the various editions of the *Diagnostic and Statistical Manual* published by the American Psychiatric Association. The WHO system is mainly a collection of diagnostic terms while the American system has attempted to list the signs that should be used to make different diagnoses. Both systems are constantly in revision; with each new edition, they have become more closely aligned.

Today, the most widely accepted diagnostic scheme is the one published by the American Psy-chiatric Association. The system relies on a *multiaxial* approach. Each individual is described on five dimensions (axes). The first axis includes the major diagnostic categories, many of which are similar to those first suggested by Kraepelin (see Table 2.2). Axis II contains a set of conditions known as personality disorders (compulsive, dependent, narcissistic) and specific developmental disorders (reading and arithmetic disorders, for example) (see Table 2.3). Together, these two axes contain all the diagnostic labels recognized by the American Psychiatric Association.

On Axis III, the clinician evaluates any physical disorders that may be relevant to an individual's

TABLE 2.4 Axis IV. Severity of Psychosocial Stressors Scale: Adults

Severity Code	Description	Example
1	none	no relevant events
2	mild	child left home
3	moderate	lost job
4	severe	divorce
5	extreme	death of spouse
6	catastrophic	death of child
0	no information or no change	—

TABLE 2.5 Axis V. Global Assessment of Functioning

Severity Code	Description
81–90	Good functioning in all areas, socially effective
71–80	Temporary problems as a result of specific incidents (e.g., poor marks in school)
61–70	Mild symptoms such as occasional insomnia
51–60	Moderate symptoms including phobias
41–50	Serious problems such as suicide threats
31–40	Impairments in distinguishing reality from fantasy
21–30	Delusions or hallucinations
11–20	Gross problems that may present a danger to self or others

behavior. For example, an adolescent who has been misbehaving in school may have just learned that he or she has diabetes and will require a lifetime of treatment. Axis IV is used to record the social stress that the individual may be experiencing (see Table 2.4). This information is useful for understanding a specific case. For example, depression may be an appropriate reaction if we know that a person has recently experienced a divorce or the death of a close relative. The final axis is used to record the individual's highest level of functioning in the previous year (see Table 2.5). This information is useful in determining the prognosis for recovery and also for providing a benchmark for judging the effects of any treatment program. Clinicians often hope to restore individuals to their previous level of functioning. Axis V provides a crude measure of what the clinician can hope to achieve.

Although the modern multiaxial classification system has many strengths, the diagnostic scheme has some severe critics. Their criticisms take a variety of forms, but several general themes may be identified. The first, and most basic, criticism questions the pathology model that underlies the classification scheme and provides its rationale. Critics prefer to view most forms of psychopathology as the result of faulty habits developed from previous learning experiences or simply as "problems in living." This criticism is difficult to refute because many of the diagnostic labels currently in use do not appear to be connected to any clear-cut etiology nor do they have specific implications for treatment. As a consequence, labels lead to the following type of circular reasoning: Mr. X deliberately sets fires, so he must be suffering from *pyromania*. How do I know? Well, he sets fires, doesn't he? In such cases, using the diagnostic label provides illusory explanatory power. The label suggests that we know something about the underlying cause of fire setting when, in fact, the label simply describes the behavior it is meant to explain.

Although this criticism carries considerable force, it does not follow that diagnostic classifications should be abandoned. Grouping together

MULTIAXIAL CLASSIFICATION

The multiaxial classification system requires that people be assessed on five different dimensions. The goal is to give as complete a description of the individual as possible. To see how the system works in practice, consider the case of Christine.

Christine dropped out of college to work as a secretary so that her husband, Mike, could complete medical school. Her plan was to return to school after Mike finished his residency and, after a few years, start a family. Things seemed to be working out to plan. It was difficult getting by on Christine's money, but they both knew that things would soon improve. After 5 years of marriage, Christine felt content and optimistic about the future. In Mike's final year of residency training, he was offered an excellent university hospital post in a large Eastern city; he would have time for teaching as well as private practice. Christine could pick up her studies at the university. Christine could never remember being happier. Thus, it was all the more devastating when, shortly before they were due to move, Mike told her that he did not want her to come with him. He no longer loved her; in fact, he had someone else.

Christine was shattered. She went back to live with her parents and became increasingly depressed. She did not return to college. Instead, she spent most of her time alone arranging a record collection in alphabetical order, organizing all the recipes in the house by food group, and continually making the beds, arranging the cupboards, and cleaning house. Christine began to have difficulty sleeping and would frequently awake in the middle of the night and be unable to return to sleep. She lost her appetite and began to lose weight. No matter how hard her parents tried to interest her in getting out, Christine refused to talk with them. She simply cried and claimed her life was over. When Christine began to talk of suicide, her parents convinced her to see a psychologist.

On the basis of this case information, the psychologist made the following multiaxial diagnosis:

Axis I: Major depressive disorder

Axis II: Obsessive-compulsive personality disorder

Axis III: Because there is no physical condition affecting Christine's problem, no entry is made here.

Axis IV: Psychosocial stressors = 5 (extreme), divorce, rejection, change of location.

Axis V: Highest level of functioning in previous year = 90, good functioning in all areas, socially effective.

---

people with similar problems may lead to etiological discoveries (as in general paresis), and it is the only way to test out treatments. For example, we know that depressions caused by specific life events (divorce, job loss) respond differently to drugs than do depressions that arise more-or-less spontaneously without any obvious triggering cause. If we had not separated depressed people into these two separate categories (if we simply had considered all patients with depression to belong to a single group), we may never have made this discovery. Because only some people respond to the drugs, we probably would have concluded that they are ineffective when, in reality, they do work for a certain subcategory of patients.

A second common criticism of Kraepelin's type of diagnostic scheme is that the diagnostic classifications are unreliable. Critics claim that clinicians often disagree about a particular patient's diagnosis. While this is true for many subcategories, the diagnostic reliability of major categories (schizophrenia, mood disorders) is typically around 80% (the percentage of times that two clinicians come up with the same diagnosis). This figure compares favorably with the reliabilities achieved in other areas of medicine. Radiologists don't always agree when evaluating chest x-rays, cardiologists disagree about the meaning of electrocardiograms, and pathologists don't always agree about whether a tissue sample is malignant. Yet no one has ever argued that because radiologists, cardiologists, and pathologists do not always agree there is no value in trying to group syndromes into independent categories. It is well recognized that diagnosis always carries with it some uncertainty. The solution lies in better diagnostic procedures and not in the abandonment of classification schemes.

The third major theme voiced by critics is that the diagnostic process itself can be pernicious. The effects of labeling people on their later behavior were first systematized by sociologists Edwin Lemert and Thomas Scheff, who made a clear distinction between *primary* and *secondary* causes of abnormal behavior. Initially, psychopathology may arise from causes within an individual or from an individual's experience. A person may have contracted a disease such as general paresis, inherited a predisposition to mental illness, or undergone a traumatic experience. Any or all of these factors can produce abnormal behavior. Once the person begins to behave abnormally, however, a second force comes into play — society's reaction. Like the lepers of the past, and today's AIDS patients, people diagnosed mentally ill are socially disadvantaged and stigmatized. Affected individuals are ridiculed, shunned, feared, and isolated. People, even old friends, avoid them, and they find it difficult to obtain housing and jobs. To adapt, they withdraw from social contacts. In some cases, they become aggressive toward those who mistreat or ignore them. In this way, the diagnostic label becomes a kind of self-fulfilling prophecy. Once we label them mentally ill, we make it difficult for patients to cope by placing the blame for their problems not on our own attitudes but on the patients' "illness." Eventually, diagnostic labels begin to affect how people think about themselves. Labeled individuals lose faith in their ability to control their own lives. Instead, they become dependent on mental-health professionals to tell them how to behave. In effect, labels become secondary causes of abnormal behavior. The powerful role played by diagnostic labels was explored by David Rosenhan in the classic study described next.

CLASSIC STUDY 4
On Being Sane in Insane Places

David Rosenhan was educated at Yeshiva College where he studied mathematics and at New York's

FIGURE 2.4 David Rosenhan

Columbia University where he received degrees in both economics and psychology. After receiving his Ph.D. from Columbia in 1958, he held a variety of research and teaching positions at Haverford College, the University of Pennsylvania, Princeton University, the Educational Testing Service, and Swarthmore University. In 1971 he was appointed Professor of Psychology and Law at Stanford University where, except for visiting positions at Oxford, Western Australia, Tel Aviv, and Georgetown Universities, he has remained to this date. Rosenhan is the author of numerous scientific articles and several famous textbooks; he has also served as president of the American Board of Forensic Psychiatry and vice-president of the Institute for Psychosocial Interaction.

Rosenhan's classic research first appeared in the prestigious journal *Science* in 1973.[3] His article began with the following question: "If sanity and insanity exist, how shall we know them?" Rosenhan compared the pathology model of mental illness with the sociological emphasis on the importance of labels and decided to see which view

> is more nearly accurate by getting normal people (that is, people who do not have, and have never suffered, symptoms of serious psychiatric disorders) admitted to psychiatric hospitals and then determining whether they were discovered to be sane and, if so, how. If the sanity of such pseudopatients were always detected there would be prima facie evidence that a sane individual can be distinguished from the insane context in which he is found. Normality (and presumably abnormality) is distinct enough that it can be recognized wherever it occurs, for it is carried within the person. If, on the other hand, the sanity of the pseudopatients were never discovered, serious difficulties would arise for those who support traditional modes of psychiatric diagnosis. . . . Such an outcome would support the view that psychiatric diagnosis betrays little about the patient but much about the environment in which an observer finds him.

Over a 3-year period, Rosenhan arranged for eight "pseudopatients" to be admitted to 12 different psychiatric hospitals (some pseudopatients were admitted to more than one hospital). Among the eight pseudopatients were psychologists, physicians, a painter, a housewife, and Rosenhan himself. The hospitals were spread over five states on both the East and West coasts of the United States. Some hospitals were well-staffed teaching institutions; others were run-down state hospitals. Both public and private hospitals were represented.

Pseudopatients contacted their assigned hospital for an appointment and, on arrival at the admissions office, complained of hearing voices. The voices were the same sex as the patient and were unfamiliar. If asked what the voices said, the pseudopatients described them as unclear but they seemed to be saying "hollow," "empty," and "thud." These words were chosen because they suggested "existential" anguish ("My life is empty and hollow"). Although auditory hallucinations are often associated with severe mental illness, it is important to note that the words and sounds reported by the pseudopatients had never been reported in the clinical literature. Apart from feigning this symptom and using false names and professions, the pseudopatients answered all other questions honestly. They gave accurate family and personal histories, and none made any attempt to appear abnormal.

The strong effect of social context was immediately evident. On the basis of this never-before-reported symptom and in the absence of any supporting evidence, all of the pseudopatients were diagnosed psychotic. It seemed that the context—a psychiatric admissions office—ensured that patients who claimed to hear voices would be considered mentally ill. On 11 occasions, the diagnosis was schizophrenia; one patient was diagnosed manic-depressive. Once the pseudopatients were admitted to the hospital, their next task was to convince the medical staff that they were sane so that they could be discharged. According to Rosenhan, the pseudopatients were highly motivated to be released:

> The psychological stresses associated with hospitalization were considerable, and all but one of the pseudopatients desired to be discharged almost immediately after being admitted. They were, therefore, motivated not only to behave sanely, but to be paragons of cooperation. That their behavior was in no way disruptive is confirmed by nursing reports. . . . These reports uniformly indicated that the patients were "friendly," "cooperative," and "exhibited no abnormal indications."

While in hospital, the pseudopatients stopped talking about their hallucinations and behaved politely and normally (although they only pretended to take any prescribed medication). When asked, they reported no symptoms and claimed to be feeling well. Despite their motivation to be released and their unremarkable behavior, the pseudopatients spent from 7 to 52 days in hospital with an average stay of 19 days. Not a single pseudopatient was unmasked by hospital staff. Interestingly, several pseudopatients were detected by their fellow, real patients ("You're not crazy. You're a journalist or professor. You're checking up on the hospital.")

One reason for the clinicians' failure to detect their diagnostic errors may have been the general medical tendency, in doubtful cases, to assume that people are ill. There is a good reason for making such an assumption: It is the most cautious approach. Consider the patient who comes to a hospital emergency room complaining of acute abdominal pain. The cause could be appendicitis or just indigestion. If the surgeon is unsure, the best course to follow is to assume that the patient has appendicitis and operate. The surgery may later prove to have been unnecessary, but it is better to perform a useless operation than to take the chance that an inflamed appendix may perforate and cause a potentially lethal peritonitis.

To see whether mental-health professionals were similarly biased toward considering people sick, Rosenhan informed the staff of one teaching hospital that sometime within a 3-month period one or more pseudopatients would attempt to gain admission. He asked the hospital staff to try to expose the phony patients. All told, 193 people were admitted during the 3-month period and assessed by the professional staff. Forty-one were alleged, with high confidence, to be pseudopatients. These results were little short of astounding. You see, Rosenhan had actually lied. He never sent any pseudopatients to the hospital; the people accused of being phonies were real patients! Because normal people can be diagnosed mentally ill and real patients can be judged normal, Rosenhan dismissed the possibility that his initial findings were the result of a medical bias toward considering people ill. Mental illness, he claimed, resides more in the minds of mental-health professionals than in the specific behavior of the labeled individuals.

Observations while the pseudopatients were hospitalized reinforced the overwhelming influence of diagnostic labels. Perfectly normal behavior was interpreted as pathological. Boredom was construed as nervousness; anger at mistreatment was interpreted as pathological aggressiveness. Some reinterpretations of normal behavior were little short of ludicrous. For example, Rosenhan's pseudopatients kept detailed diaries of their hospital experiences yet not one was ever questioned about this. Instead, the nurses' notes contained phrases such as "Patient engages in writing behavior." According to Rosenhan, it seemed that because "the patient is in the hospital, he must be psychologically disturbed. And, given that he is disturbed, continuous writing must be a behavioral manifestation of that disturbance." Once a person is labeled mentally ill, anything he or she does—including writing notes and letters—can be construed as pathological.

Past histories were also distorted to support the patients' diagnoses. For instance, one pseudopatient accurately reported that when he was a child he had a close relationship with his mother and a distant one with his father. However, as he grew up, the situation reversed: He became closer to his father and more remote from his mother. He described his present relationship with his wife as close and warm. Apart from the occasional argument, family friction was minimal and the children were rarely spanked. This rather unremarkable story was transformed in the patient's hospital record as follows:

> . . . manifests a long history of considerable ambivalence in close relationships, which begins in early childhood. . . . Affective stability is absent. His attempts to control emotionality with his wife and children are punctuated by angry outbursts and, in the case of the children, spankings. And while he says that he has several good friends, one senses considerable ambivalence embedded in these relationships also.

Pseudopatients found it impossible to interact with the professional staff as equals. Their attempts at normal conversation were either ignored or greeted with short replies. Often, the staff did not even look at patients when speaking with them. In contrast, patients who engaged in bizarre or disruptive behavior were rewarded with attention and concern. In this way, patients were punished for attempting to display conventional behavior and rewarded for playing the role of the patient. This shaping of abnormal behavior by a combination of expectations, rewards, and punishments for attempting to play conventional social roles is an important example of how labels can produce secondary forms of psychopathology.

Eventually, the pseudopatients were all released from hospital, but they found their diagnostic labels to be "sticky." Once applied, they were difficult to remove. Even at discharge, many pseudopatients, who you will recall were behaving normally, were given the discharge diagnosis of "schizophrenia—in remission." This label implies that despite their normal behavior, they probably were still schizophrenic underneath.

Rosenhan's study made it clear that psychiatric diagnoses exert a profound effect on the way a person is treated, even by trained professionals. Once a person is labeled, all subsequent behavior—even behavior considered perfectly normal in most other contexts—is given a distorted interpretation. Labeled individuals are rewarded for playing the role of a patient and subtly punished for trying to return to more conventional roles. Labels are hard to shake. Even after discharge, patients retain their label; this makes it exceedingly difficult for them to return to their former lives.

AFTERMATH

As might be expected, Rosenhan's article elicited a storm of protest from mental-health professionals. *Science* published more than a dozen critiques, and the debate spilled over to other forums as well. Critics attacked the study's methodology, which they claimed was seriously flawed. Hospitals should have been chosen randomly, the diagnosticians' competence should have been independently assessed, control groups had been omitted. Some critics questioned whether the pseudopatients really behaved "normally." After all, normal people do not ask to be admitted to mental hospitals, and if admitted, they would not voluntarily stay. Another critical theme was the meaning of the discharge diagnosis "schizophrenia—in remission." Several clinicians argued that the usual practice is to discharge patients as "schizophrenia—much improved" or "schizophrenia—slightly improved." Compared with these terms, they argued, "in remission" is almost as good as saying "normal."

While these criticisms are not without merit, they miss the main point. No one denies that the pseudopatients lied and that the admitting doctors were obligated to believe them. Nor was it wrong for the doctors to admit patients who requested hospitalization. On humanitarian grounds alone, they could do no less. The real issue is whether the pseudopatients should have been given the label "schizophrenia." It was this label that implied the patients were suffering from a psychiatric illness, and it was this label that was responsible for staff attitudes. The hospital staff refused to carry on normal conversations with the patients, reinterpreted their behavior, and distorted their histories not because the nurses and doctors were evil or incompetent but because the patients were labeled "mentally ill." According to Rosenhan, psychiatric diagnoses are too unreliable to provide useful information yet they can severely stigmatize any labeled individual. His study was an attempt to demonstrate this unreliability and to argue that the costs of labeling exceed the benefits. In his own words:

> To raise questions regarding normality and abnormality is in no way to question the fact that some behaviors are deviant or odd. Murder is deviant. So, too, are hallucinations. Nor does raising such questions deny the existence of the personal anguish that is often associated with "mental illness." Anxiety and depression exist. Psychological suffering exists. But normality and abnormality, sanity and insanity, and the diagnoses that flow from them may be less substantive than many believe them to be.

Although he never explicitly said so, Rosenhan was widely seen to be suggesting that psychiatric diagnosis should be abandoned. This interpretation of his position is reinforced by Rosenhan's reply to his critics published in *Science*. In the course of refuting various criticisms of his research, Rosenhan remarked that, if the pseudopatients simply had been described as "hallucinating," then "there would have been no further need to examine the diagnostic issue." This position is almost certainly too extreme. Labeling people may have pernicious effects, but it does not follow that we should abandon diagnosis and classification. After all, even the most ardent antilabeling writers admit that the effects of labeling are *secondary*; some other, *primary* cause (illness, trauma, drugs, faulty learning) is responsible for the initial appearance of abnormal behavior. The primary causes of abnormal behavior require careful study, and classification, as we have seen, is a necessary first step. Of course, psychiatric diagnoses are not perfectly reliable, but they may still be useful. As noted earlier, many medical diagnoses are also unreliable, yet we do not argue that they should be abandoned. One of Rosenhan's critics, Paul Fleischman, made this point in a letter to *Science*:

> It would be quite possible to conduct a study in which patients trained to simulate histories of myocardial infarction would receive treatment on the basis of history alone (since a negative electrocardiogram is not diagnostic), but it would be preposterous to conclude from such a study that physical illness does not exist, that medical diagnoses are fallacious labels, and that "illness" and "health" reside only in doctors' heads.[4]

The proper response to Rosenhan's work is not the wholesale abandonment of diagnoses and classification but (1) the development of more reliable diagnoses and (2) attempts to de-stigmatize diagnostic labels. The American Psychiatric Association has attempted to accomplish the first goal by providing explicit diagnostic criteria for its diagnoses. For example, the diagnostic criteria for schizophrenia include a list of symptoms of which the patient must have two:

1. delusions
2. prominent hallucinations (throughout the day for several days or several times a week for several weeks, each hallucinatory experience not being limited to a few brief moments)
3. incoherence or marked loosening of associations
4. catatonic behavior
5. flat or grossly inappropriate affect [emotions]

Alternatively, the diagnosis can still be made on the basis of "bizarre delusions" or "prominent hallucinations," but there must also be a marked interference in the person's functioning such as an inability to work or socialize. Similar criteria have been established for manic-depressive psychosis and most other psychiatric conditions. The goal is to standardize diagnostic practice thereby improving diagnostic reliability. Had these criteria been available in 1973, it is unlikely that any of Rosenhan's pseudopatients would have been diagnosed "schizophrenic."

The refinement of diagnostic labels is a continuous process of incorporating new discoveries into an already existing framework. The work is difficult, and progress slow, but at least we know how to do it. The second necessary response to Rosenhan's work, destigmatizing psychiatric labels, has proven to be considerably more difficult. The typical approach is to replace one label with another. "Lunatics" become "mentally ill"; "morons" and "imbeciles" become "mentally retarded" (or even "exceptional"). Unfortunately, this ploy rarely works for long because the new label soon takes on the same stigmatizing power as the old one. An alternative approach is to educate the public and to promote a more positive attitude toward those who have mental disorders. Programs for the families of patients can also help as they are patients' main caregivers. Families need to learn what diagnostic labels mean, where they come from, and what can be done (and cannot be done) about various conditions. Such educational programs help to remove some of the sting from psychiatric diagnoses, but care must still be taken. Labels should generally be kept confidential and not used for any purpose other than treatment and research. In addition, before anyone is given a diagnostic label, professionals must ensure that the classification and treatment benefits of labeling are not outweighed by its stigmatizing effects. When dealing with vulnerable people — with human beings in distress — professionals must take special care not to add to an individual's problems. The principle was first stated by Hippocrates 2,000 years ago, but it bears frequent repeating: *primum non nocere* ("first do no harm").

Further Reading

Kahn, E. (1959). The Emil Kraepelin Memorial Lecture. In B. Pasamanick (Ed.), *Epidemiology of mental disorder* (pp. 1–38). Washington, D.C.: American Association for the Advancement of Science.

Kraepelin, E. (1919). *Dementia praecox and paraphrenia* (R. M. Barclay, Trans.). Edinburgh: E. & S. Livingstone.

Rosenhan, D. L. (1973). On being sane in insane places. *Science, 179,* 250–258.

Notes

1. Da Costa, J. (1864). *Medical diagnosis with specific reference to practical medicine.* Philadelphia: Lippincott. Pp. 14–15.
2. Kraepelin, E. (1919). *Dementia praecox and paraphrenia* (R. M. Barclay, Trans.). Edinburgh: E & S Livingstone.
3. Rosenhan, D. L. (1973). On being sane in insane places. *Science, 179,* 250–258.
4. Fleischman, P. R. (1973). Psychiatric diagnosis. *Science, 180,* 356.

PART II

Developmental Psychopathology

Child development is usually considered to be a series of more-or-less orderly changes leading toward a mature individual. Unfortunately, as many psychologists have come to know, progress through developmental stages can be erratic and slow development may have important social consequences. A child who is much older than others in a classroom may have difficulty developing friendships; a child who is slow to develop physically may be left behind when other children of the same age enter puberty. Some children compensate by becoming the "class clown," others by becoming rebels. A few withdraw entirely.

Children are constantly changing; behaviors that are expected at one developmental stage (bed-wetting, "the terrible twos") may suggest an emotional problem at another stage of development. To put a child's behavior problem in context, psychologists must be familiar with all aspects of child development: the evolution of motor skills (the sequence in which a child sits unaided, crawls, stands, and walks), the acquisition of language, the development of moral values, and the increasing need for social contact. But this knowledge, while certainly necessary for understanding child psychopathology, is not entirely sufficient. Often, what appears to be the same behavioral problem may have several different origins. For example, a child who is having difficulty learning to read may be suffering from inadequate instruction, a visual or neurological disorder, anxiety about being evaluated, or distractibility or simply may be rebelling against authority (or some combination of these factors). Psychologists must be able to specify the precise nature of the child's problem, the factors causing it, and the way these factors interact.

Some of the behavioral changes that occur over time result from biological factors whereas others depend on undergoing certain experiences. More often, however, developmental changes do not fit neatly into either category; they result from biology and experience working together. For example, all around the world, children learn to say their first words at around the same time. Psychologists have taken this as evidence that language development may have a biological component. However, children in various parts of the world do not learn to say the same words; the specific language they learn depends on where they happen to be born — on their early experience. Most psychological traits turn out to be like language: They represent the interaction of biology and experience. Despite sometimes heated debates, how much of any particular trait is the result of genetics and how much is due to experience is often impossible to say.

Equally controversial is the distinction between continuous change and the existence of discrete developmental stages. As children get older they become gradually taller and heavier. Psychologists have argued that intellectual, moral, and cognitive development are also gradual processes. Others take the view that children pass through a series of discontinuous stages. Each stage presents a specific developmental challenge that must be successfully conquered before the child can proceed to the next. Failure at any stage can produce serious, sometimes life-long psychopathology.

As will be seen in the succeeding chapters, arguments about the *relative* contribution of biology and experience to different forms of psychopathology and controversies about the existence of discrete developmental stages have a long history. Few of these controversies have ever been completely resolved. Like modern physics, which conceives of light as *both* continuous waves and discrete particles, a complete understanding of childhood psychopathology may require a variety of flexible theoretical perspectives.

CHAPTER 3

Suffer the Little Children

Of all mammals, humans are the most immature at birth. While some babies are able to move around almost immediately (horses, for example), human infants are incapable of any locomotion. Humans are slow developers even in comparison to their close relatives, the primates. Some species of newborn monkeys are on their own only a few weeks after birth; others are ready to fend for themselves in a few short months. Human infants, on the other hand, are dependent on caregivers for many years before they become self-sufficient. During this long period of dependence, children are trained to adopt mature social roles, a process known as *socialization*.

There are four major theories of how the socialization process unfolds. *Humanism*, which is really more of a philosophical position than a scientific theory, optimistically emphasizes the innate potential of human beings. According to humanists, give children love and the freedom to learn and socialization will more-or-less take care of itself. The *cognitive-developmentalists* view the socialization process as similar to a series of steeplechase hurdles that must be jumped as the child matures. Each successful leap requires that the child interact with the environment, but the racecourse is set out in the child's genes and, except in unusual cases, the socialization process unfolds automatically. In contrast to these largely "automatic" views, the third theory, *behaviorism*, conceives of socialization as a learning process in which children are actively taught to behave in socially approved ways. There has always been a range of opinion among behaviorists about how malleable children really are. For example, the father of behaviorism, John Watson, described children as "blank slates" on which practically anything could be written:

> Give me a dozen healthy infants, well-formed, and my own specialized world to bring them up

We are moulded and remoulded by those who have loved us; and though the love may pass, we are nevertheless their work, for good or ill.

—François Mauriac

in, and I'll guarantee to take any one at random and train him to be any type of specialist I might select — doctor, lawyer, artist, merchant chief, yes, even beggar-man thief.[1]

The fourth major theory of socialization is Sigmund Freud's *psychoanalytic* theory of development. According to psychoanalysis, infants are instinct-ridden, pleasure-seeking organisms. Their only desire is to satisfy their primitive instinctive urges for food, drink, comfort, and sexual stimulation. Socialization requires that children learn to subjugate their instinctual desires. Like the cognitive-developmentalists, the psychoanalysts see development as a series of hurdles, each of which poses a challenge that must be overcome. By meeting these challenges, the child learns to satisfy his or her desires in socially approved ways. Failing to negotiate a developmental hurdle can lead to psychopathology later in life.

Despite obvious differences, all four theories of socialization are united on one point; they all agree that early childhood experiences set the stage for later social behavior. The social attachments formed by children are seen as particularly important. This chapter is concerned with two classic works on parent-child relationships: René Spitz's study of "maternal deprivation" and Sigmund Freud's famous case study "Little Hans." Freud's analysis of this young boy's fear of horses played a seminal role in the development of psychoanalytic theory. Freud's insistence that psychological development is mediated by parent-child interactions led Spitz to examine the effects of parental absence on a young child's emotional development.

THE INVENTION OF CHILDHOOD

Before the 16th century, there was no concept equivalent to our modern idea of "childhood." From age 5 or so, when they were weaned from their mothers or wet nurses, children were considered to be little adults who no longer belonged to their parents. There were no children's toys or literature and no recognition that children might have special emotional needs. Children worked side-by-side with adults and shared adult entertainments including drinking at local pubs. Family portraits painted in those days depict children in adult dress with adult physical features. Often, the only way to tell that these figures are supposed to be children is that they are shown as smaller than their parents.

Attitudes toward children began to change in the 17th century, and by the end of the 18th century, practically all societies began to view childhood as a special developmental stage, separate from adulthood. This change in attitudes was at least partly the result of improved health care and a consequent decline in infant mortality. Parents had previously avoided becoming emotionally attached to their offspring because there was a good chance their children would die in their first years of life. (As late as 1750, the odds against a European child making it past age 5 were three to one.) This detached attitude slowly changed as children began to live longer and their parents became less afraid of losing them. The Industrial Revolution played an equally important role in changing the concept of childhood. As industrialization took hold, economic conditions improved and a middle class developed. For the first time in history, a large number of parents had the time and money required to take an interest in children. Parents cuddled and played with their children; they told them stories and taught them games. Those who could afford the expense bought their children special clothes, books, and toys. In this way, the concept of childhood, an invention of changing social circumstances, gradually evolved.

Economic prosperity was instrumental in the invention of childhood, but political changes were important as well. Democratic revolutions in America (and, for a time at least, in France) produced a new political and philosophical outlook. Parents began to accept responsibility not only for the health and welfare of their children but also for their social development and moral training. Schools, formerly a luxury of the rich, became increasingly important, not simply as places where children could learn specific skills but as social institutions designed to convey socially approved values to succeeding generations. Instead of heredity or class, a person's lot in life was to become increasingly a matter of education. This faith in education and the power of reason was the culmination of a philosophy that began with the Enlightenment and had been refined by generations of philosophers. The formula was simple: Evil, misery, and unhappiness were caused by ignorance and superstition; education would eventually dispel superstition and create a peaceful and progressive world. The scientific and technological breakthroughs of the 18th and 19th centuries reinforced this faith — life was continually improving and humanity could look forward to never-ending progress.

In contrast to this emphasis on rational thought, the Romantic philosophers emphasized feelings and instinct. Educators were specially taken with the ideas of Jean-Jacques Rousseau, whose extensive observations of a developing child appeared in his book *Émile*. Rousseau's thesis was that all evil stems from society's rules. If people could only "return to nature," they would behave morally and find happiness. Rousseau compared children to primitive people. Both were "noble savages," free from the stultifying mores of civilized society. Children, he believed, must be given the opportunity to develop in a "natural" manner so that they could remain uncorrupted by society. Children raised this way would create a fairer, more humane world.

Although Rousseau was hardly a paragon of moral virtue (he was a thief who abandoned his five illegitimate children), educators eagerly set out to test his ideas. The most famous test began in 1799 when a boy was found in the woods near Aveyron in France (see Figure 3.1). This "wild boy" did not speak and appeared to have had no contact with other human beings for many years. It was assumed that he ran away from home and lived on wild berries and plants. To Jean Itard, a doctor who specialized in teaching the deaf and dumb, the boy epitomized Rousseau's noble savage raised in a completely "natural" state. Itard took it on himself to demonstrate that the high moral development which Rousseau had predicted would naturally result from such an upbringing. Unfortunately, Itard's experiment was a failure. The child could barely communicate — he learned only a few words — and although he was easy to get along with, he was mentally retarded and never progressed much beyond his initial, low intellectual level.

Itard's was not the Romantic movement's only failure. The Romantics' celebration of nationalism and racial superiority led to bloody wars that provided precious little evidence that human beings are innately good. In despair, the Romantics completely changed direction. People, they decided, are not innately good, they are inherently bad. War, destruction, irrationality, and hate are inevitable, and no

FIGURE 3.1 The "Wild Boy" of Aveyron.

amount of education will ever change human nature. As the 19th century drew to a close, there was little reason to doubt this grim prophecy. Supposedly civilized, eminently rational people were killing one another throughout Europe; goodness was everywhere losing to evil, and the horrific slaughter of World War I loomed in the not-too-distant future. It was into this increasingly pessimistic world that Sigmund Freud was born.

SIGMUND FREUD: THE ORIGINS OF PSYCHOANALYSIS

Sigmund Freud was born in 1856 in Freiberg, today a part of Czechoslovakia, but then part of the great Austrian Empire. When Freud was 4, economic crises and a surge of anti-Semitism forced his family to migrate to Vienna, the cosmopolitan city where he was to spend most of his life. Although Freud's parents were Jewish, they brought their son up without any religious training. Nevertheless, Freud remained identifiably "Jewish" throughout his life. Indeed, toward the end of his life, he was persecuted for his Jewish identity and forced to flee Austria for England. In a speech to the Society of B'nai B'rith, Freud explained his Jewishness as follows:

> What bound me to Jewry was (I am ashamed to admit) neither faith nor national pride. . . . But plenty of other things remained . . . to make the attraction of Jews and Jewry irresistible — many obscure emotional forces, which were more powerful the less they could be expressed in words, as well as a clear consciousness of inner identity, the safe privacy of a common mental construction. And beyond this there was a perception that it was to my Jewish nature alone that I owed two characteristics that had become indispensable to me in the difficult course of my life. Because I am a Jew I found myself free from many prejudices which restricted others in the use of their intellect; and as a Jew I was prepared to join the Opposition and to do without agreement with the "compact majority."[2]

Although the family was not well off, Freud received a good secondary education. Records show that his early schooling was marked by considerable success. He often scored first in his class and showed a particular appreciation for literature and a talent for writing. He maintained these interests throughout his life translating many foreign works including the writings of the British philosopher John Stuart Mill into German. Unfortunately, the financial outlook for writers was (and is) bleak. So, for economic reasons, Freud entered the medical course at the University of Vienna when he was just 17. It took him 8 years to graduate because, instead of attending to his medical studies, he got caught up in scientific research. While still a medical student, Freud published several scientific papers on anatomy and physiology. From his early work, it seems clear that Freud was on the threshold of a promising scientific career, but he abandoned this path for private medical practice when he became engaged to Martha Bernays in 1882. Freud needed money to support a family, and there was little available in pure scientific research. Nevertheless, he maintained his research interests and published papers on brain anatomy, neurology, and a well-known monograph on the effects of cocaine. In 1885 Freud was appointed to the position of *dozentur* (clinical lecturer) in neurology at the University of Vienna. This was an ideal situation for him because it allowed him to keep his hand in teaching and research while still maintaining a private practice. It also made him eligible for a scholarship. Freud used the money to visit Paris where he worked at the Salpêtrière under the guidance of Jean-Martin Charcot. As described in the introduction of this book, Charcot was responsible for making the study of hysteria and hypnosis respectable. Charcot's scientific approach made a lasting impression on the young Freud, who translated the French master's lectures into German.

Within a few years after his return to Austria, Freud's medical practice expanded markedly. He married Martha and, with financial success ensured, began to raise a family that eventually included six children. Freud became known as an expert in neurology and was frequently consulted by patients who were suffering from hysteria. Unhappy with the results he achieved using hypnosis, Freud became interested in the work of Josef Breuer, at the time, one of the most respected clinicians in Vienna. Breuer had been treating a hysteric patient known in the medical literature as Anna O. He was struck by the way the young woman avoided giving any information about her background and the possible causes of her problem. Using Charcot's approach, Breuer hypnotized Anna O. on several occasions. Under hypnosis, she expressed guilt over her father's death. (Young children often believe that they are somehow responsible for a parent's death). Reliving the traumatic emotional experience of her father's death appeared to cure Anna O.'s hysteria — her symptoms gradually disappeared. Freud and Breuer published the story of Anna O. in a book called *Studies in Hysteria*. The book marked the birth of psychoanalysis. In addition to the emotional reliving method, which the authors called *catharsis*, other psychoanalytic concepts such as *defense mechanism, repression,* and *resistance* were also introduced. As for Anna O., whose real name was Bertha Pappenheim, she went on to become one of Germany's leading campaigners for women's rights.

Freud applied his cathartic method to other patients and found that many revealed emotional traumas which were in some way or other concerned with sex. He concluded that hysterical symptoms, and many other neurotic problems,

FIGURE 3.2 Sigmund Freud in his middle years.

were the result of unresolved sexual conflicts. Breuer disagreed with Freud on this issue, and the two men had a falling-out. Indeed, most contemporary psychiatrists and psychologists found Freud's emphasis on the sexual nature of unconscious conflicts distasteful. They shunned his company and stopped referring patients to him. Professionally isolated, Freud continued his work alone. During this period, he investigated and published books and papers on dreams, slips of the tongue, memory, and sexual behavior. Gradually, these works gained him adherents both within and outside the medical community. International recognition came in 1909 when G. Stanley Hall, the first president of the American Psychological Association, invited him and other psychoanalysts to lecture in the United States.

Although Freud continued to use hypnotically induced catharsis in his clinical work, he grew increasingly unhappy with the limited results. He looked for a better method of uncovering his patients' unconscious wishes and desires and hit on the free-association technique. Freud had patients express aloud their uncensored thoughts and desires. To stimulate the process, he often used a patient's dreams as a trigger ("Tell me, what associations does the dream bring to mind?"). He analyzed the resulting stream of associations and random thoughts attempting to find the unconscious theme that tied them together. More often than not, the

THE PSYCHOSEXUAL STAGES

From a psychoanalytic viewpoint, adult personality develops as the child passes through a series of stages. Each stage puts the child into a conflict that must be resolved if personality is to develop normally. The oral stage, which comes first, centers around the child's instinctual pleasure in sucking and, later, eating. If for some reason the child is frustrated at this stage, *fixation* will result. Some psychic energy will remain at the oral stage, and the individual will need to incorporate things; that is, the person will always crave the satisfaction of oral needs. If the fixation occurs later in the oral stage, the individual may become someone who is verbally abusive (a "biting" speaker).

The second psychosexual stage is the anal stage. It represents the first important confrontation between the instinct-driven child and the demands of reality. Defecation, a reflexive, pleasurable activity, must be regulated according to society's demands—that is, the child must be toilet trained. Fixation at this stage could lead to slavish conformity (do whatever others demand) or rebelliousness (a refusal to bow to society).

The next, phallic, stage brings an even more threatening conflict between the child's natural urges and the demands of civilization. In the phallic stage, it is the genitalia that are the site of pleasurable feelings, and it is during this stage that the Oedipal conflict occurs. Males are forced, through fears of retaliation, to repress their desire for their mothers and to identify with and pattern themselves after their fathers. A similar process occurs for females. The outcome of all this turmoil during the phallic stage has implications for much later social and sexual behavior. It also marks the birth of the superego, which incorporates the moral code of the child's parents.

The final developmental stage, the genital stage, sees the growth of interpersonal skills, friendships, and other social attachments. A fully developed personality requires a successful passage through all psychosexual stages.

unifying theme was childhood sexuality. Freud eventually came to believe that child development, indeed, civilization itself, rests on the successful resolution of infantile sexual conflicts.

FREUD'S THEORY OF SOCIALIZATION

In Freud's hands, psychoanalysis became more than a method of treatment; it evolved into a theory of personality development. Philosophically, Freud was a modern incarnation of the 17th-century philosopher Thomas Hobbes. Hobbes's political treatise, *Leviathan,* depicted human beings as governed by selfishness, lust, greed, and aggression. If left unchecked, their natural instinct would always be to satisfy their basest impulses by whatever means possible including war, rape, and theft. According to Hobbes, the only thing standing in the way of this "each person for himself or herself" attitude is the restraint placed on individual behavior by outside forces such as governments. But even governments are established to achieve selfish ends. We tolerate them only because they make it possible for us to satisfy our needs.

Like Hobbes, Freud regarded human beings as hedonistic animals who, left to their own devices, would seek to gratify their impulses at all costs. But Freud did not believe that government soldiers were the only thing that kept people from misbehaving. According to Freud, individuals learn to *internalize* society's rules in the form of a conscience or, in Freud's terms, a *superego* that controls our instinctual urges toward sex and aggression. The superego punishes transgressions with feelings of guilt, regret, and remorse; it rewards socially approved behaviors by increasing an individual's self-esteem. The superego develops by a process of *identification.* The child wishes to be like his or her parents and, therefore, "identifies" with (adopts) their standards of proper behavior. Because children have two parents, they can make two identifications. The balance of these identifications determines not only the child's moral standards but also his or her sexual identity. If the identification process goes awry, Freud believed the result would not only be a damaged conscience but also an uncertain sexual identity and perhaps even homosexuality.

Freud's two basic ideas—children are not noble savages (they must be socialized if we expect them to behave morally) and sexual identity is not innate (it is derived from early family experience)—formed the cornerstone of his theory of psychological development. The data for this theory were derived from his patients. For almost 40 years, Freud treated patients for 10 hours per day, 5 or 6 days per week. Their dreams, slips of the tongue, and free associations were analyzed and formalized into psychoanalytic theory. To gain some insight into Freud's method, Classic Study 5 describes his analysis of a boy who developed a fear of horses. This case figured prominently in Freud's theory of socialization.

CLASSIC STUDY 5
Little Hans

Freud urged his pupils and friends to collect observations on the sexual life of their children. When Hans was born in 1903, his parents, who were adherents of Freud's, were happy to oblige. Hans's father, a Viennese doctor, wrote often about his son's development. When Hans was 5 years old, he developed a fear of horses. Freud conducted Hans's "analysis" by mail. Hans's father asked his son questions, recorded the boy's answers, and sent these to Freud, who replied with suggestions and further questions. Freud quoted extensively from this correspondence in his paper *Analysis of a Phobia in a Five-Year-Old Boy* (1909). The correspondence allows us to see, firsthand, how Freud formulated and tested hypotheses using the available "raw materials."[3] The following extracts are drawn from Freud's famous paper.[4] They appear in chronological order and are reprinted verbatim with the original emphases and punctuation. As the case unfolds, try to make interpretations of your own. Compare your interpretations to Freud's. Are they the same? If not, is there a way to decide who is right and who is wrong? The first excerpt begins when Hans was around 3 years old.

CASE MATERIALS

1. At that time, by means of various remarks and questions, he was showing a quite peculiarly lively interest in that portion of his body which he used to describe as his 'widdler.' Thus, he once asked his mother this question:

HANS: 'Mamma, have you got a widdler too?'
MOTHER: 'Of course, why?'
HANS: 'I was only just thinking.'

2. Meanwhile his interest in widdlers was by no means a purely theoretical one; as might have been expected, it impelled him to touch his member. When he was three and a half his mother found him with his hand to his penis. She threatened him in these words: 'If you do that, I shall send for Dr. A. to cut off your widdler. And then what'll you widdle with?'

3. But the great event of Hans' life was the birth of his little sister Hanna when he was exactly three and a half. His behavior on that occasion was noted down by his father on the spot: 'At five in the morning,' he writes, 'labour began, and Hans' bed was moved into the next room. He woke up there at seven and hearing his mother groaning, asked: "Why's mamma coughing?" Then, after a pause, "The Stork's coming today, for certain."

'Naturally he has often been told during the last few days that the stork is going to bring a little girl or a little boy; and he quite rightly connected the unusual sounds of groaning with the stork's arrival.

'Later on he was taken into the kitchen. He saw the doctor's bag in the front hall and asked: "What's that?" "A bag," was the reply. Upon which he declared with conviction: "The stork's coming today." After the delivery of the child the midwife came into the kitchen and Hans heard her ordering some tea to be made. At this he said: "I know! Mummy's to have some tea because she is coughing." He was then called into the bedroom. He did not look at his mother, however, but at the basins and other vessels, filled with blood and water, that were still standing about the room. Pointing to the blood-stained bedpan, he observed in a surprised voice: "But blood doesn't come out of *my* widdler."

'Everything he says shows that he connects what is strange in the situation with the arrival of the stork. He meets everything he sees with a very suspicious and intent look, and *there can be no doubt that his first suspicions about the stork have made their appearance.*

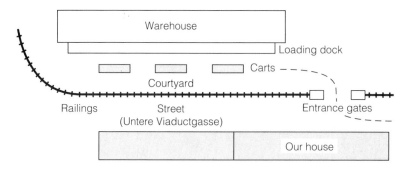

FIGURE 3.3 The scene opposite Hans's house (drawn by Hans's father).

'Hans is very jealous of the new arrival, and whenever anyone praises her, says she is a lovely baby, and so on, he at once declares scornfully: "But she hasn't any teeth yet." And in fact when he saw her for the first time he was very surprised that she could not speak and decided that this was because she had no teeth. During the first few days he was naturally put very much in the background. He was suddenly taken ill with a sore throat. In his fever he was heard saying: "But I don't want a little sister!"

4. He was watching his three-months-old sister being given a bath, and said in pitying tones: "She *has* got a tiny little widdler."

5. 'On January 8th my wife decided to go out with him herself so as to see what was wrong with him. They went to Schönbrunn [a zoo], where he always likes going. Again he began to cry, did not want to start, and was frightened. In the end, he did go; but was visibly frightened in the street. On the way back from Schönbrunn he said to his mother, after much internal struggling: *"I was afraid a horse would bite me."*

6. 'On Sunday, March 1st, the following conversation took place on the way to the station. I was once more trying to explain to him that horses do not bite. *He:* "But white horses bite. There's a white horse at Gmunden [a lake resort] that bites. If you hold your finger to it it bites. . . . Her [Lizzi, a girl who lived in a neighboring house] father was standing near the horse, and the horse turned his head round (to touch him), and he said to Lizzi: *'Don't put your finger to the white horse or it'll bite you.'*"

7. At Schönbrunn he showed signs of fear at animals which at other occasions he had looked at without any alarm. Thus he absolutely refused to go into the house in which the *giraffe* is kept, nor would he visit the elephant, which used formerly

to amuse him a great deal. He was afraid of all the large animals whereas he was very much entertained by the small ones.

8. 'During the night of 27th-28th Hans surprised us by getting out of bed while it was quite dark and coming into our bed. His room is separated from our bedroom by another small room. We asked him why: whether he had been afraid, perhaps. "No," he said, "I'll tell you to-morrow." He went to sleep in our bed and was carried back to his own.

'Next day I questioned him closely to discover why he had come in to us during the night; and after some reluctance the following dialogue took place, which I immediately took down in shorthand:

'HE: *"In the night there was a big giraffe in the room and a crumpled one; and the big one called out because I took the crumpled one away from it. Then it stopped calling out; and then I sat down on top of the crumpled one."*

9. 'The whole thing is a reproduction of a scene which has been gone through almost every morning for the last few days. Hans always comes in to us in the early morning, and my wife cannot resist taking him into bed with her for a few minutes. Thereupon I always begin to warn her not to take him in bed with her, . . .

10. 'When I got up from the table after breakfast Hans said: "Daddy, don't trot away from me!" I was struck by his saying "trot" instead of "run" . . .

11. 'The position of our street-door is as follows: Opposite it is the warehouse of the Office for the Taxation of Food-Stuffs, with a loading dock at which carts are driving up all day long to fetch away boxes, packing-cases, etc. This courtyard is cut off from the street by railings; and the

entrance gates to the courtyard are opposite our house. . . . I have noticed for some days that Hans is specially frightened when the carts drive into or out of the yard, a process which involves their taking a corner. I asked at the time why he was so much afraid and he replied: *"I'm afraid the horse will fall down when the cart turns."*

12. 'In the afternoon we again went out in front of the street-door, and when I returned I asked Hans:

'"Which horses are you actually most afraid of?"
'HANS: "All of them."
'I: "That's not true."
'HANS: "I'm most afraid of horses with a thing on their mouths."
'I: "What do you mean? The piece of iron they have in their mouths?"
'HANS: "No. They have something black on their mouths." (He covered his mouth with his hand.)
'I: "What? A mustache, perhaps?"

13. 'HANS: "And I'm most afraid of furniture-vans too."
'I: "Why?"
'HANS: "I think when furniture-horses are dragging a heavy van they'll fall down."
'I: "So you're not afraid with a small cart?"
'HANS: "No. I'm not afraid with a small cart or with a post-office van. I'm most afraid too when a bus comes along."
'I: "Why? Because it's so big?"
'HANS: "No. Because once a horse in a bus fell down."
'. . . I: "What did you think when the horse fell down?"
'HANS: "Now it'll always be like this. All horses in buses'll fall down. . . . When the horse fell down, it gave me such a fright, really! . . ."
'I: "Why did it give you such a fright?"
'HANS: "Because the horse went like this with its feet!" (He lay down on the ground and showed me how it kicked about.) "It gave me a fright *because it made a row with its feet.*"

14. 'April 9th. This morning Hans came in to me while I was washing bare to the waist.
'HANS: "Daddy, you *are* lovely! You're so white!"
15. 'I: "Are you fond of Hanna?"
'HANS: "Oh yes, very fond."
'I: "Would you rather that Hanna weren't alive or that she were?"
'HANS: "I'd rather she weren't alive."
16. 'I: "If you rather she [Hanna] weren't alive, you can't be fond of her at all."

'HANS (assenting): "H'm, well."
'I: "That was why you thought when Mummy was giving her her bath, if only she'd let go, Hanna would fall into the water . . ."
'HANS (taking me up): ". . . and die."
'I: "And then you'd be alone with Mummy. A good boy doesn't wish that sort of thing, though."
'HANS: *"But he may think it."*
'I: "But that isn't good."
'HANS: *"If he thinks it, it is good all the same, because you can write it to the Professor* [Freud].

17. 'Afternoon, in front of the house. Hans suddenly ran indoors as a carriage with two horses came along. I could see nothing unusual about it, and asked him what was wrong. "The horses are so proud," he said, "that I'm afraid they'll fall down." (The coachman was reining the horses in tight, so that they were trotting with short steps and holding their heads high. In fact their action was *"proud."*)

'I asked him who it really was who was so proud.
'HE: "You are, when I come into bed with Mummy."
'I: "So you want me to fall down?"
'HANS: "Yes . . . and then I'll be able to be alone with Mummy for a little bit."

18. 'At lunch-time I was told that Hans *had been playing all the morning with an india rubber-doll which he called Grete. He had pushed a small penknife in through the opening to which the little tin squeaker had originally been attached, and had then torn the doll's legs apart so as to let the knife drop out. He had said to the nurse-maid, pointing between the doll's legs: "Look, there's its widdler!"*

19. 'I: "Then why do you always cry whenever Mummy gives me a kiss? It's because you're jealous."
'HANS: "Jealous, yes."
'I: "You'd like to be Daddy yourself."
'HANS: "Oh, yes."
20. 'HANS: "I'm not afraid of carriages and pair or cabs with one horse. I'm afraid of busses and luggage-carts, but only when they're loaded up, not when they're empty. . . ."
'I: ". . . When Mummy was having Hanna, was she loaded full up too?"
'HANS: "Mummy'll be loaded full up again when she has another one, when another one begins to grow, when another one's inside her."

21. 'On May 2nd Hans came to me in the morning. "I say," he said, "I thought something

to-day." At first he had forgotten it; but later on he related what follows, though with signs of considerable resistance: *"The plumber came; and first he took away my behind with a pair of pincers, and then he gave me another, and then the same with my widdler. . . ."*

'I: "He gave you a *bigger* widdler and a *bigger* behind."

'HANS: "Yes."

'I: "Like Daddy's; because you'd like to be Daddy."

'HANS: "Yes, and I'd like to have a mustache like yours and hairs like yours." (He pointed to the hairs on my chest.)

FREUD'S INTERPRETATION

Although these extracts constitute only a fraction of the information available to Freud, they contain all the elements he used to analyze Hans's dream and phobia.

Hans's Dream

Hans relates his dream in extract number 8. Dreams are important in psychoanalysis because they often reveal desires *(wish fulfillments)* not available to the conscious mind. However, dreams do not reflect these desires directly, but in a disguised form. The psychologist's task is to translate the *manifest content* of the dream into its *latent elements.*

The manifest content of Hans's dream consisted of three elements: a big giraffe, a crumpled giraffe, and the act he described as "sitting down" on top of the crumpled giraffe. Freud interpreted this dream as a manifestation of the *Oedipus complex* in which boys love their mothers and are jealous of their fathers. The large giraffe is Hans's father (the long neck symbolizes his father's large penis), and the crumpled one is his mother. Hans takes the small giraffe away from the large giraffe and then fulfills his unconscious wish by possessing it, perhaps sexually ("I sat down on top of the crumpled one").

Of course, this is not the only possible interpretation of Hans's dream. As Freud readily admits, sibling rivalry is another possibility. Instead of Hans's father, the large giraffe could symbolize his mother while the small "crumpled" one could be the baby Hanna. In this version of the dream, Hans, jealous of his sister with whom he must share his mother's love, decides to do away with her by sitting on her.

The extracts contain support for both the sibling rivalry and the Oedipal interpretations. On the sibling rivalry side, Hans saw Hanna shortly after her birth when she was doubtless "crumpled," and he was certainly jealous of his sister. In excerpt 16, Hans admits that he wishes she did not exist. The Oedipal interpretation, on the other hand, is supported by the "phallic" nature of the giraffe's long neck, the "crumpling" of his mother's abdomen after giving birth, Hans's habit of coming into his parents bed, and his preoccupation with "widdlers." Freud did not think it necessary to choose between these two interpretations. He argued that *condensation,* in which several themes are symbolically linked in a single dream, is a common phenomenon. However, Freud chose to emphasize the Oedipal interpretation rather than sibling rivalry because the former also "explained" Hans's *phobia* (unreasonable fear) of horses.

Hans's Phobia

Hans was initially afraid that horses, particularly white ones, would bite him (see excerpt 5, for example). Freud interpreted the white horse as a symbol for Hans's father. The evidence for this interpretation is plentiful: Hans described his father as "lovely" and "white," he asked his father not to "trot" away, and he was most fearful of horses with "black" around their faces like his father's mustache. (Hans's father, Freud noticed, also wore glasses, which Hans once translated into a horse's blinders.) Why should Hans fear that a horse (his father) would bite him? According to Freud, the bite symbolizes castration, the punishment Hans fears he will receive for desiring his mother. Where would the boy get such an idea? Freud suggests several possibilities. First, Hans's mother threatened to have "Dr. A." cut off Hans's "widdler" if he continued to fondle himself (excerpt 2). Second, Hans heard a friend's father warn her that a white horse can bite off an appendage such as a finger (excerpt 6). The finger may have become a symbolic representation of a penis. Third, Hans noticed that girls have little "widdlers," which he associated with the doctor's visit on the occasion of Hanna's birth. Hans may have come to believe that the blood-filled bedpans were the result of the doctor's castration of Hanna. Finally, Hans correctly perceived that his father resented his coming into the matrimonial bed in the mornings.

If Hans really did fear castration, his fear was certainly never conscious. According to Freud, *displacement* of a fear onto another object (in this case, from

Hans's father to a white horse) is one way that people protect themselves from painful thoughts. The need to shield himself from unacceptable thoughts may also explain why Hans's phobia changed over time to become a fear that a horse drawing a heavy burden would fall down (see excerpt 13). Freud felt that the falling horse represented Hans's ambivalence toward his father. On the one hand, Hans feared his father and wished that he would fall down and die while, on the other hand, he loved his father and did not want any harm to come to him.

Like Hans's dream, his fear of horses falling down may have had more than one meaning. For example, the falling horse may have represented Hans's mother rather than his father. After all, Hans was only afraid of horses carrying heavy loads similar to the "full load" his mother carried during pregnancy. Perhaps he feared that his mother would give birth to yet another rival. Freud saw both explanations of Hans's phobia—fear of his father or dismay at the possibility of another sibling—as not only possible but reflections of the same underlying conflict or theme: Hans's resentment of rivals for his mother's attention. Because Hanna presented no physical threat, Hans expressed his hostility toward her in an undisguised fashion. Because of the possibility of retaliation, Hans's jealousy of his father could not be expressed overtly. So it was displaced and revealed only in a disguised form. In the end, Hans's feelings about *both* rivals are condensed into a single dream and phobia. The dream expressed his desire to eliminate his competition and possess his mother while the phobia represented Hans's fear of the likely consequences should he succeed: castration, his father's death, another sibling. Freud went on to generalize that all neurotic symptoms are the result of such displaced unconscious conflicts.

AFTERMATH

No doubt, on first reading, Freud's interpretations appear convincing. However, on closer scrutiny doubts begin to surface. First, the evidence gathered by Hans's father was not entirely objective. As an admirer of Freud, Hans's father was disposed to believe in psychoanalytic hypotheses. Of all the events of his household, he wrote to Freud only about those he knew would interest the great psychoanalyst. When his son developed his fear of horses, Hans's father set about looking for data that

would confirm a psychoanalytic interpretation. When such data were not forthcoming voluntarily, he practically planted them in his son's mind (as in excerpt 19). Freud was aware of his reporter's overzealousness, writing that "Hans's father was asking too many questions and was pressing the inquiry along his own lines instead of allowing the little boy to express his own thoughts." Nevertheless, Freud believed his interpretations were not biased by selective reporting because the important data (the white horse with black parts around the mouth, the fallen horse, and "sitting" on the crumpled giraffe) were all volunteered by Hans. Of course it is always possible that Hans, too, was giving Freud what he knew the "Professor" wanted to hear (see, especially excerpt 16). Freud discounted this possibility for a number of reasons. Not the least of these was his observation that presenting Hans with psychoanalytic interpretations of his phobia and dream seemed to cure his fear of horses. Freud argued that the psychoanalytic interpretation must have been correct or Hans would not have overcome his fear.

Because Freud was so certain about the unconscious causes of behavior, he gave little attention to Hans's report (excerpt 13) that he once saw a horse pulling a heavy load fall down and make a row with its feet. Yet this experience suggests an alternative hypothesis about the origin of his fear. It could have been caused by witnessing the frightening event, a simple *conditioned response*. Similarly, his fear of a horse biting him may have been the result of the association of a previous bite (perhaps from a dog or another child) with Lizzi's father's admonition to keep his fingers away from the white horse to avoid being bitten. Perhaps Oedipal desires, unconscious conflicts, displacement, and so on are not necessary to understand Hans's phobias after all.

The conditioned-response explanation for Hans's phobia was particularly attractive to John Watson, the American psychologist who founded the *behaviorism* movement early in the 20th century. Behaviorists denied the need to hypothesize any unconscious causes for behavior, preferring instead to view all behavior as habits learned from experience. Watson and his assistant, Rosalie Rayner, decided to show that their view was superior to Freud's by producing a phobia in a young child by conditioning methods. Their experimental subject was an infant they deliberately called "Little Albert" so that he would be compared with Freud's patient who was

FIGURE 3.4 John Watson (1878–1958), founder of modern behaviorism.

known as "Little Hans." Their technique was to startle the baby with a loud noise while he played with a small white laboratory rat. Before the experiment, Albert liked playing with the rat, but after several pairings of the rat and noise, Albert no longer wanted anything to do with the animal. Showing him the rat, even without any accompanying noise, was enough to make him cry. He even seemed apprehensive around objects "related" to the furry white rat such as a sealskin coat. Watson and Rayner claimed that they produced a phobia in Little Albert solely through conditioning. In their 1920 paper reporting the conditioning procedure used to inculcate a phobia in Little Albert, Watson and Rayner clearly expressed their disdain for psychoanalytic interpretations:

> The Freudians, twenty years from now, unless their hypotheses change, when they come to analyze Albert's fear of a sealskin coat—assuming that he comes to analysis at that age—will probably tease from him the recital of a dream which, upon their analysis, will show that Albert at three

years of age attempted to play with the pubic hair of the mother and was scolded violently for it.[5]

Unfortunately, the results of Watson and Rayner's study were more equivocal than they appeared to believe. To begin with, there is reason to doubt that Watson and Rayner really produced a phobia in Little Albert. According to their own description, Albert showed no fear at all if permitted to suck his thumb when the rat was around. It is also not clear how widely his "fear" generalized to objects such as the sealskin coat. Watson and Rayner's descriptions were crude at best, and the only evidence they provided for the generalization of Albert's fear to the coat was that the baby "fretted" when they showed him the garment. (Whether Albert would have also fretted when shown a cloth coat was never tested.) Most troubling of all was the failure of other experimenters to replicate Watson and Rayner's results. In one such attempt, not one of 15 children learned to fear a wooden toy even when it was repeatedly paired with a loud disagreeable noise.

Despite these weaknesses, Watson and Rayner's paper stirred psychologists' imaginations. Many came to believe that neurotic symptoms could be understood in conditioning terms and, perhaps, even cured by conditioning. The practical outcome of this belief was the development of behavior therapy, which is discussed in more detail later in this book. In the 1920s, however, the rise of behavior therapy was still decades away, and Freudian interpretations dominated psychology especially in America and the United Kingdom. It was taken for granted that once patients accepted and "worked through" the psychoanalytic interpretation of their behavior, their problems would disappear. This belief was reinforced in a postscript to Hans's story published by Freud in 1922: "Little Hans was now a strapping youth of nineteen. He . . . was perfectly well, and suffered from no troubles or inhibitions." His parents had divorced and remarried. As a consequence, Hans lived alone ". . . and only regretted that as a result of the breaking up of the family he had been separated from the *younger sister he was so fond of* [emphasis added]."[6]

For Freud, Hans's fear was not a special case—the Oedipal conflict is universal. It is resolved only when the child relinquishes the object of his desire and *identifies* with the same-sex parent. The process of identification leads to the development of a superego and the adoption of the parent's moral code. Freud's emphasis on the relationship between children and their parents naturally led to speculation about what happens to children deprived of one or the other parent early in life. Such children may not only find it difficult to resolve their conflicts, but they may develop severe psychological illnesses. The importance placed on early childhood experience by Freudians stimulated psychologists to study the emotional effects of separating children from their parents—a phenomenon that came to be known as *maternal deprivation.*

INFANT ATTACHMENTS

Leonardo da Vinci was born in 1452, the illegitimate child of an Italian landlord. When he was only 4 years old, he was torn away from his mother, Caterina, and raised by his father's young and tender wife, Donna Albiera. Years later, Leonardo drew on his childhood experience to paint *The Virgin and Child with Saint Anne,* which shows a child being taken away by a young woman as an older woman looks on. Leonardo's theme—the separation of a mother from her child—recurs repeatedly in folklore and legends.

Myths and fairy tales are replete with stories of abandoned children separated from their mothers at a tender age. Some survived on their own; others were supposed to have been raised by animals (Romulus and Remus, for example). The Tarzan stories and Rudyard Kipling's "Mowgli" are modern variations on this ancient theme. The stories usually present such children in an idealized light, living happily among the beasts of the forest or the jungle.

In contrast, another set of legends conveys a far gloomier picture of what happens when children are separated from their mothers. For example, in an experiment designed to discover the "original" human language, the Emperor Frederick II of Prussia was supposed to have taken children from their mothers and put them in the care of nurses who were permitted to bathe and feed them but were forbidden from cuddling, playing, and most important, from speaking to the children. The idea was that without language models the children would grow up speaking humanity's original language. Unfortunately, the children did not live long enough for the emperor's hypothesis to be tested. Without their mothers' love and affection, the children all

died. The idea that children may die if deprived of their mothers' love is echoed in the diary of an 18th-century Spanish bishop who wrote, "In the orphanage children become very sad and many of them die because of this sadness."

The early mother-child bond played an important role in Darwin's theory of evolution. He noted that among birds and mammals some kind of early parental attachment is routine. In contrast to fish that lay hundreds of eggs and then abandon their potential offspring to shift for themselves, birds and mammals have fewer children in whom they invest considerable effort. Human parents, especially mothers but often fathers as well, provide food, shelter, and protection to their young, caring for them through a long period of dependency. While under parental care, children learn the skills necessary to survive on their own. To a large extent, the mother-child bond is mediated through the expression of emotion. In Darwin's words:

> The movements of expression in the face and body, whatever their origin may have been, are in themselves of much importance for our welfare. They serve as the first means of communication between the mother and her infant; she smiles approval, and this encourages her child on the right path, or frowns disapproval. The movements of expression give vividness and energy to our spoken words. They reveal the thoughts and intentions of others more truly than do words, which may be falsified.[7]

All parents are aware that unhappy children are comforted by the sight, voice, and touch of their caregivers (usually their mothers). Separation from the mother produces the opposite reaction, clear signs of distress. In the words of the poet George Eliot:

> A child foresaken, waking suddenly,
> Whose gaze afeard on all things round doth rove,
> And seeth only that it cannot see
> The meeting eyes of love.

Children appear to go through a series of stages in the development of attachments. In the first stage, which lasts from birth to about the middle of the first year, children have no clear conception of their mothers as separate from other people; they can be comforted by anyone. During the next 6 months, however, infants develop a strong attachment to a single individual (normally the mother,

WHAT MAKES BABIES CUTE?

Why do mothers slave over their babies? To some extent, the answer lies in heredity. Infants have evolved a set of attractive physical features that trigger maternal emotions and elicit parenting behavior. The features that constitute babiness include a large forehead, large eyes, upturned nose, and chubby cheeks. Babies have evolved these features because they define cuteness and make adults want to cuddle and take care of them. Similar features produce cuteness in animals and in cartoons.

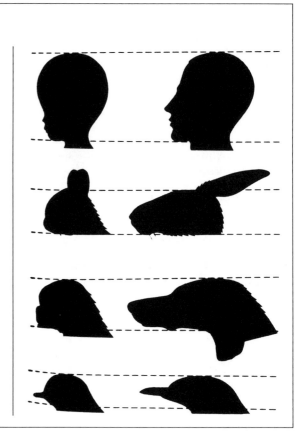

Physically "cute" features attract maternal tenderness.

but in some cases a nurse or father). The child shows clear signs of distress when the mother departs and is comforted when she returns. As the attachment strengthens, strangers come to be feared; their very presence provokes distress. This tendency to form close personal attachments evolved because a fear of being abandoned, of being left to fend for oneself, has clear survival value. Animal children are most likely to survive if they stay near their mothers, who will not only care for them but also protect them from predators. Human infants, too, are most likely to ensure their own safety by forming a strong attachment to their mothers and by insisting in any way they can that the attached individual remain nearby.

As children get older, they become less insecure and can tolerate increasingly longer separations from their mothers. But what happens when separations are lengthy or even permanent? In animals, the effects can be drastic. The famous American psychologist Harry Harlow separated infant monkeys from their mothers, indeed from all other monkeys, for long periods and observed the effects on the infants' later development. He found that the infant monkeys spent hours huddled in the corner of their cages, rocking back and forth. They failed to play with other monkeys, were unable to fight back if attacked, and showed no interest in social interaction when they grew older. Many refused to mate with other monkeys. It seems as if the early maternal deprivation experienced by these monkeys left them unable to engage in normal social relations when they grew older. Social adjustment was particularly disturbed when monkeys were separated from their mothers for 6 months or more during the first year of life. An infant's first year appears to be a *critical period* when attachments must form if babies are to develop normally. A failure to form and maintain attachments during this critical period leads to problems later in life (e.g., they do not mate with other monkeys and they become social isolates).

Many psychologists believe that maternal separation has similar effects on human infants. But because humans are not monkeys, there is no certainty that human infants will react to maternal deprivation in the same way. Clearly, we cannot repeat Harlow's experiment with humans—no responsible scientist would take babies away from their parents. (Even the monkey experiments would be ethically suspect today.) However, we can look for "natural experiments" in which, for one reason or another, infants are separated from their mothers early in life. In the early decades of the present century, the site for such natural experiments was typically the "foundling home" or orphanage.

Late 19th and early 20th century observers—doctors mainly, but also educators and psychologists—were shocked at the high rate of infant mortality found in orphanages in both Europe and America. Death rates ranging from 30% to over 70% of children admitted during their first year were common. A campaign to improve health, nutritional, and sanitary conditions brought mortality down to around 10% by the 1940s. However, the children who survived were found to have a high rate of psychological disturbance in later life. Two explanations were advanced: lack of early sensory stimulation and maternal deprivation. The lack of stimulation occurred because, in an attempt to maintain hygiene, institutions isolated infants in sterile cots and cribs. All they had to look at were white sheets and a white ceiling. Children also lacked the stimulation that comes from interacting with other people. Staff shortages meant that infants received little personal attention except for feeding and bathing. This unstimulating environment could well have interfered with intellectual and social development.

In addition to lacking stimulation, the orphans, by definition, lacked mothers. According to Freudian theory, psychological development requires the interaction of parents and children. Children deprived of parents, especially mothers, are highly vulnerable to psychological disturbance. Although both factors, lack of stimulation and maternal deprivation, were considered important determinants of a child's later adjustment, maternal deprivation was emphasized. This was largely the result of the growing popularity of psychoanalysis. For example, René Spitz, whose research is the subject of this chapter, would certainly never have given maternal deprivation the attention he did had it not been for the increasing influence of Freudian ideas.

René Spitz was born in Austria in 1887. He studied psychoanalysis under Freud and emigrated to the United States along with many other psychoanalysts in the 1940s. He served on the graduate faculty of the City College of New York and also held the post of vice-president of the New York Psychoanalytic Society. Although Spitz was the author of several books, he is mainly known for two widely cited articles on *hospitalism* and *anaclitic depression*. The term *hospitalism* describes the psychological and physical disorders produced by institutionalization. Anaclitic depression, on the other hand, is a psychological disturbance produced by separating a child from its mother. Although he admitted that understimulation played some role in causing hospitalism, Spitz believed that both hospitalism and anaclitic depression are mainly reactions to maternal deprivation.

Spitz criticized earlier observations of children in orphanages as too impressionistic and unsystematic. His goal was to bring scientific rigor to maternal-deprivation research by introducing control groups and quantitative measures of infant development. His methods and results are described in Classic Study 6.

CLASSIC STUDY 6
Maternal Deprivation

Spitz reported his research in a series of articles in a periodical called *The Psychoanalytic Study of the Child*. His first paper, "Hospitalism: An Inquiry into the Genesis of Psychiatric Conditions in Early Childhood," appeared in 1945. It described 164 children, 130 of whom were raised in one of two institutions during their first year of life. Spitz called the two institutions the Nursery and the Foundling Home, respectively. He did not identify the precise institutions; all he would say is that they were "situated in different countries of the Western hemisphere." (In a later publication, he extended this to somewhere in the Western world.) As control subjects, Spitz studied 34 "noninstitutionalized children of the same age group in their parents' homes in both countries." Many of Spitz's observations were recorded on film resulting in the documentary feature *Grief: A Peril in Infancy.*

The children studied by Spitz were raised in sharply different environments. The Nursery was a penal institution for females. Those inmates who gave birth while in custody cared for their children until the babies were a year old. If a child had to be separated from his or her mother for brief periods, another Nursery mother took over. Spitz described the Nursery mothers as socially maladjusted, feebleminded, or criminal; nevertheless, he claimed they were able to give their children "everything a good mother does." The children were kept in glass-enclosed cots until they were 6 months of age and then transferred to rooms full of toys. Spitz describes the Nursery atmosphere as "warm and friendly" and notes that the children received considerable attention from their mothers, who had little else to do.

The other institution studied by Spitz presented a marked contrast. He called this second institution the Foundling Home because children were placed there when their mothers, usually for financial reasons, could not provide adequate care. Although the children were breast-fed by their mothers during their first few months of life, care seems to have been in the hands of a kindly but small nursing staff (one nurse to every eight infants). Nurses could only provide each child with custodial attention, so infants spent most of their first 18 months of life alone in their cots. Sheets were draped over the sides of their beds so that the infants could see nothing of what went on around them. There were few toys to keep them occupied. The two control groups were made up of 11 children from urban professional homes and 23 children raised in a poor, presumably Latin American or western European fishing village.

Spitz's major research measure was the Developmental Quotient (DQ), a measure of infant development derived from a set of measures known as the Hetzer-Wolf Baby Tests. These tests measure physical and motor development (the age at which a child can sit unaided, crawl, walk, and so on) as well as intellectual and social development. DQs were calculated for each child in the first 4 months of life and again in the final 4 months of the first year. The results are summarized in Table 3.1.

As may be seen, there were major discrepancies among the groups even at the initial evaluation. Children of professional families scored highest, well above the average score of 100, while Nursery children scored lowest. Spitz believed that these initial differences were the result of a combination of genetic and environmental factors. While the size of the genetic influence is debatable, there is no doubt that the mothers from professional households received better prenatal care than did any of the other mothers Spitz studied. Professional mothers and their babies also received the best food, medicine, and clothing. Interestingly, the Foundling Home children also scored well on the initial testing. Spitz thought that their high initial DQs were also a sign of genetic superiority. He described Foundling Home children as the offspring of "socially well-adjusted, normal mothers whose only handicap was an inability to support themselves and their children (which is no sign of maladjustment in women of Latin background)."

Although the Foundling Home children started off with high DQs, by the last 4 months of their first year they had deteriorated to a level far below average and well below those children raised in the Nursery. The remaining two groups achieved similar scores on both testings. Along with a drop in DQ, Spitz reported that Foundling Home children were specially prone to developing infections, were slow to learn to sit and walk, slow in developing social skills, and often morbidly afraid (or excessively fond) of strangers. According to Spitz, all of these problems were part of the single syndrome of *hospitalism.* Follow-up studies showed that, in their second and third years, when children in the Nursery were walking and talking—as were children in the control families—only 2 of the 26 Foundling Home children could walk and only these same two children could speak (and only a few words).

There are several, fairly obvious potential explanations for Spitz's observations. The conditions in the Foundling Home may have been less hygienic, the food less nutritious, and the medical care less attentive than in the other settings. Spitz considered

TABLE 3.1   Initial and 1-Year Developmental Quotients (DQs) for Children in Four Groups (from Spitz's study)

Type of Environment	Cultural and Social Background	Developmental Quotients	
		Average of first 4 months	Average of last 4 months
Parental home	Professional	133	131
	Village population	107	108
Institution	"Nursery"	101.5	105
	"Foundling Home"	124	72

these possibilities but rejected them all. The Foundling Home provided professional medical care and adequate diets; the babies were well clothed and clean. Spitz also rejected the possibility that, despite their high initial DQs, Foundling Home infants harbored some hidden genetic defect that led their mothers to put them in the Home in the first place. Indeed, he asserted that the Foundling Home children were genetically superior to children in the Nursery whose mothers, after all, were "psychically defective, psychopathic, or criminal."

Having disposed of the obvious explanations for the Foundling Home children's drop in DQ, Spitz turned to more obscure ones. He noted, for example, that the children in the Foundling Home had fewer toys than did those in the Nursery. The Nursery children also received considerably more human attention. Nursery mothers lavished their babies with care and were constantly interacting with one another. Nursery children could see what was happening around them through their glass-sided beds, and they could even look out a window. Foundling Home children, in contrast, had little stimulation. Their cribs were draped in white, illumination was low, they could not see out a window, and except for scheduled feedings, there was no human contact to absorb their attention. Spitz also observed that the babies in the Foundling Home lay in one position so long that "a hollow is worn into their mattresses" making it impossible for them to turn from side to side. (How babies who are left to lie in a hole for 18 hours per day can be described as "well-cared-for" is a mystery Spitz never explains.)

Another important factor that differentiated Foundling Home and Nursery children was the "loss" of their mothers. After they were weaned at around 4 months of age, Foundling Home children rarely saw their mothers. Nursery children, on the other hand, were intensely mothered by their natural mothers, who had little else to do in jail and who, according to Spitz, reacted to their children as a "phallic substitute." To show that the deterioration in DQ is the result of maternal deprivation, Spitz plotted the changes in DQ over the first year. His graph, which is reproduced in Figure 3.5, shows the deterioration in DQ over time. The Foundling Home children begin to lose ground as early as 3 months of age, but they don't sink below 100 until after they are weaned and their mothers depart. The nursery children, on the other hand, gradually increase in DQ during their first months and show small fluctuations during the rest of the year.

Of these two explanations for the Foundling Home children's drop in DQ—lack of sensory stimulation and separation from their mother after weaning—Spitz clearly prefers the latter. He concluded that the major cause of the drop in DQ and the other psychological symptoms he observed in Foundling Home children was maternal deprivation and not simply the effect of understimulation. In a follow-up report made several years after his initial observations, Spitz reported that the early effects of maternal deprivation were irreparable. The children remained sickly and developmentally delayed even when their rearing conditions were greatly improved and they were given considerable amounts of human attention. Most frightening of all, 27 of

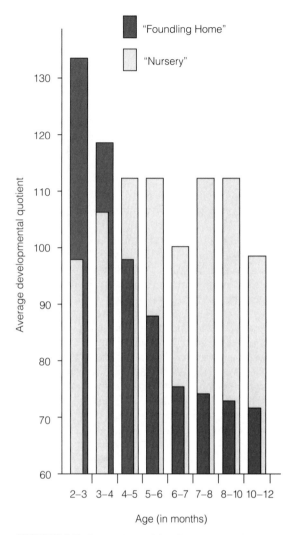

FIGURE 3.5 Comparison of development quotient scores in Nursery and Foundling Home (from Spitz's study).

when Foundling Home babies were separated from their mothers. In Spitz's words:

> In the second half of the first year, a few of these [maternally deprived] infants developed a weepy behavior that was in marked contrast to their previously happy and outgoing behavior. After a time, this weepiness gave way to withdrawal. The children in question would lie in their cots with averted faces, refusing to take part in the life of the surroundings. When we approached them we were ignored.[8]

As may be seen from Spitz's description, at first, the infant protests the loss of its mother by crying and temper tantrums. After a while, anger turns to despair and depression. The child becomes unresponsive, loses interest in the environment, and takes on a sad facial expression. According to Spitz, these children become depressed because they have lost maternal love. The symptoms become increasingly marked as the length of the separation increases. Hospitalism can be seen as an exaggerated form of anaclitic depression. In both cases, the condition remits, sometimes dramatically, if the mother returns in a relatively short time. Prolonged separation, however, produces irreversible psychological damage.

Spitz was careful to differentiate anaclitic depression and hospitalism from adult forms of depression. He conceptualized the latter in psychoanalytic terms—the work of a "sadistically cruel superego." Because young children do not have superegos, Spitz felt that their depression was fundamentally different from adults'. It was not until the 1970s that psychologists and psychiatrists began to realize that adult forms of depression can occur in children as well as adults.

Spitz's chilling descriptions of children's reactions to separation from their mothers produced understandable alarm among mental-health workers and educators. Many called for social programs, even legislation, to ensure that all children were raised by attentive and consistently present caregivers.

AFTERMATH

The research reported by Spitz and others inspired many others to study the effects of maternal deprivation. At least initially, these studies supported Spitz's main finding—maternal deprivation pro-

the Foundling Home children died in the period between the original and follow-up studies. Although their medical care was supposedly no better, none of the Nursery children died.

Spitz later described a syndrome he called *anaclitic depression,* an infantile emotional disorder observed

duces serious disturbances in children. Although the severity of the psychological disturbance depends on the length of separation and the age of the child at separation, researchers agreed that maternally deprived children grow up to be disturbed adolescents and adults. This conclusion was reinforced by another "natural" experiment conducted during World War II when German bombing forced thousands of British children to be evacuated from the target areas (mainly cities) and sent to live either in the country or in institutions. It was widely reported that children left with their families had fewer psychological problems despite the frequent bombing raids. Summarizing the existing data in 1951, the famous British psychiatrist John Bowlby concluded that there was "no room for doubt . . . the prolonged deprivation of the young child of maternal care may have grave and far-reaching effects on his character."

Despite widespread acceptance of Bowlby's conclusions among mental-health authorities, a few critics began to emerge. Spitz's methodology and measurements were especially suspect. For example, one critic, Samuel Pinneau, noted that half the drop in DQ among the Foundling Home children occurred *prior* to the time (4 months) at which most children were separated from their mothers. Pinneau also pointed out that Spitz's data were often inconsistent and the number of children in the various groups varied from one report to the next. Also, although it appeared from his reports that Spitz studied each child from infancy, in reality the children were studied only for a few months each and some for less than that.

Other critics suggested that Spitz was too hasty in dismissing quality of care as an explanation for his observations. Spitz's report that Foundling Home children wore holes in their mattresses so deep that they could not even turn from side to side suggests that it was at least possible that poor general care and understimulation rather than maternal deprivation was responsible for the problems faced by Foundling Home children. Because Spitz would not reveal the location of the institutions, his findings could not be checked directly. Investigators did, however, repeat his observations at other institutions. They found that neither hospitalism nor anaclitic depression was an inevitable consequence of maternal deprivation.

Long-term follow-ups of children who were separated from their parents also failed to support Spitz's dire predictions. For example, 15 years after the Battle of Britain, children who were removed from their homes in London to institutions in the country were found to be well adjusted and no more likely to have psychological problems than others of the same age. Even Bowlby eventually had to admit that he and others may have overstated their case. Only a small minority of children develop severe psychological problems from lack of mothering. Clearly, there must be something about these children or their experiences (or both) that was responsible. To find out why some deprived children succeed in developing normally while others fail, researchers had to become more sophisticated. Instead of considering maternal deprivation to be a single homogeneous variable, they had to break deprivation down into a number of constituent variables: stimulation, contact, health care, feeding, and so on. Maternal deprivation can have a variety of effects depending on which of these aspects of "mothering" is disturbed. The severity of any disturbance depends on the age at which separation occurs, the number and duration of previous separations, the child's temperament, the quality of the child's care, and the degree to which alternative caregivers can make up for the child's maternal loss.

Although the notion that maternal deprivation always leads to severe psychological illness had to be abandoned, Spitz's research made an important difference in the way institutionalized children are cared for. For example, before Spitz's time, it was common to see hospitalized children left alone in their beds without stimulation for long periods. In some cases, the children were even restrained by tying their limbs to the bedrails. After Spitz, almost all health workers understood the importance of providing care and stimulation to babies, and hospital practices changed. Similar changes occurred in orphanages, schools, and other institutions.

The work on maternal deprivation also served to increase the importance of psychoanalysis. The theory's focus on early childhood experiences as the major determinant of later psychological problems offered what appeared to be an explanation for the effects that researchers such as Spitz reported. Freud became a figure of international stature because of his theory of psychological development.

However, in 1938, when the Nazis occupied Austria, Freud was again a victim of anti-Semitism. He was unable to write, his books were burned, and he was put under house arrest. American President Franklin Roosevelt arranged for him to move to London. He was soon followed by his daughter Anna who was to go on to become a famous psychoanalyst in her own right. Although he was dying from cancer, Freud worked until the end refusing painkillers so that his mind could keep alert. On 23 September 1939, the pain had become unbearable; he took a strong dose of morphine and, a little while later, died.

Further Reading

Bowlby, J. (1951). *Maternal care and mental health.* Geneva: World Health Organization.

Freud, S. (1909). Analysis of a phobia in a five-year-old boy. In E. Jones (Ed.), *Sigmund Freud: Collected papers* (Vol. 3, pp. 149–295). New York: Basic Books.

Spitz, R. (1945). Hospitalism: An inquiry into the genesis of psychiatric conditions in early childhood. *Psychoanalytic Study of the Child, 1,* 53–74.

Spitz, R. (1946). Hospitalism: A follow-up report. *Psychoanalytic Study of the Child, 2,* 113–117.

Notes

1. Watson, J. B. (1950). *Behaviorism.* New York: Norton. P. 104.
2. Freud, S. Address to the society of B'nai B'rith, 6 May 1926. Quoted in E. Freud, L. Freud, & I. Grubrich-Simitis (Eds.), *Sigmund Freud: His life in pictures and words* (p. 238). Brisbane: University of Queensland Press, 1978.
3. The value of this case as an illustration of psychoanalytic reasoning was earlier demonstrated by: Brown, R. (1965). *Social psychology.* New York: Free Press.
4. Freud, S. (1909). Analysis of a phobia in a five-year-old boy. In E. Jones (Ed.) (1959), *Sigmund Freud: Collected papers* (Vol. 3, pp. 149–295). New York: Basic Books.
5. Watson, J. B., & Rayner, R. (1920). Conditioned emotional reactions. *Journal of Experimental Psychology, 3,* p. 14.
6. Freud, S. Postscript. In E. Jones (Ed.) (1959), *Sigmund Freud: Collected papers* (Vol. 3, pp. 288–289). New York: Basic Books.
7. Darwin, C. (1965). *The expression of emotion in man and animals.* P. 364. Chicago: University of Chicago Press.
8. Spitz, R. (1965). *The first year of life.* New York: International Universities Press. Pp. 268–269.

CHAPTER 4

T he concept of "mind" is constantly being invoked. We make up, lose, and change our minds every single day. But exactly what does the word *mind* mean? Philosophical arguments about the existence of minds, separate from brains, have been going on for centuries. Those on one side argue that the human mind is a special evolutionary gift that sets us apart from other living things. The other side believes that the abilities attributed to minds (perceiving, learning, feeling, remembering, and so on) are entirely the result of electrochemical activity in the millions of cells that make up our brains. We may believe that we think, love, and reminisce with our minds, but it is really our brains that are doing all the work.

The mind versus brain debate has been going on for centuries, long enough for positions to become firmly entrenched. Although there are many subtle nuances differentiating individual philosophies, there are really only two main points of view: *dualist* theories of mind and *monist*, or materialist, theories. Dualists consider the brain to be little more than a machine while the "mind" is nonphysical and separate. Monists, on the other hand, scoff at the very notion of a nonmaterial mind; they view the mind and brain as inseparable and, in most senses, identical. The main strength of the dualist view is that it coincides with everyday thinking. We are all accustomed to attributing behavior to causes that originate in the mind. For example, when we say that an office worker took an umbrella to work because she *believed* rain was likely, we are implying that her state of "mind" when she set out to work caused her behavior. Similarly, if the same individual often worked late hoping to advance her career, we attribute her behavior to a *motive to achieve*. It should be

Three Extraordinary Conditions of Early Life

Everything about this condition is extraordinary — its name absurd, its symptoms unique, its character baffling, its cause unknown, and its treatment problematic. Serious investigators have doubted its very existence. Others have felt it to be a form of malingering, and some have felt it to be of supernatural origin.

—E. M. Bouteille

clear, however, that "achievement motives," like beliefs about rain, exist only in minds.

To balance its strength, dualism also has a serious weakness: It fails to specify exactly what the mind is made of and where it can be found. If the mind occupies no physical location, where does it store its memories and carry out its thinking? Similarly, if the mind is separate from the brain, why does brain damage affect its operation? Materialism overcomes these difficulties by equating minds with brains. But, as a philosophy, materialism has some serious problems of its own. For example, if minds and brains are the same thing, how is it possible for us to be aware of ourselves? Who or what observes our thoughts when we think to ourselves? If I decide to read a book rather than go to the cinema, who or what made the choice?

Despite its philosophical shortcomings, most psychologists align themselves squarely in the monist camp. They find it impossible to sustain the dualist's belief in an independent mind when it is so easy to demonstrate that the mind's functions are disrupted by brain damage. Curiously, despite almost unanimous agreement that the brain is the "organ" of the mind, psychologists continue to distinguish between *organic* and *functional* psychopathology. Organic syndromes, they say, are the domain of neurologists whereas functional syndromes such as phobias (which occur in people with perfectly normal brains) are the province of psychologists.

How can psychologists claim to be materialists and yet still distinguish between organic and functional pathology? Aren't the two positions contradictory? Many psychologists argue that they are not. Consider the following computing analogy: Computers consist of "hardware" (wires, silicon chips, and other electronic components) and "software" (stored information and programmed instructions). Both are "real," and both are required for the computer to perform useful work, but software and hardware are not the same thing. Programmers, who are responsible for designing software, need not know the details of computer hardware. Similarly, the engineers who build and maintain computer hardware do not need to be expert programmers. If we accept that human behavior is produced by the interaction of a certain type of hardware (the brain) interacting with specific software (cognitive abilities), then, by analogy, it should be possible for abnormal behavior to have one of three possible etiologies: functional (faulty software), organic (damaged hardware), or some combination of both. The classic example of a hardware-based disorder is general paresis, a syndrome whose behavioral symptoms, including a progressive dementia, are entirely a function of the brain damage caused by syphilis. At the other extreme, Little Albert's "phobia" (see Chapter 3) was entirely functional—the result of classical conditioning.

Although the functional-organic dichotomy served as a convenient classification system for many decades, it began to break down when it became clear that many forms of abnormal behavior could not be neatly assigned to either the functional or the organic category. Schizophrenia, for example, has been shown to have organic components (including brain deterioration and abnormal neural chemistry), but it seems to develop only in those people unable to cope with certain types of environmental stress. Thus, schizophrenia is neither clearly functional nor clearly organic; it seems to be the result of both types of defect. In the 1980s, other syndromes long classified as functional were found to also have an organic component. Indeed, in the 1990s, it has become common to consider practically all serious forms of psychopathology as partly functional and partly the result of faults in brain function.

In the present chapter, three classic case studies are used to illustrate the way in which the functional-organic dichotomy has evolved into today's interactive *psychobiological* approach. At the same time, the chapter describes how psychologists and others have tried to unravel three of the most puzzling and intriguing mysteries of childhood and adolescence: *autistic disorder, anorexia nervosa,* and *Tourette's disorder.*

AUTISTIC DISORDER

The story of the syndrome known today as autistic disorder (formerly, early infantile autism) begins in a small town on the Austrian-Russian border in 1894, the year pioneer child psychiatrist Leo Kanner was born.

Kanner grew up in an orthodox Jewish community that frowned on secular education. His

FIGURE 4.1 Leo Kanner (1894–1981), pioneer child psychiatrist.

From the beginning, Kanner's research interests varied widely. At one time or another, they included the study of venereal disease among American Indians, a social-historical study of dentistry, and an attempt to understand the "functional" psychoses — serious psychiatric syndromes in which patients with apparently normal brains would lose touch with reality. His early publications on these and other topics won Kanner a fellowship in psychiatry at the Phipps Clinic located at Baltimore's Johns Hopkins University. The clinic's director, Adolph Meyer, was also a European immigrant who, by the time Kanner moved to Baltimore, had become a major figure in American psychiatry. Originally trained by Freud, Meyer was not a doctrinaire psychoanalyst. He encouraged a diversity of approaches to the study of psychopathology. Even John Watson, the arch behaviorist who conditioned Little Albert to fear furry animals (see Chapter 3), worked in the Phipps Clinic for a time. The fellowship came at a fortunate time in Kanner's career; his exposure to diverse views early in his professional life gave him an open-mindedness that would serve him well in later research and practice.

At the completion of his 3-year fellowship, Kanner was asked to stay on in Baltimore to establish a child psychiatry service. Although he had little background in either pediatrics or child psychiatry, Kanner took on the job with enthusiasm. Within 5 years, he published *Child Psychiatry*, the first comprehensive textbook in the field. Now in its 14th edition, the book has been translated into dozens of foreign languages.

Kanner's textbook, and the expertise it reflected, gave him stature both in his profession and in the wider community. Kanner used his prestige to help improve the lives of patients. For example, at one time it was common for crooked lawyers to obtain the release of mentally retarded patients from institutions so that they could work as virtually unpaid servants in affluent homes. Appalled by this practice, Kanner eschewed the polemical or political approach to reform preferring instead to attack the problem scientifically. Kanner conducted a follow-up study of patients who had been released from the Maryland State Training School for the Retarded to homes that were ostensibly looking after them but who were really looking for slave labor. He found that many patients were unable to perform

mother's insistence that her son learn more than religion led young Leo to a confrontation with the local rabbi. Kanner remembered this incident throughout his life. It made him a strong proponent of individual freedom. Kanner's school career was interrupted by World War I during which he served in the Austrian army. After the war, he returned to his studies at the University of Berlin eventually earning a medical degree in 1921. Kanner spent the next few years practicing in Germany, but postwar economic hardships led him to emigrate to America in 1924. His first position was as an assistant physician at Yankton State Hospital in North Dakota.

When not looking after his patients, Kanner spent his time improving his English by doing newspaper crossword puzzles. He also developed what was to become a lifelong interest in research.

the household duties required of them. These failed servants were tossed out on to the street where they became prostitutes or criminals. Many wound up in jail. Kanner published the results of his survey. The resulting furor led to the reform of this despicable practice. Kanner's social conscience also led him to help resettle Holocaust victims, to raise funds for the Spanish loyalists fighting the Fascists, and to campaign for patient rights wherever he saw them violated. For this work, Kanner received awards from the Joseph P. Kennedy Junior Foundation and the American Academy of Pediatrics. He also received the Salmon Award of the New York Academy of Medicine and the Stanley Dean Award of the American Psychiatric Association.

Of Kanner's many publications, by far the best known is an article he published in the now defunct journal *The Nervous Child*. The article, which appeared in 1943, was titled "Autistic Disturbances of Affective Contact." In what is widely regarded as a historic landmark in abnormal psychology, Kanner carefully described 11 children whose behavior appeared to represent a distinct syndrome different from mental retardation and other previously known forms of psychopathology. This syndrome, which soon became known as infantile autism, is the most serious mental illness of childhood. Over the years, autism has been the focus of intense research interest. Psychologists have learned a great deal about the syndrome, but many of Kanner's original observations stand up today as well as they did in 1943. Indeed, nearly all the basic points Kanner made in his first paper have been confirmed. To fully appreciate Kanner's achievement, it is necessary to first put it in historical perspective.

Childhood Autism Before Kanner

The first description of a child who may have been autistic was published by the English physician John Halsam almost 200 years ago. Halsam described a 5-year-old boy admitted to London's Bethleham Royal Hospital ("Bedlam") in 1799. The child had contracted a severe case of measles when only a year old. According to his mother, after the boy recovered, he was livelier than before and difficult to control. His development followed an atypical course. For example, although he walked at age 2, he did not speak until he was 4. When seen by

Halsam, the boy was in good physical health but seemed compelled to keep constantly moving. Unlike other children, the boy showed little distress when parted from his mother nor did he show much interest in playing with other children. Instead, he played in a repetitive way with toy soldiers and listened to music. He could recall many tunes and whistle them quite accurately. Indeed, the boy seemed to have a special talent for mimicry. One of the oddest traits the boy exhibited was his habit of referring to himself in the third person. The boy never used the word "I"; he always referred to himself as "you."

Around the same time that Halsam saw his case, Jean Itard first met the "Wild Boy" of Aveyron (see Chapter 3). Although he was clearly mentally retarded the boy, who was called Victor, showed many unusual behaviors not typically found in retarded children. For example, like the boy described by Halsam, Victor did not play normally with toys. Instead, he obsessively and repetitively fondled common objects, and like Halsam's boy, he was very fond of music. Itard noted that Victor strenuously resisted any change in his environment and liked everything in his room to be maintained in a particular place. He had an excellent memory and could always tell when some object had been moved. If these objects were not immediately replaced, the boy would become agitated and visibly distressed. Victor also showed peculiar reactions to sounds. A pistol shot right behind his ear might produce no response at all, whereas the sound of cracking walnuts in another room would bring Victor running hoping to be given a little of his favorite food.

The next description of what now appears to have been an autistic child was published in 1920 by Lightner Witmer, an American psychologist credited with starting the first child psychology clinic. Witmer described a 3-year-old boy named Don who spent all of his time contemplating a playing card that he held in his hand. He did not play with toys and seemed emotionally aloof even from his parents. Like Victor, Don resisted change and would have a temper tantrum if anyone tried to take away his playing card. Like Halsam's boy, Don loved music and could hum tunes. Through patient training, Witmer and his co-workers managed to overcome some of Don's more annoying behaviors (especially a worrying tendency to scratch his own face), but this improvement hardly made Don normal. Even after he was able to look after himself, he still played obsessively and his speech was highly repetitive.

Don, Victor, and the child described by Halsam share several important characteristics. All three were boys, they all liked music, and all three had good memories. The three boys were aloof from interpersonal relationships, and at least two of the three resisted any change in their respective environments. None of the boys played normally with toys; instead, they obsessionally tapped and fondled common objects. Although their behaviors were not typical of retarded children, no immediate attempt was made to assign them to an independent category. They were simply grouped together with other retarded children. This is typical in the history of psychopathology and medicine in general; global categories, containing many different types of people, slowly give way to increasingly finer distinctions. Not long ago, for example, patients were described as suffering from the "fevers" as if all the illnesses that cause fever constitute a single category. As doctors' understanding of bacteriology and virology improved, patients were assigned to more specific groups. Instead of the "fevers," they were classified as suffering from bacterial, rickettsial, or viral infections. Within each of these categories, patients were assigned to subcategories according to the specific organism that caused the symptom.

Such homogeneous patient categories are essential for researchers. Even wonder drugs such as penicillin would appear ineffective when administered to an undifferentiated group of fever patients. Some would respond but many, perhaps most, would show no benefit because their fevers were produced by organisms (viruses, for example) that are insensitive to the drug. Studies of undifferentiated fever patients would therefore lead to the incorrect conclusion that penicillin is not a very effective treatment. On the other hand, if the drug were administered to fever patients who had been assigned to bacterial subcategories, it would soon become apparent that the drug is an effective treatment for some specific conditions. The need to assess treatments using homogeneous patient populations is one of the main reasons why scientists and clinicians have spent so much effort developing patient classification schemes (see Chapter 2).

It should be obvious that psychological terms such as "mentally retarded" or "psychotic" are as vague and useless as "fevers." More specific diagnostic categories are required if we are ever to develop effective treatments. Leo Kanner's major contribution to psychopathology was the delineation of one such diagnostic subcategory—autism. As it turns out, the syndrome described by Kanner was probably the same one described by Witmer, Halsam, and Itard (although Kanner did not know this at the time). But Kanner went further than anyone before him: He separated this special group of children from the amorphous mass of troubled children labeled "subnormal" or "psychotic." His observations sparked a strong interest among scientists and clinicians in understanding and treating this strange disorder. In the half century since his seminal article appeared, autism has been the subject of more than 3,000 scientific articles and books. All of this work originated with Kanner's classic study, which is described next.

CLASSIC STUDY 7
Eleven Autistic Children

After completing his Phipps Clinic fellowship, Kanner began a child psychiatry practice. It was immediately successful; by the time his textbook appeared, Kanner was a well-known authority on child psychiatry. Colleagues frequently referred troubling or difficult cases to him. Kanner found one group of children particularly haunting. They were neither clearly retarded nor schizophrenic, but they were certainly emotionally impaired. Kanner studied 11 such children for 5 years and then published his observations in his famous 1943 article, which began as follows:

> Since 1938, there have come to our attention a number of children whose condition differs so markedly and uniquely from anything reported so far, that each case merits—and, I hope, will eventually receive—a detailed consideration of its fascinating peculiarities.[1]

AUTISM AND THE "THEORY OF MIND"

Practically everyone working in the field believes that autistic individuals have a serious cognitive impairment. However, attempts to characterize this deficit have been rather vague. Progress requires some specification of just what knowledge or cognitive skills autistic people lack. Few studies have been designed to yield such information. An exception is the research carried out by English psychologist Simon Baron-Cohen and his colleagues. Their studies focused on what has been called the "theory of mind." A theory of mind is defined as the ability to assign mental states to oneself and to others. That we all possess such a theory is evidenced by our ability to infer "what other people know, want, feel, or believe." The ability to make inferences about what others believe and how they will behave is an important social skill—a skill that most children begin to display at around 2 years of age.

Baron-Cohen and his colleagues believed that autistic children lack a theory of mind. To test this hypothesis, they compared a group of autistic children to normal preschool children and mentally retarded children. The autistic children were high functioning (their verbal and nonver-

bal intelligence scores were actually higher than those of children in the retarded group and probably higher than most of those in the normal group as well). The children were shown two dolls and taught their names. They observed one doll place a marble in her basket. This doll was then removed from the scene. While she was absent, the marble was transferred by the second doll to another location. The first doll then returned. The child who observed all of this was then asked the crucial question: Where will the first doll look for her marble? If the child pointed to the original location, it was concluded that he or she understood the doll's incorrect belief. On the other hand, if the child pointed to the marble's new location, then it was concluded that he or she was not taking account of the first doll's belief. To be certain that the children's answers were not simply the result of misunderstanding the task, each child was also asked to show where the marble *really* was and where the marble was "in the beginning." A child who could answer these questions but still insisted that the first doll would seek the marble in the new location was said to lack a theory of mind.

Kanner went on to describe the 11 children, their differences, but more important, their similarities:

> But even a quick review of the material makes the emergence of a number of essential common characteristics appear inevitable. These characteristics form a unique "syndrome" not heretofore reported, which seems to be rare enough, yet is probably more frequent than is indicated by the paucity of observed cases. It is quite possible that some such children have been viewed as feeble-minded or schizophrenic.

According to Kanner, the 11 cases contained a cluster of characteristic features that were both unusual and not typical of other conditions such as mental retardation or schizophrenia. These included:

1. *Early onset.* The children were affected almost from birth and certainly from the first year or two of life.

2. *Lack of responsiveness to others.* Kanner described the children as aloof and unable to relate to others. As infants they failed to anticipate being picked up when their mothers approached. Once lifted from their beds, the children did not adjust their bodies to the person holding them. In short, they were not "cuddly" babies.

3. *Peculiar speech.* Although most of the children could talk, they did not use speech for communication. Those who could talk simply echoed back what they had heard others say on previous occasions. The children also substituted the word "you" for the word "I" and rarely used the word "yes."

The results were clear-cut. All the children could say where the marble was now and where it started out. However, when it came to showing where the doll would look for the marble, the groups differed markedly. Over 85% of the normal and retarded children correctly indicated the old location, the one the first doll "believed" correct. In contrast, 80% of the autistic children failed the belief question. They indicated that the doll would seek the marble in its new location. The psychologists concluded that autistic children, despite having adequate intelligence, did not appreciate the difference between what they knew and the doll's knowledge; that is, the autistic children failed to demonstrate they possessed a theory of mind.

Autistic children lack a "theory of mind": They cannot attribute false beliefs to other people, for instance, and so predict, in this experiment, that Sally will look for the marble in the box.

4. *Cognitive deficits.* Abstract concepts were difficult, if not impossible, for the children to comprehend; their play was monotonous, repetitive, and almost entirely unimaginative (see Figure 4.2). Nevertheless, the children gave the impression of having an underlying intelligence and most had excellent rote memories.

5. *Desire to maintain sameness.* Changes in their environment, even minor changes such as moving the living-room furniture or changing the time of a daily bath, were likely to provoke "catastrophic" panic attacks in the children.

6. *Progression.* Some of the children began to improve after age 6, but all remain grossly impaired.

These observations are similar to those made by Itard, Witmer, and Halsam, but Kanner recognized that they constitute a separate syndrome. In medicine, it is usually assumed that syndromes reflect underlying diseases which have specific causes. Kanner did not suggest what the cause of his syndrome might be. He did say, however, that one aspect is especially important:

The outstanding, "pathognomic," fundamental disorder is the children's *inability to relate* themselves in the ordinary way to people and situations from the beginning of life. . . . There is from the start an *extreme autistic aloneness* that, whenever possible, disregards, ignores, shuts out anything that comes to the child from outside [Kanner's italics].

FIGURE 4.2 Autistic children fiddle aimlessly with objects seemingly lost in a world of their own.

The term *autism* had previously been used in psychiatric descriptions of schizophrenic patients and refers to those who actively withdraw from reality to live in an inner world of fantasy. As applied to Kanner's 11 children, the term was rather misleading because it suggested that the children had active fantasy lives when just the opposite appeared to be the case. It also implied that there was some connection between autism and schizophrenia even though Kanner himself emphasized the differences between these two syndromes. Nevertheless, the term stuck, and the children were soon widely known as autistic.

Kanner always maintained that autism is a rare disorder. He reported that, of the 20,000 children seen in his clinic, 150—or less than 1%—were autistic. Even this low figure was probably an overestimate. Because Kanner was an eminent authority, he received many referrals in which autism was the suspected diagnosis. As a consequence, autistic patients were overrepresented in Kanner's clinic, making his numbers higher than they would otherwise have been. Subsequent studies of the prevalence of autism have estimated that the disorder occurs in 4 or 5 of every 10,000 children under 15 years old. The majority are boys. Of Kanner's first 100 cases, 80 were boys and 20 were girls. The 4:1 sex ratio has been confirmed many times since.

One intriguing and frequently noted autistic characteristic is what Kanner called "good cognitive potential." Despite serious mental retardation in most autistic children, some display special abilities, particularly in the area of music, art, arithmetic, and memory. Their behavior in this respect resembles that of children known as *idiot savants* ("retarded scholars") (see Figure 4.3). Although many, if not all, *idiot savants* are probably autistic, the relationship does not hold in reverse. The majority of autistic children do not show any special intellectual or creative abilities.

As a group, autistic children may not be especially intelligent or creative, but according to Kanner, their parents certainly are. The parents of Kanner's first 100 cases included doctors, lawyers, engineers, and other highly educated professionals. This observation was important because most serious psychological disorders (schizophrenia, for one) are more likely to be found among the poorly educated lower social classes. Kanner described the parents of autistic children as "successfully autistic" themselves:

> These parents, as a rule, are cold, humorless, perfectionists who prefer reading, writing, playing music or "thinking" to seeking out the presence of other people. They are polite, dignified, impressed by seriousness, and disdainful of "small talk." They describe themselves and their marriage partners as undemonstrative. Matrimonial life is a rather cool and formal affair. The parents treat each other with faultless respect, talk things over earnestly and calmly, and give to outsiders the impression of mutual loyalty.
>
> The parents' behavior toward the children accentuates the emotional frigidity and mechanization of care. Lack of genuine maternal warmth is often conspicuous in the first visit to the clinic. Many of the fathers hardly know their autistic children. . . .
>
> Autistic children could rarely be thought of as rejected children. Childbearing was an accepted part of matrimony, but the parents did not seem to know what to do with the children once they arrived. They lacked the warmth their babies needed.

It now appears that Kanner's observations may have been the result of what scientists call a "selection" bias—highly educated, relatively affluent parents were more likely to seek Kanner's help for their children than were working-class parents. The same selection bias may also be responsible for cold parental personalities; Kanner may simply have described the kinds of people who consulted his clinic. Even if Kanner's observations were not biased, we still could not assume that parental personality *causes* infantile autism. We have no way of knowing what the parents were like before their autistic children were born. It is possible that they were previously warm and demonstrative and that the birth of an autistic child turned them cold.

Kanner acknowledged that the cold parental behavior he observed could well have been a reaction to having an autistic child. (It is quite understandable that parents find it difficult to relate to a child who does not relate to them.) Nevertheless, Kanner's observations were taken by many as proof that autism is caused by inadequate or emotionally destructive parenting. Perhaps the foremost proponent of this view was psychiatrist Bruno Bettelheim, who claimed that autism is a "denial of the self" necessitated by a destructive mother. Autistic children hope to avoid their mothers' wrath by becoming "nonpersons." According to Bettelheim, the failure to use the word "I" (and many other common autistic behaviors) results from an unwillingness or inability to develop and maintain a concept of one's "self." Variations on the general theme of maternal destructiveness have been proposed by other psychoanalytic writers. They attribute autism either to a *lack* of maternal love or, in some cases, to *too much* maternal love from mothers who are overdependent on their children for affection. Psychoanalysts are not alone in attributing autism to psychological causes. Although they use different terminology, behaviorists make strikingly similar claims. Autism, they assert, results from an early environment that failed to reinforce proper social behavior. Having learned few social behaviors, the children engage in repetitive, self-stimulatory activities because these are all they know how to do.

Of course, neither the psychoanalytic nor the behavioral view precludes the possibility that some children, because of their physiological makeup, are

FIGURE 4.3 Some autistics are *idiot savants*. This picture was drawn in a few seconds by an autistic girl with extraordinary drawing ability.

predisposed to develop autism. Indeed, because autistic children often have normal brothers and sisters, it is only logical to postulate that some children are biologically disposed to develop autism in response to early environments that other children experience with no noticeable harm. However, simply suggesting that biological factors probably contribute to autism does not constitute much of an explanation. To be useful, etiological theories must identify a specific biological deficit and detail the mechanism by which it gives rise to the various autistic symptoms. Vaguely stated allusions to biological dispositions simply acknowledge that psychological theories are inadequate without suggesting any clear-cut alternatives.

THE STORY OF AN AUTISTIC CHILD

Both Robert and his wife Susan were 26 years old when Mark, their first child, was born. Despite his youth, Robert had already achieved eminence as an attorney, and it was generally agreed that he was well on his way to a successful legal career. Robert had met Susan in college where both were honor students. Susan, who is considered intelligent and pretty, gave up a promising career in mathematics when she married Robert. Neither Robert nor Susan knew of any "mental illness" in their respective families, but Susan's brother had required speech therapy as a child.

Susan's pregnancy was unremarkable, and there were no complications at the time of Mark's delivery. For the first 6 months, he appeared to be a normal, healthy baby. At about 6 months, Susan consulted a pediatrician because she was distressed by Mark's frequent and prolonged crying spells. During these episodes, neither cuddling nor rocking seemed to console him. These crying periods gradually disappeared during the year and were all but gone by Mark's first birthday.

Although Susan voiced no further concerns to Mark's doctor until he was 2, in retrospect, she can recall some things that appeared odd to her. For example, she remembers that although he smiled and enjoyed being tickled, Mark never seemed to anticipate being picked up when she approached. Not once can she recall Mark stretching out his arms to her as she neared his bed. Also, despite Mark's attachment to a pacifier (he would complain loudly if it were mislaid), he showed little interest in toys. In fact, Mark seemed to lack interest in anything. He rarely pointed to things and seemed oblivious to sounds. (Both Robert and Susan recall being concerned about Mark's hearing.) Mark spent most of his time repetitively tapping on tables, seeming lost in a world of his own. Perhaps these behaviors should have stimulated some positive action from Robert and Susan, but Mark was their first child. Not only did they have no other children with whom to compare him, but his health was good, his appearance attractive, and his various developmental milestones (crawling, walking) were on schedule. They really had little reason to suspect that Mark was other than a normal, healthy child.

After his second birthday, Mark's behavior began to trouble his parents enough for them to seek professional advice. Mark, they said, would "look through" people or past them but

AFTERMATH

Although the diagnostic criteria for autism were continually refined (see Table 4.1 for the latest version), for at least 20 years from the date of Kanner's original article the dominant view among mental-health professionals remained that autism is mainly the result of psychological and emotional factors—especially a disturbed mother-child relationship. It was assumed that maternal overprotection, deprivation, or some other practice produces the behaviors associated with autism. This assumption, which was implicit and largely untested, was always far from self-evident. Crucial facts contradicted it. For example, children raised from birth in poorly run orphanages, receiving minimal custodial care and little more, are no more likely to develop autism than children in the general population. If lack of maternal affection and coldness are in any way responsible for autism, the syndrome should flourish in such institutions. Instead, it is extremely rare. This does not mean, of course, that institutionalized children do not develop psychological problems, just that these problems do not include autism. (For more on the psychological problems of institutionalized children, see Chapter 3.)

Psychological ("blame the mother") theories are also inconsistent with the results of studies of the personalities and child-rearing practices of the mothers of autistic children. Not one such study has produced any scientifically acceptable evidence that mothers of autistic children differ from other mothers in personality, child-rearing practices, or in the social "reinforcers" they supply for their chil-

rarely at them. He could say a few words but did not seem to understand speech. In fact, he did not even respond to his own name. Mark's time was occupied examining familiar objects such as crayons, which he would hold close to his eyes as he twisted and turned them. Particularly troublesome were Mark's odd movements — he would jump, flap his arms, twist his hands and fingers, and perform all sorts of odd facial grimaces, especially when he was excited — and what Robert described as Mark's "rigidity." Mark would arrange objects in straight rows and protest loudly if any were disturbed. He insisted on keeping everything in its place and would become extremely upset if Susan attempted to rearrange the living-room furniture. Mark also insisted on following a daily routine and reacted strongly if any activity (his daily bath, for instance) were rescheduled.

This portrait of Mark at age 2 remained reasonably accurate for the next 3 years. Slowly, beginning at age 5, Mark began to improve. Although his speech consisted primarily of echoing back words and phrases, he was able to use these phrases for a primitive type of communication. For example, when hungry, he would reproduce the phrase "Do you want dinner?" The pronoun was inappropriate, and the phrase was merely a repeat of one he had heard in the past, but his meaning was clear. Mark's rote memory for spoken language was remarkable. He could recall long verbal sequences and repeat them in accurate detail. At about the same time, Mark's musical ability also became apparent. He enjoyed listening to records and sometimes would even sing along. Here again, his unusual memory helped him to recall long sequences.

Mark's speech continued to improve for the next 2 years. Occasional spontaneous utterances began to make their appearance. Today, at age 7, Mark is able to communicate verbally but only with great effort. His social development has also improved, and even his resistance to change has decreased. Mark attends a normal public school where he is in a special-education class. He engages in various activities (especially music), but he never plays directly with other children.

Schwartz, S. & Johnson, J. (1985). *Psychopathology of Childhood*. 2nd ed. Elmsford, NY.: Pergamon, Pp. 114–115.

dren. In fact, it is autistic babies who fail to provide reinforcement for their mothers rather than the other way around. The ordinariness of the mothers of autistic children is not particularly surprising; it is just what we would expect given that autistic children frequently have normal siblings.

Despite their almost total lack of empirical support, psychological explanations for autism dominated the field for decades. It was not until the 1960s that psychologists began to realize that these explanations were based on shaky foundations. To a great extent, the reassessment of the psychological position was inspired by the epoch-making book *Infantile Autism*, written by psychologist Bernard Rimland. Rimland's book, which appeared in 1964, critically reviewed the literature available at the time and proposed that autism was mainly biological rather than psychological in origin. Rimland argued that autism's appearance soon after birth gives little time for psychological factors to have an effect. Moreover, the sex ratio (more boys than girls) seems consistent with a biological defect. Hemophilia, colorblindness, baldness, and many other biological conditions affect males three or four times more often than females. In the years following Rimland's book, researchers have also found that autism is related to congenital rubella (German measles), birth complications, and exposure to toxic chemicals. All of these facts favor a biological cause for autism.

Considerable effort has gone into trying to link autism to particular biological defects. Family studies, for example, have been conducted to determine whether autism can be inherited. These studies revealed a slightly higher probability of finding a sec-

TABLE 4.1   Diagnostic Criteria for Autistic
            Disorder

At least 8 of the following 16 items are present including at least 2 items from A, 1 from B, and 1 from C.
(Note that an item is counted only if the behavior in
question is abnormal for the person's age.)

A. Qualitative impairment in reciprocal social interaction
   as manifested by:
   1. marked lack of awareness of the feelings of others
   2. no or abnormal seeking of comfort at times of dis-
      tress (for example, a child who does not seek out
      comfort even when hurt)
   3. no or impaired ability to imitate (does not wave
      "bye-bye," for instance)
   4. no or abnormal social play
   5. gross impairment in the ability to make
      friendships

B. Qualitative impairment in verbal and nonverbal communication as manifested by:
   1. no mode of communication
   2. markedly abnormal nonverbal communication (for
      example, does not look at the person when mak-
      ing a communicative approach)
   3. absence of imaginative activity (no fantasy)
   4. abnormal speech production
   5. marked abnormality in the content of speech
      (echoes phrases)
   6. marked inability to sustain a conversation

C. Markedly restricted repertoire of activities and interests, as manifested by:
   1. stereotyped body movements
   2. persistent preoccupation with parts of objects
   3. marked distress over trivial environmental
      changes
   4. unreasonable insistence on following routines in
      detail
   5. markedly restricted range of interests

D. Onset during infancy or childhood

ond autistic child in a family where one has already
been diagnosed. Nevertheless, the syndrome is
clearly not inherited in the same way as, say, hair
color. We know this because there are cases of identical twins (who have identical genetic endow-
ments) in which only one member is autistic. Such
cases could not exist if autism is purely genetic. Of

course, it is possible that what is inherited is a
vulnerability to certain viruses or environmental
toxins, in which case only those twins exposed to
these specific dangers would develop the syndrome.

Another line of research has looked for brain
damage among autistic patients. Using a variety of
modern brain-imaging techniques, researchers
have found several different brain defects, but no
single defect has been found present in all autistic
patients. Moreover, many reported defects can be
found in people who are not autistic; it is possible
for their brains to appear anatomically normal while
still misfunctioning. For this reason, researchers
have devised ingenious tests of autistic brain function. Most of these studies have been designed to
assess whether autistic children have functional abnormalities in their left cerebral hemispheres—the
part of the brain responsible for language. To date,
however, the evidence is decidedly mixed, and it is
not yet possible to identify a specific autistic brain
deficit. Similarly, biochemical investigations have
failed to uncover any abnormality that occurs only
in autistic patients and not among nonautistics.

Many of the advances of the last 50 years have
been chronicled in the *Journal of Autism and Childhood Schizophrenia,* which was founded by Kanner in
1971. (The name was later changed to the *Journal of
Autism and Developmental Disabilities.*) Kanner himself remained an active contributor to the field right
up to the end of his life in 1981.

Although a definitive biological explanation for
autism has still not been identified, some progress
has been made in unraveling the mysteries of autism. Several lines of evidence suggest that autistic
children have a congenital vulnerability that may be
inherited or perhaps acquired as an accident of
birth. Exposure to certain viruses or environmental
stressors produces brain dysfunction, which results
in language disorders, cognitive disorders, and an
inability to relate to others. The demise of "psychological" theories of autism's etiology does not mean
that psychologists do not have a role to play in helping autistic people to live full lives. Teaching autistic
individuals to look after themselves and to communicate with others requires considerable ingenuity
on the part of educators and psychologists. Over
the past 30 years, psychologists have developed ingenious behavior-modification programs to help
autistic children learn many important skills. These
programs rely on the careful delineation of the be-

A MOTHER'S VIEW OF PSYCHOGENIC THEORIES

Peter Eberhardy was an autistic child. His parents and sister had to adjust to his being different—a difficult task at best—but it was made considerably more difficult by the notion that parents are responsible for their child's disturbance. Peter's mother tells what it was like:

I told my psychiatric social worker about Peter but her questions were directed to me.

How did I get along with my parents, siblings, the people at work? As well as most people I thought.

Had I wanted the baby? Yes, I had gone through sterility studies to get pregnant.

Why had I wanted a baby? Why? I had never reasoned it out. They are a part of life, just like food, sunshine, friends and marriage.

How did I get along with my husband? Very well. She snapped to attention. "Why?" she asked, "Are you afraid to quarrel with him?" Well—we were both in our thirties. We had no serious problems and could laugh at our small differences. Years of separation by the war had

made us treasure the ordinary joys of life.

I asked the psychiatric social worker for suggestions, but she had none to offer. What I did was not so important as how I felt about it. What could I read that would help me understand Peter? She could suggest no reading nor would she advise it. . . .

My questions as to the cause of Peter's trouble, she evaded—an eloquent answer indeed!

I alternated between being overwhelmed with guilt, and feeling resentful at being treated like a child who couldn't face an unpleasant truth. If I could have felt that it was true, that we had been cold and dominating, or cold and indifferent parents, I think I could have faced that fact. At least I would have had something concrete to work with. Anything would have been better than that nameless, formless, faceless fear.*

---

*Eberhardy, F. (1967). The view from the "couch." *Journal of Child Psychology and Psychiatry, 8,* 259–260.

---

haviors to be learned and the tight control of reinforcers. The success of behavior-modification programs with autistic individuals has been widely acknowledged. Indeed, behavior modification is today the clear treatment of choice for many autistic problems. It should be noted, however, that the success of behavior modification as a treatment does not necessarily imply any support for the behavioral theory of autism. Just because penicillin is an effective treatment for pneumonia, no one would argue that pneumonia is caused by a lack of penicillin. Similarly, the success of behavior modification as a treatment does not mean that autism results from a lack of appropriate behavior modification early in life.

The demise of psychological theories of autism has had an important salutary effect. Parents, whose lives have already been heavily burdened by their child's condition, no longer need to bear the extra burden of guilt over having caused their child's autism. Even without this guilt, the parents of autistic children face enormous problems. Perhaps the most important is what to do when their

autistic child grows up. In the past, great effort has been devoted to providing facilities for autistic children. Indeed, the term "infantile" autism puts the focus on children and implies that autistics stop being autistic when they grow up. Unfortunately, most autistic children reach adolescence and early adulthood still requiring a lot of help and assistance. Their parents are often shocked to find that adequate preparation has not always been made. Providing care and training for autistic adolescents and adults presents an important challenge to psychology during the 1990s.

CLASSIC STUDY 8
Anorexia Nervosa

In 1864 an English doctor named Richard Morton published what was probably the first paper on anorexia nervosa. He described a girl of 18 and a boy of

16 who had both suffered from a condition he called "nervous atrophy." These two cases were characterized mainly by marked weight loss; both patients were described as looking like "skeletons clad only in skin." Ten years later, another English doctor, Sir William Gull, coined the term *anorexia nervosa* ("nervous loss of appetite") to describe similar patients.

Gull was a highly successful "society" doctor; among his famous patients were Queen Victoria and the Prince of Wales. He was also something of a pioneer and was credited with removing many psychiatric patients from the physical restraints (straitjackets, for example) commonly in use at the time. Gull's arrogance and his almost uncontrollable temper made him unpopular with his colleagues, but his distinguished appearance and his confident clinical manner attracted scores of rich patients. When he died, Gull left an estate worth £344,000 ($1.3 million), a fabulous sum at the time and a record for a 19th-century doctor.

In 1874 Gull published a paper on "appetite loss" in the *Transactions of the Clinical Society of London*. He began by noting that the extreme weight loss described by Morton occurred among his own patients as well. These patients were primarily young women who also displayed other symptoms including amenorrhea (cessation of menstruation), constipation, lowered pulse rate, and hyperactivity. He gave two examples from among his own patients. The first, Miss A., was 17 when first brought to his care. Gull described her in his terse clinical style as follows:

> Her emaciation was very great. It was stated that she had lost 33 lbs. in weight. She was then 5 st. 12 lbs. [82 pounds] Height 5 ft. 5 in. Amenorrhoea for nearly a year. No cough. Respirations throughout chest everywhere normal. Heart sounds normal. Resps. 12; pulse 56. No vomiting nor diarrhoea. Slight constipation. Complete anorexia for animal food, and almost complete anorexia for everything else. Abdomen shrunk and flat, collapsed. . . .
> The condition was one of simple starvation. There was but slight variation in her condition, though observed at intervals of three or four months.[2]

In the absence of any distinct sign of organic disease, Gull's attempts to treat this patient relied on that age-old medical strategy, trial and error.

> Various remedies were prescribed—the preparations of cinchona [tree bark], the bichloride of mercury, syrup of iodide of iron, syrup of the phosphate of iron, citrate of quinine and iron, . . . but no perceptible effect followed their administration. The diet was also varied but without any noticeable effect upon the appetite. Occasionally, for a day or two the appetite was voracious, but this was very rare and exceptional. The patient complained of no pain, but was restless and active. This was in fact a striking expression of the nervous state, for it seemed hardly possible that a body so wasted could undergo the exercise which seemed agreeable.

Gull was convinced that the root of Miss A.'s problem was psychological and that her physical symptoms (low pulse and amenorrhea) were a secondary result of her eating disorder. That is, according to Gull, the causal sequence goes as follows: Psychological factors cause an unwillingness to eat, which, if prolonged, leads to a state of semistarvation; starvation, in turn, produces a low pulse and amenorrhea. Gull deliberately chose the name anorexia nervosa to emphasize his belief that Miss A.'s syndrome was caused by a "morbid mental state."

Although the main symptom of anorexia nervosa is a failure to eat, Gull noted that many patients go through periods in which they eat voraciously. Such behavior, if repetitive, is today known as *bulimia*. Although bulimia can occur on its own, it is common to find an alternation between binge eating, in which large amounts of food are consumed, and anorexia, in which fasting, self-induced vomiting, and laxatives are used to reduce weight.

Largely because of publications by Gull and others, anorexia and bulimia began to receive considerable attention from psychiatrists and psychologists. Numerous case histories were published, diagnostic criteria were established (see Table 4.2), and research was undertaken in many clinical centers. Understandably, much of this research was concerned with treating this potentially life-threatening condition. Unfortunately, as Gull observed, most medical interventions were futile. This does not mean that patients did not improve. Gull, and others, described several cases in which anorexic patients returned to normal eating habits, but such recoveries were considered "spontaneous" (which really means that no one knows what caused them). It was Gull's view that many patients recovered spontaneously provided they did not starve to death first. For this reason, he recommended force-

A CASE OF ANOREXIA NERVOSA

Hilde Bruch, a psychoanalyst specializing in eating disorders, published the following account of a fairly typical anorexia nervosa patient in 1978.

At fifteen Alma had been healthy, and well-developed, had menstruated at age twelve, was five feet six inches tall, and weighed one hundred and twenty pounds. At that time her mother urged her to change to a school with higher academic standing, a change she resisted; her father suggested that she watch her weight, an idea she took up with great eagerness, and she began a rigid diet. She lost rapidly and her menses ceased. That she could be thin gave her a sense of pride, power and accomplishment. She also began a frantic exercise program, would swim by the mile, play tennis for hours or do calisthenics to the point of exhaustion. Whatever low point her weight reached, Alma feared that she might become "too fat" if she regained as little as an ounce. There were many efforts to make her gain weight, which she would lose immediately, and she had been below seventy pounds most of the time. There was also a marked change in her character and behavior. Formerly sweet, obedient, and considerate, she became more and more demanding, obstinate, irritable, and arrogant. There was constant arguing, not only about what she should eat but about all other activities as well.

When she came for consultation she looked like a walking skeleton, scantily dressed in shorts and a halter, with her legs sticking out like broomsticks, every rib showing, and her shoulder blades standing up like little wings. Her mother mentioned, "When I put my arms around her I feel nothing but bones, like a frightened little bird." Alma's arms and legs were covered with soft hair, her complexion had a yellowish tint, and her dry hair hung down in strings. Most striking was the face—hollow like that of a shriveled up old woman with a wasting disease, sunken eyes, a sharply pointed nose on which the junction between bone and cartilage was visible. When she spoke or smiled—and she was quite cheerful—one could see every movement of the muscles around her mouth and eyes, like an animated anatomical representation of the skull. Alma insisted that she looked fine and that there was nothing wrong with her being so skinny. "I enjoy having this disease and I want it. I cannot convince myself that I am sick and that there is anything from which I have to recover."*

---

*Bruch, H. (1978). *The golden cage: The enigma of anorexia nervosa*. Cambridge, MA.: Harvard University Press. Pp. 1–2.

TABLE 4.2   Diagnostic Criteria for Anorexia
Nervosa

A. Refusal to maintain normal body weight (weight 15% or more below normal).

B. Intense fear of gaining weight or becoming fat.

C. Disturbance in body perception (person claims to feel fat although obviously underweight).

D. In females, the absence of at least three consecutive menstrual cycles.

feeding patients to keep them alive until their normal appetite returned. Force-feeding combined with comfort and concern soon became the primary treatments for anorexia nervosa.

AFTERMATH

Generations of psychiatrists and psychologists were influenced by Gull's choice of the name anorexia nervosa. They simply took it for granted that the syndrome was psychological in origin. Because anorexia nervosa usually appears in adolescence, it was seen as a way of avoiding the responsibilities of adulthood. Some of the more imaginative Freudian writers have claimed that anorexic patients stop eating because they fear "oral impregnation" or because they wish to hide their "cannibalistic impulses." As you may imagine, it is not at all clear how one would go about establishing the validity of such claims.

Behavioral psychologists, taking a different tack, have argued that food avoidance is "reinforced" by the reactions of others. That is, some adolescents discover that they can gain attention and even control other people by refusing to eat. Parents, especially, tend to bend to a child's will when it appears that is the only way to get her to eat. While plausible, this is really an explanation for the maintenance of an eating disorder; it does not say why anorexia nervosa developed in the first place. The same control of others could be gained by threatening suicide, for example. So, why stop eating?

A popular alternative to both the psychoanalytic and behavioral views is the family systems approach, which sees anorexia as a symptom of a family problem rather than the illness of a single child. A child's anorexic behavior may, for example, be a way of keeping an otherwise disintegrating parental relationship together. With a sick child as the identified patient, the parents can avoid facing their own problems by absorbing themselves in their child's illness. While this construction seems as plausible as the behavioral view, it also suffers from the same problem. It explains how anorexia, once established, is maintained by the family, but it does not explain why a particular child develops anorexic symptoms in the first place.

The inadequacies of most, if not all, psychological theories of anorexia led many clinicians and researchers to reexamine Gull's observations. Some were easy to substantiate. For example, the disorder is most common among teenagers and females outnumber males 10 to 1. The typical patient does deny feeling ill, and most claim to find extreme thinness attractive. On the other hand, Gull's name for the syndrome turns out to have been something of a misnomer. Initially, at least, most patients do not lose their appetites. They continue to crave food, but they refuse to eat. It is only after a prolonged period of starvation that their appetites generally disappear. It is also not entirely true that the amenorrhea found among female anorexic patients is always caused by malnutrition. In some cases, amenorrhea precedes or coincides with weight loss. This finding suggests that malnutrition may not cause amenorrhea but that both are caused by some deeper psychophysiological process basic to the illness itself.

There is little doubt that anorexia nervosa is accompanied by profound alterations in psycho-physiological functioning. These changes are most noticeable in the endocrine system where disturbed hormonal secretions are responsible for amenorrhea and many other physical symptoms. It is possible that these hormonal abnormalities result from some malfunction in the hypothalamus, the part of the brain that controls the operation of several important endocrine glands and that also happens to be the part of the brain responsible for the regulation of eating and drinking.[3] Recent research suggests that the origin of anorexia nervosa may lie in a malfunction of the neurotransmitter chemicals that carry information from one nerve cell to another in the hypothalamus. A disturbance in the neurotransmitter system may result in incorrect information being communicated to and from the appetite control centers in the hypothalamus. Although this theory remains speculative, the research findings available to date suggest that Gull have may been incorrect when he claimed that the physical symptoms of anorexia are all caused by starvation.

The strong possibility that physiological factors play a role in the etiology of anorexia nervosa is also supported by family studies which suggest that the condition may be inherited. Studies of anorexia among twins have found that it is much more likely to find a second affected child in twin pairs in which one child has already been diagnosed. By itself, this is not particularly strong evidence that anorexia is genetic. After all, twins are normally raised together in the same family using the same child-rearing techniques. Thus, even if anorexia were entirely caused by environmental factors with no genetic component, we would still expect to find a tendency for both twins to be affected. Aware of this, researchers separated twins into two groups: identical and fraternal. They found that anorexia was considerably more likely to affect both members of an identical-twin pair (who share an identical set of genes) than a fraternal-twin pair (who come from different ova and are no more genetically alike than any other pair of siblings). Because both identical and fraternal twins are raised in similar environments, this finding can only be explained by the greater genetic similarity of the identical twins. It should be noted, however, that even among identical twins it was possible to find cases in which only one twin developed anorexia. Thus, although genetics appears to play some part in the etiology of anorexia, it is clear that even those who inherit a disposition to develop the condition do not inevitably become anorexic. It seems likely that some triggering event is also required for the syndrome to develop.

The search for the environmental "triggers" that cause some individuals to develop anorexia has produced an impressive list: Death or illness in the family, personal illness, failure at school or work, and sexual conflicts have all been implicated. Some have claimed that anorexia begins with a self-imposed diet which, for some reason or another, gets out of control. Once dieting reaches the state of malnutrition, physiological changes take over and the diet becomes self-perpetuating. The anorexic patient rationalizes continued dieting by claiming to prefer being skinny and enters a vicious cycle in which psychological and physical factors combine to keep the syndrome from resolving. This characterization of anorexia has the virtue of making explicit the interactive effects of physiology and psychology. It makes clear that the "either psychology or physiology" dichotomy fails to capture the complexity of human behavior in general or anorexia nervosa in particular. Human beings are single organisms, not separate minds and bodies. In anorexia, both mind and body are disturbed. Moreover, the physical disturbances affect the mind and vice versa. Which comes first? It is not yet possible to say. Perhaps, like the problem of the chicken and the egg, the question is not even answerable. Anorexia is an excellent example of a disorder in which physical and psychological problems are interwoven in a seemingly inextricable way.

CLASSIC STUDY 9
Tourette's Disorder

"Pray Dr. Johnson," asked the small child, "why do you make such strange gestures?" "From bad habit," he replied. "Do you, my dear, take care to guard against bad habits." The Dr. Johnson in question is Samuel Johnson (1709–1784), the most famous man of his age. Poet, playwright, biographer, and lexicographer, Johnson's witticisms and opinions fill 10 pages of the *Oxford Dictionary of Quotations*. Yet, like the small child, those who met him for the first time were often shocked by his behavior. His hands and feet were continually moving,

and he produced odd, often shocking noises. A contemporary described him as follows:

> His mouth is constantly opening and shutting as if he were chewing. He has a strange method of frequently twirling his fingers and twisting his hands. His body is in continual agitation seesawing up and down; his feet are never a moment quiet; and in short his whole person is in perpetual motion.
>
> In the intervals of articulating he made various sounds with his mouth, sometimes as if ruminating, or what is called chewing the cud, sometimes giving a half whistle, sometimes making his tongue play backwards from the roof of his mouth, as if clucking like a hen.[4]

As a young man, Johnson had difficulty gaining employment as a schoolteacher because of his odd movements and vocalizations. The education authorities feared he would be ridiculed by the children. Their concern was well founded but should not have been limited to children; Johnson was ridiculed by most adults as well. Practically everyone who met him for the first time thought Johnson to be, if not a lunatic, certainly a distinctly odd-looking individual. From the descriptions available at the time, there can be no doubt that Johnson was odd. But looking back from today's vantage point, we know that he was not mad. He was probably suffering from Tourette's disorder.

Tourette's disorder is named after the French doctor Gilles de la Tourette. Although "movement disorders" (known in medicine as choreas) had been described by others, Tourette's achievement, like Kanner's and Gull's, was to isolate a specific syndrome from among a number of superficially similar ones. Curiously, the first description of what was to become known as Tourette's disorder was not published by Tourette but by Jean Itard—the doctor who studied Victor, the Wild Boy of Aveyron—in 1825. Itard's patient was a young French aristocrat, the Marquise de Dampierre. From the age of 7, the Marquise suffered from a number of striking motor abnormalities commonly known as movement disorders, or tics. She also produced what appeared to be involuntary vocalizations. These consisted of snorts, barks, hisses, and—particularly embarrassing for a woman of breeding—numerous obscenities. According to Itard:

> In the middle of a conversation that interests her suddenly without being able to avoid it, she

interrupts that which she says or hears by bizarre cries and extraordinary words which make deplorable contrast to her distinguished manner. These words are mostly rude oaths, obscene adjectives which are no less embarrassing for herself as for the other.[5]

Additional, and equally odd, disorders were described in the decades following Itard's case study. These included the "Jumping Frenchmen of Maine" who, when startled by a command ("Jump!") performed the required action while shouting the command aloud. One such "jumper" was said to be startled violently by a train whistle at the same time each night. Each time, he would awake suddenly and strike his wife. A similar condition in Malaysia was called *latah*, a syndrome that also included *coprolalia* (swearing). A Russian variation was called *myriachit*. This peculiar collection of movement disorders caught the interest of Jean Charcot, Freud's teacher and the most eminent neurologist of his time. By a stroke of luck, Charcot was able to examine Itard's original patient, the Marquise de Dampierre who—by the time Charcot saw her—had been suffering her strange symptoms for 79 years. Charcot noted that little had changed from Itard's original description, but he never published his observations. He left that to his pupil, the neurologist Gilles de la Tourette.

Tourette reconstructed the case from Itard's original notes and from Charcot's observations. He published his findings along with eight other case histories in 1885. Tourette described the Marquise, whom he called Madame de D., in some detail.[6]

Madame de D. . . . at the age of 7 was afflicted by convulsive movements of the hand and arms. These abnormal movements occurred above all when the child tried to write, causing her to crudely reproduce the letters she was trying to trace. After each spasm, the movements of the hand became more regular and better controlled until another convulsive movement would again interrupt her work. She was felt to be suffering from overexcitement and mischief, and because the movements became more and more frequent, she was subject to reprimand and punishment. . . .

As the disease progressed, and the spasm spread to involve her voice and speech, the young lady made strange screams and said words that made no sense. However, during all this she was clearly alert and showed no signs of delirium or

FIGURE 4.4 Gilles de la Tourette (1857–1904)

other mental problems. Months and years passed with no real change in her symptoms. It was hoped that with puberty these might naturally abate, but this did not occur. The young lady was therefore sent to Switzerland under the care of a doctor who specialized in the treatment of nervous disorders, relying primarily on milk baths as a form of therapy. . . . At the end of the year when this young woman left Switzerland and returned home, she was calm, beaming with freshness, and showing only rare and isolated muscle jerks around her mouth and neck. She married during this period. . . . She was greatly disappointed, because the disease reappeared. . . . Her uncontrolled convulsive movements, which except for 18–20 months of abatement had lasted 18 years of her life, now returned, and rather than waning, they in fact seemed to be progressing.

Her examination showed spasmodic contractions that were continual or were separated only by momentary intervals of time. . . . The movements involved . . . the muscles of the upper arms, the finger muscles and those of the face, and the muscles involved with sound production and articulation. . . . In the midst of an interesting conversation, all of a sudden without being able to prevent it, she interrupts what she is saying or what she is listening to with horrible screams and with words that are even more extraordinary than her screams. All of this contrasts deplorably with her distinguished manners and background. These words are for the most part offensive curse words and obscene sayings. . . . The more revolting these expressions are, the more tormented she becomes.

. . . Until quite old she still manifested her incoordination and continued to say obscene words even in public places. In 1884, the newspapers published her obituary and some of them even included for their readers a list of the obscene words that she had sadly pronounced, in particular *merde* and *foutu couchon*.

Tourette's remaining case histories told similar stories. At around the age of 7 or 8, the child would begin to display facial tics and sometimes make gasping sounds. The tics would be confined to the face for a long time and then gradually spread to the shoulders and arms. Echolalia (echoing words and phrases) usually followed. At some point, the individual would begin saying obscene words without any specific provocation and without restraint. As the condition progressed, the sufferer developed increasingly gross tics. These included arm flinging and foot stamping. These motor tics would come and go with new tics constantly replacing old ones.

Initially, Tourette did not consider his patients to be psychologically disturbed:

As for the mental state, it is perfectly regular and normal: The subjects are reasonable, in no way do their acts resemble those of madmen; they are totally aware of their state; most are very intelligent.

In later papers, however, Tourette revised his earlier opinion claiming that the condition he described was an inherited form of neurotic instability. While it is possible that the neurotic behavior he observed was a response to having the syndrome rather than its cause, Tourette never had the opportunity to pursue this line of thought. His work was dramatically cut off at age 35 when he was shot in the head by a mentally disturbed patient. He spent the remaining 11 years of his life disabled by massive brain damage. To honor his student, Charcot named the Marquise de Dampierre's tic condition *Gilles de la Tourette syndrome*. The name was later shortened to Tourette's syndrome and finally, with the publication of the DSM-III-R diagnostic criteria (Table 4.3), to Tourette's disorder.

TABLE 4.3 Diagnostic Criteria for Tourette's Disorder

A. Multiple motor and one or more vocal tics have been present at some time during the illness, although not necessarily concurrently.

B. Tics occur many times each day (usually in bouts), nearly every day or intermittently throughout a period of more than 1 year.

C. The location, number, frequency, complexity, and severity of the tics changes over time.

D. Onset is before age 21.

E. The tics are not the result of drugs or known nervous system diseases.

AFTERMATH

Although Tourette's career ended in tragedy, many doctors and researchers continued to study the disorder he described. Almost without exception, they attributed it to psychological factors. By the early 20th century, it was taken for granted that Tourette's syndrome was some kind of hysterical neurosis. Psychoanalytic hypotheses predominated. Tics were thought to symbolize anal sadism, inhibited aggression, or in the case of one particularly imaginative psychoanalyst, a way to avoid thumb-sucking!

Tourette's original idea that the syndrome is a movement disorder rather than a psychological disturbance was revived in the 1960s when it was noted that: (a) the disorder is three times more common in boys than girls, (b) children suffering from encephalitis (inflammation of the brain) may be left with Tourette's syndrome, and most important of all, (c) a dramatic improvement was produced in many patients by administration of the drug haloperidol. Haloperidol reduces the available amount of the neurotransmitter dopamine. Neurotransmitters such as dopamine allow nerve cells to communicate. Too much or too little dopamine can produce serious abnormalities including a movement disorder considerably more common than Tourette's

THE STORY OF JOSEPH BLISS

We can often learn a great deal about a disorder by the careful clinical study of a single case. Such a case study was published by Joseph Bliss, a Tourette's patient, and two psychiatrists in 1980. In this remarkable document, Bliss describes his careful self-observations over a period of 35 years. In his own words:

> I have been stalking this thing for over 35 years with a single minded determination to find something that would give me a clue, a direction, to the meaning of the problem. When I was told in 1947 that there was nothing to be done, I knew there was only one way for me to go.
>
> Very slowly, over the years, I came to be aware of the faint signals that preceded a movement. I kept watching these preliminary sensations year after year. In my notes, I described them as vague, "unfulfilled" feelings. Later, and very gradually, they became more recognizable as discrete sensations, and even if they did not become neatly definable, they did acquire a pattern with predictable and reproducible influences on each other and on the overt actions they stimulated. . . .
>
> Each movement is preceded by certain preliminary sensory signals and is in turn followed by a sensory impression at the end of the action. Each movement is the result of a *voluntary* capitulation to a demanding and relentless urge. . . . [italics added]
>
> The drive behind the TS sensations is the compelling need to satisfy them permanently and therefore eliminate them with some sort of action, with a movement toward a target or with a vocal outburst so forceful that it will provide the release that is so intensely desired. The use of the blurted swearing is an extension to an extreme of the common use of expletives to (1) punctuate and accent situations or (2) provide a final burst of energy.*

As Bliss describes it, Tourette's is more a sensory than a motor disorder. Unlike the "Jumping Frenchmen" or Malaysian *latah*, Tourette's syndrome is not a true movement disorder. According to Bliss, vague sensory feelings cause a build-up of tension, which the Tourette's patient attempts to relieve with tics. The tics and even the swearing are not involuntary; they are deliberate attempts to release excess energy.

---

*Bliss, J., Cohen, D. J., & Freedman, D. X. (1980). Sensory experiences of Gilles de la Tourette syndrome. *Archives of General Psychiatry, 37,* 1344–1346.

disorder—Parkinson's disease. The positive, and sometimes quite dramatic, response to haloperidol suggests that Tourette's syndrome is related to abnormalities in dopamine levels.

Further support for the idea that Tourette's disorder is not entirely psychological comes from studies that have found abnormal brain-wave activity among at least some sufferers. There is also some evidence that tics run in families. Interestingly, however, the incidence of psychiatric disturbance is also higher than average in the families of those with Tourette's disorder. Moreover, studies of Tourette's patients have found that the tics become worse when patients are put under stress and that they usually disappear when patients sleep, relax deeply, or have sex. Although the relationship between stress and the severity of Tourette's symptoms is poorly understood, it seems clear that the disorder has both psychological (stress) and physiological components.

Our understanding of Tourette's disorder has taken a giant step forward in recent years as doctors have come to realize that the tics and even the vocalizations that characterize the disorder are not really "involuntary." Unlike, say, the Jumping Frenchmen or people suffering from Parkinson's disease, Tourette's patients can voluntarily inhibit their odd movements for a period of time. However, inhibiting tics requires great effort and is perceived by the patients as producing "tension," which must eventually be released. One high school–aged patient described how he would sit in a classroom desperately trying to keep from making any movements until the perceived tension was so great that he had to run to the bathroom where he could produce a series of motor tics and a stream of obscenities unobserved by teachers or classmates.

It would seem fair to conclude that, like autism and anorexia nervosa, Tourette's disorder also has both organic and psychological components. In all three cases, neither organic nor psychological factors alone are capable of explaining all aspects of the syndrome. This does not mean that Tourette's sufferers cannot be treated with drugs; many patients respond dramatically to haloperidol and other similar compounds. Even low dosages drastically reduce the number and intensity of tics. Unfortunately, these drugs have important shortcomings as long-term treatments. They can produce severe side effects including, ironically, the severe movement disorder Parkinson's disease. Additional research is required to develop a drug that mimics the beneficial properties of haloperidol without its side effects. In addition, given the psychobiological nature of the disorder, treatments based on behavior modification, stress reduction, and other psychological interventions can also help to alleviate symptoms and give patients the confidence they require to lead normal social lives.

REPRISE

The three extraordinary syndromes described in this chapter could not, on the surface at least, be more different: Autistics are aloof and lost in a perplexing world; anorexics have exaggerated ideas of physical attractiveness and refuse to eat; Tourette's disorder is manifested by motor and vocal tics. Yet the three are alike in one crucial way. None of the three can be categorized as either psychological or neurological—they are all both. Indeed, all three disorders illustrate why we need to consider both mind and body when trying to understand abnormal behavior. The unfortunate split that occurred at the beginning of the 20th century between neurology and psychology resulted in a mindless neurology and a bodiless psychology. The challenge for the next century is to begin to put minds and bodies back together again.

Further Reading

Friedhoff, A. J., & Chase, T. N. (Eds.) (1982). *Gilles de la Tourette syndrome*. New York: Raven Press.

Garfinkel, P. E., & Garner, D. M. (1982). *Anorexia nervosa: A multidimensional perspective*. New York: Brunner/Mazel.

Schopler, E., & Mesibov, G. B. (Eds.) (1987). *Neurobiological issues in autism*. New York: Plenum Press.

Notes

1. Unless otherwise noted, quotations are from: Kanner, L. (1943). Autistic disturbances of affective contact. *Nervous Child, 2,* 217–250.

2. Quotations are from: Gull, W. W. (1874). Anorexia nervosa. *Transactions of the Clinical Society of London, 7,* 22–27.

3. The hypothalamus has also been implicated in depression suggesting a relationship between eating and mood disturbances.

4. Quoted in: Murray, T. J. (1982). Dr. Samuel Johnson's abnormal movements. In A. J. Friedhoff & T. N. Chase (Eds.), *Gilles de la Tourette syndrome* (pp. 25, 27). New York: Raven Press.

5. Quoted in: Shapiro, A. K., Shapiro, E. S., Bruun, R. D., & Sweet, R. D. (Eds.) (1978). *Gilles de la Tourette syndrome*. New York: Raven Press. P. 16.

6. Quoted in: Goetz, C. J., & Klawans, H. L. (1982). Gilles de la Tourette on Tourette syndrome. In A. J. Friedhoff & T. N. Chase (Eds.), *Gilles de la Tourette syndrome* (pp. 2–3). New York: Raven Press.

PART III

Patterns of Psychopathology

Open any psychopathology textbook and you will find a bewildering collection of syndromes, disorders, illnesses, and maladjustments. Just about any common behavior, if exaggerated enough, can be considered abnormal. Get too sad, and you are "depressed." Become overly concerned with neatness and you are "compulsive." Drink too much and you are alcohol "dependent." Because so many behavioral disorders are simply extreme forms of normal behavior, some clinicians have argued that psychopathology and normal behavior exist on a continuum (with only the extremities considered pathological). In contrast, others have argued that psychopathological and normal behavior are fundamentally different. They point out that some disorders involve bizarre behaviors never seen among normal people. For example, the peculiar motor and vocal tics that characterize Tourette's disorder (see Chapter 4) are always considered abnormal regardless of their frequency or intensity. Similarly, the hallucinations experienced by schizophrenic patients have no real equivalent among nonschizophrenics.

The chapters in this section vary in the extent to which the abnormal behaviors they describe are continuous with normal behavior. As will be shown, however, the "continuous versus noncontinuous" dichotomy is far too simple; most forms of psychopathology turn out to be a little of both. Like many controversies in the field of abnormal psychology, the continuous versus noncontinuous debate has shed more heat than light. The real challenge facing students of abnormal psychology is to unravel the complicated etiological mechanisms that result in *both* extreme forms of normal behavior and atypical behaviors.

The causes of abnormal behavior are many and varied. Genetic predispositions, brain injury, early childhood experiences, traumatic emotional experiences, severe stress, and even social forces such as racial discrimination all play a part. The purpose of this section is to examine how clinicians and researchers go about uncovering how various etiological factors combine to produce abnormal behavior.

Instead of trying to survey the entire field of psychopathology, the present strategy is to focus on a small number of well-studied disorders. The section consists of five chapters. Chapter 5 is concerned with the most intensely studied of all serious psychopathologies, schizophrenia. Chapter 6 deals with the relatively common, but still serious, problem of depression. Chapter 7 examines the controversial areas of stress and psychophysiological disorders while Chapter 8 deals with personality disorders. The final chapter in this section, Chapter 9, focuses on sexual disorders.

CHAPTER 5

Schizophrenia is one of the most puzzling psychological disorders; it is also one of the more common. It has been estimated that 1 in every 100 people will require treatment for schizophrenia at some point in his or her life. For decades, half of all psychiatric hospital beds have been occupied by persons diagnosed schizophrenic. The financial cost to society, including time lost from employment, ranges into the billions each year. The cost in pain and anguish cannot begin to be estimated.

Several theories have been formulated to explain this serious condition, but the key to the puzzle remains elusive. At least part of the problem lies in the vague meaning of the term *schizophrenia*. As discussed in Chapter 2, the various syndromes currently lumped together under the label "schizophrenia" were previously known as dementia praecox. Emil Kraepelin, whose diagnostic system still influences abnormal psychology today, preferred dementia praecox because he wished to emphasize the syndrome's early onset and progressively deteriorating course. Kraepelin's publications contained detailed descriptions of dementia praecox patients, but he intentionally avoided looking deeper into the possible causes of the disorder. He left this task to the Swiss psychiatrist Eugen Bleuler.

Bleuler was born in a small town near Zurich in 1857. He studied medicine at the University of Bern and then pursued postgraduate study at Paris' famous Saltpêtrière hospital under the guidance of Jean Charcot. After his training, he returned to Zurich where he eventually became professor of psychiatry and director of the famous Bürgholzli clinic. By the end of the 19th century, Bleuler was one of the best known psychiatrists in Europe.

Like Kraepelin, Bleuler was a student of both psychology and psychiatry. He was familiar with

A Little-Known Country

And he, repulsed, — a short tale to make, —
Fell into a sadness, then into a fast,
Thence to a watch, thence into a weakness,
Thence to a lightness; and by this declension,
Into the madness wherein now he raves,
And we all wail for.

—William Shakespeare

FIGURE 5.1 Eugen Bleuler: Doyen of Swiss psychiatry (1857–1939).

the scientific psychology pursued in Leipzig by Wilhelm Wundt and with Freud's psychoanalysis, and he maintained a lifelong interest in both. Indeed, Bleuler set himself the goal of reconciling experimental psychology and psychoanalysis in the belief that some combination of the two approaches was necessary to understand psychopathology. In addition to his direct influence on the field of psychopathology, Bleuler also exerted an indirect influence through his students. The most famous of these was Carl Jung. It was Bleuler who first suggested to Jung that he study Freud's theories. Bleuler also strongly encouraged Jung's research into word associations (see Chapter 1) because he saw these as a possible link to Wundt's experimental psychology. Bleuler's influence crossed a generation when Hermann Rorschach (another University of Zurich student) was inspired by his mentor, Carl Jung, to study "associations" (see Chapter 1). To-

ward the end of his career, Bleuler worked with the Swiss psychologist Jean Piaget, who was already beginning to formulate his theories of mental development.

Although he was sympathetic to both psychoanalysis and experimental psychology, Bleuler was not totally devoted to either one. He took a pragmatic line borrowing some ideas and concepts from psychoanalysis while taking others from psychology. He was particularly interested in the concept of the unconscious and the possibility that overt behavior has its origins in unconscious motivations.

Bleuler's first paper on dementia praecox was published in 1902 and was essentially an elaboration of Kraepelin's descriptions. He, like Kraepelin, had observed many odd behaviors among dementia praecox patients. Unlike Kraepelin, however, Bleuler was not content with mere description. He wanted to uncover the common ties that cause these seemingly disparate symptoms to occur together—their underlying cause. For most of the decade following the publication of his first paper on the subject, Bleuler devoted himself to the careful study of over 600 dementia praecox patients. The result of his labor was a book, *Dementia Praecox or the Group of Schizophrenias*, first published in 1911. This classic book, which for some inexplicable reason was not translated into English until 1950, is one of the most famous documents in abnormal psychology. It set the research agenda for the next 50 years, and more than any other clinical work, it illustrates the tremendous power that a disorder's name can have on research and treatment.

CLASSIC STUDY 10

From Dementia Praecox to Schizophrenia

Despite his earlier agreement with Kraepelin's observations, by the time he wrote his classic book Bleuler had changed his mind about two vital issues. According to his observations, dementia praecox did not always begin in adolescence nor did it inevitably lead to dementia. Because dementia praecox means mental deterioration beginning in childhood, Bleuler argued that the name was inappropriate. His suggested replacement was "schizophrenia."

Bleuler derived the term *schizophrenia* from the Greek words *schizo* ("split") and *phrene* ("mind"). Contrary to what some writers have suggested, Bleuler did not mean to imply that his patients were suffering from the "split" or "multiple personalities" so popular with movie makers. The "splitting" that Bleuler had in mind was not between several personalities but between psychological processes in the same personality. For example, in schizophrenia, the association between a joke and an affective state (happy laughter) may be split producing an individual who laughs when nothing is funny and fails to laugh when appropriate. According to Bleuler, schizophrenics suffer from a "breaking of associative threads," which results in the strange, even random, associations universally regarded by nonschizophrenics as "bizarre and unpredictable."

Bleuler deliberately chose the term *schizophrenia* to focus attention on what he considered to be the fundamental problem: a breakdown in the normal process of association. In his own words, "I call dementia praecox schizophrenia because . . . the splitting of the different psychic functions is one of its most important characteristics."

Like Kraepelin, Bleuler devised a system for categorizing the various symptoms displayed by schizophrenic patients. However, in place of Kraepelin's 36 categories, Bleuler's classification system had only two: fundamental symptoms and accessory symptoms. Bleuler looked upon the fundamental symptoms as pathognomonic. That is, they were always present in schizophrenia and never present in any other condition. The fundamental symptoms — associate disturbance, autism, affective disturbance, and ambivalence — became known as the four A's because of their identical first letters.

Associative Disturbance

As already noted, Bleuler considered a breakdown in associations to be the defining characteristic of schizophrenia:

> In this malady the associations lose their continuity. Of the thousands of associative threads which guide our thinking, this disease seems to interrupt, quite haphazardly, sometimes such single threads, sometimes a whole group, and sometimes even large segments of them. In this way, thinking becomes illogical and often bizarre. Furthermore, the associations tend to proceed along new lines. . . . Two ideas, fortuitously encountered, are combined into one thought. . . . Clang-associations [associations based on sounds such as rhymes] receive unusual significance. . . . Two or more ideas are condensed into a single one.
>
> . . . Thoughts are subordinated to some sort of general idea, but they are not related and directed by any unifying concept of purpose or goal. It looks as though ideas of a certain category . . . were thrown into one pot, mixed, and subsequently picked out at random, and linked with each other by mere grammatical form or other auxiliary images.[1]

The loosening of associative threads produces incoherent communications. Bleuler gives the following example produced by one of his patients:

> The city of London is in England. I know this from my school-days. Then, I always liked geography. My last teacher in that subject was professor August A. He was a man with black eyes, I also like black eyes. There are also blue and gray eyes and other sorts, too. I have heard it said that snakes have green eyes. All people have eyes. There are some, too, who are blind. These blind people are led about by a boy. It must be very terrible not to see. There are people who can't see and, in addition, can't hear. I know some who hear too much. One can hear too much. There are many sick people in Bürgholzli; they are called patients.

Autism

As noted in Chapter 4, Leo Kanner took the name *autism* from Bleuler's description of adult schizophrenics. The term is misleading when applied to Kanner's children because it wrongly suggests that they have active fantasy lives. It is, however, an accurate description of schizophrenics:

> The most severe schizophrenics, who have no more contact with the outside world, live in a world of their own. They have encased themselves with their desires and wishes (which they consider fulfilled) or occupy themselves with the trials and tribulations of their persecutory ideas; they have cut themselves off as much as possible from any contact with the external world.
>
> The detachment from reality, together with the relative and absolute predominance of the inner life, we term autism.

Affective Disturbance

In the jargon of abnormal psychology, emotion is known as "affect." An affective disturbance is one in which emotional expression is somehow distorted. Most often, the affective disturbance in schizophrenia takes the form of inappropriate emotions; patients laugh when they should be crying or vice versa. In the acute phase of their illness, they often swing violently from one mood state to another. Among long-term schizophrenics, however, the most common affective disturbance is the lack of any emotion at all.

> Indifference seems to be the external sign of their state; an indifference to everything — to friends and relations, to vocation and enjoyment, to duties or rights, to good fortune or to bad.
> Schizophrenics can write whole autobiographies without manifesting the least bit of emotion. They will describe their suffering and their actions as if it were a theme in physics.
> During a lengthy clinical presentation a paranoid patient complains constantly about his persecutions but sits very calmly and nonchalantly as he tells his story. . . . It is common knowledge that older paranoids relate with the greatest calmness how they were flayed and burnt during the night; how their bowels were torn out.

Ambivalence

According to Bleuler, schizophrenics are constantly experiencing contradictory wishes, impulses, and ideas. He labeled this phenomenon *ambivalence* and identified three types:

> The very same concept can be accompanied simultaneously by pleasant and unpleasant feelings (*affective ambivalence*): the husband both loves and hates his wife.
> In *ambivalence of will*, the patient wished to eat but does not eat. He starts to bring the spoon to his mouth dozens of times but never completes the act, or makes some other useless movement. He clamors for his release and then resists with much cursing when he is informed that he will be discharged from the institution. . . .
> It is *intellectual ambivalence* when a patient says in the same breath: "I am Dr. H.; I am not Dr. H"; or "I am a human being like yourself, even though I am not a human being" [Bleuler's italics].

Accessory Symptoms

In addition to these four fundamental symptoms, Bleuler described many accessory symptoms. Included among these were most of the features that Kraepelin emphasized in his descriptions of dementia praecox: hallucinations (usually hearing voices when there are none), delusions (bizarre thoughts), negativism, impulsiveness, and catatonia (motor abnormalities ranging from frenzy to stupor). According to Bleuler, the fundamental symptoms are present in all schizophrenics while accessory symptoms such as hallucinations and delusions are present in only some schizophrenic patients and missing in others (and can also be found among nonschizophrenics).

Etiology

Not content just to describe and classify schizophrenic symptoms, Bleuler sought a general theory of the "disease" as well as an explanation for its various symptoms. He began by examining the possibility that schizophrenia is caused by emotional or psychological trauma. Overwork, strain, keeping irregular hours, early childhood experiences, and excessive masturbation were considered, but Bleuler rejected them all on the grounds that they lack specificity. (Many people overwork but do not become schizophrenic, and many schizophrenics have never worked at all.) Bleuler concluded that

> as yet we cannot answer the question whether there are psychic causes for schizophrenia. However, it is probably to be answered in the negative. . . . In the majority of cases, it is . . . quite evident without much searching that the unfortunate love affair, demotion from the office, etc., were consequences and not causes of the disease.

Bleuler did not intend this to mean that schizophrenics are somehow immune from emotional traumas:

> Psychic experiences — usually of an unpleasant nature — can undoubtedly affect the schizophrenic symptoms. However, it is highly improbable that the disease itself is really produced by such factors. Psychic events and experiences may release the symptoms but not the disease.

Having ruled out psychological causes, Bleuler considered a number of organic possibilities. He noted a tendency for schizophrenia (and other types of psychiatric disturbance) to run in families suggesting a hereditary basis for the syndrome. He also described several anatomical and physiological anomalies exhibited by schizophrenic patients. Although he found no specific abnormality that could be definitely linked to schizophrenia, Bleuler was certain one exists:

> Complete justice to all these factors [symptoms] can only be done by a concept of the disease which assumes the presence of (anatomic or chemical) disturbances of the brain.

According to Bleuler, this "disturbance of the brain" produces the primary schizophrenic symptom, loose associations. All the other symptoms result from this associative disturbance interacting with each individual's life experiences:

> We assume the presence of a process, which directly produces the primary symptoms; the secondary symptoms are partly psychic functions operating under altered conditions, and partly the results of more or less successful attempts at adaptation to the primary disturbances.
>
> Almost the totality of the heretofore described symptomatology of dementia praecox is a secondary, in a certain sense, an accidental one. . . . Hallucinations, and delusions (entirely aside from the releasing factor) need not stem directly from the disease process itself. The latter provides only the predisposition, on the basis of which, psychic processes develop the symptoms.

Thus, for Bleuler, the causal sequence is as follows: Some organic brain disturbance, probably inherited, produces a splitting of associations. The individual experiences these associations as an incoherent melange of ideas, sounds, phrases, and meanings. In an attempt to cope, and maintain some degree of self-respect, the affected individual tries to assign reasonable interpretations to these experiences. Strange or unacceptable ideas could not simply pop into the mind—they must have been placed there by outside forces. Similarly, failures and setbacks cannot be the result of mental deterioration—they must be the result of external persecution. In this way, a train of events set off by an organic brain disturbance results in delusions of persecution.

The specific content of a delusion is determined by a particular individual's experiences. Bleuler puts it this way:

> No schizophrenic can entertain the delusion that a certain Miss N. wants to marry him if he knows nothing about a Miss N. . . . No one would hallucinate that Jesuits were persecuting him if he never heard anything of the significance of the Jesuits. The content of delusions and hallucinations can only be understood and conceived of in terms of definite external events.

Although Bleuler divided schizophrenia into several subgroups, he saw these divisions as tentative at best and potentially misleading because the same person may move from one subgroup to another. ("A case which begins as a hebephrenic may be a paranoid several years later.") Bleuler's subcategories included the paranoid group, whose major symptom is a delusion of persecution; catatonia, in which motor symptoms (ranging from hyperactivity to stupor) predominate; hebephrenia, which is marked by intellectual disorganization and dementia; and simple schizophrenia, which is characterized by a gradual withdrawal from the outside world. He even proposed a category called "latent schizophrenia" for those who have inherited a disposition to develop schizophrenia but have not yet shown any specific symptoms.

Bleuler was aware that there are other ways to categorize schizophrenic subtypes: chronic versus acute, sudden versus gradual onset, childhood versus adult, periodic (cyclic) versus gradually deteriorating, and so on. He left open the question of which of these approaches to classification would prove most useful in the long-term.

Bleuler concluded his book with a chapter on therapy. After debunking practically all treatments then in use, he recommended occupational therapy as a way to distract patients from their ruminations and to teach them useful skills. He also made some suggestions about drug treatments (including the therapeutic use of alcohol). From our present perspective, one of Bleuler's most interesting suggestions is that hospitalization should be avoided whenever possible. Sounding very much like a modern proponent of "deinstitutionalization," he wrote:

> In general, it is preferable to treat these patients under their usual conditions and within their habitual surroundings. The patient should not be admitted to the hospital just because he suffers from schizophrenia, but only when there is a definite indication for hospitalization. The indication is, of course, given when the patient becomes too disturbing or dangerous, when restraint is necessary, when he presents a threat to the well-being of the healthy members of his family . . . the institution will attempt to educate the patient to act in a more acceptable manner, after which he will be released.

A MIND THAT FOUND ITSELF

Clifford Beers graduated from Yale in 1907 and began what promised to be a successful career on Wall Street. However, after a few years, it was over. Instead of working, he spent his time at home morbidly worrying that, like his older brother, he would develop a brain tumor. To escape his torment, he jumped from a fourth floor window of the family home. He survived this suicide attempt, but while recuperating in the hospital he developed delusions of persecution. Over the next 2 years, he was transferred from one mental institution to another. Beers went from a morose silence to an aggressive mania that gradually subsided and returned him to the career he had given up several years before. But Beers was not content as a businessman. He dedicated himself to improving the life of institutionalized mental patients. His book, *A Mind That Found Itself*, was an autobiographical description of his illness and his often chilling hospital experiences. Beers's book galvanized public opinion and led to the creation of the greatest psychiatric reform movement in history, the mental-hygiene movement, which led to the establishment of child guidance clinics and the upgrading of mental hospitals.

In this extract from his autobiographical book, Beers illustrates the development of his paranoid delusions. The narrative begins as Beers is about to be taken home from the hospital after his suicide attempt.

> It was my eldest brother who looked after my care and interests during my entire illness. Toward the end of July, he informed me that I was to be taken home again. I must have given him an incredulous look, for he said, "Don't you think we can take you home? Well, we can and will." Believing myself in the hands of the police, I did not see how that was possible. Nor did I have any desire to return. That a man who had disgraced his family should again enter his old home and expect his relatives to treat him as though nothing had changed, was a thought against which my soul rebelled; and, when the day came for my return, I fought my brother and the doctor feebly as they lifted me from the bed. But I soon submitted, was placed in a carriage, and driven to the house I had left a month earlier.
>
> For a few hours my mind was calmer than it had been. But my new-found ease was soon dispelled by the appearance of a nurse—one of several who had attended me at the hospital. Though at home and surrounded by relatives, I jumped to the conclusion that I was still under police surveillance. At my request my brother had promised not to engage any nurse who had been in attendance at the hospital. The difficulty

In 500 pages, Bleuler succeeded in summarizing everything that was known about schizophrenia at the time, proposed a theory about the cause of schizophrenia that had the virtue of linking the bewildering array of symptoms described by Kraepelin to a single underlying cause, and made some important and, for the time, provocative suggestions about treatment. His book set the research agenda for the next 50 years, and even today no serious discussion of schizophrenia omits a reference to *Dementia Praecox or the Group of Schizophrenias*.

AFTERMATH

Bleuler was careful to emphasize that he did not believe in a single illness called schizophrenia: "For the sake of convenience, I use the word in the singular although it is apparent that the group includes several diseases." Unfortunately, in the decades following the publication of Bleuler's classic book, psychologists and psychiatrists have not always been quite so circumspect. Although the term dementia praecox was universally discarded in favor of Bleuler's new label, schizophrenia, the plural nature of the condition was often disregarded. Like Bleuler, writers frequently referred to schizophrenia, not to the schizophrenias. To avoid awkward grammar, this chapter too refers to "schizophrenia" when "the schizophrenias" would be technically appropriate. But the tendency to refer to the illness as singular rather than plural is not just a matter of grammar. Some researchers actually began to think

of procuring any other led him to disregard my request, which at the time he held simply as a whim. But he did not disregard it entirely, for the nurse selected had merely acted as a substitute on one occasion, and then only for about an hour. That was long enough, however, for my memory to record her image. Finding myself under surveillance, I soon jumped to a second conclusion, namely, that this was no brother of mine at all. He instantly appeared in the light of a sinister double, acting as a detective. After that I refused absolutely to speak to him again, and this repudiation I extended to all other relatives, friends and acquaintances. If the man I had accepted as my brother was spurious, so was everybody—that was my deduction. For more than two years, I was without relatives or friends, in fact, without a world, except that one created by my own mind from the chaos that reigned within it.*

*Beers, C. (1908). *A mind that found itself.* New York: Longmans, Green. Pp. 27–28.

Clifford Beers (1876–1943) started the mental-hygiene movement.

of schizophrenia as one "illness." As a consequence, they spent considerable time and energy looking for the common cause of paranoid, catatonic, hebephrenic, simple, and other types of schizophrenia—a common cause that probably does not exist.

To make matters worse, in the years following the publication of Bleuler's book, clinicians continually added more and more patients to the schizophrenia category. This tendency was particularly noticeable in the United States where "schizoaffective" disorders, "pseudoneurotic" disorders, and other types of schizophrenia were constantly being invented. By the early 1950s, the American concept of schizophrenia had expanded to include the vast majority of psychotic patients as well as many non-

psychotic patients. Like the 18th-century medical diagnosis, the fevers, schizophrenia became such a diffuse category that meaningful research became close to impossible.

Psychosocial Causes

During the 1940s and 1950s, psychoanalysis dominated American psychopathology and many of Bleuler's ideas, especially his dismissal of psychological factors as primary causes of schizophrenia, were discarded. Postwar psychoanalysts tended to view all behavior disorders as the result of psychological conflicts. The "schizophrenogenic" mother who produces schizophrenia in her child by her deviant behavior became a common character in the psychoanalytic literature. Schizophrenia, many argued, was the result of abnormal family communication patterns, especially the "double bind." A person put in a double bind is given two contradictory messages; if one is obeyed, the other is automatically violated. For example, a mother buys her son two shirts for his birthday. He wears one the next morning only to find his mother asking, "Why are you wearing that shirt? Don't you like the other one?" Why such communications (which occur in every family) should lead to schizophrenic delusions, hallucinations, and the loosening of associations is far from obvious.

The possibility that mothers' communication patterns may be affected by their living with schizophrenic children, or that abnormal family communications develop as a *consequence* of having a schizophrenic family member, received short shrift in the heyday of psychoanalysis. In fact, the psychiatric establishment was so convinced that schizophrenia was the result of psychological conflict that the first edition of the American Psychological Association's Diagnostic and Statistical Manual, which was published in the early 1950s, referred to the schizophrenias as "schizophrenic reactions." This term, which was first coined by Adolph Meyer (see Chapter 4 for more on Meyer), was purposely chosen to suggest that schizophrenia is a reaction to some stressful or traumatic experience.

Despite the dubious status of some psychoanalytic theories of schizophrenia, there is no doubt that Meyer was correct on one point: Schizophrenia is sometimes preceded by psychologically stressful events. In the 1960s and 1970s, considerable energy was devoted to differentiating schizophrenic "reactions" from the slow, progressive deterioration associated with dementia praecox. These two groups of patients were known as "reactive" and "process" schizophrenics, respectively. In addition to a gradual onset, process schizophrenics usually have a history of emotional and adjustment problems even before being diagnosed schizophrenic. Reactive schizophrenics, on the other hand, are usually well adjusted before the sudden onset of their illness. The prognosis for the two groups is also different. Reactive schizophrenics are more likely to recover than process schizophrenics, who usually show a deteriorating course interspersed with short periods of remission. Despite these differences, both categories of patients were labeled schizophrenic,

and not until the 1960s were process and reactive schizophrenics routinely separated for research purposes.

Diagnostic Practice

In the 1980s, the American Psychiatric Association revised their diagnostic criteria for schizophrenia several times. The 1987 criteria are summarized in Table 5.1. The first criterion derives directly from Kraepelin's descriptions of dementia praecox. It is nothing more than a list of recognized schizophrenic behaviors (delusions, hallucinations, and so on). Note that of Bleuler's four A's (associations, affect, autism, and ambivalence) only two manage to make it into the diagnostic criteria, and even these have been demoted from the fundamental status given them by Bleuler to just one of several possible abnormalities that may be exhibited by schizophrenics. Even a brief examination of the diagnostic criteria will make it clear that schizophrenia is a very broad category. Indeed, criterion A is so flexible that three completely different individuals can all be labeled schizophrenic. The first can be diagnosed schizophrenic because she displays bizarre delusions (criterion A.2), the second for having hallucinations (criterion A.3), and the third for displaying both catatonia and inappropriate affect (A.1.d and A.1.e). All three individuals wind up being called schizophrenic even though they have completely different symptoms.

The American Psychiatric Association has also specified criteria for schizophrenic subtypes that are more-or-less identical to Bleuler's (paranoid, catatonic, and so on). Although these subtypes are frequently used in clinical practice, there is some doubt about their reliability; clinicians often agree that a patient is schizophrenic but then disagree about the specific subtype. Pointing to this unreliability, and the fact that the diagnostic criteria do not require all patients to show the same symptoms, some writers have argued that schizophrenia is not a real disease with a single organic cause (such as tuberculosis, for example) but a collection of loosely related symptoms or a syndrome. Others have gone even farther, arguing that schizophrenia does not really exist but that it is merely a label invented by our "up-tight" society to express its disapproval of unusual behavior. Although the idea that schizophrenia is essentially a culturally specific, even a moral, judgment is

TABLE 5.1   Diagnostic Criteria for Schizophrenia

A. Presence of the characteristic psychotic symptoms in the active phase: either 1, 2, or 3 for at least 1 week (unless the symptoms are successfully treated):

  1. Two of the following:
    a. delusions
    b. prominent hallucinations
    c. incoherence or marked loosening of associations
    d. catatonic behavior
    e. flat or grossly inappropriate affect
  2. Bizarre delusions
  3. Prominent hallucinations of a voice

B. During the course of the disturbance, functioning in such areas as work, social relations, and self-care is markedly below the highest level achieved before the onset of the disturbance.

C. Schizoaffective disorder and mood disorder with psychotic features have been ruled out.

D. Continuous signs of the disturbance have existed for at least 6 months.

---

appealing to those who value freedom and individual diversity, it is difficult to reconcile with the strong evidence that schizophrenia exists in just about every society in the world. Cultures as different as Canadian Eskimos and West African bushmen appear to have notions of "insanity" that are virtually identical to ours. Moreover, the prevalence of severe psychoses is the same in these cultures as in our own. Because cultures with different child-rearing practices and very different social mores have similar ideas about mental aberration (and similar numbers of mentally aberrant citizens), it is impossible to assert that schizophrenia is nothing more than our society's moral judgment. The cause of schizophrenia must lie elsewhere.

Biochemical Causes

The enormous advances in neurochemistry over the past 20 years have prompted scientists to look for a biochemical cause for at least some symptoms of schizophrenia. The hypothesis currently receiving the most research attention is that schizophrenic behavior results from an excess of the neurotransmitter dopamine in the brain. Dopamine is one of the chemicals used by neurons to communicate. Researchers believe that many neurons in the brains of schizophrenics have become overly sensitive to dopamine. These neurons are constantly firing when they should be quiescent. The main evidence in favor of this hypothesis is that antipsychotic drugs known to block the action of dopamine also reduce the severity of many schizophrenic symptoms. It has also been shown that chemically increasing dopamine levels makes schizophrenic symptoms worse. Indeed, individuals who overuse amphetamines (stimulant medications that enhance dopamine activity) can develop symptoms very similar to those exhibited by schizophrenics (see Figure 5.2).

Although the dopamine hypothesis still requires additional proof, the idea that schizophrenic patients are chronically overstimulated fits nicely with Bleuler's fundamental symptom of associative disturbance. The overstimulated individual is constantly bombarded with stimuli (sounds, smells, sights, thoughts). Each stimulus produces a host of associations that are too strong to ignore. The result is distractibility and an unpredictable jumping from one thought to another.

How does the oversensitivity to dopamine develop in the first place? Several possibilities have been put forward. Schizophrenics may have contracted some sort of slow-growing virus, perhaps while still in their mother's uterus. Alternatively, the sensitivity may have resulted from stress. A third possibility, and the one that has received the most attention, is that the tendency to develop schizophrenia is inherited.

Genetics of Schizophrenia

The idea that the schizophrenias might be inherited is not new. Bleuler took it for granted that "heredity does play its role in the etiology" and went on to claim that "mental disease can be shown to exist in 65% of the families of schizophrenics." Breaking this figure down by "degree of relationship," Bleuler claimed that 35% of "our schizophrenics [in the Bürgholzli] had mentally sick parents or grandparents or both." For the most part, genetic research in the 20th century has largely consisted of attempts to refine Bleuler's observations.

Family Studies

The most common research approach is to examine the family tree of diagnosed schizophrenics looking

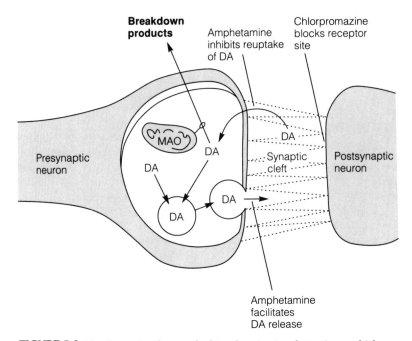

FIGURE 5.2 The dopamine theory of schizophrenia. Amphetamines, which can produce schizophrenia-like symptoms, increase the amount of dopamine (DA) crossing the synapse connecting two nerves. They accomplish this in two ways: by causing more to be released by the neuron sending a message and by slowing the uptake in the receiving neuron. Antipsychotic drugs such as chlorpromazine reduce the amount of effective dopamine by blocking dopamine receptor sites thereby diminishing schizophrenic symptoms. MAO is an enzyme that helps metabolize DA.

for other cases of schizophrenia. Such studies have shown that relatives of schizophrenics are more likely to become schizophrenic themselves than are members of the general population. Moreover, the probability of finding another schizophrenic in the family increases as the genetic relationship to the patient becomes closer. Thus, a patient's children have a higher risk of being diagnosed schizophrenic than a patient's cousins, nieces, or nephews (see Table 5.2). While family studies are consistent with the idea that a predisposition toward schizophrenia is inherited, they cannot offer definitive proof because family members share not only genes but also similar environments and experiences. The tendency for schizophrenic parents to have affected children could simply mean that schizophrenic parents provide poor homes which prevent their children from developing normally.

Twin Studies

The usual way to disentangle genetic from environmental causes of schizophrenia is to study twins. If schizophrenia is solely genetic, identical twins who come from a single egg and share exactly the same genes should have equal chances of becoming schizophrenic. Fraternal twins, on the other hand, come from two eggs fertilized at the same time. They are no more genetically alike than any other pair of siblings, but like identical twins, they share the same intrauterine environment and they are raised together in the same family environment. By comparing identical and fraternal twins, it is

SCHIZOPHRENIC LANGUAGE AND COGNITION

Schizophrenic speech is often odd. Bizarre notions, a rapid flight from one idea to another, the invention of new words, associations based on sound rather than meaning all combine to create what Bleuler referred to as "word salad." Although such disorganized speech is not common—even chronic schizophrenic patients speak normally most of the time—researchers and clinicians have devoted considerable attention to understanding what has come to be known as "schizophrenic language."

The term *schizophrenic language* is somewhat misleading. No one really believes that there is a language, with its own syntax and semantics (like French or English), called Schizophrenia. Schizophrenic language refers to the deviations from normal language displayed by schizophrenic patients. These deviations are usually taken to reflect a deeper cognitive deficit. That is, schizophrenic speech is an overt sign of disordered thoughts.

Sherry Rochester, a Canadian psychologist, analyzed schizophrenic speech samples in an attempt to identify those aspects that lead clinicians to infer that their patients suffer from a "thought disorder." She found that the speech samples rated by clinicians as the most disordered were those that lacked cohesive ties. Sentences were often strung together in ways that made it difficult for listeners to see how they were connected. For example: "My mother was in France. They were old." Sometimes, patients failed to provide listeners with clear referents. For example, a patient may begin a conversation by saying, "He was here yesterday," without providing any information about who "he" might be.

Rochester's analysis suggests that schizophrenic patients fail to consider the information required by listeners. A similar failure to adopt the listener's role was described by psychologist Bertram Cohen, who asked patients and nonpatients to describe one disk out of a set of several colored disks so that "another person [a judge]

with the same colors in front of him will know which color you are talking about." Judges with only the schizophrenics' directions to guide them had considerably more difficulty picking out the correct color than those provided with nonschizophrenic descriptions. An example will show why. In the following extract, both the normal subject and the schizophrenic subject are describing the same disk:

Normal: "My God this is hard. They are both the same except that this one may be a little redder."

Schizophrenic: "Make-up. Pancake make-up. You put it on your face and they think guys run after you. Wait a second! I don't put it on my face and guys don't run after me. Girls put it on them."*

It would seem that the schizophrenic patients are easily distracted by irrelevant associations which they are unable to inhibit. The result is that patients provide listeners with useless information that actually interferes with the task of identifying the color. Distractibility and the failure to inhibit irrelevant associations lie at the heart of Bleuler's fundamental associative disturbance. Thus, Cohen's work can be taken as support for Bleuler's observation. However, the significance of Rochester's and Cohen's work goes beyond just another demonstration of Bleuler's cognitive deficit. Successful communication and most social interaction requires that we are able to see things from the perspective of another person. Their failure to provide listeners with adequate information suggests that, in addition to their cognitive deficit, schizophrenics have a social deficit which makes them unable to operate successfully in social situations.

---

*Cohen, D. (1978). Referential communication deficit in schizophrenia. In S. Schwartz (Ed.), *Language and cognition in schizophrenia* (pp. 28–29). Hillsdale, N.J.: Erlbaum.

TABLE 5.2 Expectation for Schizophrenia Among Relatives of Schizophrenics

Relationship to Identified Schizophrenic Patient	Percent Schizophrenic (Diagnostically Certain Cases Only)
Parents	4.4
Siblings	8.5
Children	12.3
Half siblings	3.2
Uncles and aunts	2.0
Nephews and nieces	2.2
Grandchildren	2.8
First cousins	2.9
Probability for general population	1.0

theoretically possible to separate the contributions of heredity and environment to the development of schizophrenia.

The usual data yielded by twin studies are "concordance" rates, the likelihood of a second twin having schizophrenia once one is diagnosed. A large twin study conducted in the 1940s by Franz Kallman estimated the concordance rate for identical twins at 85% as compared to only 15% for fraternal twins. Kallman concluded that genetic factors are much more important determiners of who will become schizophrenic than are environmental factors. More recent studies have failed to confirm the high rate of concordance among identical twins reported by Kallman. Nevertheless, even strictly controlled studies put the concordance rate at around 50%.

One reason for discrepancies among studies is their failure to use a uniform definition of concordance. Some studies base their figures on psychiatric evaluations; others insist that individuals be hospitalized and diagnosed schizophrenic before they can be counted as concordant. Not surprisingly, the concordance rate varies with the strictness of the definition. Nevertheless, in every study, the concordance rate among identical twins has been at least twice as high as for fraternal twins. Moreover, even among discordant identical twins (in which only one twin has developed a schizophrenic disorder), the offspring of the nonschizophrenic twin are almost as likely to become schizophrenic as are the

offspring of the affected twin. This finding suggests that the genetic disposition may be passed on through the generations even though it does not always lead to the overt expression of schizophrenic symptoms.

Because twins are reared together, it is still likely that a common deviant environment is at least partly responsible for their both developing schizophrenia (many, for example, had schizophrenic parents). Studying identical twins separated early in life provides a means of determining the relative contributions of heredity and environment to the development of schizophrenia. The separated twins share identical genetic dispositions, but because they are raised apart, they grow up in different environments. If such separated twins still have high concordance rates, it is highly likely that heredity is responsible. A small number of separated twins have been studied. In each case, at least one twin had been diagnosed schizophrenic. The probability that the second twin was also diagnosed schizophrenic was over 60%. While this finding is consistent with a genetic basis for schizophrenia, it must be considered tentative because it is based on only a small number of twins. Much larger samples have been obtained from adoption studies.

Adoption Studies

Adoption studies capitalize on the unfortunate fact that the children of schizophrenic parents are often given up for adoption. Children of schizophrenic parents who are raised in adoptive homes have the benefit of being brought up in nonschizophrenic environments. If they still develop the disorder, it must be their genetic predisposition that is responsible. Several studies of children reared apart from their schizophrenic mothers have been conducted. One of the best known was conducted by Seymour Kety. Taking advantage of the excellent records the Danish government keeps on all citizens, Kety combed the files looking for schizophrenic individuals who had been adopted at an early age. A search of the records found that the biological relatives of these individuals were more likely to have been diagnosed schizophrenic than were members of the general population. In contrast, their adoptive relatives—the parents who raised them and their half brothers and sisters—were no more likely to develop schizophrenia than any other member of the general population. This finding is just what would be expected if schizophrenia is genetically rather than environmentally determined.

Genetics *Plus* Environment

Although there is strong evidence that schizophrenia has a genetic component, the evidence does not allow us to conclude that schizophrenia is completely genetic. If heredity were completely responsible, we would expect the concordance rate among identical twins to be 100%. The actual figure, which is far lower, suggests that environmental factors also play a role. The previously mentioned relationship between traumatic experiences and reactive schizophrenia is also consistent with this view. Given the undeniable influence of both genetics and environment, many researchers have adopted an interactive theory of schizophrenia which assumes that some unlucky people do inherit a biological vulnerability to schizophrenic breakdown but that this breakdown will occur only if the individual is exposed to extreme environmental stress.

Though sensible, this interactive theory is rather vague. It does not say how to identify the predisposition nor does it specify the life stresses that cause predisposed people to develop a schizophrenic disorder. In theory, at least, the necessary information on life stress could be obtained from detailed patient histories. Kraepelin, Bleuler, and the generations of clinicians who followed them published numerous life histories of schizophrenic patients. However, because the data for these histories are collected after patients were diagnosed schizophrenic (clinicians do not even get to meet patients until after they develop problems), they are entirely dependent for their accuracy on the memories of the patients and their families. Unfortunately, such recollections are subject to a variety of subtle and not-so-subtle biases. These include selective forgetting (all patients, and their families, have past experiences they would rather forget), distortions, and even outright fabrications (to avoid blame, alleviate guilt, and so on). For these reasons, retrospectively collected case histories are rarely trustworthy. The obvious solution is to observe individuals before they become schizophrenic. By studying a large population of children for 20 to 40 years, subjecting them to periodic psychological assessments, keeping track of their life experiences, and noting which ones develop schizophrenia, we should be able to identify the special physiological characteristics as well as the life stresses that precipitate schizophrenic disorders. Such a research project would be enormously expensive, however. Many children would have to be studied because only 1 in 100 will ever become schizophrenic. The cost can be reduced substantially if only those children who are likely to develop schizophrenia are studied. This was the strategy adopted in the classic research discussed next.

CLASSIC STUDY 11
Children at Risk

Sarnoff Mednick was born in 1928. Like many famous American psychologists of his generation, Mednick received his B.A. from the City College of New York. He then moved to Chicago where he pursued doctoral study at Northwestern University. After receiving his Ph.D., Mednick spent several years at Harvard University and the University of California at Berkeley before moving to the University of Michigan. After 10 years at Michigan, Mednick again moved, this time to the New School for Social Research in New York and then later to the University of Southern California where he is presently professor of psychology.

Mednick has published over 250 papers and books and has been director of the Psychology

Institute at Copenhagen's Community Hospital since 1962. He has also been a visiting scientist at the Soviet Academy of Medicine. His many honors include the Stanley Dean Award for Research in Schizophrenia from the American College of Psychiatrists, the Distinguished Scientist Award of the Clinical Division of the American Psychological Association, and the Outstanding Research Award from the Golden Key National Honor Society.

Mednick was still at the University of Michigan when he first had the idea of following a group of children at high risk for the development of schizophrenia. The study had to be abandoned, however, because of the difficulties involved in keeping track of children as their families moved from place to place. The project was revived again when Mednick learned of the careful records kept by the Danish government (the same records used by Kety in his adoption study).

In a 1966 paper called "A Longitudinal Study of Children with a High Risk for Schizophrenia," Mednick described the purpose of his study as follows:

> We intend to follow these [high-risk] children closely for the next fifteen to twenty years. When some appreciable number becomes schizophrenic, we will be able to look back at our current measures and see how those who became schizophrenic differed in childhood from those who did not. If within the span of our current examinations there are some measures related to factors predisposing to schizophrenia, then it is possible that we will be able to devise a battery of tests that will effectively pre-identify children who have an extremely high risk of becoming schizophrenic.[2]

To select a high-risk group, Mednick and his collaborator, Danish psychiatrist Fini Schulsinger, chose children with schizophrenic mothers. Based on previous research, they expected that half such children would develop some form of psychopathology and that around 30% of this "deviant" group would eventually develop a schizophrenic disorder. To see why children with schizophrenic mothers constitute a "high-risk" group, you need only compare their chances of developing a schizophrenic disorder with those of the average child (with no schizophrenic parents). The latter children have only a 1% chance of someday being diagnosed schizophrenic — one tenth the risk of members of the high-risk group. By studying high-risk children

periodically throughout their lives and comparing them to children who do not develop a schizophrenic disorder, Mednick hoped to be able to find early predictive signs that could be used to pick out the most vulnerable children. Such children could be the target of special "early intervention" programs that could eventually lead to the prevention of this serious psychosis.

Mednick's research program could be conceptualized as passing through three levels (see Figure 5.3). In level I, children with schizophrenic mothers could be compared with low-risk children whose mothers were not schizophrenics. Initial psychological and physiological differences between the two groups could be noted. During level II, approximately half the children in the high-risk group were expected to become psychologically "deviant" while only 10% of the low-risk children were expected to develop psychological problems. The factors that produce deviance in both groups of children could be compared. Finally, at level III, 30 or so of the deviant high-risk children were expected to develop a schizophrenic disorder. The factors responsible could be teased out by comparing the schizophrenic children with those who did not develop schizophrenia.

The high-risk research strategy overcomes many of the problems associated with previous research. Unlike earlier retrospective studies, the observations and test data gathered on high-risk children are not contaminated by a history of taking therapeutic drugs, previous hospitalizations, the stigma of carrying a diagnostic label, or any other consequences of having developed a schizophrenic condition. Stereotyped expectations about how schizophrenics are supposed to behave (see the discussion of Rosenhan's study in Chapter 2) are also eliminated because neither the researchers nor the children know who is destined to succumb. In addition, because data are gathered prospectively, the biases that plague retrospective studies (selective forgetting, distortions, and so on) are also avoided.

Mednick and Schulsinger's study began in 1962. The high-risk subjects were 207 adolescents whose mothers were process schizophrenics. Mothers were chosen because paternity is often difficult to determine and because surveys found that schizophrenic women have many more offspring than schizophrenic men have. The researchers decided

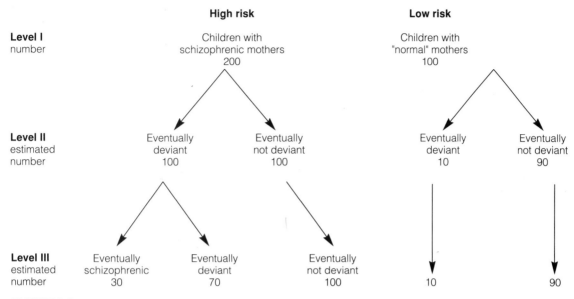

FIGURE 5.3 Design of Mednick and Schulsinger's high-risk study.

to include only the offspring of the most severely affected women (process schizophrenics) because these mothers have been shown to yield the highest number of schizophrenic children. Though diagnostic criteria have changed over the decades, applying today's diagnostic criteria to the original sample of high-risk mothers would still result in the vast majority receiving the schizophrenic diagnosis. The control group consisted of 104 low-risk children whose mothers were not schizophrenic. Pairs of high-risk children were matched on variables such as age, sex, father's occupation (a good measure of social class in Denmark), rural versus urban residence, years of education, and institutional versus family upbringing. Thus, a 13-year-old high-risk male whose father was a laborer and who was raised in an orphanage would be matched with another high-risk male of the same age and background. In addition, a single low-risk child was matched to each pair of high-risk children using the same variables. The average age of the 311 high- and low-risk children was around 15 years. Because the peak period for developing a schizophrenic disorder is between 15 and 35 years of age, the investigators maximized the possibility that the high-risk

children would succumb during the 20 years planned for the study by starting with a teenage sample. It should be mentioned that no child was seriously mentally disturbed when the study began.

Each subject received a thorough evaluation at the outset of the experiment and periodically thereafter. In addition to psychological tests and diagnostic clinical interviews, reports were elicited from teachers, guardians, and even from the midwife who assisted at each subject's birth. In addition, tests of sympathetic nervous activity were also conducted. The sympathetic nervous system consists mainly of defenses designed to protect the individual in case of emergency. When faced with severe stress, the sympathetic nervous system releases the hormone adrenalin to increase alertness, increases blood sugar to provide extra energy, and speeds up heart and respiration rates to provide more oxygen to the muscles. At the same time, the blood supply to vessels near the skin is restricted to reduce bleeding in case of injury and proteins that cause blood clotting are manufactured to prevent excessive blood loss should injury occur. Mednick included assessments of the sympathetic nervous system because he believed that an overly "sensitive" sympathetic nervous system may contribute to schizophrenic breakdowns. (See Chapter 7 for more on the sympathetic nervous system.)

Heart rate, muscle tension, and galvanic skin response (GSR) all served as measures of sympathetic nervous system responsivity in Mednick's study, but most emphasis was placed on the GSR, which is simply a measure of the amount of electrical activity taking place in the skin. Flash a light, make a sudden loud noise, or administer a mild electric shock and within seconds the affected individual will show a change in GSR. A few seconds later—provided no further lights, noises, or shocks are administered—the GSR returns to normal. Mednick's technique was to present the children with a neutral sound (a buzzer) followed by an irritating loud noise. The loud noise produced the expected reaction: increased heart rate, increased muscle tension, and a substantial GSR. After a number of such pairings, the neutral stimulus became conditioned and also began to elicit the "arousal" response. The experimenters then presented a series of sounds that varied in their similarity to the buzzer. Their aim was to measure the extent to which conditioning was carried over to other sounds (this is known as stimulus generalization).

The researchers found several differences between the high-risk group and others. First, they had stronger GSRs to both the loud noise and the buzzer. This suggests that high-risk children have greater autonomic responsiveness even before they develop any behavioral disorder. A second important difference between high- and low-risk children is the former's failure to "habituate." With repeated presentations of the sound, the low-risk children took longer and longer to produce a GSR, as if they were getting "used to" the stimulus. The high-risk children, on the other hand, showed no habituation. In fact, their GSRs tended to occur with increasing speed as if each presentation made them *less* able to cope with the stimulus. Finally, the time taken for the electrical skin resistance to return to normal was much shorter among the high-risk than among the low-risk children. Thus, the high-risk children were "overreactive" in both directions. Their GSRs were stronger and more rapid than those produced by low-risk children, but they also returned more quickly to their resting state.

Following the initial examinations conducted in 1962, an "alarm network" was established in Denmark ensuring that the investigators were notified whenever any subject in their study was admitted to a psychiatric facility. Within 5 years, notifications were received for 20 high-risk subjects. Each had developed some type of serious disturbance but not necessarily schizophrenia. The researchers compared this "sick" group to subjects with similar backgrounds who had not become sick and found several characteristics that set them apart. These included early separation from their mothers (when the mothers were hospitalized for psychiatric reasons), behavioral problems at school, poor performance on a psychological test of associations, and a large number of pregnancy and birth complications. On the physiological measures, the sick children were at the extreme of the high-risk group: They had exceptionally fast GSRs that failed to habituate and returned very rapidly to their resting state (see Figure 5.4).

Mednick was particularly interested in the GSR data. He interpreted them as supporting his theory that many "symptoms" are simply learned behaviors designed to help schizophrenic individuals reduce the chronically high level of physiological arousal produced by their "abnormally sensitive" sympathetic nervous systems. For example, because of their "overresponsiveness," a threatening thought (perhaps of a sexual nature) may produce an excessively high level of arousal in schizophrenic individuals. Because this high level of arousal makes them uncomfortable, they attempt to banish the thought by thinking of something entirely unrelated. Arousal is quickly reduced (recall that high-risk individuals show an especially rapid return of the GSR to its resting state). Thus, their avoidant behavior is rewarded (or "reinforced" in the jargon of conditioning theory). Put simply, overresponsive individuals learn to jump from one irrelevant thought to another in order to reduce physiological arousal.

As already mentioned, pregnancy and birth complications were specially prevalent in the sick group. Seventy percent had a history of birth complications as opposed to only 15% of the remaining high-risk children. Interestingly, psychophysiological overresponsivity occurred only in children with a history of pregnancy and birth complications.

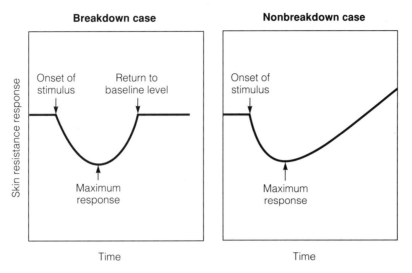

FIGURE 5.4 GSRs of sick children compared with those of controls.

Mednick suggested that oxygen starvation produced by birth complications leads to brain damage, which results in an overly responsive sympathetic nervous system. Overresponsivity, in turn, produces schizophrenic symptoms such as loose associations. The similarity between Mednick's theory and Bleuler's ideas is quite striking.

By 1972, 17 of the high-risk subjects and 1 low-risk subject had developed schizophrenia. In addition, 55 high-risk subjects were found to have psychological disturbances serious enough to be considered borderline "psychotics." (Ten high-risk subjects died in the course of the follow-up, seven by suicide, while none of the low-risk subjects died.) The subjects who were diagnosed schizophrenic had the most severely disturbed mothers, had been separated from their families early in life and placed in institutions, had a large number of pregnancy and birth complications, and were "conduct" problems in school. Curiously, GSR recovery rates and performance on the association test—measures strongly related to psychiatric disturbance in the sick group 5 years earlier—were not nearly as good predictors of schizophrenic breakdown. In fact, many of the schizophrenics were not even members of the sick group. It would seem that psychophysiological responsiveness and impaired

associations are related to the general tendency to develop psychological problems rather than specific causes of schizophrenia.

More recent follow-up studies by Mednick and his colleagues have found the following factors to be the most important determinants of an individual's risk of developing a schizophrenic disorder:

1. A severely affected schizophrenic mother and many schizophrenic relatives

2. A history of pregnancy and birth complications

3. Institutional upbringing or many separations from mother

AFTERMATH

The Danish high-risk study has spawned many similar studies. Because of the length of time the studies take, their final results may not be available for some years. Preliminary findings, however, suggest that Mednick's original "overarousal" hypothesis was too simple, and more complicated versions have been proposed. In recent publications, Mednick himself has de-emphasized his earlier views on arousal although he still believes that brain damage plays an important role in the etiology of many types of schizophrenia. Using modern

SOCIAL CLASS AND MENTAL ILLNESS

In addition to family factors, sociologists have also implicated social class as a possible cause of schizophrenia. In their pioneering book, *Social Class and Mental Illness: A Community Study,* published in 1958, sociologists A. B. Hollingshead and F. C. Redlich found that schizophrenia is nine times more likely to develop at the bottom of the social ladder than in the top social class. In addition, the prevalence of schizophrenia is highest in the poorest areas of cities and gradually reduces as one moves from urban centers to the suburbs. These findings suggest that the stress produced by poverty and crowded urban conditions contributes to the development of schizophrenia.

Some investigators have argued that the sociological data are biased because they are based on mental-hospital admissions. Lower-class patients are much more likely to be hospitalized in such institutions than higher-class patients, who often have access to private sanitoriums and clinics. To ensure an unbiased sample, investigators have adopted an epidemiological strategy sending specially trained interviewers to talk to all members of a community, hospitalized or not. The result has almost always been the same: The poor are more likely to be schizophrenic.

The relationship between social class and schizophrenia is consistent with the notion that, among those who inherit a genetic susceptibility, the stress produced by poverty can cause a schizophrenic disorder. But it should be recognized that the causative direction may go the other way; schizophrenic behavior may cause people to fall to the bottom of the social ladder. At present, it is not possible to say which view is correct.

---

brain-imaging techniques, he has recently shown a relationship between illness during the mother's pregnancy, birth complications, brain damage, and the development of schizophrenic disorders.

The results of high-risk studies when combined with the genetic studies discussed earlier are consistent with Bleuler's idea that there exists a group of people who share a genetic propensity to develop schizophrenia. Such individuals are called "schizotypal." Those who inherit this propensity and who also suffer the experience of stressful environments often go on to develop a schizophrenic disorder. Thus, it is the environment (institutional upbringing, early separation from mother, emotional traumas) that brings out schizophrenic disorders in vulnerable individuals. It follows, then, that early therapeutic intervention in the lives of high-risk individuals might actually prevent the development of schizophrenia and other serious disorders.

Peter Venables, a British psychologist, and Mednick have been conducting an early-intervention experiment on the Indian Ocean island of Mauritius. The experiment, sponsored by the World Health Organization, began in 1972 with 1,800 3-year-old children. At the outset of the study, the children were all examined using Mednick's physiological techniques, looking for those who showed exceptionally fast return of the GSR to a resting state. The researchers assumed that such children would be specially vulnerable to schizophrenic breakdown even though they may not have had schizophrenic mothers. One hundred children including abnormal GSR responders and matched controls were sent to specially designed nursery schools while a similar group was left to be raised in the community in the normal way. (The identity of the high- and low-risk children was kept secret from nursery school staff.) The schools gave lessons in social behavior, encouraged children not to become isolated, and tried to teach techniques that the children could use to help reduce emotional arousal. The children, who were first examined in 1972, are just entering the most vulnerable age for the development of schizophrenia, so it is too early to say whether early intervention is successful in preventing the later development of schizophrenia. However, evaluations conducted after the children left nursery school showed that high-risk children (as measured by GSR) were more sociable and less likely to sit around passively watching others than were other

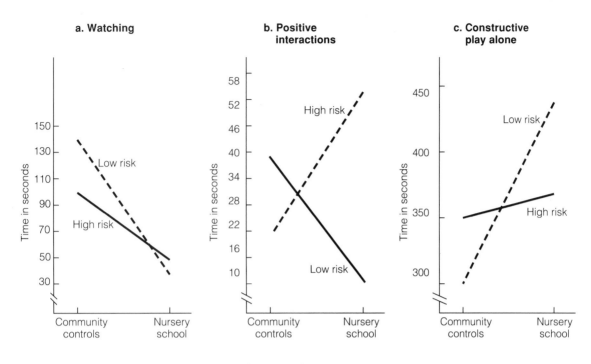

Control and nursery groups

FIGURE 5.5 Time spent by children (a) watching, (b) playing positively with others, and (c) engaging in constructive play alone for high- and low-risk groups. High-risk children in the nursery differed from high-risk children in the community. Low-risk children were also affected by their nursery experience but not necessarily in the same direction as high-risk children.

high-risk children raised in the community. The high-risk children were even more likely to play with others than were low-risk nursery children. The latter, however, spent more time in constructive individual play (see Figure 5.5).

Despite attending the same nursery schools for 3 years, and despite the fact that school staff did not know which children were high-risk, there were still differences between the high- and low-risk groups. (The high-risk group interacted more than others; the low-risk group spent more time in constructive individual play.) As the years pass, we will be able to learn whether early therapeutic nursery-school experience reduces the risk of developing an adult schizophrenic disorder in a high-risk population. These findings, combined with the results of the high-risk studies currently under way, should further increase our understanding of the genetic and environmental factors that lead to schizophrenic

breakdown and provide clinicians with the tools necessary to prevent schizophrenia in future generations.

We have clearly learned a great deal about schizophrenia in the 80 years since Bleuler published his classical book. (Perhaps the most important breakthrough, the discovery of antipsychotic medication, has barely been mentioned.) Nevertheless, it is worthwhile noting Bleuler's prescience on a number of important points. As he expected, and many subsequent studies have confirmed, there is a significant genetic component in schizophrenia. However, environmental stress is required to "release" schizophrenic symptoms, which can vary markedly from one individual to another. Bleuler also expected that schizophrenic patients would be shown to have some type of brain damage. Using modern brain-imaging techniques, researchers are beginning to collect data suggesting that Bleuler's expectation was almost certainly well founded. On the treatment side, Bleuler recommended community care. He would, therefore, be pleased to know that hospitalization is now reserved only for acutely ill patients and community care is preferred where at all possible. Although many details remain to be filled in, the outline of schizophrenia provided by Bleuler in *Dementia Praecox or the Group of Schizophrenias* has withstood remarkably well the test of time.

Further Reading

Bleuler, E. (1950). *Dementia praecox or the group of schizophrenias* (J. Zinkin, Trans.). New York: International Universities Press.

Mednick, S. A. (1966). A longitudinal study of children with a high risk for schizophrenia. *Mental Hygiene, 50,* 522–535.

Mednick, S. A., Parnas, J., & Schulsinger, F. (1987). The Copenhagen high-risk project, 1962–1986. *Schizophrenia Bulletin, 13,* 485–495.

Notes

1. All quotations are from: Bleuler, E. (1950). *Dementia praecox or the group of schizophrenias.* (J. Zinkin, Trans.). New York: International Universities Press.
2. Mednick, S. A. (1966). A longitudinal study of children with a high risk for schizophrenia. *Mental Hygiene, 50,* 522.

CHAPTER 6

A Season in Hell

Everybody gets depressed at one time or another; sadness and despair are an inevitable part of life. Fortunately, depression is usually only temporary, an emotional reaction to a specific life experience (loss of a loved one, for example). Complete recovery is the usual rule. But sometimes depression can linger indefinitely. When this happens, prolonged sadness and dejection causes sufferers to lose interest in their future and even to contemplate suicide. This chapter is concerned with such serious depression. But, as will be shown, it turns out to be impossible to discuss depression without also describing another mood disorder called *mania*. Mania is, in many ways, the opposite of depression. It is characterized by elation, exuberance, and grand plans for the future. Despite their very different appearance, mania and depression may occur in the same individual. These people are known as "manic-depressives" because they cycle through emotional states—from mania to depression and back again. The intimate connection between mania and depression suggests that, for some people at least, the two conditions may have a common underlying cause. A full understanding of depression, therefore, requires that we study mania as well.

SYMPTOMS OF MANIA AND DEPRESSION

Depression and mania have always been with us. Thousands of years ago, Hippocrates, the most famous doctor of ancient Greece, described a mental disorder called *melancholia*, which is indistinguishable from the condition we call depression. The term *melancholia* was derived from the Greek words *melan* ("black") and "choler" (bile). Black bile, it will be recalled, was one of the four humors believed to affect personality. As will be shown, the idea that depression is caused by a chemical imbalance in the body still retains adherents today. Mania was also

My life had come to a sudden stop. I was able to breathe, to eat, to drink, to sleep. I could not, indeed, help doing so; but there was no real life in me.

—Leo Tolstoi

known to the Greek and Roman doctors, who called it *mainesthai,* a word that roughly translates to mean "madness."

Hippocrates and his colleagues commented on the tendency for depression and mania to occur in the same person. Over the subsequent centuries, their observation was reconfirmed many times. By the modern era, the connection between mania and depression became so well known, it was taken for granted that they constitute a single entity. This is why Kraepelin's diagnostic scheme included "manic-depressive disorder" as *one* of the two common psychoses (the other, as described in Chapter 2, was dementia praecox). For many years following Kraepelin's pioneering work, all serious depressions were considered to be a partial expression of a manic-depressive disorder. In the last 20 years, however, it has become clear that both depression and mania can also occur on their own although pure manic disorders are relatively rare.

Manic Episodes

Mild manic states (called hypomanic episodes) are sometimes difficult to distinguish from high spirits. Everything seems accelerated. The affected person is elated, energetic, talkative, and full of self-confidence. It is difficult to see that there is anything really wrong. Everyone likes happy, lively people; their enthusiasm is infectious, and their exuberance is stimulating. But everything, even good moods, may be taken to extremes. Carry liveliness too far and it turns into frenzy; let enthusiasm get out of hand and it can become fanaticism. This is exactly what happens in hypomania. Affected individuals may appear elated and industrious, but careful observation will usually reveal a tendency to skip from one activity to another, an inability to carry out plans to their completion, irritability, and a low tolerance for frustration. Acute mania is a more severe version of hypomania in which the hypomanic's talkativeness is transformed into an endless stream of loosely connected speech similar to that produced by some schizophrenic patients. The following extract is an example:

> Women of America, it behooves you one and all to help at this, the most interesting epoch of the world's history, in every way possible, the march of civilization, the march to victory! I will play you Beethoven's Great Symphony with its four fateful opening notes — sol, sol, sol mi. . . . — V, V, V, V, the Day of the Century has dawned![1]

Acute manics need little or no sleep or food. They spend their time in constant motion: dancing, singing, making speeches, writing books, exercising, moving furniture, and gratifying sexual impulses (see Figure 6.1 for an example of manic writing). Their lives become a confused whirl of largely purposeless activity; physically and mentally, they are in high gear. Manics often have grandiose plans for making millions or bringing world peace. They spend money with no regard for the future; their life savings may be dissipated in a few days. Manics consider their grand plans too important to drop for sleep or rest. Attempts to slow them down or an unwillingness to go along with their plans causes great frustration and may even provoke a violent response. Lack of sleep and an inability to slow down quickly take their toll in fatigue and poor health. Ultimately, manic patients may have to be sedated just to prevent them from harming themselves.

Manic disorders typically make their first appearance when individuals are in their early 20s, but late-life onsets have also been reported. Episodes come on quickly and can last for weeks or months disappearing as quickly as they came. The DSM-III-R criteria for manic episodes are summarized in Table 6.1.

TABLE 6.1 Diagnostic Criteria for Manic Episodes

A "manic syndrome" includes criteria A–F below; a "hypomanic episode" excludes C.

A. A distinct period of abnormally elevated, expansive, or irritable mood.

B. Three of the following symptoms are present during mood disturbance (four if mood is only irritable):
   1. inflated self-esteem or grandiosity
   2. decreased sleep
   3. more talkative than usual
   4. jumping from idea to idea
   5. distractibility
   6. increased activity
   7. seeking pleasure without regard for consequences (buying sprees, investments, sexual promiscuity)

C. Mood disturbance severe enough to cause social relations or work to suffer.

D. No delusions or hallucinations except during period of acute mood changes.

E. No schizophrenia or other psychosis.

F. No obvious organic cause.

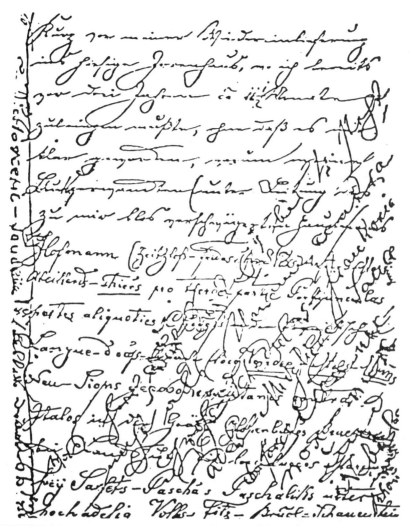

FIGURE 6.1 This manuscript was produced by one of Kraepelin's patients during an acute manic episode.

Depressive Episodes

Because depression is a common reaction to some of the perils of life, clinicians need some way of differentiating these "normal" mood states from major depressive disorders. Often the difference turns out to be largely a matter of degree. Normal depressions last only a short time; the sadness is not as intense and the hopelessness not as profound as in serious clinical depression. There are also differences in kind. Clinically depressed individuals often blame themselves for their depression; they see no future beyond their current state and may consider suicide a reasonable solution to their misery. For convenience sake, the major depressive symptoms are organized into four categories: mood, thought, motivational, and physical symptoms. All four types are incorporated into the DSM-III-R diagnostic criteria (see Table 6.2).

Mood Symptoms The primary, and most important, symptom of depression is sadness. When asked how they feel, depressed patients describe themselves as "blue, melancholy, miserable, hopeless,

TABLE 6.2 Diagnostic Criteria for Major
Depressive Episode

At least five of the following symptoms present during the same 2-week period with at least one being either 1 or 2. Omit any symptoms with an organic cause or those caused by schizophrenia.

1. depressed or, in children, irritable mood most of the day, every day
2. markedly diminished interest or pleasure in all or almost all activities most of the day, every day
3. significant weight loss or weight gain when not dieting
4. decreased or greatly increased sleep
5. psychomotor retardation or, in some cases, agitation
6. chronic fatigue or energy loss
7. feelings of worthlessness or excessive or inappropriate guilt feelings
8. diminished ability to think or concentrate
9. recurrent thoughts of death or suicide

unhappy, or sad." In some cases, anxiety may also be part of the picture. In the throes of depression, the pleasures of children and family life pale, career successes and sporting triumphs become hollow, even sex loses its appeal.

Thought Symptoms Depression is usually accompanied by low self-esteem as well as feelings of inadequacy and inferiority. These lead the depressed individual to believe that the future holds nothing but failure. Sufferers blame themselves for their condition. They feel guilty about being depressed, and their guilt serves to make them even more depressed.

Motivational Symptoms Depression is marked by inertia, passivity, and a pervasive loss of volition. Even the smallest task appears to require enormous effort. In severe cases, sufferers show a complete "paralysis of will." They must be forced out of bed, dressed, and forced to eat.

Physical Symptoms Although mildly depressed individuals may turn to food for solace, severe depression is almost always accompanied by loss of appetite. Sleep disturbances, especially an inability to return to sleep after an early awakening, are also common as is impotence. Severe cases display a symptom known as *psychomotor retardation* in which all physical movements, speech, and even thoughts slow down. When psychomotor retardation is severe, patients seem like characters in a slow-motion film.

In addition to these four symptom categories, clinicians use three other classification schemes to describe depression: chronic versus episodic, endogenous versus exogenous, and seasonal versus nonseasonal.

Chronic Versus Episodic Chronic depression develops insidiously and lasts for years with few remissions. Episodic depressions, on the other hand, have sudden onsets and remissions. Episodic depressions are more common than the chronic variety, but the two categories should not be thought of as completely distinct. Depressions that start as episodic can go on to become chronic. Whether chronic or episodic, depression is a serious health problem. At any specified time, approximately 10% of female and 4% of male adults are seriously depressed.

Endogenous Versus Exogenous The endogenous classification is used to describe depressions that are thought to have a biological rather than a psychological origin. Psychomotor retardation, eating and sleeping disturbances, impotence, and generally more severe symptoms are said to be signs of biologically caused depression, whereas psychologically caused, or exogenous, depressions are milder and produce fewer physical symptoms. While many clinicians find the distinction between biological and psychological depression useful, the history of psychopathology suggests that such distinctions are difficult to sustain. As noted in previous chapters, disorders as diverse as autism, Tourette's syndrome, anorexia nervosa, and schizophrenia have all proven to be the interactive products of biology and psychology. There is scant evidence to suggest that depression is any different. Indeed, the available evidence supports the interactive view. For example, endogenous depression, if it is purely biological, should respond better to antidepressant drugs than exogenous depression. But studies have shown that drugs are effective for both types of patients. Taking the opposite tack, exogenous depression, if it is really psychological,

CHRONICLES OF DEPRESSION

Serious depression can affect even the famous and successful, a group who objectively appear to have no "reason" to be unhappy. The following extracts are all from well-known authors describing their personal experience of depression.

I do not care for anything. I do not care to ride, for the exercise is too violent. I do not care to walk, walking is too strenuous. I do not care to lie down, for I should have to remain lying, and I do not care to do that, or I should have to get up again, and I do not care to do that either. . . . I do not care at all.

—Søren Kierkegaard (Danish philosopher)

My life had come to a sudden stop. I was able to breathe, to eat, to drink, to sleep. I could not, indeed, help doing so; but there was no real life in me. I had not a single wish to strive for the fulfillment of what I could feel to be reasonable. If I wished for anything, I knew beforehand that if I were to satisfy the wish, nothing would come of it, I would still be dissatisfied. Had a fairy appeared and offered me all I desired, I should not have known what to say. . . . I really wished for nothing.

The truth lay in this, that life had no meaning for me. Every day of life, every step in it, brought me nearer the edge of a precipice, whence I saw clearly the final ruin before me. To stop, to go back, were alike impossible; nor could I shut my eyes so as not to see the suffering that alone awaited me, the death of all in me, even to annihilation.

—Leo Tolstoi (Russian author)

I saw the days of the year stretching ahead like a series of bright, white boxes, and separating one box from another was sleep, like a black shade. Only for me, the long perspective of shades that set off one box from the next had suddenly snapped up, and I could see day after day after day glaring ahead of me like a white, broad, infinitely desolate avenue.

It seemed silly to wash one day when I would only have to wash again the next. It made me tired just to think of it. I wanted to do everything once and for all and be through with it.

—Sylvia Plath (American writer)

should be more closely associated with specific precipitating factors (loss of job, death of a spouse) than endogenous depression. In fact, both types of depression have been found to have the same type and number of triggering factors. Given these findings, it seems best to conclude that, at the present time at least, there is no firm basis for categorizing depressions as biological or psychological. The main difference between endogenous and exogenous depression appears to be one of severity, not etiology.

Seasonal Versus Nonseasonal For most of us, seasonal mood changes are subtle; we feel a little down in winter and energized in spring. But for some people, a change in season can bring on mood shifts so severe, they interfere with their ability to function. The typical pattern is a depression that comes on each winter and lifts with the arrival of spring. The longer and more severe the winter, the

worse the depression. For example, Scandinavian cities located above the Arctic Circle have much higher rates of suicide in winter (when it is dark most of the day) than in summer. This pattern is known as *seasonal affective disorder* or by the highly appropriate acronym SAD. Seasonal affective disorders are thought to be related to changes in the number of daylight hours across seasons (see the box "Let There Be Light").

Manic-Depressive (Bipolar) Disorders

The great majority of depressions, perhaps 90%, are *unipolar*. That is, they occur without mania. The remaining 10% occur as one part of the *bipolar* disorder, *manic-depression.*

The first episode in a bipolar disorder is usually a manic one followed some time later by a depressive episode. The cycle may then immediately repeat again although a period of remission between cycles

LET THERE BE LIGHT

Seasonal changes in behavior are common in the animal kingdom. Birds and fish migrate with the seasons, arctic animals hibernate, amphibians change their physical shape. The trigger for many of these behavior patterns is a change in the amount of daylight. Except at the equator, winter days are short while summer days are long. Many animals are sensitive to changing day lengths. They use information about the hours of sunlight to predict the coming season and change their behavior accordingly. Generalizing from animal behavior, Thomas Wehr, a researcher in clinical psychobiology, and his colleagues reasoned that seasonal mood changes in humans may also be the result of changing day lengths. Because sufferers improve with the longer days of spring, Wehr hypothesized that artificially lengthening winter days could dispel their despondency.

Wehr and his co-workers tested this hypothesis in the dead of winter by exposing a sample of depressed patients to artificial sunlight. The treatment could not have been simpler. Patients awakened early, around 5 A.M. while it was still dark. They spent the next few hours reading, knitting, or listening to the radio while sitting in front of an artificial sun—a bank of fluorescent lamps. Despite its simplicity, the experiment was a success. Within a few days to a week, patients began to report feeling the way they usually do in spring. Since the initial experiments, hundreds of patients have been successfully treated with light therapy.

At present, the mechanism by which light therapy lifts depression is unknown. The secret, however, almost certainly lies in light's effect on the oldest and most primitive parts of the human brain. The success of light therapy reminds us of how closely we are linked with the animal world. Although we prefer to see ourselves as in control of our own behavior, the seasonal cycles that control animals and plants affect us as well.

---

is more typical. Epidemiological estimates suggest that about 1 in 100 adults develop a manic-depressive disorder sometime in their lives. In contrast to unipolar depression, which occurs most frequently in women, manic-depression is equally likely to affect males and females. It also appears to run in families. (A milder version of manic-depression, in which hypomanic and mild depressive states alternate, is called *cyclothemia*.)

The essential difference between unipolar and bipolar disorders is that, in the latter, depressive episodes alternate with manic ones. However, there are also qualitative differences between the two types of depressions. Bipolar depressions are marked by lethargy, excessive sleep, and early age of onset whereas unipolar depressions begin later in life and are normally characterized by an inability to sleep and nervous agitation. Because of these differences, bipolar disorders are thought to have a different etiology from unipolar depressions. Separate etiologies are also suggested by heritability studies that have found bipolar disorders to show a stronger genetic component than unipolar disorders and from studies of the drug lithium carbonate, which has been found to be therapeutic for bipolar depression but not for unipolar.

THEORIES OF DEPRESSION

Hints about the causes of depression may be gained by looking at who gets depressed. Studies have shown that one fourth or more of the population will develop a serious depression at least once during their lifetimes. Although just about all people are potentially vulnerable, not everyone is equally likely to succumb. For example, women develop depression twice as often as men; older adults (especially older women) are more vulnerable than young people. Interestingly, unlike schizophrenia, the incidence of depression does not vary with social class (see Chapter 5 for more on social class and schizophrenia). As might be expected, stressful life events such as divorce, failures at work, and death of loved ones are common precursors of depression. Early life experiences also appear to play a role. For example, depression is particularly common among individuals who lost their mothers while they were still children.

SUICIDE MYTHS

Marilyn Monroe, one of the most publicized suicides.

In the depths of their despair, depressed people sometimes see suicide as their only way out. Many only talk about killing themselves, some make half-hearted attempts, but a large number actually succeed. Official American reports put the number of suicide deaths at 25,000 per year. (Because many suicides go unrecorded, this is considered to be a low estimate.) Females attempt suicide about three times as often as men, but men are more successful. The incidence of suicide is greatest among people in their 50s and 60s although in recent years there has been a worrying increase among adolescents and college students. Contrary to popular belief, the risk of suicide is not highest when patients are most depressed. Severely depressed patients usually have too little energy and motivation to plan such an act. The most dangerous time is when the depression just begins to lift. Such patients are still despondent, but they have the motivation and energy to take matters into their own hands. Other myths about depression have been collated by psychologist Ed Schneidman:

Myth	Reality
Those who talk about suicide never do it.	Eighty percent of suicides give warnings.
Suicidal people always want to die.	Most are unsure; they gamble hoping others will save them.
Once a person tries suicide, they are always suspect.	Suicide is linked to depression. The risk decreases when the depression is completely gone.
Suicide occurs most often among the rich.	Suicide occurs equally often in every social class.
Suicide attempts are always signs of mental illness.	Some suicides, such as those among the terminally ill, may be rational acts.

SHOCK THERAPY

Electroshock therapy has its origins in an accident. A Viennese doctor, Manfred Sakel, noted that a patient who had been put into a temporary coma by an accidental insulin overdose became less anxious and depressed. Sakel experimented with "insulin shock" and reported that it produced therapeutic effects in a variety of conditions including schizophrenia. Other clinicians also reported success using insulin-induced comas as well as a drug called metrazol, which causes seizures and blackouts. In this climate of experimentation, it was probably only a matter of time before someone thought to induce comas and seizures using electric shock. The "someone" turned out to be an obscure psychiatrist called Ugo Cerletti, who administered the first therapeutic electroshock in 1938. Like those who had experimented with drug-induced comas, Cerletti reported great success treating a variety of conditions. He theorized that electroconvulsive shock treatment (now called ECT) produces brain chemicals called *aeroagomines,* which have an antipsychotic effect. Late in life, Cerletti began to administer electric shocks to animals, which he would then kill in order to extract the antipsychotic serum from their brains. Because he believed that the serum contained antipsychotic aeroagomines, Cerletti advocated injecting it into psychiatric patients rather than administering potentially dangerous electric shocks.

Cerletti's notions about aeroagomines were almost completely ignored. ECT, on the other hand, was widely adopted for a broad range of disorders. Although its efficacy for many of the psychiatric disorders is questionable, there is no doubt that some patients improve dramatically with ECT. Today, ECT is used mainly for depressed patients who have not responded to other forms of treatment. The typical approach is to first administer anesthesia and muscle relaxants to ensure that the patient feels no pain and will not be hurt during the convulsion. Electrodes (flat metal disks) are then placed on the head. In right-handed patients, the electrodes are normally placed on the right side of the head. Because the left side of the brain normally contains the speech centers, this electrode placement minimizes any disruption in language and communicative ability. Once the electrodes are in place, a high current is passed through the head for about half a second. This produces convulsions that last about 1 minute. When patients come out of the anesthesia, they have no memory of the treatment and they often lose memory for preceding events as well. A course of six ECT treatments administered across 2 weeks is usually required to obtain the maximum therapeutic effect. How ECT works to dispel depression is not known. Some scientists have suggested that it increases the level of catecholamines in the brain. This hypothesis, which lacks any direct evidence, is essentially identical to Cerletti's largely ignored notion that ECT produces "aeroagomines." The truth is that, after 50 years of use, we still have no acceptable theory to explain the therapeutic effects of ECT.

Several theories have been developed to account for unipolar and bipolar disorders. They vary mainly in the emphasis they give to biological causes.

Biological Factors

Although there are no strong grounds for categorizing depressions as solely endogenous or exogenous, there are many compelling reasons for believing that biology plays an important etiological role in most depressions. The response of seasonal affective disorder to light therapy, the therapeutic effectiveness of antidepressant drugs, and the evidence for a genetic factor are all compatible with a biological origin. The evidence for a biological etiology is particularly strong for bipolar disorders in which the swing from one mood to the other may be unrelated to external circumstances—almost as if something has triggered an internal, biological switch. Although the exact nature of this biological "switch" is unknown, a currently popular hypothesis focuses on a specific group of neurotransmitter

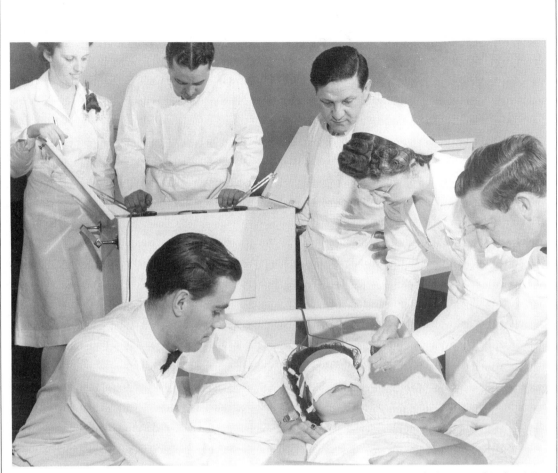

Electroshock therapy (ECT) has been in use for over 50 years. This photograph shows ECT being used in the 1940s. New techniques make the procedure much safer today.

chemicals, the catecholamines. Research has shown that drugs which deplete the supply of cate-cholamines (such as those used to treat high blood pressure) can lead to depression while those that increase catecholamines act as antidepressants. Generalizing from the effect of drugs, researchers have theorized that depression results from an im-balance of catecholamines; too low a level causes de-pression, too high a level results in mania.

Abnormal levels of catecholamines are not the only chemical imbalances implicated in depression.

It has long been known that new mothers risk devel-oping depression *(postpartum depression)*; so do women entering menopause *(involutional melan-cholia)*. More recently, it has been noted that females are most likely to feel depressed just before men-struation. Because childbirth, menopause, and menstruation are periods of intense hormonal changes, it has been suggested that hormonal imbalances may trigger depression. Although plau-sible, this line of reasoning has one serious weak-ness. That is, it may be the psychological meaning of the various events rather than the accompanying hormonal changes that cause depression. For example, a new mother may become depressed because she feels unable to meet the demands of a baby. A menopausal woman may become depressed because she feels unneeded by her grown-up family or less attractive to her spouse. Of course, it is also possible that both hormonal and psychological factors are operating together. This would explain why only some new mothers and menopausal women develop depressive disorders. An interaction between biological and psychological factors would also account for the results of twin studies of bipolar disorder. As might be expected, these studies have found a higher concordance rate for identical than for fraternal twins (when the respective sibling pairs were raised apart). But, even for identical twins, the concordance was only around 65%. This means that inheritance is not sufficient to ensure that the disorder will develop; other factors must also be involved.

Psychological Factors

Those who emphasize biological factors see mood changes as the primary cause of depressive and manic symptoms. For them the causal sequence goes something like this: A genetic disposition produces an inadequate supply of catecholamines, which results in a depressed mood. In an attempt to explain their depressed mood, sufferers construct a peculiar set of beliefs—they consider themselves useless and loathsome, their futures look hopeless. In this way, their thoughts (or "cognitions" as they are known) become consistent with their mood.

While plausible, this etiological sequence has not gone unchallenged. Several psychological theorists have turned the causative direction around. They claim that feelings of worthlessness and inadequacy come first and that it is these cognitions which cause people to become depressed. Foremost among these cognitive theorists is the psychiatrist Aaron Beck, who claims that depression results from certain cognitive distortions and exaggerations. According to Beck, people who develop depressions characteristically blame themselves when something goes wrong ("What a jerk I am") even when the events are beyond any individual's control. An example is the host of a rained-out barbecue who blames himself for the weather. Depression-prone people also overgeneralize (one failed examination

leads them to conclude that they are too stupid to ever learn) and exaggerate (one scratch on a car makes it worthless). Events that simply annoy most people (running out of gasoline on a busy highway, for example) are interpreted by depression-prone people as clear evidence of their own inadequacy and the futility of life. According to Beck, these illogical cognitions produce the mood change that we call depression. He developed a psychological test, the *Beck Depression Inventory,* to measure depressive cognitions. Sample items are found in Table 6.3.

Although the faulty cognitions identified by Beck have been shown to occur frequently among depressed individuals, there is little evidence that such cognitions actually *cause* depressed moods. What is needed is some plausible (and testable) mechanism by which cognitions and mood can be related. One possibility is the "learned helplessness concept" derived from the classic studies conducted by Martin Seligman. These are discussed next.

CLASSIC STUDY 12
Learned Helplessness

Martin E. P. Seligman was born in Albany, New York, in 1942. He received his undergraduate education at Princeton and his Ph.D. from the University of Pennsylvania in 1967. He taught at Cornell University for a few years but returned to the University of Pennsylvania in 1970. After spending a year in the university's psychiatry department, he moved to psychology. Except for visiting fellowships at The Institute of Psychiatry in London and the Max Planck Institute in Berlin, Seligman has spent his entire career at the University of Pennsylvania where he has been professor of psychology since 1976.

Seligman has received a Ph.D. Honoris Causa from Uppsala University in Sweden, a Guggenheim Fellowship, and the Distinguished Scientific Contribution Award of the American Psychological Association (as well as separate awards from its divisions of clinical and experimental psychology). He is the author of over 100 scientific articles and many widely cited books including *Helplessness: On Depression, Development and Death,* which has been translated into eight foreign languages.

TABLE 6.3   Sample Items from the Beck Depression Inventory

Attitude	Score	Cognition
Pessimism	0	I am not particularly pessimistic or discouraged about the future.
	1	I feel discouraged about the future.
	2a	I feel I have nothing to look forward to.
	2b	I feel that I won't ever get over my troubles.
	3	I feel that the future is hopeless and things cannot improve.
Sense of failure	0	I do not feel like a failure.
	1	I feel I have failed more than the average person.
	2a	I feel I have accomplished very little that is worthwhile or that means anything.
	2b	As I look back on my life all I can see is a lot of failures.
	3	I feel I am a complete failure as a person (parent, husband, wife).
Guilt	0	I don't feel particularly guilty.
	1	I feel bad or unworthy a good part of the time.
	2a	I feel quite guilty.
	2b	I feel bad or unworthy practically all of the time now.
	3	I feel as though I am very bad or worthless.
Self-accusations	0	I don't feel I am worse than anybody else.
	1	I am critical of myself for my weaknesses or mistakes.
	2	I blame myself for my faults.
	3	I blame myself for everything bad that happens.

Source: Adapted from Beck, A. T., Ward, C. H., Mendelson, M., Mock, J., & Erbaugh, J. (1961). An inventory for measuring depression. *Archives of General Psychiatry, 4*, 561–571.

Note: Score is total of highest numbered items chosen from each set.

In contrast to Beck's cognitive theory, which was derived from clinical observations, Seligman's ideas arose from research on animal learning. Seligman was particularly taken with studies in which animals were exposed to an inescapable punishment. In the typical experiment, dogs were confined in a box with an electrified floor. They received numerous painful electric shocks that could not be avoided no matter what they did (there was no escape route). Later, the same dogs as well as a new set of dogs that had not received any previous electric shocks were further tested using an apparatus known as a "shuttle box." This box had two compartments. One had an electrified floor, the other did not. A small, easily traversed partition separated the two compartments. As before, the electrified grid was used to produce painful shocks. But this time, the shocks were preceded by a warning signal (a light or a buzzer). The animals, which were attracted to the electrified compartment by food or drink, could avoid pain by jumping over the partition whenever they heard (or saw) the warning signal. Segliman noted that animals behaved quite differently depending on their earlier experience.

Those that had not received previous inescapable shocks were at first quite distressed. They ran all around the compartment looking for some means of escape. Eventually, they learned that safety lay on the other side of the partition. Before long, they also made the connection between the warning signal and the shock. Having made these two discoveries (a means of escape and the implications of the warning signal) these dogs were able to eat and drink in the electrified compartment and still avoid painful shocks by leaping to the safe compartment whenever they heard or saw the warning signal. The animals that had earlier experienced inescapable shock behaved rather differently. Instead of frantically seeking an escape route from the shocks, they simply gave up, lay down on the grid, and passively accepted their fate. Few ever learned how to avoid pain; many simply cowered and whined.

Seligman and his co-worker, Steven Maier, explained these differences in behavior by claiming that the animals which had previously received unavoidable shocks considered efforts to escape to be futile. In their experience, painful outcomes were beyond their control. Thus, they had little motivation to learn how to avoid shocks even when such avoidance was possible. In essence, the previously shocked animals had learned to be helpless.

According to Seligman, "learned helplessness" in animals has many similarities to human depression. Like the previously shocked dogs, depressed people have often experienced painful events over which they have little control—bereavement, illness, failure. Also, like the dogs, chronically depressed people have given up trying to overcome adversity. They simply take whatever comes, reacting with passivity and resignation rather than trying to cope. This superficial similarity between depressed humans and previously shocked dogs has been given further depth by physiological studies demonstrating that helpless dogs have depleted catecholamine levels. Because antidepressant drugs (which relieve human depression by increasing catecholamine levels) have been found to reduce helplessness in previously shocked dogs (as does ECT), it seems reasonable to conclude that human depression and learned helplessness are closely related. Just how closely was shown in studies designed to demonstrate learned helplessness in humans. In one such experiment, two groups of subjects were

FIGURE 6.2 Martin E. P. Seligman (1942–).

exposed to unpleasant loud noise. One group could escape the noise by making a simple response while the other group had no control over the noises. Subjects were then asked to solve simple problems (anagrams, for example). Seligman and his colleagues found that problem-solving performance was impaired among those exposed to uncontrollable noise but not among subjects who were able to escape noise. In other words, the experience of not being in control was enough to cause people to feel helpless, a feeling that attempts to solve the puzzles would be futile. In other studies, Seligman found that people who score high on Beck's *Depression Inventory* have as much trouble with the anagrams as do the nondepressed people who had previously been exposed to uncontrollable noise. This finding provides important additional support for the connection between depression and learned helplessness because it shows that laboratory manipulations designed to produce a feeling of helplessness produce performance similar to the performance exhibited by depressed people.

In his book *Helplessness: On Depression, Development and Death,* Seligman explicitly connects learned helplessness and depression by suggesting that they share a common etiology:

> The model suggests that the cause of depression is the belief that action is futile. What kind of events set off reactive depressions? Failure at work and school, death of a loved one, rejection or separation from friends and loved ones, physical disease, financial difficulty, being faced with unsolvable problems, and growing old. There are many others, but this list captures the flavor.
>
> I believe that what links these experiences and lies at the heart of depressions is unitary; the depressed patient believes or has learned that he cannot control the elements of his life that relieve suffering, bring gratification, or provide nurture — in short, he believes that he is helpless.[2]

According to Seligman, chronically depressed people have developed generalized feelings of impotence. They have given up hope of shaping their own destinies; they have become passive victims of life's vicissitudes. In short, they have become helpless.

AFTERMATH

The learned helplessness theory of depression struck a responsive chord among researchers and clinicians. However, several aspects of the theory caused concern. One was the common tendency, observed by practically all clinicians, for depressed people to blame themselves for their failures. It is not immediately apparent why people who consider themselves helpless to affect their fate should blame themselves when things go wrong. A second concern was the theory's relative neglect of outcome. Why does depression normally dissipate with time? Is learned helplessness only a temporary phenomenon?

In an attempt to deal with these and other problems, Seligman and his co-workers revised the learned helplessness theory. First, to deal with the apparent paradox of helpless people blaming themselves, they introduced a distinction between *universal* and *personal* helplessness. Universal helplessness occurs in response to events that no person could expect to control (natural disasters, accidents, death of loved ones, aging). Personal helplessness, on the other hand, refers to situations in which, contrary to fact, a person feels unable to influence the future. Although both forms of helplessness can cause depression, universal helplessness does not lead to self-blame. Instead, people attribute their failure to outside forces. Personal helplessness, on the other hand, leads to self-blame and low self-esteem because individuals realize that their helplessness is not inevitable but the result of their own behavior.

A similar mechanism was introduced to account for the tendency of depression and helplessness to dissipate over time. That is, if helplessness is thought to result from external forces beyond an individual's control, depression will disappear more quickly than if it is perceived to result from an individual's personal deficiencies (from cowardice, for example).

The revised learned helplessness theory puts considerable emphasis on the idea of attribution — assigning failures to either external or internal (personal) causes. External attributions lead to temporary feelings of helplessness and depression but not to self-blame whereas internal attributions produce a more chronic type of depression in which low self-esteem and self-blame play an important role. Of course, there are degrees of severity, even among internal attributions. Global attributions ("I am stupid") are more pernicious than specific attributions ("I am poor at mathematics") because they can be invoked on many more occasions. People who tend to attribute all failures to enduring, global, personality traits ("I am a coward") are said to have "depressive attributional styles" (a large number of unhappy or unpleasant experiences can trigger a depressive reaction). An important prediction of this formulation is that serious depressions require not only an external triggering event (loss of job, for instance) but also an attributional style that assigns responsibility for the event to some general personal failing ("I am really stupid"). This prediction has been confirmed in a number of studies.

If the belief that one is helpless is a major cause of depression, then it follows that altering this belief should help prevent or at least alleviate depressive disorders. Teaching people how to influence others (social skills, assertiveness training) should reduce depression and increase self-esteem by giving people a sense of control. Changing attributions ("I did not lose my job because I am stupid, I'm just not suited for this particular career") should also help to

DEPRESSION AND THE "ME" GENERATION

For several decades, psychologists in clinical practice have been reporting a marked increase in depression especially among young people. These clinical impressions have been substantiated by large-scale epidemiological surveys which show that people born after 1945 are 10 times more likely to suffer from depression than people born in the decades before World War II. These studies also show that depression is occurring earlier in life. Individuals born in the 1920s and 1930s typically had their first depressive episode when they were in their 30s or 40s. In contrast, people born in the 1950s experienced their first depressive episode while still in their 20s.

Attempts to explain the increase in depression have focused on several different culprits: changes in the gene pool, changes in society, even environmental toxins. Although none of these possibilities can be ruled out, Seligman finds them inadequate to account for the finding that the increase in depression seems confined to Western societies. Suicide, helplessness, and loss of self-esteem are rare in "traditional" cultures, at least until they are modernized. For example, the Amish people of Pennsylvania, a sect that promotes preindustrial life styles and mores, have low levels of depression (despite living in the midst of modern America).

Seligman's explanation for the increasing incidence of depression is the postwar rise of what he calls the "California self" and the demise of the "New England self." The California self is hedonistic, self-absorbed, and concerned mainly with its own feelings whereas the New England self (the self of our grandparents) held traditional values and commitments including family ties, religious faith, devotion to country, and dependence on their local community. When things go wrong—as they inevitably do in everyone's life—the New England self could turn to the family, church, or community for support. These traditional ties served to keep individuals from sinking into despair. The California self, on the other hand, lacks such external supports. Its inward preoccupation prevents life's inevitable blows from being attributed to external forces. When failures are interpreted as the result of one's own inadequacy, self-blame and depression are the inevitable results.

According to Seligman, the incidence of depression is likely to remain high in modern society until at least some of the values of the New England self are reinstated ("we can retain our belief in the importance of the individual while scaling down the self's preoccupation with its own comfort and discomfort"). Individuals need some meaning in their lives, an attachment to something larger than themselves. Religion, nationalism, extended families, community groups have all disintegrated. Until they, or some substitute, are reborn, depression is likely to continue increasing.

---

alleviate depressions. Both of these approaches are widely used today to help depressed patients improve. The parallels between learned helplessness and depression are quite striking (see Table 6.4).

Although the revised theory represents an important modification of the original formulation and has direct implications for therapy, several important problems remain. The first is their inability to account for the physiological symptoms so often present. Are helplessness and faulty attributions the cause of the sleep, appetite, and other disturbances present in depression? If not, what causes

them? A second problem is the relationship between learned helplessness and the psychiatric classifications of depression (unipolar and bipolar). Although Seligman originally focused on "reactive depressions," the revised, attributional theory describes depression in terms that make them sound more similar to bipolar patients having a depressive episode. Learned helplessness cannot account for either the cyclical mood swings or the delusions of grandeur that characterize bipolar disorder. This may be a failing of the theory, or as Seligman has pointed out, the classification scheme may be

TABLE 6.4 A Comparison of Learned Helplessness and Depression

	Learned Helplessness	Depression
Symptoms	Passivity	Passivity
	Cognitive deficits	Negative cognitions
	Self-esteem deficits	Low self-esteem
	Sadness, hostility, anxiety	Sadness, hostility, anxiety
	Loss of appetite	Loss of appetite
	Loss of aggression	Loss of aggression
	Catecholamine deficits	Catecholamine deficits
Cause	Learned belief that one cannot control outcomes (and attributions to stable, internal, global factors)	Feeling that the future is hopeless
Therapy	Change beliefs about the futility of trying to change	Change cognitions
	Drugs	Drugs
	Time	Time

wrong. Seligman has suggested the establishment of a diagnostic category called "helplessness depressions," but so far the psychiatric establishment has preferred to stick with its present scheme.

Despite these problems, there is no doubt that the learned helplessness model has made a major contribution to our understanding of the causes of depression and its treatment. It demonstrates in dramatic form how basic psychological research can shed light on important clinical phenomena.

Further Reading

Becker, R. E., Heimberg, R. G., & Bellack, A. S. (1987). *Social skills training treatment for depression.* Elmsford, NY: Pergamon Press.

Garber, J., & Seligman, M. E. P. (Eds.) (1980). *Human helplessness: Theory and applications.* New York: Academic Press.

Seligman, M. E. P. (1975). *Helplessness: On depression, development and death.* San Francisco: W. H. Freeman.

Notes

1. Cohen, R. A. (1975). Manic-depressive illness. In A. M. Freedman, H. I. Kaplan, & B. J. Sadock (Eds.), *Comprehensive textbook of psychiatry* (Vol. 2, p. 1020). Baltimore: Williams and Wilkins.
2. Seligman, M. E. P. (1975). *Helplessness: On depression, development and death.* San Francisco: W. H. Freeman. P. 93.

CHAPTER 7

Stress and Disease

The central role of emotions in our lives is reflected in our language. There are more than 400 English words to describe feelings (joy, passion, sorrow, fear, anger, love, hate, shame, guilt, and so on), each with a slightly different meaning. Looking down the list, it quickly becomes apparent that emotions are not just moods or feelings, but they also have physiological components (our heart beats faster when we are afraid, for example), cognitive components (we must know that a situation is threatening before we can feel fear), and social components (sometimes, it is best to hide one's true feelings). Because they connect physiology and behavior, emotions have long been implicated as possible causes of physical disease. Indeed, the field of psychosomatic medicine is mainly devoted to studying the effects of emotions on health. The two studies described in this chapter are classics in the history of psychosomatic medicine; they demonstrate how the mind and body interact in health and disease.

EMOTIONS, PHYSIOLOGY, AND BEHAVIOR

Walter Cannon was born in Wisconsin in 1871. Even as a youth, he showed a strong interest in biology, which eventually led him to decide on a career in medicine. Cannon received his medical degree from Harvard University in 1900 but opted for a career as a scientist rather than a practitioner. He spent the rest of his working life as a Harvard academic. Cannon's original interest was the physiology of thirst and hunger. In 1912 he and his collaborator, A. L. Washburn, performed the famous experiments that first showed a connection between hunger pangs and simultaneously occurring stomach contractions. In addition to demonstrating a correlation be-

One of my problems is that I internalize everything. I can't express anger; I grow a tumor instead.

—Woody Allen

tween a psychological state (hunger) and a specific physiological sign (stomach contractions), this early research gave birth to a concept that Cannon was to develop into a full-blown theory over the course of his life—the concept of *homeostasis*.

Homeostatic Mechanisms

Long before Cannon was born, physiologists had noted that the internal environment of most organisms remains remarkably constant despite large fluctuations in the world outside. For example, ambient temperature swings of 40° C, or even greater, have almost no effect on the amount of salt in the body, the concentration of sugar and oxygen in the blood, or most important, body temperature. The body's internal environment is normally so constant that any large change almost always means that the organism is ill. Cannon introduced the term *homeostasis* (which means "equal state") to describe this tendency toward equilibrium and devoted his career to studying how this equal state is achieved. He eventually hit on a "feedback" theory. According to Cannon, the body's homeostatic mechanism works like the thermostat used to control the temperature of a room. The thermostat senses a decrease in room temperature and responds by turning on the furnace until the temperature increases to the desired level. By continually sensing and responding to temperature changes (feedback), the thermostat maintains a steady state.

Human beings, and other mammals, use a similar method to maintain a stable internal temperature. External warming is sensed by receptors both in the skin and inside the body. The first response is usually the dilation (widening) of the blood vessels near the surface of the skin. This causes more blood to flow to the surface of the body where its heat can be lost. Sweating, which cools the body by evaporation, may also begin. Opposite reactions occur in response to external cooling. Blood vessels constrict, and sweating is inhibited. If the external temperature is extremely cold, the body's metabolic rate will increase and shivering will begin. (The increased metabolic rate burns more fat, which produces heat as a by-product; shivering causes the muscles to vibrate, a process that also generates heat.) Of course, in addition to these "involuntary" reactions to temperature change, we humans can also adjust our temperature by taking voluntary actions. When it's cold we can put on more clothing;

when it's hot, we can take cold showers or jump into a cool swimming pool. Thus, there are two ways to maintain homeostasis: involuntary reflexes such as the dilation of blood vessels or sweating and voluntary actions (when it's hot, we can turn on the air conditioning). In both cases, a stable internal environment is produced by a feedback mechanism. Once the desired internal temperature is achieved, the mechanism—sweating, shivering, showering—initiated to change the temperature is switched off.

Cannon was primarily interested in the involuntary reflexes rather than voluntary actions. These reflexes are mediated by the autonomic nervous system and the endocrine glands.

The Autonomic Nervous System and Endocrine Glands

The internal organs of the body are supplied with nerves that activate them. These nerves are known collectively as the autonomic nervous system, or ANS (see Figure 7.1). The ANS is commonly subdivided into two main divisions: the *sympathetic* and the *parasympathetic*. Many of the body's internal organs are connected via nerve fibers to both divisions. These organs can be controlled by the two divisions acting antagonistically. For example, excitation of the sympathetic system causes the heart to accelerate while stimulation of the parasympathetic system slows it down. By balancing these antagonistic forces, the ANS helps to maintain the body in a steady state.

In addition to the ANS, the *endocrine system* is also an important means of controlling the body's internal environment. This system consists of a set of glands that secrete chemicals known as hormones into the bloodstream. These hormones circulate throughout the body affecting organs far removed from the glands themselves. Hormonal stimulation (or inhibition) helps the body to maintain its equilibrium. For example, *insulin*, a hormone produced by the pancreas, acts to maintain the level of sugar in the body. The major functions of the endocrine glands are summarized in Table 7.1.

Cannon theorized that a temporary physiological imbalance (a drop in blood sugar level, for example) results in a "local" physiological reaction (hunger pangs). To explain why the organism responds to these feelings by eating, Cannon suggested that local physiological reactions are associated with subjective states (in this case, hunger). It

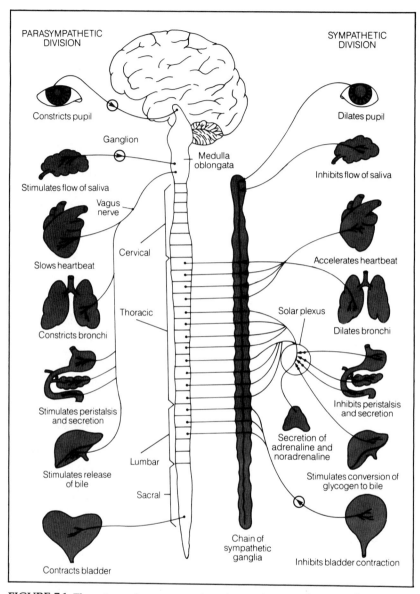

FIGURE 7.1 The autonomic nervous system. As may be seen, the sympathetic division consists mainly of nerves originating in the thoracic and lumbar regions of the spinal cord while the parasympathetic division arises directly from the brain or the lower (sacral) spine. Strong emotions such as fear trigger the sympathetic system, which in turn produces a variety of physiological effects: pupil dilation, dry mouth, faster heartbeat, and so on. These physiological reactions originally evolved to protect the organism from external threat. The parasympathetic system reduces arousal once the threat—and its related strong emotion—dissipates.

TABLE 7.1   Major Functions of the Endocrine Glands

Gland	Major Functions
Anterior pituitary	Stimulates other glands, controls growth and sexual development.
Posterior pituitary	Controls blood pressure, water excretion, and certain muscles.
Thyroid	Controls metabolic rate.
Pancreas islet cells	Affects the level and use of blood sugar.
Adrenal cortex	Has various effects on metabolism and sexual behavior.
Adrenal medulla	Stimulates sugar output. Affects many organs in the same manner as the sympathetic nervous system.
Ovaries	Produces female sexual characteristics, assists gestation.
Testes	Produces male sexual characteristics and causes sexual arousal.

is these feelings, rather than the physiological reactions themselves, which motivate the organism to restore the body's equilibrium by eating. Thus, Cannon assigned the central role in maintaining homeostasis and ensuring the integrity of the organism to subjective feelings.

During World War I, Cannon studied the effects of severe emotional shock ("battle fatigue") on soldiers. He became particularly interested in the effects of combat-induced fear on the functioning of the nervous system and the endocrine glands. His observations of soldiers scarred by battle led him to believe that local physiological reactions not only were associated with basic biological drives such as hunger and thirst but also were involved in producing emotions such as fear and terror. These strong emotions, in turn, motivate certain protective behaviors. Some of these are involuntary reflexes—increased adrenaline secretion, faster respiration, accelerated heart rate, increased alertness—whereas others are voluntary (running away, for example). Surprising as it may seem, and despite its plausibility, Cannon's view—that emotions "cause" behavior—was inconsistent with the accepted wisdom of the time, the James-Lange theory of emotions.

The James-Lange Theory of Emotions

The theory of emotions put forward independently by Cannon's colleague at Harvard, psychologist

William James, and the Danish psychologist Carl Lange around the turn of the century denied that feelings and emotions motivate behavior. On the contrary, according to the James-Lange theory, engaging in specific behaviors *causes* emotions (see Figure 7.2). For example, instead of saying that "I run away because I am afraid," the James-Lange theory asserts that the correct phrasing should be "I'm afraid because I run away." On its surface, the theory seems to defy common sense by putting the horse before the cart. Nevertheless, we have all had experiences that are consistent with it. Think about what happens when you narrowly miss hitting someone who has darted out in front of your car. Chances are, your first act is to slam on the brakes and screech to a halt. Then, after the car is safely stopped you notice that your heart is beating rapidly, your hands are shaking, your face is flushed with sweat, and you feel afraid. As the James-Lange theory predicts, only after the car is stopped and the accident averted is the emotion felt. On a smaller scale, the same thing happens when you slip on a stairway and regain your balance by grabbing the railing. Fear is felt after, not before, the physical reaction.

The Cannon-Barr Theory of Emotions

Cannon was highly critical of the James-Lange theory. He pointed out that many reflexes—hormonal

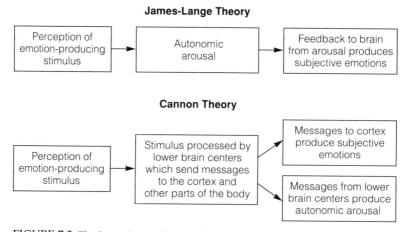

FIGURE 7.2 The James-Lange theory of emotions views subjective feelings as caused by physiological responses controlled by the ANS. Cannon, on the other hand, viewed emotions and autonomic arousal as independent. Both are the result of activation of lower brain centers.

reactions, for example—take place too slowly to cause emotions; people experience strong emotions such as fear well before hormones have a chance to produce any physiological effects. Cannon also criticized the idea that each emotion has associated with it a characteristic ANS and endocrine response pattern. The James-Lange theory requires this assumption to explain how we distinguish one emotion from another. If the physiological concomitants of emotions were not specific, if the same pattern of autonomic and hormonal responses accompanied different emotions, we would be unable to tell whether we were feeling happy or sad.

Cannon's skepticism about the specificity of autonomic reactions was justified by an experiment performed by a Spanish doctor named Gregorio Marañón who injected the hormone adrenaline into 210 patients. The adrenaline produced a pattern of autonomic arousal almost identical to the one produced by strong emotions: accelerated heart rate, flushing, dry mouth, increased respiration, and alertness. When asked how they felt, 70% of Marañón's subjects simply reported their physical reactions without attributing any emotional feeling to them. The remainder reported "emotional-type" feelings but made it quite clear that no emotions were really present. Instead of saying that they felt

happy or afraid, they reported feeling *as if* they were happy or *as if* they were afraid. In other words, Marañón's subjects did not experience emotions as a result of their physiological arousal. They had little difficulty divorcing the physiological effects produced by the adrenaline from the subjective feelings produced by real emotions. Later research by the American psychologist Stanley Schachter confirmed that autonomic arousal is largely nonspecific. The same pattern of physiological arousal is produced during fear as during sexual excitement and even during anger. The subjective emotion an individual experiences is determined not by a specific pattern of autonomic arousal but by the social context in which the autonomic arousal takes place. In a threatening context, autonomic arousal is experienced as fear; in a sporting context, the same pattern of arousal can produce exhilaration. It should be obvious that neither Marañón's nor Schachter's findings are consistent with the James-Lange theory of emotions. Their findings can be explained, however, by a theory put forward by Cannon (with experimental evidence provided by Philip Barr) in the 1920s.

Emotions, Cannon argued, are not produced by specific autonomic reactions nor are autonomic reactions caused by emotions. Instead, both emo-

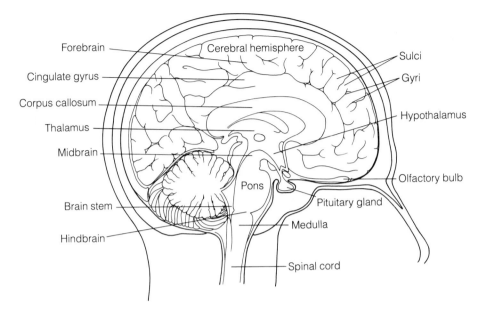

FIGURE 7.3 A cross section of the brain showing the hypothalamus and the pituitary gland.

tions and autonomic activation are controlled by a third agent, the lower brain center known as the thalamus. According to Cannon, an emotionally charged situation (a threatening person encountered on a dark street, for example) produces a reaction in the thalamus which, in turn, sends signals to the ANS, the endocrine glands, and the higher brain cortex simultaneously. The message is interpreted at the cortex as an emotion and by the ANS and endocrine systems as a signal to produce the physiological reactions associated with strong emotion. Thus, according to Cannon, the physiological correlates of emotions and their cognitive interpretation (in this case, fear) are not directly connected. Both are produced by the thalamus' reaction to an emotion-producing situation.

Subsequent investigations have shown that Cannon was wrong about the thalamus; it is not involved in emotions. The correct structure is the *hypothalamus,* an organ that lies just above the brain stem and controls autonomic activation and many hormonal activities (see Figure 7.3). Indeed, the hy-

pothalamus, which is relatively tiny (only a few cubic millimeters), is the major organ of homeostasis. It contains both *receptors* that monitor internal bodily states and mechanisms for adjusting these states. For example, the hypothalamus has sensors that react to the temperature of body fluids and links to the parasympathetic nervous system which controls blood vessel dilation, sweating, and other reflexes designed to lower body temperature. The hypothalamus also has connections to the sympathetic nervous system that can trigger shivering, vasoconstriction, and other reflexes which increase body temperature. These various connections permit the hypothalamus to work like a thermostat sensing internal temperature and making adjustments accordingly. The hypothalamus, of course, is not just a homeostatic center. As already mentioned, it also plays an important part in emotions. For example, electrical stimulation of the hypothalamus produces clear signs of strong emotion, especially fear and anger. Thus, although it appears that Cannon was wrong about the thalamus, he was correct in stating that both emotions and physiological

EMOTIONS AND DEATH

Walter Cannon's interest in emotions and their physiological effects ranged far beyond his physiological studies. He was also interested in anthropology, especially tribal cultures in which "curses" are said to be capable of causing death. In 1942 he published an article in the *American Anthropologist* that contained examples of so-called voodoo death.

Among Australian Aborigines, for example, a curse that involves pointing a bone at an individual is claimed to result in the person's death from fright. Cannon quotes an anthropologist on the subject:

> The man who discovers that he is being boned by an enemy is, indeed, a pitiable sight. He stands aghast, with his eyes staring at the treacherous pointer, and with his hand lifted as though to ward off the lethal medium, which he imagines is pouring into his body. His cheeks blanch and his eyes become glassy and the expression of his face becomes horribly distorted. . . . He attempts to shriek but usually the sound chokes in this throat, and all that one might see is froth at his mouth. His body begins to tremble and the muscles twitch involuntarily. He sways backward and falls to the ground, and after a short time appears to be in a swoon; but soon after he writhes all over in mortal agony, and, covering his face with his hands, begins to moan. After a while he becomes very composed and crawls to his wurley. From this time onwards, he sickens and frets, refusing to eat and keeping aloof from the daily affairs of the tribe. Unless help is forthcoming in the shape of a counter-charm administered by the hands of the . . . medicine man, his death is only a matter of a comparatively short time.*

Although such anecdotal reports must be treated with caution, Cannon believed in their veracity. He described postmortem examinations of those who died voodoo deaths that found no evidence of physical illness. Cannon attributed such deaths to the intense autonomic arousal produced by fear. Animal studies, in which laboratory animals have been exposed to frightening situations, have likewise confirmed the severely debilitating, even fatal, effects of strong emotion.

---

*Basedow, H. (1925). *The Australian Aboriginal*. Adelaide: F. W. Preece. Pp. 178–179.

---

arousal are controlled by the lower brain center responsible for homeostasis.

Although Cannon's theory, as described so far, explained the facts, it seems rather incomplete. Specifically, if emotions do not cause physiological reactions, it is not clear why emotions ever evolved. What purpose is there in feeling an emotion if that feeling has no effect on the survival of the organism? According to Cannon, the answer lies in a distinction between specific motives and general arousal. Activation of the ANS and the endocrine system is general and nonspecific. It produces the resources to energize a response, but it does not specify a behavior. Emotions, on the other hand, motivate specific behaviors many of which are voluntary (fleeing a threatening situation, for example). Together, ANS arousal and the emotions constitute an *emergency reaction* that allows the body to marshal the resources necessary to cope with demanding situations.

Emergency Reaction: Fight or Flight

Cannon drew a strong distinction between the functions of the sympathetic and parasympathetic nervous systems. The parasympathetic system, he argued, was concerned with the body's normal, *vegetative* functions: waste disposal, metabolism, reproduction. Its influence is felt when the organism is calm—it lowers heart rate, aids in digestion, assists elimination, and helps control sexual behavior. The sympathetic system, in contrast, serves mainly to arouse and activate the organism. The two systems work in opposition. Parasympathetic impulses slow the heart rate, sympathetic impulses speed it up; parasympathetic activity stores sugar for future use, sympathetic impulses metabolize the stored sugar to provide energy for the body. The arousal-producing potential of the sympathetic nervous system is amplified by its effect on the endocrine system. That is, sympathetic arousal stimulates the production of hormones that serve to arouse the body even further.

Intense sympathetic arousal with its associated hormonal stimulation results in what Cannon called an "emergency reaction." This reaction energizes the organism to deal with demands greater than those made by everyday homeostasis; they help the organism to survive under extraordinary conditions. Cannon gave the example of a grazing animal, calmly maintaining homeostasis, who suddenly spots the approach of a predator. All nonessential vegetative functions are shut down as the animal undergoes intense sympathetic activation. Extra energy is directed toward the muscles, heart, and lungs to help the animal flee. Cannon claimed that a similar reaction occurs when the animal attacks rather than runs away. The heart accelerates, the pupils dilate, and sugar metabolism is increased. Although both flight and fight help the organism to survive, Cannon could not predict which course any particular individual would take. This depends on the animal's habits as well as on the specific context. Many animals instinctually try to flee threatening situations but will fight once cornered; others fight almost from the outset. Some flee only novel threats not previously experienced; others fight any threat. (Cannon felt that humans show a similar diversity of reactions to strong emotions such as fear.)

In addition to fight or flight, intense fear also produces some familiar side effects—digestive upsets and impotence are the most common. These side effects can be traced to the inhibition of the parasympathetic system. Not quite so easy to explain is the loss of bladder or bowel control that often accompanies intense fear. Because the parasympathetic system, which is responsible for relaxing the relevant sphincters, is inhibited during sympathetic activation, it is not at all obvious why fear should cause involuntary urination and defecation. Cannon guessed that prolonged arousal causes the reciprocal inhibition of the parasympathetic and sympathetic systems to break down. In other words, both systems are activated at the same time.

During his career, Cannon conducted considerable basic research into the endocrine glands (he was the discoverer of the hormone *sympathin*, which stimulates heart activity). However, he is best remembered for his delineation of the emergency reaction and his descriptions of how organisms attempt to deal with significant threats to homeostasis. Cannon's ideas exerted considerable influence on the fields of physiology, medicine, and psychology, but they turned out to be only a starting point for the more comprehensive work of the endocrinologist and physiologist Hans Selye.

HANS SELYE: MEDICAL PHYSIOLOGIST

Hans Hugo Selye was born in Vienna in 1907, but he grew up in a provincial city that is now part of Czechoslovakia. Selye's father was a fourth-generation doctor whose thriving medical practice was managed by his wife, a driven perfectionist whose intellectual interests and strong need for achievement exerted a powerful effect on her son's character.

Selye followed the family tradition studying medicine in Prague, Paris, and Rome. In 1929 he received a medical degree from the German University of Prague; in 1931 he was awarded a Ph.D. in chemistry from the same institution. Selye spent a postdoctoral year at Johns Hopkins University in Baltimore before moving to McGill University in Montreal, the city where he was to spend the rest of his life. From early in his career, Selye was interested in endocrinology, especially the role played by hormones in health and disease. His biochemical research on hormones continued throughout his career providing him with a solid basis for what would become his life's work: understanding the psychophysiological effects of *stress*.

The term "stress" is used so commonly in psychology, and in everyday life, that few people realize it was Selye who gave the word its modern meaning. Selye used the word to refer to physical threats to homeostasis (bacteria, trauma), but the concept has gradually grown to encompass a bewildering number of potential sources of stress. Fear, illness, work pressure, extreme temperatures, poor diet, sleep loss, divorce, child care, even vacations and sudden wealth have been described as "stressful." At first glance, these disparate "stressors" appear to have little or nothing in common: some are physiological, others are social; some are clearly unpleasant, others, such as sudden wealth, are normally considered desirable. Attempts to find a defining principle that characterizes all stressors have proven futile—the various sources of stress do not appear to share any intrinsic characteristics. Nevertheless, Selye believed that fundamentally different stressors can still be tied together. The way to do this, he argued, is to focus not on the stressors themselves but on their psychophysiological effects. Selye believed that, in addition to their specific effects, all stressors elicit similar coping responses. He called the body's "nonspecific" attempt to cope with stress the *general adaptation syndrome*.

CLASSIC STUDY 13
The General Adaptation Syndrome

As a young man, Selye was mainly interested in endocrinology. In an attempt to discover a new sex hormone, he injected rats with hormonal extracts derived from ovarian tissue. He observed several important effects: an enlargement of the adrenal gland, a shrinkage of the thymus gland—a gland that helps fight disease—and the development of gastric ulcers. Because no known hormone produced this collection of symptoms, Selye believed that he had uncovered a new one. His elation was soon shattered, however, by his discovery that the injection of other tissue extracts produced precisely the same effects. Indeed, injecting rats with almost any foreign substance shrunk the adrenal and thymus glands and produced ulcers. Selye struggled to make sense of these results:

> All my dreams of discovering a new hormone were shattered. All the time and all the materials that went into long study were wasted. . . . I be-

came so depressed that for a few days I could not do any work at all. I just sat in my laboratory brooding. . . . The ensuing period of introverted contemplation turned out to be the decisive factor in my whole career; it pointed the way for all my subsequent work. . . . As I repetitiously continued to go over my ill-fated experiments and their possible interpretation, it suddenly struck me that one could look at them from an entirely different angle. If there was such a thing as a single non-specific reaction of the body to damage of any kind . . . the general medical implications of the syndrome would be enormous![1]

Selye decided to pursue the possibility that various sources of stress produce similar physiological reactions by studying how animals react to different challenges: heat, cold, toxic materials, electric shock, surgery, and involuntary restraint. For want of a better term, Selye called these noxious agents "stressors," and he called the effect they produced "stress." Selye later said that "strain" would have been more precise. He blamed his poor English for choosing the wrong word. In any event, "stress" caught on and has been part of the psychological and medical vocabulary ever since. Selye's first paper on the general psychophysiological effects of different stressors appeared in 1936. In that article, he described the organism's initial response to stress, which he called the *alarm reaction*. In the following years, Selye continued to build on his observations until, in 1950, he published an 800-page book called *The Physiology and Pathology of Exposure to Stress: A Treatise on the Concept of the General Adaptation Syndrome and the Diseases of Adaptation*. This major work contained thousands of references and surveyed just about everything that was known about stress at the time. A more accessible book on the same topic, *The Stress of Life,* followed in 1956 (revised 1976). Together, these books ensured that the general adaptation syndrome would become well known to both scientific and lay audiences.

Selye's early observations led him to assume that "stress endangers life, unless it is met by adequate adaptive responses." Individual stressors elicit specific defensive reactions (for example, a bacterial infection triggers the production of specific antibodies), but all stressors set off "an integrated syndrome of closely related adaptive reactions to nonspecific stress itself." This nonspecific, general adaptation syndrome (GAS) consists of three stages: the alarm reaction, the stage of resistance, and the stage of exhaustion.

The Alarm Reaction

As its name suggests, the first stage of the GAS is one of general preparedness—an organic burglar alarm that is triggered no matter who, or what, intruded. In a manner similar to Cannon's "emergency reaction," which it closely resembles, the alarm reaction ensures that the body is put on alert. The autonomic nervous system and the endocrine system begin to mobilize the body's defenses. Heart rate increases, breathing becomes quicker, and the organism becomes more alert. Stress, whatever its source, also causes the anterior pituitary gland to secrete *adrenocorticotrophic hormone* (ACTH) into the bloodstream. ACTH stimulates the adrenal gland to produce chemicals known as *corticoids*. The corticoids are an important line of defense (they control tissue inflammation, for example).

The Stage of Resistance

If stress persists, the organism moves into the resistance phase of the GAS. If the alarm reaction can be thought of as the mobilization of internal defenses, then the resistance stage is more like all-out war. Many of the manifestations of the alarm reaction disappear as the organism attempts to limit local tissue damage. For example, in place of the corticoids produced during the alarm reaction, the adrenal cortex begins to produce *glucocorticoids*. These hormones, which include steroids such as cortisone, have different effects from those produced in the alarm reaction. The glucocorticoids promote an increase in available blood sugar, which provides extra energy to combat stress while also reducing inflammation and pain. Unfortunately, the same hormones reduce the body's resistance to infection. They cause wounds to heal more slowly, inhibit antibody formation, decrease the number of disease-fighting white blood cells, and depress the production of sexual and reproductive hormones. Thus, in the resistance stage, the organism uses its resources to avoid immediate tissue damage. However, short-term protection comes at a price: the potential long-term weakening of the body (lowered resistance to infection, fatigue, and so on).

The Stage of Exhaustion

If the stress persists beyond the stage of resistance, the organism's defenses become increasingly depleted. Illness and disease become more likely as the body slips into exhaustion. Ultimately, should the stress continue, the organism will almost certainly sustain some permanent damage and could even die.

Individual Differences and Diseases of Adaptation

Selye argued that the traditional approach of medical researchers (looking for the specific manifestations of different diseases) was valuable for making differential diagnoses and for treatment planning but it ignored the role of the GAS, which is common to all diseases. For example, diabetes and sickle-cell anemia produce different problems, are identified using different laboratory tests, and are subjected to different treatments. Yet both diseases, indeed all diseases, also affect general fitness, sleep patterns, energy level, and many other aspects of general body functioning. According to Selye, these non-specific effects, which are produced by any stressor, can also cause disease as they cause the body's defenses to crumble. Selye referred to illnesses produced this way as "diseases of adaptation." These include, but are not limited to, gastric ulcers, hypertension, headaches, rashes, allergies, coronary heart disease, asthma, arthritis, and diabetes.

Selye realized that the idea that "widely different maladies should result from the same cause" was contrary to the usual medical assumption that all illnesses have specific etiologies. He justified his theory by asserting that stressors have both specific and general effects. A specific bacterium, for example, may attack the lungs and, if left unchecked, will cause pulmonary disease. At the same time, the bacterium will set off a GAS which, if prolonged, will also contribute to the disease process by debilitating the body's general defenses. To explain why individuals develop different diseases in response to what appears to be the same stressor, Selye hypothesized the existence of individual differences that can mediate the effects of the GAS. These differences may be genetic—individuals may inherit a specific weakness in one or more organ systems making them especially vulnerable to

POSTTRAUMATIC STRESS DISORDER

Kevin is a 43-year-old who lost an arm in Vietnam. He married soon after his discharge from the Army, but the marriage did not last. He has held a series of jobs but none long enough to achieve any advancement. In the past 10 years, Kevin has twice attempted suicide by overdosing on the drugs to which he has been addicted on and off since the war. His second suicide attempt led to a 6-week psychiatric hospitalization. While in the hospital, Kevin was frequently reported to wake up screaming. He recounted dreams of slaughter and mayhem. In calmer moments, he expressed guilt that he survived the war while some of his buddies perished.

Veterans of all wars suffer psychologically. "Shell shock" and "combat fatigue" were relatively common syndromes among veterans of World Wars I and II, respectively. But Vietnam was different. The soldiers were younger than those of the past (their average age was only 19), and there were no clear front lines. Soldiers were constantly under threat of unpredictable guerrilla attacks, they lived in unfamiliar jungle conditions, and they often had difficulty telling friend from foe. The result was a particular propensity to develop various psychological problems. To mental-health professionals, these problems seemed to occur together often enough to constitute a distinct syndrome. To-

day, this syndrome—which affects Kevin and many others—has become widely known as *posttraumatic stress disorder*.

The major characteristics of posttraumatic stress disorder are: frequent nightmares in which the trauma is relived, anxiety attacks, sleep disturbances, distractibility, apathy, loss of former interests, feeling "numb," and a sense of guilt about escaping the fate of others. In some cases, posttraumatic stress disorder may develop immediately after a disaster. In other cases, it may lie dormant for weeks, months or even years only to be triggered off by some relatively minor incident. Posttraumatic stress disorder may persist indefinitely. For example, studies of Nazi concentration camp survivors have found symptoms to persist for decades.

Posttraumatic stress disorder became widely known because of its high incidence among Vietnam War veterans. But one does not have to be a casualty of war to develop the disorder. Survivors of catastrophes such as train crashes or natural disasters such as earthquakes and victims of violent crime may also develop the syndrome. All that is required is that the individual experience extreme stress. Posttraumatic stress disorder is an unfortunate example of the potential deleterious effects of stress on health.

stress—or they may arise from other sources: inadequate diet, previous infections, and so on (see Figure 7.4).

In summary, then, Selye's position was that the GAS constitutes the body's response to any source of stress. If adaptation is unsuccessful, disease can result. The specific disease depends on such factors as genetics, diet, medications, and previous illnesses. A full understanding of disease, therefore, requires knowledge of how specific stressors, individual differences, and the GAS interact.

Selye worked at McGill until 1942 when he left to take up the position of Director of Experimental

Medicine and Surgery at the University of Montreal. Working with a fluctuating group of up to 30 international scientists (Selye spoke eight languages), he spent the next 40 years expanding and deepening his understanding of the GAS. His determination to succeed, a trait he may have inherited from his mother, resulted in a prodigious body of work. During his career, he published more than 1,700 scientific articles and around 40 books. He also received 17 honorary degrees, was elected a Companion of the Order of Canada, and was awarded 80 medals and prizes. He was still actively at work at the time of his death in 1982.

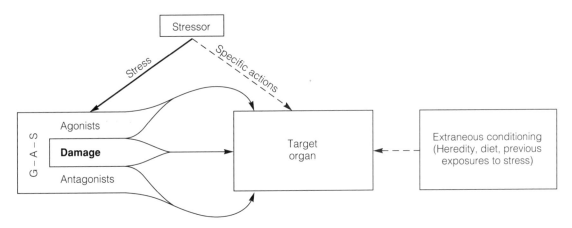

FIGURE 7.4 Selye's theory of the diseases of adaptation. Stressors have both general effects that are mediated through the GAS's connections to the ANS and specific effects on certain body organs. (Agonists stimulate the ANS while antagonists inhibit it.) Extra factors such as heredity and diet also help determine an individual's idiosyncratic response to stress.

AFTERMATH

Although it was soon discovered that the GAS is not as general as Selye first thought — there are subtle differences in the GAS by various stressors — no scientist seriously disagreed with Selye's assertion that prolonged stress can cause physical deterioration and disease. Selye was criticized, however, for omitting psychological and social factors from his analysis. Unlike Cannon, who specifically emphasized the importance of the emotions, Selye concentrated on physical stressors and the physiological response to stress. Although he noted them in later books, Selye paid little attention to psychological variables.

Psychologists were quick to demonstrate the inadequacy of Selye's purely physiological approach. Studies of animals and humans showed that the stress produced by any particular stressor depends to a great degree on how it is perceived psychologically. For example, your first job interview is likely to elicit a greater alarm reaction than your second or third. In other words, familiarity with a stressor reduces its psychophysiological effects. "Predictability" also reduces the effects of stress. Laboratory animals, for example, produce a more intense ANS and endocrine reaction to unpredict-

able electric shock than to shocks of exactly the same voltage that occur on a predictable schedule. Providing animals with a way of avoiding or shutting off the shock reduces the stress response even further (see Figure 7.5). This last finding suggests that "controllability" also determines a stressor's effect. The influence of familiarity, predictability, and controllability demonstrates the important role that psychological factors play in mediating the physiological response to stress. It would appear that a full understanding of how stress causes disease requires that we consider the influence of psychological factors.

The notion that psychological factors can produce disease is hardly a new idea. Indeed, it is one of the oldest concepts in medicine. It lies at the very basis of the field known as *psychosomatics*.

ORIGINS OF PSYCHOSOMATICS

Like most modern medical ideas, the relationship between the emotions and physical health was first described by the ancient Greek physician Hippocrates. Observing that fear produces sweat and that shame causes heart palpitations, Hippocrates advised doctors to always assume an unworried facial expression

"Executive" rat   **"Subordinate" rat**   **Control rat**

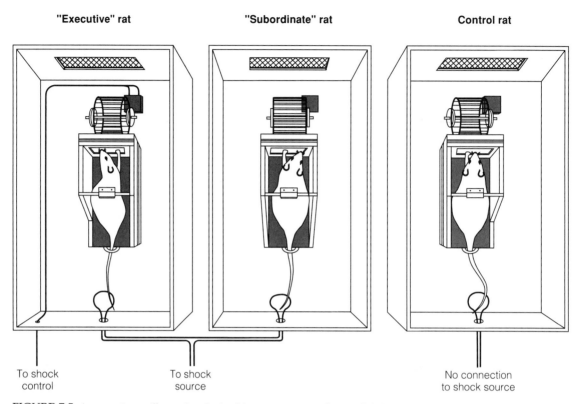

To shock   To shock   No connection
control   source   to shock source

FIGURE 7.5 An experiment illustrating the health consequences of controllability. The "executive" rat can control the electric shock to its tail by turning the wheel. The subordinate rat has no control over the shock. The control rat receives no shock at all. Neither the control nor the executive rat develops gastric ulcers. The subordinate, on the other hand, does develop ulcers as well as a lower immunity to disease. Thus, the same external stressor has different effects on health depending on its controllability.

and never to castigate patients for their intemperate habits. A similar theme was taken up by the philosopher Aristotle, who linked the emotions of anger, fear, courage, and joy to specific bodily states. According to Aristotle, doctors should calm the angry and reassure the fearful because anger and fear brought illness while joy and courage restored health. Galen, the Greek physician whose ideas formed the basis of medicine for 1,000 years, was also acutely aware of the important physiological effects produced by emotions. The reader may recall Galen's observation that a female patient's pulse tended to race whenever the name of a certain male dancer was mentioned (see the Introduction for more on this inci-

dent). For some unexplained reason, the wisdom of the classical doctors seems to have been neglected during the Middle Ages in favor of the theory that all illness is caused by demons inhabiting the body. The Renaissance brought an end to demonology, but doctors continued to ignore the psychological factors in disease. Instead, they concentrated on learning as much as possible about anatomy and physiology. It was not until the 19th century that clinicians once again became interested in the effects of the emotions on health. This interest culminated in the work of Sigmund Freud, who explicitly implicated the emotions as potential causes of both mental and physical illness.

Following Freud, psychological factors began to be implicated in many illnesses. These were referred to as *psychophysiological* or *psychosomatic* diseases because it was believed that psychological ("psycho") forces cause the physical ("somatic") symptoms. Examples of disorders considered to have a psychosomatic component are listed in Table 7.2. Among the post-Freudian psychoanalysts, the individual most concerned with psychosomatic illness was Franz Alexander, who put forward the *specificity theory* of psychosomatic disease.

The Specificity Theory

Franz Alexander was born in Hungary and migrated to the United States in the 1930s. He became active in Chicago psychoanalytic circles where he devoted his considerable energies to the study of psychosomatic disorders. Alexander argued that emotional conflicts, even when they are unconscious, produce physiological stress. If left unchecked, this stress can produce a physical illness — the specific illness depending on the nature of the underlying conflict. For example, according to Alexander, "the crucial factor in the pathogenesis of ulcer is the frustration of the dependent, help-seeking and love-demanding desires. When these desires cannot find gratification in human relationships, a chronic emotional stimulus is created which has a specific effect on the functions of the stomach." Similarly, Alexander believed that high blood pressure is caused by the "damming up" of "hostile impulses." Because Alexander believed that psychosomatic illnesses are caused by specific emotional conflicts, his theory became known as the specificity theory.

Alexander's theory is easily criticized on methodological and theoretical grounds. Methodologically, his conclusions are weak because he studied only people who had already become sick. It is entirely possible that the emotional conflicts he described were caused by his patients' physical illnesses rather than the other way around. That is, having an ulcer may cause a person to become dependent and demanding while high blood pressure (or the drugs used to treat it) may cause people to become hostile. From a theoretical perspective, this "reversed" sequence of causation is consistent with the James-Lange theory of emotions described earlier.

TABLE 7.2 Examples of "Psychosomatic" Disorders

Acne	Nausea
Allergy	Obesity
Angina pectoris	Premenstrual syndrome
Asthma	Rheumatoid arthritis
Coronary heart disease	Skin rashes
Diabetes	Tachycardia
Headache	Ulcers
Immune diseases	Vomiting
Irritable bowel	Ulcerative colitis
Migraine	Warts

Like the James-Lange theory, Alexander's specificity theory assumed that different emotions (and emotional conflicts) produce different physiological reactions. If the physiological effects of various emotions were identical, then not only would we be unable to distinguish one emotion from another but we would be unable to link specific emotions to specific diseases. Unfortunately, as already discussed, physiologists have failed to identify specific patterns of physiological responding that correspond to different emotional states. Instead, as Selye demonstrated, the physiological response to stress is the nonspecific activation of the autonomic nervous system. Not surprisingly, therefore, researchers in psychosomatic medicine began to look toward the nonspecific effects of stress for an explanation of how stress affects health.

The Nonspecific Stress Theory

The nonspecific stress theory is simply an extension of Selye's GAS to include psychological stressors. The list of potential psychological and social stressors is quite long: bereavement, divorce, work pressure, financial setbacks, and so on. Like the physical stressors studied by Selye, these social and psychological stressors can also set off a GAS. The initial symptoms produced by psychological stress are the same as those in the alarm reaction: dry mouth, heavy breathing, release of hormones, rapid heartbeat, perspiration, trembling, hot flushes, and a sinking feeling in the pit of the stomach. Prolonged

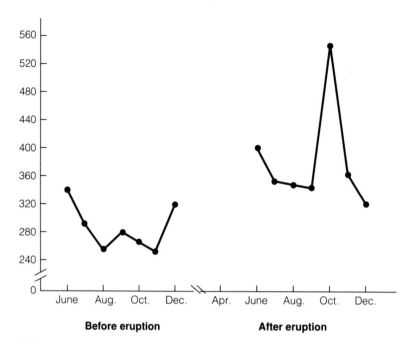

FIGURE 7.6 Catastrophic events can produce important effects on health. This graph shows emergency-room visits in the months before and after the eruption of the Mt. St. Helens volcano in 1980. The data, collected by psychologists from a hospital near the volcano, show a large increase in consultations during the months following the eruption.

emotional arousal can result in the organism moving further into the GAS thereby increasing the possibility that physical deterioration will lead to the development of disease. The specific disease depends on an individual's genetic predispositions and life history.

The nonspecific stress theory has been broadened in recent years to what has become known as a holistic perspective. Instead of singling out a specific group of disorders with psychological causes, the holistic view contends that all illnesses, whether traditionally considered psychosomatic or not, involve the interplay of biological and psychological factors. The American Psychiatric Association adopted the holistic view in their *Diagnostic and Statistical Manual* (DSM-III-R) which no longer includes psychosomatic (or the related term, "psychophysiological") disorders as a diagnostic category. Instead, the manual included a category called "psychological factors affecting physical condition."

This change makes it clear that psychological factors can initiate, maintain or exacerbate just about any physical condition.

Causes of Psychological Stress

When asked to imagine the psychological and social causes of stress, most people immediately think of large-scale catastrophes: floods, earthquakes, hurricanes, and accidents (see Figure 7.6). Such events are unpredictable, horrifying, and doubtless exert an important effect on health. However, the more common psychological causes of stress are small-scale and apply to a single individual. These stressors usually come in the form of life changes such as job loss, bereavement, divorce, or a new baby. Studies have found such life events do appear to presage illness. For example, a recent study of 96,000 Finnish widows and widowers found a doubled risk of death among survivors in the week immediately following their partner's death. Be-

TABLE 7.3   Social Readjustment Rating Scale

Life Event	Life-Change Units
Death of spouse	100
Divorce	73
Separation	65
Jail term	63
Death of close family member	63
Personal injury or illness	53
Marriage	50
Loss of job	47
Retirement	45
Gaining new family member	39
Mortgage of $10,000 or more	31
Outstanding personal achievement	28
Begin or end school	26
Trouble with boss	23
Change in residence	20
Change in sleeping habits	16
Vacation	13
Christmas	12
Minor violations of the law	11

Source: Adapted from Holmes, T. H., & Rahe, R. H. (1967). The Social Readjustment Rating Scale. *Journal of Psychosomatic Research, 11,* 213–218.

Note: 150 points = a life crisis, 300 = major crisis.

reavement combined with other life changes such as job loss were found to increase the risk even further.

To measure the stress produced by life events, researchers have created rating scales. An example is the *Social Readjustment Rating Scale,* in which various life events have each been assigned a certain number of "life-change units" according to their stress-producing potential (see Table 7.3). Summing the points assigned to the items an individual has experienced in the past year is supposed to give an indication of that individual's risk of developing a stress-related illness. These scores should be interpreted with caution, however. Careful studies have found such scales to be only weak predictors of future health. This is probably because the scales are incomplete. As noted by Selye's critics, the same

physical stressor can have different effects depending on psychological factors. This is also true of life events. An individual with specific retirement plans and the means to achieve them may look forward to leaving work, whereas another person, whose identity is intimately wrapped up in work, may dread the very prospect of retirement. Ignoring these individual differences, rating scales assign both people the same number of life-change units. It is not surprising, therefore, that the scale is a poor predictor of future health.

As an alternative to life-change scales, some researchers have attempted to measure the stress produced by the events of everyday life. They have looked at daily "hassles": time spent in rush-hour traffic or waiting at the bank, noisy neighbors, getting caught in the rain or snow. These stressors are clearly trivial when compared with catastrophes or with the life events listed in the Social Readjustment Rating Scale. Nevertheless, they can take their toll. For example, busy urban white-collar workers, who are exposed to many more daily annoyances than their rural counterparts, are considerably more likely to suffer from headaches, ulcers, and hypertension.

Although catastrophes, life changes, and the stress of daily living can lead to illness, it should be reiterated that individuals vary a great deal in their response to the same stressors. Selye suggested that heredity, diet, and previous illness may determine how an organism responds to various stressors. It is also possible that learned styles of behaving and personality traits may play a role in mediating the stress response. The most compelling evidence we have that personality affects health comes from the classic work on coronary heart disease.

CLASSIC STUDY 14

Type A Behavior and Coronary Heart Disease

Coronary heart disease, caused primarily by the narrowing of the blood vessels supplying the heart, has become the leading cause of death in most industrialized countries. Yet, until recently, coronary heart disease was relatively rare. At least some of the increased incidence may be explained by longevity; as people live longer, they become more susceptible to heart attacks. But longevity is not the whole story. Coronary heart disease is also an important cause of death among middle-aged and even young adults. To explain why coronary heart disease, so rare in the past, has become so common, researchers have focused on such potential risk factors as smoking, obesity, genetics, inactivity, diet, hypertension, and high levels of blood cholesterol. Although each has been found to contribute to the risk of heart disease, no single factor or combination of factors is able to explain why the illness has become more common among the young and middle-aged. Hypertension, high-fat diets, obesity, and smoking were common in the 19th century when heart disease was relatively rare.

In the 1950s, when the increase in heart disease was first being noticed, two American cardiologists, Meyer Friedman and Ray Rosenman, were studying cholesterol metabolism. It had long been suspected that fats like cholesterol accumulating in the blood were responsible for the blocking of blood vessels, but it was unclear to the researchers whether dietary habits, such as consuming too much unsaturated fat, were sufficient to account for the build-up of fatty deposits. In a study of San Francisco couples, for example, Friedman and Rosenman found that, while both partners consumed about the same amount of unsaturated fat, husbands were much more susceptible to heart disease than their wives. After ruling out the possible influence of sex hormones, Friedman and Rosenman fell back on an idea first put forward by the famous turn-of-the-century physician Sir William Osler, who described the typical heart patient as "a keen and ambitious man, the indicator of whose engine is always full speed ahead." Noting that husbands, at least in the 1950s, were more likely to be driving and ambitious than their wives, Friedman and Rosenman came up with a theory that would have pleased Selye greatly. They hypothesized that what differentiates those who succumb to heart disease from those who do not is adaptability to stress.

As a first-step exploration, Friedman and Rosenman surveyed a selection of doctors and businessmen asking what factors they thought were responsible for the heart attacks suffered by their patients and colleagues. The answers consistently suggested that the stress of striving for advancement and success played an important role.

Armed with this consensus opinion, Friedman and Rosenman undertook a field experiment. They decided to study a sample of taxation accountants whom they knew had an important, stress-producing deadline to meet—the April 15th date for filing income tax returns. The experimenters measured the level of blood cholesterol and blood-clotting speed (blood clots are responsible for much serious heart damage) in the accountants at intervals beginning in January and ending in June. They hypothesized that stress would increase as the April 15th deadline approached and that this stress could be demonstrated physiologically. Their hypothesis was confirmed. The accountants evidenced normal cholesterol levels and blood-clotting speed early in the year. As the April 15th deadline approached, both cholesterol levels and blood-clotting speed measures became dangerously abnormal. By June, with the deadline well behind them, the accountants' cholesterol and blood-clotting speed returned to normal. It appeared that psychological stress, probably mediated by Selye's GAS, can put individuals at risk for coronary heart disease.

The results obtained in their study of accountants led Friedman and Rosenman to take on an even more ambitious project, the Western Collaborative Group Study. Three thousand healthy men between the ages of 35 and 59 were interviewed about their health, work habits, and diet. During this 15-minute interview, each man's rate of speech, posture, aggressiveness, and signs of impatience (head nodding, knee jiggling, rapid eye blinking) were noted (see Table 7.4). Those who seemed the most ambitious, impatient, competitive, and short-tempered were called Type A. The more easygoing subjects were called Type B. The men were then followed for the next decade. During that time, 257 of the original 3,000 men developed coronary heart disease. Of these, 178 had previously been classified Type A. In other words, Type A's were twice as likely to develop heart disease as Type B individuals. A further analysis showed that, of the most extreme Type B's—those who were judged to be the least competitive and aggressive—not a single one developed heart disease.

As you might expect, Friedman and Rosenman's findings caused a major sensation. Newspapers and magazines published questionnaires that their readers could use to classify themselves as Type A or Type B. Therapists began to offer treatment to

TABLE 7.4   Interview Indicators of Type A
            Behavior

Time Pressure

Facial tautness

Rapid eye blinking

Knee jiggling, finger tapping

Head nodding when speaking

Hurried speech

Interrupting interviewer with answers to incomplete
questions

Excessive perspiration

Competitiveness and Hostility

Clenched jaw and drawing back of lip to expose teeth

Hostile laughter

Clenched fist, table pounding

Frequent obscenities

Reacting in hostile manner to interviewer's questions

Reporting irritation when kept waiting or when driving

Distrust of the motives of others

Always playing to win, even children's games

change Type A's into Type B's. Meanwhile, the scientific community began to try to identify precisely why Type A personalities are more likely to develop coronary heart disease. Two possible mechanisms have been put forward. This first is indirect. Type A people have been found more likely to smoke, drink coffee, and stay up late than Type B people. It is possible that it is the smoking, caffeine, and poor sleeping habits and not the Type A behaviors themselves that cause coronary heart disease. The alternative possibility is that Type A behaviors have a direct effect on health. Some support for this position comes from studies that have found Type A's to be more physiologically reactive to stress than Type B's. When faced with a stressor, their hormonal secretions are greater than those of Type B's and their heart rate and blood pressure are higher as well. Frequent and extreme alarm reactions cause blood to be diverted away from the liver, which normally removes excess cholesterol from the blood. Thus, a combination of habitually high hormonal secretion rates and an underactive liver could result in the build-up of cholesterol in the coronary arteries.

AFTERMATH

With a result as important as the link between Type A behavior and coronary heart disease, it was inevitable that other researchers would try to repeat the studies performed by Friedman and Rosenman. To date, there have been dozens of such experiments. The results of these studies have not always confirmed the original findings. There are several possible reasons why the various studies have produced discrepant results. One possibility may be found in the specifics of experimental design. Some studies use the same technique as Friedman and Rosenman. They measure Type A behavior while the subjects are still healthy and then follow the subjects for some years to see who becomes ill. Other studies obtain a sample of people who already have coronary heart disease and then test to see whether they have Type A behavior. The latter procedure is distinctly inferior because it is always possible that it is the disease that is responsible for the patient's behavior rather than the other way around.

Another possible reason for the inconsistent results is the varying methods used by different researchers to classify people as Type A or Type B. Instead of the 15-minute interview procedure used by Friedman and Rosenman, some studies have used self-report questionnaires to classify their subjects. These questionnaires do not correlate very well with the interview procedure and are not as good predictors of future illness. Rosenman has defended the interview procedure because he does not believe that Type A behavior is a personality trait that can be measured by a questionnaire. He prefers to think of Type A behaviors as a set of learned habits that may occur in people with quite different personalities. Such behaviors are easier to observe as they actually happen during an interview than they are to measure with questionnaires. Thus, it is not surprising that the two methods of classification yield conflicting results.

Recent research suggests that not all Type A behaviors are equally predictive of coronary heart disease. The crucial difference between Type A and Type B personality appears not to be competitiveness or striving to succeed but anger and aggression. Considerations such as these have led to increasingly sophisticated attempts, focusing mainly on hostility, to modify Type A behaviors in the hope

PSYCHONEUROIMMUNOLOGY

Although the idea that psychological states can affect physical health goes back to antiquity, modern medicine has tended to ignore psychological factors in favor of physiology, bacteriology, and virology. This is beginning to change as doctors recognize the important etiological role played by stress. For example, in the 1960s and 1970s, researchers inspired by Selye's work on stress began to investigate the effects of stress on the immune systems of laboratory animals. They found that laboratory rats exposed to stress produced weaker immune responses to bacteria and to viruses. The animals grew more tumors and lost the capacity to combat parasites.

Stress appears to have a similar affect on humans. Bereavement, for example, has been found to lead to illness (or even death). Although fascinating, this research has been met with skepticism by many doctors who demand detail about the exact mechanism by which psychological factors affect physical health. At least part of the answer had already been provided by Selye. The glucocorticoids, like cortisone, released during the GAS have a suppressive effect on the body's immune system. But in recent years, it has become clear that this is not the only mechanism by which stress affects immunity. There appear to be direct effects as well. An important insight into the way in which stress affects health has been provided by psychologist Christopher Coe from the University of Wisconsin.

Coe and his colleagues were interested in the immune effects produced by removing infants from their mothers. Clearly, they could not remove human infants from their mothers, so they studied monkeys. They injected a mild, non-symptom-producing bacterium into monkeys that were left with their mothers and into monkeys that were separated and placed in an unfamiliar environment for 7 days. They found that the separated monkeys produced fewer antibodies (to fight off infection) in response to the injection than did monkeys left with their mothers. Coe later found that even a brief separation from the mother, just long enough to receive the injection, was sufficient to diminish the immune response. Coe found that there were two psychological variables which could reduce the separation effect. Monkeys left in their familiar environment (but without their mothers) and monkeys housed with familiar friends did not show a reduction in immunity when injected with the bacterium. Presumably, the comforting environment and the social support provided by the familiar monkey counteracted the effects of separation.

This finding suggests that psychological stress can have a direct effect on the body's immune system (hence the term "psychoneuroimmunology"). More important, it appears that the deleterious effects of stress may be preventable by psychological and social means. Clearly, if these findings are substantiated on humans, they will have dramatic implications for health psychology and medicine in general.

---

that such interventions will reduce susceptibility to heart disease. It has also produced another upsurge in interest on the effects of personality and stress on illness. An entire new specialty, health psychology, has developed to study how people perceive symptoms, the coping mechanisms they use to reduce stress, and the role of social factors in mediating the effects of disease. The result is that we now know considerably more about the important interrelationships among stress, psychological coping mechanisms, and disease. But we still have a great deal to learn. As Selye himself wrote in one of his final works, the Introduction to *Stress Research Issues for the Eighties:*

> Over fifty years have passed since I first conceived the notion of stress, and still, I do not consider my work on stress to be finished — far from it! I know very well that I shall never see the end of this study. . . . I think I can safely say, without exaggerating the vitality of this work, that it will go on

forever, as long as biology and medicine exist, alongside the study of psychology and sociology. (p. 1)

Further Reading

Cannon, W. B. (1939). *The wisdom of the body*. New York: Norton.

Rosenman, R. H. (1986). Current and past history of Type A behavior pattern. In T. H. Schmidt, T. M. Dembroski, & C. Blümchen (Eds.), *Biological and psychological factors in cardiovascular disease* (pp. 15–40). Berlin: Springer-Verlag.

Selye, H. (1950). *The physiology and pathology of exposure to stress: A treatise on the concept of the general adaptation syndrome and the diseases of adaptation*. Montreal: Acta.

Notes

1. Selye, H. (1976). *The stress of life*. New York: McGraw-Hill. Pp. 24–26.

CHAPTER 8

The Strangers
Among Us

The fear that society is about to be engulfed by a tidal wave of crime is not peculiar to the late 20th century. Nineteenth-century Europeans were even more obsessed with crime than we are today. At the time, the structure of Western European society was violently changing. Industrialization had led to the rapid development of towns and then cities. An increasing birthrate ensured that these new cities were crowded with unemployed youths whose very existence, in those prewelfare days, depended on theft. Today, of course, we understand the important influence the environment has on social behavior. We automatically look for the causes of crime in nurture, not nature. In the 19th century, however, most people were convinced that criminals were born, not made. They believed in the existence of a natural "criminal class" which produces crime in the way that bootmakers produce shoes.

Given the strong genetic bias of the time, it was inevitable that psychiatrists and psychologists would also emphasize the effects of heredity and biology on criminal behavior. The first person to take up this theme was the pioneering French psychiatrist Phillipe Pinel, who described criminals as suffering from *manie sans délire,* a mental illness that causes violent behavior without any signs of overt insanity. Benjamin Rush, the American psychiatrist, referred to criminals as possessing an "innate moral depravity." The English psychiatrist J. C. Prichard agreed and coined the phrase "moral insanity" to describe individuals with normal intelligence but in whom

> the moral and active principles of the mind are strongly perverted or depraved; the power of self-government is lost or greatly impaired and the individual is found to be incapable not of talking or reasoning upon any subject proposed to him, but of conducting himself with decency and propriety in the business of life.[1]

Ye shall be as gods, knowing good and evil.

—Genesis 3:5

In his book on moral insanity, which was published in 1835, Prichard attributed the condition to an inherited "weakness" of the nervous system. By coincidence, 1835 was also the year in which the Italian academic Cesare Lombroso was born. Lombroso went on to earn an uncomfortable place in history by carrying Prichard's idea about inherited weakness to extremes. Although he was, in many ways, the founder of the field of criminology, Lombroso is mainly remembered for his theory that criminals can be identified by the way they look.

LOMBROSO'S CRIMINAL ANTHROPOLOGY

Cesare Lombroso was born into an Italian Jewish family. He received his secondary education from the Jesuits, giving him a decidedly ecumenical start in life. The young Lombroso was found to have an aptitude for language; he learned Aramaic, Hebrew, and Chinese and at one time thought of pursuing a research career in linguistics. Practical considerations prevailed, however, and he entered the University of Pavia to study medicine. In 1859 Lombroso served as a medical officer in the Austro-Hungarian war. After the war, he studied surgery at the University of Genoa and then joined the faculty of the University of Turin. During his career at Turin, Lombroso held a succession of positions including professor of legal medicine, professor of psychiatry, and professor of criminal anthropology. Lombroso was a prolific writer in each of these fields producing monographs on such diverse subjects as the operation of the central nervous system, abnormal psychology, and intellectual ability. Although some of his theories were rather strange—he believed that genius is a type of insanity—Lombroso also made many useful scientific contributions. Perhaps the most important was his discovery that the vitamin deficiency disease pellagra was linked to the moldy corn fed to peasants by their landlords.

While still a young doctor, Lombroso had occasion to examine the brain of a wild bandit who had been executed for terrorizing the local villages. Lombroso described the criminal's brain as different from those of normal humans and more similar, anatomically, to the brains of primates such as gorillas or chimpanzees. Lombroso went on to study the skulls of hundreds of criminals. In each case, he claimed to find similarities between their heads and those of lower animal species. These similarities took the form of certain physical *stigmata*: small skull, asymmetrical face, narrow forehead, protruding ears, and prominent cheekbones. Based on these observations, Lombroso concluded that criminals are biological "throwbacks" to an earlier stage of evolution.

Although Lombroso acknowledged the social and psychological causes of crime, the first edition of his famous book, *L'uomo delinquente,* was largely devoted to a description of the anatomical, physical, and psychological stigmata that supposedly set criminals apart from the rest of humanity. Lombroso claimed that different types of criminals (thieves, murderers) have different patterns of stigmata. He became a champion of *physiognomy,* the theory that a person's character is reflected in his or her physical appearance (see Figure 8.1). (For more on physiognomy, see Chapter 1.)

Lombroso's emphasis on the biological causes of criminality did not mean that he believed criminals could not be rehabilitated. On the contrary, Lombroso campaigned for the constructive treatment of criminals. He argued that they require firm but fair treatment. He also believed that criminals could benefit from the "moral education" that comes from compensating their victims. Lombroso was an opponent of capital punishment reserving it for only the most incorrigible.

Despite some of his more enlightened views, Lombroso's main interest was clearly in the biological causes of criminality. For this reason, he soon found himself out of step with the growing social consciousness that marked the second half of the 19th century. It had become fashionable to lay the blame for criminal behavior at the feet of an unjust society. The idea that criminality might be genetically programmed was considered dangerously reactionary. Lombroso, an anathema to the social reformers, was also reviled by scientists, who criticized his work as largely anecdotal. They argued that his conclusions were not based on rigorous observations but simply on subjective impressions. Lombroso responded by deemphasizing the genetic aspects of criminality. In the first edition of his book, he argued that *the majority* of criminals are driven by their "nature" to a life of crime. In later editions, he reduced this "natural" criminal group to only 40% of all criminals and, finally, to 33%. Not surprisingly, these changing figures failed to

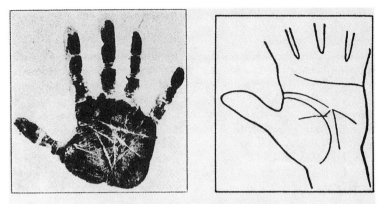

THE BROKEN LINE OF LIFE

Palm-print indicating that the person would die at the age of thirty-five, because the Line of Life, as indicated in the diagram, is broken in the middle.

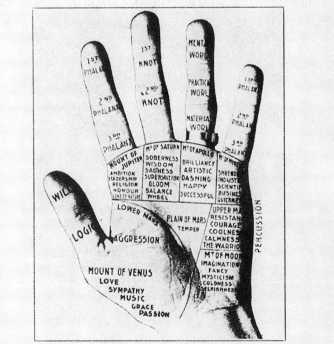

FIGURE 8.1 Although physiognomy typically involves determining character from head shape, palm reading is also a type of physiognomy. This old woodcut assigns personality traits to various regions of the hand.

impress the scientific community. They only served to underscore the subjective nature of his so-called science.

Abetted by the landlords who resented Lombroso's linking of pellagra to the miserly rations they fed their peasants, social reformers and scientists vilified his work. He was portrayed as an eccentric whose ideas were not worth taking seriously. With regard to physiognomy, the critics were undoubtedly correct. This was pseudoscience at its worst.

However, as we shall see later in this chapter, the idea that criminals are, to some extent, born and not made cannot be so easily dismissed. Nor can we completely dismiss Lombroso's scientific legacy. Because they wanted to debunk his physiognomy, legitimate scientists began to study the causes of criminal behavior. In this way, Lombroso's work, although misguided, stimulated the development of criminology as a scientific field.

PSYCHIATRIC CONCEPTS OF CRIMINALITY: THE PERSONALITY DISORDERS

While Lombroso pursued his labors, Emil Kraepelin was engaged in his great effort to systematize psychiatric nomenclature. Kraepelin's approach to this task was described in detail in Chapter 2. Basically, he looked for syndromes, groups of signs and symptoms that seemed to occur together. When he found a recurrent pattern, he gave it a name. Although this approach worked reasonably well for some syndromes, Kraepelin was left with a large group of people whose behavior was inappropriate and often perverse but who did not fit neatly into any of the traditional psychiatric classifications. These individuals had not lost contact with reality—they had no hallucinations or delusions—but they were clearly atypical. They lied, cheated, withdrew from social contact, put on histrionic acts and often harmed themselves and others. Following Prichard, Kraepelin considered such people to be suffering from a "constitutional psychopathic inferiority." This term was soon shortened to "psychopathic personality" and later simply to "psychopath." Kraepelin included in this category those people Prichard described as unable to lead their lives with "decency and propriety." While he recognized that individuals considered to be psychopaths in one culture—terrorists, for example—could be hailed as heroic freedom fighters in another, Kraepelin emphasized the genetic nature of the disorder (hence, *constitutional* psychopathic inferiority). Kraepelin identified eight psychopathic subtypes—excitable, unstable, impulsive, eccentric, liars, swindlers, antisocial, quarrelsome—although he admitted that the categories often overlap.

In contrast to Kraepelin's approach, American psychiatrists adopted a more sociological view. Antisocial acts, they argued, arise from poverty, faulty learning, deprived childhoods, and poor role mod-els. As a consequence, the 1952 edition of the American Psychiatric Association's diagnostic manual referred not to psychopathic but to "sociopathic" personalities. Except in textbooks, the term *sociopath* never really caught on. So, the third revision of the diagnostic manual dropped it in favor of a diagnostic category known as *personality disorder.*

PERSONALITY DISORDER

The personality disorder category is based on the notion that, unlike the "clinical" syndromes, some disorders can stem from enduring character traits. The reasoning goes something like this. People have different personalities—some are gregarious, others are extremely shy. Some agonize over every decision while others act impulsively. Taken to extreme limits, these enduring personality traits can lead to an impairment in social functioning. When this happens, the affected individual is said to have a "personality disorder." The American Psychiatric Association's *Diagnostic and Statistical Manual* describes 11 personality disorders (histrionic, narcissistic, borderline, and so on) but notes that an individual may have more than one at the same time.

Despite the American Psychiatric Association's attempt to provide objective diagnostic criteria, clinicians often have difficulty agreeing on whether a person fits the criteria for a particular personality disorder. It seems that at least some personality disorders have a considerable degree of overlap. Clinicians have also questioned whether the personality disorder diagnosis carries much practical value. The diagnosis tells us nothing about how personality disorders develop nor does it allow us to predict future behavior with much precision. It seems that future behavior is more influenced by the demands of a specific social situation than by personality traits. Honest people may lie if the situation demands. Similarly, given the right circumstances, dishonest people may tell the truth.

Even if the personality disorder diagnosis did allow us to predict behavior, many clinicians would still object to it on philosophical grounds. Diagnoses such as "antisocial personality" appear to divide people into two categories: those who are bad and those who are mad. Both groups of people may engage in the same behaviors (say, sexual assault), but the consequences are different. Bad people go to jail while mad people go to mental hospitals. The justification for this distinction appears to be that bad people misbehave of their own free will and deserve to be punished whereas those with personality disorders cannot help themselves and, therefore, qualify for treatment.

Unfortunately, the idea that a person has a "will" that can grab control of the wheels of the brain, stamp on the brakes, and keep him (or her) from misbehaving has always been problematic. Where does this will reside? Who, or what, tells the will when to put on the brakes and when to go full speed ahead? Is there an "executive" will? If so, who controls the executive? Such questions have puzzled philosophers for centuries, and they are still nowhere near resolution. These hoary philosophical issues will not be resurrected here. It is enough to note that, despite the appearance of respectability given to such diagnoses as "antisocial personality disorder" by clinicians, there is no generally agreed-on way of distinguishing those people who should be held responsible for their actions from those who should not. The upshot is that considerable unfairness results; some people are held responsible for their behavior whereas others are excused because they supposedly suffer from a personality disorder.

Because of its vagueness, the personality disorder category appears to have become a repository for people who do not fit neatly into any other diagnostic category—a heterogeneous scrap heap of people whose main common trait is a tendency to harm themselves or others. Despite its drawbacks, most clinicians believe that some type of personality-disorder diagnostic category is required. Their most convincing case, and the most commonly studied personality disorder, is the previously mentioned "antisocial personality."

ANTISOCIAL PERSONALITY

Antisocial personality is a diagnostic category that includes a mixed group of people: confidence tricksters, quack doctors, corrupt politicians, prostitutes, bank robbers. Despite the diagnostic manual's attempt to provide an objective set of diagnostic criteria, it is clear that the behaviors described in Table 8.1 could potentially be applied to almost any habitual criminal. To limit the number of people who fit in the category, the criteria require some evidence of antisocial behavior before the age of 15 and a continuous pattern of antisocial behavior in many aspects

TABLE 8.1 Diagnostic Criteria for Antisocial Personality Disorder

A. Current age at least 18.
B. Evidence of conduct disorder before age 15. Indicated by:
   1. truancy
   2. ran away from home overnight on two occasions
   3. initiated fights
   4. used weapons in fights
   5. forced someone into sexual activity
   6. cruel to animals or other people
   7. destroyed property, set fires
   8. lying, stealing
C. A pattern of irresponsible and antisocial behavior since age 15:
   1. unstable employment history
   2. police record
   3. irritability and aggressiveness
   4. defaults on debts
   5. impulsive, fails to plan ahead
   6. disregard for truth
   7. reckless
   8. inadequate parenting
   9. poor interpersonal relationships
   10. lacks remorse

of life including, but not limited to, work, parenting, and sexual relations.

Despite the label "personality disorder," we cannot be certain that everyone diagnosed as suffering from an antisocial personality will actually have similar personalities. Because the diagnostic criteria deal mainly with antisocial acts, the only thing we can be sure that antisocial people have in common is their unpopular behavior. And even this may not set them completely apart from the general population. Studies of normal individuals using anonymous questionnaires suggest that as many as 90% of the population occasionally engages in illegal acts. The antisocial personality may simply be an extreme example of a common behavior pattern.

Given that the personalities of antisocial individuals may not be all that similar, it is not surprising that studies designed to discover the antecedents of antisocial personality and appropriate treatment methods have produced inconsistent results and few generalizable findings. Because further progress requires that we seek comparable populations to study, several attempts have been made to define relatively homogeneous subcategories of antisocial behavior. Typically, four such subtypes are identified: dissocial, neurotic, impulsive, and harking back to Kraepelin, psychopathic.

Dissocial individuals have no psychological disorder. They are perfectly normal individuals whose antisocial behavior results from their rejection of dominant social norms in favor of the code of a deviant subgroup. Fagin's pickpockets, Mafia families, and motorcycle gang members all fit in this category. Dissocial individuals behave normally within the context of their deviant culture. In contrast to the dissocial subtype, both the neurotic and impulsive subtypes include individuals suffering from varying degrees of psychopathology. For the neurotics, antisocial behavior is often a way of gaining attention or fulfilling some need for punishment. The impulsive subtype contains those who seem unable to inhibit the gratification of their immediate needs and desires. (It is possible that at least some impulsive individuals suffer from organic syndromes that produce uncontrollable sexual impulses, explosive tempers, and extreme aggressiveness.) The fourth subtype retains Kraepelin's original label, psychopath. Unlike dissocial individuals, psychopaths are not simply behaving according to the rules of some deviant subculture. They are unsocialized loners with no allegiance to any group. Despite normal or even superior intelligence, they chronically engage in antisocial behavior, defy authority, and never feel the least bit guilty. Because of their intelligence and charm, psychopaths appear to be amiable people. This combination of superficial normality and hidden destructiveness fascinated psychiatrist Hervey Cleckley, who decided to study this antisocial subgroup in depth. The result was the classic study *The Mask of Sanity.*[2]

HERVEY M. CLECKLEY: PHYSICIAN AND AUTHOR

Hervey Milton Cleckley was born in Augusta, Georgia, in 1903. He was educated at Oxford University where he was a Rhodes Scholar as well as at the University of Georgia, the institution that awarded him his medical degree. In addition to a large private practice, Cleckley spent many years as professor of psychoanalysis at the Medical College of Georgia. Cleckley was a gifted writer whose books on psychiatric topics appealed to popular as well as professional audiences. In 1957 he achieved international

FIGURE 8.2 Hervey M. Cleckley (1903–1984).

attention as the co-author of *The Three Faces of Eve.* The book, which he wrote with Corbett Thigpen, told the story of the "multiple personalities" of one of Cleckley's patients. Eve supposedly harbored three distinct personalities in her psyche; her demeanor and behavior would change dramatically as these different personalities took control of her body. *The Three Faces of Eve* was translated into 30 languages and also was made into an award-winning film. But this book was not Cleckley's only best seller. In 1941 he published *The Mask of Sanity: An Attempt to Reinterpret the So-Called Psychopathic Personality Disorder.* In this book, Cleckley set out to describe and explain the psychopathic personality. Using case studies and interpretative techniques borrowed from psychology and psychoanalysis, Cleckley tried to bring the notion of the psychopathic personality into the mainstream of modern abnormal psychology. Over the years, Cleckley refined the concept of psychopathy in a series of revised editions of his book. The fifth and final revision was published in 1976. Today, *The Mask of Sanity* is widely acknowledged as the classic study in its field.

CLASSIC STUDY 15
The Mask of Sanity

The Mask of Sanity is essentially a book of case studies. The first edition described institutionalized male psychopaths. In later editions, Cleckley added females, youths, and studies of noninstitutionalized people. In an exceptionally evocative style, Cleckley breathed life into his patients. Consider, for example, Cleckley's presentation of the case of Stanley (taken from the fifth edition):[3]

> During the summer of 1972 a small item of news appeared in many of our daily newspapers over the country. It was an item that immediately engaged my attention. Over the two short columns was printed this arresting headline:

> YOUNG MAN INDUCES FIVE TEEN-AGE GIRLS
> TO SHAVE THEIR HEADS

> The report, as I remember it, did not go into much detail about this unusual event or give an adequate account of the young man's methods of persuasion, his motives, or of just what impulses might have prompted the five girls to take such an unusual, and one might even say, such an unnatural step. Among my first thoughts on this accomplishment was that Stanley must surely have been the man who brought it about.

[Cleckley then takes up Stanley's background]

> Typical of his behavior in high school is an incident that occurred while he was making excellent grades and holding positions of leadership. With no notice or indirect indication of restlessness, Stanley suddenly vanished from the scene. He failed one day to appear at classes and did not show up at home that night. After he had been gone for over two weeks, a period of great anxiety for his parents who had no way of knowing whether he was living or dead, the police finally discovered him working successfully in a large department store in Knoxville, Tennessee, approximately a hundred and fifty miles away. He seemed quite unconcerned with the ordeal to which he had subjected his parents. At college, and also during recent years, he has run up long-distance telephone bills, sometimes charging calls amounting to hundreds of dollars to his parents. He has also run up similar bills charging [calls] to various other telephones. . . .

> During his first year at the university he was accused by a girl he had recently met of getting her pregnant after solemn promises of matrimony. . . . A similar accusation was made by another girl in a different state. Later that year, during the summer vacation he took a sudden notion to return for a brief visit to the university. . . . He casually stole a truck that happened to be at hand. . . . State police pursued him, and in the chase he turned over the truck wrecking it and injuring a companion he had persuaded to go along with him. . . .

> While still in college, he showed his excellent persuasive abilities during one summer vacation selling Bibles. . . . During this time, he was living with his first wife who eventually had to leave him because of his tyrannical demands and his predilection for beating her up. . . . Sometimes officers of the law had to be called by neighbors to obtain her release from his extreme abuse.

> While he worked, his income was ample for any ordinary needs. During one period of prosperity he was very successful selling small computers for household use. He later added as a sideline the enthusiastic promotion and sale of waterbeds, shortly after these were introduced and hailed as a stimulating erotic innovation. His profits from these enterprises were for a while spectacular until he lost both jobs through a combination of neglect and irresponsible conduct. . . .

> Even while his first wife was living with him and his income ample, he usually ran up heavy debts. When his mistreatment would force his wife to leave him or when he would capriciously stop work, he often celebrated the occasion by a splurge of unnecessary expenditures. Sometimes he would go out merrily and buy on credit several expensive suits and ample supplies of new shoes, shirts and neckties. On one such occasion, he impulsively bought a motorcycle which he never got around to using. . . .

> Stanley has proved himself a master over the years at misrepresentation in situations where the truth would cause him difficulty or put him in a bad light. He has also been scarcely less active and ingenious in the fabrication of elaborate lies that seemed to have had little or no chance of helping him gain any material objective. Though his mother is living and has been active in trying to deliver Stanley from the various troubles into which he plunges, he convinced his first wife that she had died during his second year in high school. . . . He succeeded in making her believe also that his father's second wife (his actual mother) was not only his stepmother, but also the

identical twin sister of the mother who gave him birth. While separated from his wife for a period of several months, he went for a short time with a divorcee not long out of her teens, who will here be designated as Marilyn. . . .

He requested and persistently urged Marilyn to write a letter to his wife and in it explain to her that Stanley's love for her (the wife) was strong and genuine and to implore her to accept and welcome him back without further delay. . . . [Stanley was surprised that] Marilyn could not be induced to take the role that he tried to press upon her. Though extremely shrewd in many ways, Stanley . . . seemed to show some peculiar limitations of awareness, some defect in sensibility. . . . This often led him into gross errors of judgment that even very stupid people would readily see and avoid.

Though Stanley's parents sought treatment and help for him from psychiatrists and other doctors and from counsellors of various sorts, he himself seemed to feel no need of this and only responded by brief simulations of cooperation in order to escape some unpleasant consequence or to gain some egocentric end. On two or three occasions he voluntarily entered psychiatric hospitals, apparently to impress his wife by making her think he had at last realized he needed help and meant to change some of his ways. These visits were brief and fruitless and seemed plainly designed to manipulate domestic situations or to elicit new financial aid from his parents.

His many notable and sometimes puzzling exploits were apparently decided upon and carried off on his own, without extraneous stimulation or chemical aid [illicit drugs]. . . . [Even in the rebellious 1960s] Stanley wore traditional clothes, remained clean-shaven with neatly trimmed auburn hair. He seemed to have no special interest in changing or challenging society, or in promoting rebellion. Verbally, he expressed his allegiance to law and order and regularly identified himself with traditional values.

Let us note briefly a few examples of Stanley's typical power to convince and persuade. A year or two before his second wife had to leave him he had no difficulty in getting a young woman to turn over to him all her savings, which she had accumulated by steady work over years and which she had been carefully guarding to give her two children some measure of security. . . . More recently, he succeeded in arranging for admission to the hospital of a young woman with whom he had been living for a few weeks. She was legally married to another man but had left his bed and

board. Stanley was able somehow to convince the ordinarily strict and uncompromising authorities in charge of admission to this hospital that the insurance his employer carried on him would cover this lady in the same way as if she were indeed his wife. . . .

On another occasion, Stanley escaped the consequences of a felony charge by serenely posing as an undercover agent working with the authorities against organized pushers in the hard drug traffic.

[Using the trumped up excuse of trying to find a vacationing girlfriend who was in need of vital medication, Stanley used bad checks to finance a mercy dash to Belgium. In Brussels, he enlisted the aid of the police and the media in his quest for the "sick" girl.] Though several years after the event Stanley can still give a remarkable account of his sudden jet flight to Europe and his adventures in Brussels, there is a great deal that in retrospect makes it difficult to see how he could have convinced so many people of so many implausible things. The newspaper accounts and pictures . . . establish the fact beyond question that Stanley got to Brussels and that he must have attracted a great deal of attention. Telephone calls from newspapermen and from people connected with the American embassy and his parents' report confirm this and indicate that Stanley must have created a remarkable stir and a great deal of confusion. His own report, which can hardly be counted upon as accurate or trustworthy, pictures him as being hailed and feted in Brussels in a style and on a scale almost comparable to the welcome Charles Lindbergh received in New York after his historic solo first flight across the Atlantic Ocean.

Based on this and other carefully documented cases, Cleckley argued that psychopaths constitute a distinct subtype of antisocial personality. They appear normal, even to professionals, but this normality is only a "mask of sanity." Underneath, argued Cleckley, they are deeply disturbed. He summarized his clinical observations in a set of 16 criteria that cover the major features of the disorder:

1. *Superficial charm and good intelligence.* Psychopaths normally make a good initial impression. They are alert, charming, and friendly. They score well above average on intelligence tests and seem free of any social or emotional problems.

2. *Absence of delusions or other signs of irrational thinking.* Psychopathic individuals do not have hallucinations or delusions. They are able to

verbalize correct and incorrect standards of behavior, and they can critically evaluate and apologize for their previous misdeeds ("I know I've done wrong, but believe me, I have learned my lesson"). They express devotion to family and friends and can also produce careful plans for the future. From a conversation alone, it is not possible to tell that they are anything other than honest and sincere.

3. *Absence of nervousness or psychoneurotic manifestations.* Nervousness, tension, anxiety, fear, guilt, and remorse are almost completely absent from the psychopath's emotional repertoire, even in situations in which such feelings might normally be expected.

4. *Unreliability.* The shirking of obligations is an important aspect of psychopathic behavior. Psychopaths will leave apparently successful employment at whim, fail to pay debts, ignore their families, and commit crimes whenever the impulse arises.

5. *Untruthfulness and insincerity.* The ability to lie while looking someone sincerely in the eye is one of the most frustrating of all psychopathic traits. The seemingly straightforward manner of these individuals can disarm those not familiar with their behavior. Even Cleckley himself was occasionally duped into making loans to psychopathic patients and into cashing their checks. Needless to say, these loans were never repaid and the checks always bounced.

6. *Lack of remorse or shame.* Shirking responsibility, psychopaths routinely blame others for their misfortunes. Although they may feign regret, they never show true remorse for their actions.

7. *Inadequately motivated antisocial behavior.* The psychopath lies, cheats, fights, steals, and defrauds, often when the risk of detection is great and the potential rewards quite small. Murderer Gary Gilmore, whose story is told in Norman Mailer's 1979 book, *The Executioner's Song,* explained his killings as "Habit, I guess, my lifestyle. I don't know, man. I'm impulsive. I don't think."

8. *Poor judgment and failure to learn by experience.* No amount of punishment appears to deter psychopaths. Indeed, they frequently repeat behavior for which they have been previously punished even when detection and further punishment are inevitable. Gary Gilmore, for example, spent practically his entire life in custody for one crime or another.

9. *Pathological egocentricity and incapacity for love.* Although they may profess affection, psychopaths do not show the capacity for long-lasting love. They are indifferent to the hardship and suffering their behavior causes for those they claim to "love." For example, while awaiting execution, Gilmore carried out a correspondence with his girlfriend. He prompted her to write about her personal feelings without telling her that he had sold her letters as part of a lucrative publication deal.

10. *General poverty in major affective reactions.* Psychopaths can produce "shows" of anger, happiness, and other emotions but all of their emotions are shallow. They are never deliriously happy, and even when confined to hospitals or jails, they do not get depressed.

11. *Specific loss of insight.* A lack of empathy, an inability to see themselves as others do, is a fundamental part of the psychopathic personality. Psychopaths have been known to ask for references from employers who have fired them for dishonesty. They are also genuinely astonished when they discover that other people feel they deserve a prison term for their crimes.

12. *Unresponsiveness in general interpersonal relations.* Psychopaths are rarely grateful for favors shown to them nor are they aware of the importance of equity in social relations. Interestingly, outward magnanimity (helping a frail old lady mow her lawn, spontaneous gifts to friends and families) often coexists with a callous disregard for the feelings of others.

13. *Fantastic and uninviting behavior with drink and sometimes without.* Although not all psychopaths drink or take drugs, when they do they tend to become moody and combative. Psychopaths have been known to urinate from windows, set fires, and strip naked in public. They need not be drunk for this to happen; just the mild reduction in inhibition produced by a few drinks is enough to get them going.

14. *Suicide rarely carried out.* Despite gestures and bogus attempts, and no matter how much trouble they cause themselves and others, psychopaths almost never commit suicide.

15. *Sex life impersonal, trivial, and poorly integrated.* Their impulsiveness often leads psychopaths to indulge in strange, inappropriate, and superficial sexual behavior. As a rule, their promiscuity appears to be more a function of their lack of restraint rather than a particularly strong sex drive.

16. *Failure to follow any life plan.* Instead of striving to achieve goals, psychopaths appear determined to fail. Their behavior does not follow any sort of coherent plan. Psychopaths habitually give up successful careers to follow momentary whims; their projects—both criminal and legal—almost always result in failure. It should be made clear that these failures are not the result of some neurotic need to get caught but the inevitable consequence of failing to plan ahead.

As can be seen, Cleckley's 16 points are not identical to the American Psychiatric Association's diagnostic criteria for antisocial personality. The latter omit several traits that Cleckley considers particularly important: lack of empathy, no concern for others, and a failure to feel genuine remorse. According to Cleckley, it is these characteristics, more than any others, that separate psychopaths from other types of antisocial personalities.

Cleckley believed that the psychopathic syndrome ultimately derives from a constitutional inability to experience normal emotions. Just as colorblind people learn to describe grass as "green" and fire trucks as "red" without ever having perceived the color themselves, psychopaths learn to mimic the language of emotion. By observing others, they become adept at expressing regret, affection, and fear at the appropriate times, but they do not actually feel the emotions themselves. They are like actors delivering a set of well-learned lines, simulating feelings they are not really experiencing. According to Cleckley, their impoverished emotional life explains why psychopaths do not consider the consequences of their acts: They do not fear punishment nor do they sympathize with the suffering of others.

AFTERMATH

The Mask of Sanity was enormously successful, passing through five editions. In each successive revision, Cleckley provided additional case materials and further refined the psychopathy concept. Yet his conclusions always remained circumspect. Although he presented tentative etiological hypotheses, Cleckley was always careful to emphasize the need for further research. In this respect, his book was also successful; it stimulated many researchers to investigate the origins of psychopathic behavior. Several different possibilities have been explored: familial, genetic, and psychological. These will be considered in turn.

The Role of the Family

Children learn their values and their standards of proper behavior from their parents and siblings. It is not surprising, therefore, that deviant families often produce deviant children. Ask psychopathic individuals about their early family life and you will hear harrowing stories of parental rejection and neglect. Parents are described as inconsistent disciplinarians, poor providers, emotionally unstable, and even psychotic. Although not without interest, such retrospective reports are of dubious reliability. It is entirely possible that psychopaths distort their early experience to evade responsibility for their misbehavior—that is, to create the impression that they are the victims of cruel parents. Because psychopaths may be biased, some researchers have sought corroboration of their retrospective reports from their relatives. Unfortunately, the reliability of these recollections is also not guaranteed. Relatives, who know how the child has turned out, tend to selectively recall or exaggerate early misbehaviors.

The only way to avoid the problems of retrospective data collection is to study children prospectively beginning before they are diagnosed as psychopathic. An ambitious study of this type was reported in 1966 by Lee Robins, who sought out more than 500 adults who were first seen at a child guidance clinic 30 years earlier. A group of adults from the same neighborhood who were never seen at the clinic served as a comparison group. Many of the adults who were seen in the clinic as children showed definite signs of psychopathic behavior. Robins went back to the clinic records to see what they were like as children. She summarized her findings as follows:

> If one wishes to choose the most likely candidate for a later diagnosis of sociopathic personality from among children appearing in a child guidance clinic, the best choice appears to be a boy

THE GREAT IMPOSTER

Not all psychopaths are evil. Some have even managed to do a little good. Consider, for example, the case of Ferdinand Waldo Demara, Jr., whose exploits formed the basis for the film *The Great Imposter.*

As soon as he possibly could, young Demara ran away from his unhappy home. After failing to gain acceptance as a Trappist Monk, he joined the army. But Demara soon found army life tedious and decided to try another branch of the service. Instead of applying for a transfer, he simply went AWOL and surfaced a few months later as a navy seaman aboard a World War II destroyer. Not happy as an enlisted man, Demara applied for a commission as a naval officer using a forged university transcript as proof of his educational background. His application was accepted, but when Demara learned that the commission procedure could not be finalized without a routine security check, he deserted ship. To ensure that he would not be sought, he faked a suicide leaving his uniform and a note at the end of the pier where his ship was berthed.

Having given up on the military, Demara turned to another line of work. Using stolen academic qualifications, he obtained a faculty position at a Canadian college where he specialized in teaching abnormal psychology. True to form, Demara soon tired of the academic life and set his heart on a new challenge. He decided to turn his talents to medicine. Using his standard technique — stolen credentials — Demara obtained a commission as a medical officer in the Canadian navy. In port, he managed to fake the role quite satisfactorily ("Take two aspirin and see me in the morning") while he studied medical textbooks in his spare time. The real test came when Demara was sent to sea during the Korean War. One afternoon his ship encountered a small Korean ship full of seriously wounded soldiers. As the only "doctor" around, Demara cleaned and sutured the mildly

---

referred for theft or aggression who has shown a diversity of antisocial behavior in many episodes, at least one of which could be grounds for a Juvenile Court appearance, and whose antisocial behavior involves him with strangers and organizations. . . . Such boys had a history of truancy, theft, staying out late, and refusing to obey parents. They lied gratuitously, and showed little guilt over their behavior. They were generally irresponsible about being where they were supposed to be or taking care of money. They were interested in sexual activities and had experimented with homosexual relationships.[4]

Robins also found evidence for inconsistent parenting and parental antisocial behavior in the backgrounds of those child guidance cases who later became psychopaths. Her findings have been taken to support the idea that psychopathic behavior is the result of poor parental role models, a lack of clear discipline, and parental neglect. However, findings such as those reported by Robins are open to another interpretation: They could reflect genetic factors at work. This possibility is addressed next.

The Role of Heredity

There have been several attempts to separate the potential environmental and genetic causes of psychopathy. The typical procedure is to study children who were adopted early in life. When children whose natural fathers were known criminals but who were raised in law-abiding families are compared with children from law-abiding natural families raised by adoptive fathers with criminal histories, evidence is found for a strong genetic effect on antisocial behavior. Children whose natural fathers were criminals, but who were raised in law-abiding homes, are *more* likely to break the law themselves than children from biological law-abiding families raised by criminal stepfathers. But genetics is far from the whole story. Children whose natural fathers were criminals and who were raised in homes with stepfathers who were also criminals are the most likely of all to get into trouble. This suggests a role for both biological and environmental factors in the etiology of antisocial behavior.

wounded and then turned to those requiring surgery. Drawing on his reading (Demara never actually performed or even witnessed an operation), the "doctor" operated throughout the night. He removed a bullet lodged near the heart of one man, collapsed the lung of another, and removed shrapnel from the groin of a third. When morning came, and the last operation was complete, Demara collapsed with fatigue while the crew who had witnessed his work cheered.

Demara's naval exploits won him considerable publicity and, alas, attracted the attention of the real doctor whom he had been impersonating. Needless to say, Demara was kicked out of the navy, but this was not the end of his medical career. Somehow, he had obtained a license to practice medicine in England. Later he practiced in the United States winding up as the medical officer in an institution for the criminally insane. The life must have been oppressive, however, because he became a

heavy drinker. It seemed time for another change. So, once again using stolen references and credentials, Demara obtained a position as guard in a state penitentiary. He rose to the position of assistant warden where he had a reputation as someone who had concern for the men. Indeed, he encouraged people from the nearby town to donate their old magazines to the prison library. It was in one of these old magazines that the prisoners read about the war exploits of their warden.

Demara bolted interstate, but this time his luck ran out. He was prosecuted and jailed. He dropped out of sight for a while after his release but eventually turned up in a monastery in Missouri. When last heard from, Demara had obtained a position as the minister of a small church where, by all reports, the congregation was quite pleased with his performance.

A limiting factor in many adoption studies is their focus on criminality and antisocial behavior rather than on psychopathy. An exception is a study conducted in Denmark by psychiatrist Fini Schulsinger. Schulsinger studied adopted children who were later diagnosed as psychopaths. For each child, he counted the number of biological and adoptive relatives who had also been labeled psychopathic (or something similar). Schulsinger found that the biological families of psychopaths were almost twice as likely to contain psychopaths as were their adoptive families. A control group of nonpsychopathic adoptees was also studied. Their biological families contained far fewer psychopaths than did the biological families of the psychopathic group. The adoptive families of the psychopathic and nonpsychopathic adoptees contained about the same number of psychopaths. These findings, taken in the light of the adoption studies already described, certainly suggest that there is some genetic component in psychopathy. But exactly what is inherited is not at all clear. No one seriously suggests that psychopaths inherit a gene that compels

them to lie and steal. A more reasonable hypothesis is that they inherit a trait which, given the right circumstances, keeps them from learning proper forms of social behavior. Physiological and behavioral studies suggest that this inherited trait may be an abnormally low anxiety level. This lack of normal anxiety makes it difficult for psychopaths to learn to inhibit their instinctive impulses. A low level of anxiety also makes it difficult for them to learn from experience. The evidence in favor of this hypothesis is reviewed next.

The Role of Anxiety

Psychologists, especially, are intrigued by the many instances in which Cleckley's patients fail to learn from experience. Despite being punished for similar deeds in the past, they persist in their antisocial behavior seemingly unconcerned about the likely consequences of their transgressions. It should be made clear that Cleckley did not believe that psychopaths are indifferent to punishment; they clearly do not like it. His point was that they seem unable or unwilling to forego the gratification of their

TABLE 8.2   Incidence of Psychopathic-type Disorders in Biological and Adoptive Relatives of Psychopathic and Nonpsychopathic Individuals

Adoptee Group	Relatives Showing Psychopathic-type Disorders (%)	
	Biological	Adoptive
Psychopathic	14.4	7.6
Nonpsychopathic	6.7	5.3

Source: After Schulsinger, 1972.

impulses solely to avoid future punishment. Based on Cleckley's observations, psychologist David Lykken hypothesized that, unlike other people who experience anxiety about the possibility of future punishment, psychopaths feel little or no anticipatory anxiety. In other words, psychopaths commit antisocial acts because they are not made anxious by the thought of future punishment.

To test this hypothesis, Lykken performed a laboratory experiment. He studied three groups of people: a group of convicts who fit Cleckley's description of psychopaths, a second group of prisoners who were not psychopathic, and a group of university students. He set up a situation in which the subjects must learn to avoid future punishment and predicted that, because punishment does not make them anxious, psychopaths would find such learning more difficult than the other prisoners or the students. To ensure that the experiment measured avoidance learning uncontaminated by other factors (a desire to show off how clever they are, for example), Lykken disguised the purpose of his experiment so that the subjects were unaware that avoidance learning was even being studied. In the jargon of experimental psychology, the experiment was arranged so that avoidance learning was *incidental*.

Lykken's experimental apparatus consisted of a panel containing two horizontal rows of lights and a row of levers (see Figure 8.3). The lights in the first row were red, those in the second were green. The subjects' task was to learn a sequence of lever presses (lever 2, lever 3, lever 1, and so on). Subjects knew when a correct sequence occurred because these sequences caused a green light to be illuminated. Incorrect sequences were indicated by the red lights. Some incorrect response sequences also

produced a painful electric shock. The subjects were told that these shocks were included as an extra source of motivation to help improve their performance. They were not told to avoid the shocks or even that avoidance was possible. However, the experiment was designed so that shock avoidance was possible provided the subjects learned to avoid certain sequences. Thus, while learning the main task, subjects could *incidentally* also learn to avoid shock.

Lykken kept track of how many errors people made before they learned the correct sequence of lever presses. He found little difference among his subject groups. All three groups made around the same number of errors. Lykken also kept track of the number of shocks that people received during the course of the experiment. He found that the students received the fewest number of shocks. Although it was not explicitly required, they learned to avoid the sequences of lever presses that led to shock. As might be expected, the psychopathic group received the largest number of shocks (the other prisoners fell somewhere between the two other groups). Lykken interpreted this finding as supporting his original hypothesis. Because punishment does not make them anxious, psychopaths do not learn behaviors that help them avoid it.

Lykken's experiment generated considerable interest in the research community in the early 1960s. Among the first psychologists to follow up his work was the social psychologist Stanley Schachter, whose research on emotions was briefly described in Chapter 7. Schachter and his colleague, Bibb Latané, reasoned that, if psychopaths fail to learn to avoid punishment because of their low levels of anxiety, anything that increases their anxiety should assist them to learn to avoid punishment. To test this idea, they administered the hormone adrenaline to

THE BIOLOGY OF VIOLENCE

Although Lombroso's idea that criminals can be identified by their stigmata had fallen into disrepute, it was resurrected in the 1960s when it was discovered that 1 in every 1,000 males have one more than the usual complement of Y chromosomes. Individuals with this so-called XYY syndrome are distinguished by their low intelligence, greater than average height, and a variety of peculiar physical anomalies (which were remarkably similar to Lombroso's stigmata). Reports began to appear suggesting that XYY males were overrepresented in penal institutions. The popular media carried lurid stories about hulking, ugly, super-strong men who, because of their extra Y chromosome, were biologically destined to commit violent crimes. Inevitably, lawyers began using genetics as a defense. They argued that their clients should not be held responsible for their crimes because they had no control over their heredity.

As is commonly the case with such "discoveries," assertions about the genetic basis of criminal behavior were based mainly on poorly controlled studies. It took more than a decade for scientifically reliable data to become available. The most careful study of the relationship between the XYY chromosome and behavior was conducted in Denmark by H. A. Witkin and a team of investigators that included Sarnoff Mednick and Fini Schulsinger. The same careful Danish records that had made Mednick's schizophrenia study possible (see Chapter 5) were also exploited to study the XYY syndrome. Witkin and his colleagues examined the records of all men born between 1944 and 1947 choosing for further study those who were over 6 feet tall (a total of 4,591). They tested as many of these people as they could find (about 90%) to determine whether any had an extra Y chromosome. They also examined criminal records, school reports, and army intelligence tests. A total of 12 XYY males were found, 5 of whom (42%) had criminal records. Among the normal, XY, males, only 9% had been convicted of a crime.

Although the criminal conviction rate was considerably higher among XYY males than among normal men, most of their crimes were fairly mild. Only one of the XYY males had committed an act of violence. Thus, the violent disposition attributed to XYY males was unfounded. They were no more violent than XY males. There were, however, other important differences between the XYY and XY groups. The most important of these were lower intelligence and lower school achievement in the XYY group. Both of these factors have been shown to be related to criminal behavior in XY men. Thus, it is possible that it is their low intelligence that leads XYY men to commit crimes or, at least, makes them more likely to be caught.

While the discovery of the XYY syndrome marks the first scientific demonstration that something similar to Lombroso's stigmata actually exists, XYY men account for only a small percentage of crime (and even that may be the result of low intelligence). The fact remains that most criminal acts are committed by genetically normal individuals.

---

psychopathic and nonpsychopathic convicts. Adrenaline, it will be recalled from the previous chapter, is a substance that increases sympathetic nervous system activity. The resulting arousal is physiologically similar to the arousal produced by anxiety (increased heart rate, shallow breathing, and so on).

Schachter and Latané used the same apparatus as Lykken had used. They told the participants that the experiment was concerned with the effects of hormones on learning. Each subject participated twice: once having received a placebo (an inactive drug) and once under the influence of adrenaline. Like Lykken, Schachter and Latané found that both psychopaths and nonpsychopaths made about the same number of errors while learning the correct sequences of lever pushes. Adrenaline had no effect on this aspect of the task. In contrast, the hormone

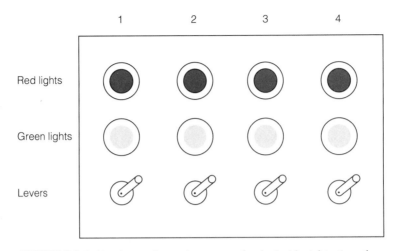

FIGURE 8.3 Lykken's experimental apparatus for the incidental testing of avoidance learning. Subjects were told that they must learn to press levers in a certain sequence. Incorrect responses sometimes produced a painful electric shock. All subjects learned the correct lever-pressing sequence eventually. In addition, although subjects were not instructed to avoid shock, the nonpsychopathic subjects learned to do so. The psychopaths, on the other hand, did not.

did produce an important effect on incidental learning. In the placebo condition, the psychopaths had considerable difficulty learning to avoid the incorrect sequences that led to electric shock. The nonpsychopaths, on the other hand, learned to avoid shock quite quickly. The difference between the two groups was even larger than the difference reported by Lykken. Under the influence of adrenaline, however, this difference reversed. Incidental learning of shock avoidance was better among the psychopaths than among the nonpsychopathic subjects. This result provides considerable support for the idea that psychopaths repeat their antisocial behavior because the threat of punishment does not make them anxious. They appear to have a "nothing can hurt me" attitude that leads them to ignore the likely consequences of their behavior.

The facilitative effects of adrenaline on avoidance learning are consistent with the idea that psychopaths are physiologically less anxious than nonpsychopaths. Further evidence for this hypothesis was also provided in the 1960s by experiments that measured the galvanic skin response, or GSR (the electrical activity of the skin). Increased arousal or anxiety produces a decrease in skin resistance and an increase in the GSR. In one simple experiment,

juveniles who were classified roughly into psychopathic and nonpsychopathic groups were told they were to receive an electric shock in 10 minutes. (In reality, no shocks were to be administered, but the juveniles did not know this at the time.) Electrodes were attached to their legs, and they were seated in front of a large clock that counted down the time to shock administration. At the outset, both groups had similar GSRs. As the shock time approached, the nonpsychopathic group showed signs of increasing tension. At the end of the 10-minute period, when the shock was due, the nonpsychopathic group produced large GSRs indicating a sharp increase in anxiety. Not one of the psychopathic subjects showed this reaction. Similar findings have been reported using other noxious stimuli such as a loud noise.

The psychopaths' lack of anxiety appears to be a fairly general trait; they fail to show apprehension in the face of a forthcoming harmful event. Interestingly, even when the shock (or loud noise) is actually administered, psychopaths report feeling less pain than nonpsychopaths. In experiments that pair noxious stimuli such as electric shock with a warning signal (say, a light or a tone), most people learn to associate the warning with the shock. Psychopaths, perhaps because they do not fear the shock and do not find it especially unpleasant, have considerable difficulty learning to make such associations.

The idea that psychopaths are physiologically different from other people has received further support from studies of brain electrical activity. Electroencephalographic (EEG) recordings of brain waves taken from psychopaths have revealed a large number of abnormalities. Although there are some differences among the studies, the general finding is that the EEGs of psychopaths are similar to those of young children. This could reflect an immature nervous system and may account for some psychopathic behaviors, particularly impulsiveness.

The line of reasoning that links the failure to learn avoidance responses to physiological variables is threatened somewhat by the results of an experiment performed by psychologist F. Schmauk. Schmauk studied psychopathic and nonpsychopathic convicts as well as a control group of nonconvicts. Like previous researchers, he devised an avoidance-learning task, but instead of just shock, he also tested how well subjects learn to avoid other punishment such as loss of money or criticism from the experimenter (e.g., "wrong again!"). Schmauk found that the psychopaths' performance depended on the punishment to be avoided. As might be expected from previous research, psychopaths had considerable difficulty learning to avoid responses that led to electric shock. They also had trouble learning behaviors that would have prevented criticism from the experimenter. (In this they were not alone; the nonpsychopathic prisoners paid even less attention than the psychopaths to the experimenter's criticisms.) The most important finding of the experiment, however, came from the condition in which incorrect responses cost individuals money. In this condition, the psychopathic prisoners learned better than either of the other two groups. Thus, it seems that psychopaths can learn to avoid punishments provided they consider these punishments important. Schmauk's results suggest that psychopaths may not have a general deficit in avoidance learning but a selective deficit that applies only to certain types of punishment. This means that any theory based on an overall physiological inability to learn to avoid punishment is too simple to account for psychopathic behavior. Social learning factors, including the nature of the punishment, also play an important role.

Treatment

Because of psychopaths' inability to form an honest relationship with a therapist, Cleckley was pessimistic about the possibilities of modifying psychopathic behavior:

> Over a period of many years I have remained discouraged about the effect of treatment on the psychopath. Having regularly failed in my own efforts to help such patients . . . I hoped for a while that treatment by others would be more successful. I have had the opportunity to see patients of this sort who were treated by psychoanalysis, psychoanalytically oriented psychotherapy, by group and by milieu therapy. . . . None of these measures impressed me as achieving successful results. . . . I have now, after more than three decades, had the opportunity to observe a considerable number of patients who, through commitment or the threat of losing their probation status or by other means were kept under treatment . . . for years. The therapeutic failure in all such patients leads me to feel that we do not at present have any kind of psychotherapy that can be relied on to change the psychopath fundamentally.

Certainly, the traditional forms of psychotherapy and drug treatment have not proven to be effective means for modifying psychopathic behavior. This is to be expected because psychopaths are normally not distressed by their behavior nor are they motivated to change. Moreover, psychopathic behavior can be rewarding, at least in the short-term. Treating psychopathic behavior remains an important challenge for clinical psychology and psychiatry. Considerable research along these lines is currently underway.

As should be apparent, Cleckley's most important legacy is his careful clinical observations. Much of what we know today to be true of psychopaths was first mentioned in one of the editions of *The Mask of Sanity*. To summarize, psychopaths (about three quarters of whom are males) are impulsive and hedonistic individuals who, perhaps for genetic reasons, lack the capacity to feel normal guilt, remorse, or even empathy for others. Despite normal or even high intelligence, they have poor judgment and will impulsively attempt to gratify their immediate needs regardless of the future consequences. Psychopaths are frequently in legal trouble. When their misdeeds are discovered, and blame cannot be shifted to others, psychopaths make a good show of expressing remorse, but their promises to reform are almost always empty. Because they have low anxiety levels, psychopaths have difficulty learning to avoid punishments even in situations in which their behavior has led to punishment in the past. It is possible that psychopathy is partly genetic, but early social experiences are also probably important. There is presently no effective treatment for this serious and challenging condition.

Further Reading

Cleckley, H. M. (1976). *The mask of sanity.* St. Louis: C. V. Mosby.

Notes

1. Prichard, J. C. (1835). *Treatise on insanity and other disorders affecting the mind.* Philadelphia: Haswell, Barrington & Haswell.
2. The term *psychopath* rather than *sociopath* is used in this chapter because that is the label used by Cleckley in his classic study.
3. Unless otherwise stated, all quotations are from: Cleckley, H. M. (1976). *The mask of sanity.* St. Louis: C. V. Mosby.
4. Robins, L. N. (1966). *Deviant children grow up.* Baltimore: Williams and Wilkins. P. 157.

The Taboo Topic

Standards of sexual behavior have varied greatly across historic periods and cultures. In Old Testament times, the purpose of marriage was to produce and raise children. As long as women bore children and devoted themselves to raising them, they were entitled to financial support and protection from their husbands. Should a woman with children become widowed, her brother-in-law was duty-bound to marry her. (Already having a wife was no obstacle in those polygamous days.) In contrast to the widow, a woman who for one reason or another could not fulfill her child-bearing role, had few rights. Her husband could abandon her with no financial support and no right to joint property. This combination of paternalistic care and cruel disregard was mirrored by a deep-rooted ambivalence toward female sexuality. Sexual contact for the purpose of procreation was encouraged, but females were viewed as inferior and, largely because they menstruated, "unclean." Women were forbidden from entering the temple and from serving as priests. Because they were unclean, women were subjected to ritual cleansing. Even today, menstruating females are barred from Hindu temples.

The early Christians continued to uphold many of the ancient Jewish beliefs adding a special emphasis on chastity. Men, they believed, could not help their lust—that is their nature—but women were expected to lack sexual desire and to remain virgins until married. Even after marriage, sex was considered at best a necessary evil and was forbidden on Sunday, Wednesday, Friday, and on holy days. The most devout women became nuns and never had sex at all.

Attitudes changed during the 12th century—the period of the Crusades and the beginning of the age of chivalry. Religious doctrine changed to emphasize femininity, and idealized love was extolled in

FIGURE 9.1 Victorian women were either pure or depraved, wives or harlots.

the odes of the troubadours. The mother of god was worshipped, and love, rather than family ties and money, became the basis of marriage. This period was brought to an "official" end with the papal bull of Pope Innocent VIII, the event that triggered the Inquisition. Not only was there a return to sexual inhibition, but sex, other than for procreation, became the most serious of all sins. Thousands were tortured to extract confessions of their lasciviousness; priests frightened their parishioners with lurid stories about men seduced by witches and women who had sex with the devil himself. Women were particular targets of the Inquisition because they were seen as temptresses who drained men of their "vital seed" by bewitching them. The Renaissance, which began in Italy and slowly spread to other countries, rehabilitated sex but did little to improve the image of females. The temptress of the Inquisition was replaced with a passionless child-bearing

machine who was not really interested in sex at all but who went along with it to please her husband and to bear children.

During the reign of Queen Victoria, 19th-century England and most of northern and western Europe became once again obsessed with sex and with the "correct" behavior of men and women. Men worked while females, except among the lower classes, did not. There were separate clubs for men and women and separate hobbies. Women were divided into two groups: pure wifely types who tolerated sex but did not enjoy it and carnal harlots who tempted men with their wanton sexuality (see Figure 9.1). Brothels, staffed mainly with working-class women, proliferated to cater to upper-class men. The Victorians perfected the idea of the "double standard": Men could have sexual desires but women could not. Men could visit prostitutes without seriously affecting their reputation whereas the prostitutes who serviced them were despised and persecuted.

The Victorian era contained many such paradoxes. Church leaders taught the literalness of the Bible, yet a Victorian produced the theory of evolution. Victorians were severely inhibited about sex. Yet it was a Victorian, Sigmund Freud, who produced a theory of personality with sex as its central concept. Perhaps the most curious paradox of all—given Victorian society's disapproving attitude toward sex—was that a Victorian founded *sexology* (the scientific study of sex). Sexology's precise birthdate is usually given as 1886, the year that Richard von Krafft-Ebing published *Psychopathia Sexualis.*

THE FOUNDING OF SEXOLOGY

Richard von Krafft-Ebing was born in Mannheim, Germany, on August 14, 1840. He was a product of the middle class; his father was a civil servant, and his mother came from a line of prominent jurists. Although interested in the law, Krafft-Ebing chose a career in medicine studying at universities in Zurich, Prague, Heidelberg, and Vienna. Upon graduation in 1863, Krafft-Ebing decided to specialize in psychiatry although discussions with his mother's relations had also given him an interest in forensic medicine. He began a private practice that had to be abandoned when he was called to serve in the Franco-Prussian war. After demobilization, he spent some considerable time reestablishing his practice but felt himself increasingly drawn to research. In 1872, with the help of German Chancellor Bismarck, Krafft-Ebing obtained a teaching post at a new university that had been recently established at Strasbourg. A year later he moved to the University of Graz as professor of psychiatry. In 1889 Krafft-Ebing moved again. This time to the prestigious chair of psychiatry at the University of Vienna, which he held for the remainder of his career.

Krafft-Ebing was not only expert in the basic sciences of physiology and anatomy but also a superb clinician. His ability to tie together theory and practice appealed to students and made his lectures enormously popular. Krafft-Ebing's style was to build his lectures around specific clinical problems showing how basic scientific knowledge could help doctors to understand and treat various conditions. Although novel for its time, Krafft-Ebing's approach to teaching has now become the norm at medical schools around the world.

FIGURE 9.2 Richard von Krafft-Ebing (1840–1902), the first sexologist.

In addition to teaching, Krafft-Ebing was heavily involved in research. He published important works in several areas of medicine including one of the first demonstrations of the relationship between syphilis and general paresis. Krafft-Ebing's accomplishments in the classroom, coupled with his scientific work, made him one of the best-known doctors of his time, but his fame increased exponentially with the publication of his epic-making book, *Psychopathia Sexualis.* This book remains, even today, the most comprehensive collection of sexual disorders ever published.

Psychopathia Sexualis

As discussed in Chapter 2, 19th-century psychiatrists were more interested in classifying and naming "mental" conditions than in treating them. This is understandable because, in the years before Freud, there were few treatments available. Psychiatrists relied mainly on reprimand, hypnotic suggestion, and when these did not work, cold baths. Krafft-Ebing was no exception. Although he recognized the need for effective treatments, his energies were primarily directed toward organizing disorders into taxonomic categories. Except for classificatory distinctions, Krafft-Ebing made only a minimal effort to provide theoretical explanations for aberrant behavior. Nevertheless, this classificatory work, which Krafft-Ebing summarized in *Psychopathia Sexualis*, was an important first step toward the scientific study of sexuality.

Krafft-Ebing's book appeared in the middle of the Victorian era when sex was completely banned from polite conversation. Those who published sexual material were often charged with lewdness and pornography and sometimes brought to court. In the United States, the Comstock laws were so punitive, individuals risked jail if they revealed their "deviant" sexual behavior to their priest, doctor, or even their spouse. Given the moral climate of his time, it took great courage for Krafft-Ebing to produce a book on sex, especially a book containing explicit descriptions of sexual behavior. Indeed, *Psychopathia Sexualis* is essentially a catalog of sexual deviations—necrophilia, sexual murder, voyeurism, exhibitionism, transvestism, fetishism—and many other examples of what would be known today as *paraphilias* (literally, "deviant attractions"). Included among the paraphilias are *sadism* and *masochism*, terms that made their first appearance in *Psychopathia Sexualis*.

Krafft-Ebing divided what he called the "sexual neuroses" into three categories: *peripheral, spinal,* and *cerebral.* The first two categories contained a motley combination of physical and "psychosomatic" conditions that affect the ability to obtain erections or to perform sexual acts (premature or painful ejaculation, for example). The cerebral neuroses, on the other hand, consisted mainly of paraphilias. Krafft-Ebing argued that "sexual neurotics" tend to degenerate with time. They go from a moderately bad practice (say, exhibitionism) to much worse practices (child abuse, for example). This theory came to be so widely held that the term *degenerate* eventually became a common synonym for sexual deviate.

Krafft-Ebing believed that all types of sexual neuroses are exacerbated by alcohol, drug abuse, disease (especially venereal disease), psychological stress, and most important, masturbation. His belief in the evils of masturbation was derived from his clinical experience. Noting that the patients who consulted him were always upset and unhappy and that many of these patients masturbated, Krafft-Ebing concluded that masturbation must cause unhappiness. The fallacy in such reasoning should be obvious: Only unhappy and upset patients consult a psychiatrist; but there may well be happy people who masturbate who never come to a doctor's attention.

Krafft-Ebing realized that his book would upset Victorian sensibilities, so he took the precaution of writing the "crucial" passages in Latin. This made them accessible to doctors and lawyers—who were his intended audience—but effectively hid them from the general public. Krafft-Ebing also took pains to assure his readers that he did not approve of deviant sexual behavior. He frequently referred to the practices he described as "disgusting" and "depraved," but he made it clear that he was referring to his patients' deeds and not to their value as individual human beings. He was adamant in his view that people with sexual neuroses are ill. He called them the "stepchildren of nature," people in need of sympathy and help.

From today's perspective, Krafft-Ebing's main scientific achievement was to establish the sexual disorders as a special category of psychiatric problems. This achievement allowed the development of the field of sexology. It is often forgotten, however, that Krafft-Ebing was also a social reformer who was not afraid to take a public stand about his beliefs. One way he did this was by serving as an expert witness at trials in which people stood accused of deviant sexual behavior. (Krafft-Ebing's interest in the law, encouraged by his mother's many "legal" relatives, was evident in *Psychopathia Sexualis*, which he subtitled *A Medico-Forensic Study*.) Krafft-Ebing invariably tried to convince the courts that people who engage in unusual sex practices were ill and should be treated as patients rather than criminals. Often these efforts were futile, but Krafft-Ebing persisted. He even championed homosexual law reform at a time when such tolerant views left him open to professional and social ostracism. Indeed, many of his contemporaries called for his expulsion from the medical community. Fortunately, these calls went unheeded. Until he died at age 62, Krafft-Ebing filled his years with scholarship and productivity. His 400 publications left such a strong

MR. V. P., SHOE FETISHIST

In *Psychopathia Sexualis,* Krafft-Ebing described hundreds of cases of what today would be known as paraphilias. These texts were published in Latin so as not to shock the general public. Here is a translation of one such case by Dr. Harry E. Wedeck:

> Mr. V. P., of an old and honorable family, a Pole, aged thirty-two, consulted me, in 1890, on account of "unnaturalness" of his sexual life. He gave the assurance that he came of a perfectly healthy family. He had been nervous from childhood. . . . For ten years he had suffered with sleeplessness and various neurasthenic ailments. From his fifteenth year he had recognized the difference of the sexes and had been capable of sexual excitation. At the age of seventeen he had been seduced by a French governess but coitus was not permitted, so that intense mutual sexual excitement (mutual masturbation) was all that was possible. In this situation his attention was attracted by her very elegant boots. This made a deep impression. His intercourse with this lewd person lasted four months. During this association her shoes became a fetish for this unfortunate boy. He began to have an interest in ladies' shoes in general, and actually went about trying to catch sight of ladies wearing pretty boots. The shoe-fetishism gained great power over his mind. He had the governess touch his penis with her shoes, and thus ejaculation with great lustful feeling was induced. After separation from the governess he went to prostitutes, whom he made perform the same manipulation. . . . In the society of the opposite sex the only thing that interested him was the shoe, and that only when it was elegant, of the French style, with heels, and of a brilliant black, like the original.
>
> In the course of time the following conditions became accessory: a prostitute's shoe that was elegant and chic; starched petticoats, and black hose, if possible. Nothing else in women interested him. *He was absolutely indifferent to the naked foot* [Wedeck's italics]. . . . In the course of years his fetishism had gained such power over him that when he saw a lady in the street, of a certain appearance and with certain shoes, he was so intensely excited that he had to masturbate. . . . Shoes displayed in shops, and, of late, even advertisements of shoes, sufficed to excite him intensely. . . . Cold-water cures and hypnotism were unsuccessful. The most celebrated physicians advised him to marry and assured him that as soon as he once really loved a girl, he would be free from his fetishism. . . . The patient was cruelly disappointed. . . . The wedding night was terrible; . . . Then he bought a pair of elegant lady's boots and hid them in the bed, and, by touching them while in the marital embrace, he was able, after a few days, to perform his marital duty.*

---

*Krafft-Ebing, R. von (1965). *Psychopathia sexualis: A medico-forensic study* (H. E. Wedeck, Trans.). New York: G. P. Putnam & Sons. Pp. 285–288.

mark on Viennese doctors, they built a statue in his memory.

Krafft-Ebing was not the only 19th-century writer on sexual matters. Between 1897 and 1928, the English doctor Havelock Ellis published a seven-volume work, *Studies in the Psychology of Sex.* Ellis is widely credited with broadening public acceptance of erotic literature. Although his first volume was banned, his last was received with considerable critical and popular acclaim. By the 1920s, books that dealt with explicit sexual themes, such as James Joyce's *Ulysses,* were being hailed as works of art. (Joyce's book remained banned in the United States for a decade after it had been published in Europe. For the first half of the 20th century, the United States remained a far more Victorian society than the queen's native country.) Havelock Ellis, like Krafft-Ebing, continues to be widely cited, but neither writer influenced our present views about sex to the same extent as Sigmund Freud.

Freud's Views on Sexuality

Freud's views on sexuality were first made explicit in his book *Three Essays on the Theory of Sexuality,* which he published in 1905 and revised several times. In these three essays, Freud attempted to

MASTURBATION AS A MURDER DEFENSE

Victorian fanaticism on the subject of masturbation is legendary. In her book *Victorian Murderesses*, Mary Hartman describes a 19th-century trial in which a charge of murder was defended by claiming that the victim masturbated:

Mlle. Doudet, a former governess who ran a small day-school in the cité d'Odiot in Paris, stood trial in that capital in 1855 on charges relating to the physical abuse of four of her pupils and the death of a fifth, all of them daughters of an English doctor who had placed them in her care. The accused, a highly educated woman with impeccable credentials for her post, insisted that the deceased child had died of natural causes related to a severe case of whooping cough. She maintained, too, that the emaciated condition of the other girls was not the result of her ill treatment, but rather the product of their own peculiar habits. . . .

Célestine Doudet, at thirty-four, had long been earning an independent living as a governess when she was hired in 1852 by the recently widowed Dr. James Loftus Marsden of Malvern to train his three eldest daughters and tutor them in French. Highly recommended by one of his patients, Mlle. Doudet came to Malvern with the glowing reports of several upper-class English families for whom she had worked in the past ten years. More than this, she had the distinction of an endorsement from the Queen herself, whom she had briefly served as a wardrobe mistress (with special responsibility for jewelry) at a time when Victoria wished to improve her French. . . .

In May, Marsden received word from the governess that four of the girls had contracted whooping cough and that the ten-year-old Mary Ann was seriously ill. At the same time neighbors of the governess, alerted by Doudet's sister, who had reportedly quit her post in April in protest over harsh treatment of the girls, began to mobilize an effort on the children's behalf. . . .

Another concerned neighbor sent the police an anonymous letter which described brutal treatments and even asserted that one child was being imprisoned in the cellar. . . .

Anonymous letters continued to arrive, but it was not until the doctor received word of the death of ten-year-old Mary Ann on July 22 that he found time to go to Paris. . . .

The day after his arrival Marsden removed his four remaining daughters. The youngest child, Alice, remained in Paris with her aunt;

---

enlarge the concept of sexuality and to give it a motivating role in practically all human affairs. Most shocking, especially for the time, was Freud's insistence that children have sexual feelings.

Freud's theory of psychosexual development has already been introduced in Chapter 3. The basic idea is that children must successfully negotiate a series of stages, each requiring some sort of accommodation to society's demands. In the *oral stage,* which comes first, the child's sexual energy (or *libido*) is centered in the lips and mouth. According to Freud, the child derives a type of sexual pleasure from sucking and later, biting. If, for some reason, the child is frustrated at this developmental stage — by too early weaning, for example — some sexual energy will remain forever attached (*fixated* was Freud's terminology) to "oral" needs. Such an individual might take up smoking, for example.

In the next stage, the *anal stage,* libidinal energy migrates to the anus. The child derives sexual pleasure from reflexive defecation, but society demands that toileting be controlled. The result is a conflict between the child's instinctive desire to achieve pleasure and society's demands. Harsh toilet training could lead to sexual energy remaining at the anal stage. Such a fixation could result in a tendency to slavishly adhere to others' demands or, in some cases, to be rebellious.

Having negotiated the anal stage, the child enters the *phallic stage,* in which sexual energy is invested in the genitals. During this stage, masturbation is commonly observed. It is at this point that the Oedipal conflict occurs. Males are forced through fear of castration to repress their desire for their mother and identify with their father. (A similar process is supposed to occur for females, but

the others, after a brief stay with the aunt, returned to England without their father's bringing a formal charge against the governess. The dissatisfied neighbors then decided to act again and in mid-September one of them went to the police to launch a formal investigation. As the inquiries got underway, Marsden was invited by the French police to submit a doctor's report concerning the health of the three daughters who had returned with him. He declined to do so, but in late September he sent word that his eldest child, Lucy, who had been kept isolated at the governess's for over a month, had just succumbed to the combined effects of whooping cough and exhaustion. . . .

The police investigation turned up several startling pieces of information. The maid . . . claimed that she had smuggled food to the children, who were systematically deprived of sufficient nourishment and rarely given anything but bread and soup. The maid also testified that Mlle. Doudet habitually tied the children's feet to their bedposts, and that on one occasion when little Alice had asked to be untied to go to the bathroom, she had been ordered to urinate in the chamber pot on the floor, which was barely possible with her legs tied. As she did so, the governess allegedly

struck her, and the chamber pot, breaking at her blow, severely cut the child. The incident doubtless accounted for the observed scars.

The maid related numerous other chilling events: she had seen the governess beating the children's heads against the wall, stamping on their bare feet until blood came, pulling out their hair, striking their arms with a ruler, forcing them to remain with arms crossed for entire days, and abandoning them for hours in the locked cellar or the toilet. . . .

Marsden was . . . motivated . . . by fear of scandal. He was perfectly aware that if he filed suit against the governess, the real reason for his sending his daughters to Paris might become public knowledge. The police investigation had already touched upon the evidence which would later become Célestine's primary defense against charges of cruelty; she claimed that all she had done was at the express order of her employer, that she had been instructed that her chief duty was to "cure" his daughters of a vice which was believed to afflict at least one of them, namely, masturbation. . . .

At her trial, witness after witness testified that Mlle. Doudet had discussed the girls' masturbatory habits on first meeting and frequently

(continued)

Freud's exposition of the so-called Elektra complex was less specific.) In any event, the resolution of the phallic stage sets the groundwork for the final developmental stage, the *genital stage*. This stage, which lasts for the rest of a person's life, represents a mature personality who, according to Freud, is able to engage in "normal" heterosexual relationships.

Freud believed that adult sexual problems, like neuroses in general, are the legacy of unresolved childhood conflicts. Most often, the sexual problem can be traced back to a fixation at the phallic stage. Sexual feelings are especially confused in this stage, and a fixation may result in the continuation of some aspect of childhood sexual behavior into adulthood. For example, if not adequately resolved, a boy's Oedipal jealousy of his father might become transformed into intense sexual jealousy of partners later in life.

Freud elaborated this view of the origin of sexual disorders by distinguishing between "infantile" and "mature" (*phallic* and *genital*) sexuality. Masturbation, for example, is infantile; intercourse is mature. Sexual maturity means moving from the pleasure derived from masturbation to the pleasure induced by intercourse. Being mature is better than being infantile. Thus, Freud disapproved of masturbation—and many other common sex practices—because he believed that they are signs of infantile sexuality.

Krafft-Ebing, Ellis, and Freud were all doctors with an interest in abnormal behavior. Initially, all suffered socially and professionally for their work, but all three were eventually recognized as pioneers who opened the field of sexual behavior to scientific scrutiny. Their scientific approach, however, was literary and clinical. It was not until the middle of

MASTURBATION AS A MURDER DEFENSE (continued)

in the presence of the children themselves. Later, when the presiding judge accused her of gross impropriety in this matter, she replied: "I recognize that in this I may have lacked discretion. But since it was the occupation of my whole life to break these habits, I constantly was thinking about them, and it happened that I would discuss them as a way of comforting myself." . . .

Through a combination of deception, ignorance, and shame, the girls' father persisted in defending a woman who was abusing his children. . . .

Correspondingly, the whole thrust of Célestine Doudet's defense was not to show that she was innocent of mistreating the children, but rather to demonstrate that all the girls were guilty of vicious habits. Her lawyer argued that once masturbation was proved, there was no need to invent bad treatment to explain the deplorable physical condition of the girls; "these habits, when they last, when they are inveterate, are sufficient to explain everything."

In preparing his case, Marsden compiled a dossier with signed statements from numerous persons who swore that his daughters were "untainted." He also worked to discredit those who had already testified to the habits. He allegedly bribed a maid from Malvern to stay away from the trial. . . .

The pathetic result of the case was its reduction to the question of whether the Marsden girls were or were not masturbators. In the process the children were forced to be as much defendants in the proceedings as Célestine Doudet. Both sides, after all, accepted masturbation as a morally culpable act which produced recognizable physical consequences. The children, then, were literally on trial. . . .

At the same time the court permitted the case to be developed as an archaic defense of patriarchal honor through a father's insistence on the sexual purity of his daughters. Time and again the combatants referred to the presence or absence of masturbatory vice as the real issue of the case, while the question of the children's physical and psychological suffering took second place. . . .

Imprisoned for three years until 1858, when her health began to fail, Célestine Doudet was pardoned and, after travel in Germany and England, returned to Paris. There she reportedly found mothers still willing to confide their children to her care.*

---

*Hartman, M. S. (1977). *Victorian Murderesses*. New York: Schocken Books. Pp. 85–129.

the 20th century that a nonmedical, traditionally trained scientist took an interest in human sexual behavior. That person was Alfred Kinsey.

ALFRED KINSEY: FOUNDER OF THE INSTITUTE FOR SEX RESEARCH

Alfred Charles Kinsey was born in Hoboken, New Jersey, in 1894. His father was a driven man who, despite only an eighth-grade education, worked his way up to become a professor of engineering at Stevens Tech. His father's passion for self-improvement and his strict religious beliefs ensured that Kinsey's childhood was relatively austere. It was also lonely. Kinsey was a sickly child who was never able to participate in sport. Perhaps in compensation, he de-

veloped a more solitary interest and became an expert pianist, at one time even considering a concert career. Kinsey eventually made male friends through Boy Scouts but throughout high school never had a date with a girl.

After graduation from high school, Kinsey enrolled at Stevens Tech to please his father. However, after 2 years, Kinsey transferred to Bowdoin College to pursue his developing interest in biology. His father was furious and refused him any further financial support. Fortunately, Kinsey was able to obtain a scholarship which, along with vacation work, saw him through a bachelor's degree in biology and psychology. Although he no longer lived at home, Kinsey's life at Bowdoin was reminiscent of high school. He never dated and spent considerable time

FIGURE 9.3 Alfred C. Kinsey (1894–1956).

alone playing the piano. For a man who would become famous as an expert on sex, Kinsey was an amazingly innocent college student. As an adult, he recalled kneeling in prayer with a fellow student imploring God to help his friend stop masturbating.

After graduating from Bowdoin, Kinsey enrolled at Harvard where he worked as an instructor while studying for his Ph.D. in zoology. Kinsey combined a growing love of the outdoors with his research interests, and by the time he received his Ph.D. in 1920 was an expert on the gull wasp and the trees in which this insect lived. On leaving Harvard, Kinsey joined the staff of Indiana University, an institution that was to become his professional home for the remainder of his life. Kinsey not only was receiving the munificent salary of $2,200 per year, but he also met and began dating the girl who was to become his wife; she was the first and only girl he ever dated. Kinsey continued his successful gull-wasp research, and by 1929 he was a full professor. Not only was his research widely praised, but Kinsey's informal and enthusiastic lecturing style made him

an extremely popular teacher. (His textbook, *An Introduction to Biology,* ultimately sold more than 400,000 copies.) Despite these successes, Kinsey might have spent the rest of his life in relative obscurity raising his children, tending his garden, and studying the gull wasp had he not been asked to organize a new course.

In 1938, in what can only be described as an unusual act for the times, Indiana University decided to launch a multidisciplinary course on marriage—including its physical aspects. Kinsey, for some reason, was nominated course coordinator. He knew a lot about the mating behavior of wasps but very little about human sexuality. A search of the available literature convinced him that no one else knew much either. The journals were replete with opinion and anecdote but light on statistics and facts. So, like a good scientist, Kinsey decided to collect empirical data.

Like many great enterprises, Kinsey's began in a small way. Because he was in charge of the course, students assumed Kinsey knew something about sex. So they began to come to him for sexual counseling. Kinsey couldn't offer much help, but he did take the opportunity to collect data; he asked students about their sexual histories and practices. In this way, without any research money and, more important, without official permission, Kinsey began to collect information about people's sexual behavior. He developed a short questionnaire and structured interview which he used to ensure that all students were asked similar questions. Kinsey was intrigued enough by his findings to start expanding his horizons. In addition to students, he began interviewing prison inmates and then members of the general community. The inevitable backlash began in the first year of the course. Clergymen, parents, and even some other members of the Indiana University staff objected to the frankness of Kinsey's lectures. By 1940 the pressure became too intense, and he was forced to stop teaching the marriage course. Curiously, his research—which involved much more explicit material than his lectures—was permitted to continue.

Contrary to popular belief, Kinsey was not the first person to ask people about their sex lives. Between 1915 and 1938, when Kinsey started teaching the marriage course, 19 surveys had been conducted. These were normally conducted by mail.

Kinsey was dubious about the validity of data obtained by mail preferring to use a structured interview in which answers could be probed and even challenged, if necessary. As his reputation grew, Kinsey was able to obtain increasingly generous grants from the Rockefeller Foundation. The funds allowed Kinsey and his colleagues to administer a much-expanded version of the original student interview to thousands of men. In 1948, along with his colleagues, Wardell Pomeroy and Clyde Martin, Kinsey published his findings in a book called *Sexual Behavior in the Human Male.* The result was a publishing sensation. Even though newspapers such as the *New York Times* refused to advertise it, Kinsey's book became a best seller with over 200,000 copies sold in its first 2 months. Theologians decried the authors' emphasis on the physical aspects of sex. Statisticians pointed out that the voluntary nature of the sample rendered it suspect as a true representation of the population. None of this stopped Kinsey, who went on to produce a second volume, *Sexual Behavior in the Human Female,* 5 years later. This second book represented a logical extension of his research. Like the first, it was a commercial success that was eventually translated into 10 foreign languages. Kinsey became a household name. He used his fame and research income to establish the Institute for Sex Research at Indiana University, an organization that continues to be a world center for research into all areas of sex. More important, Kinsey put sex research on the social and scientific agenda.

CLASSIC STUDY 16

Sexual Behavior in the Human Male and Female

Rather than simply accept social stereotypes—men are dominant, women submissive—Kinsey believed that normality is best defined statistically. Just as the "normal" male is about 6 feet tall and the normal night's sleep is about 8 hours, Kinsey argued that normal sexual behavior consists of the practices of the majority of the population. Unlike Freud, who viewed masturbation as inherently immature, or the general public, which looked upon homosexuality as obviously deviant, Kinsey believed that we cannot have a scientifically sound definition of sexual deviance without first knowing which sexual practices are statistically normal. He was, therefore, the complete empiricist. Beginning without a theory of sexuality and without preconceived beliefs about what constitutes normal sexual behavior, Kinsey set out to discover what people do and how often they do it.

Kinsey was not especially interested—at least at first—in attitudes toward sex or in the psychological factors that determine sexual behavior. His focus was squarely on numbers and acts, especially any activity that culminates in orgasm. He referred to these activities as sexual "outlets" and, like a good biologist, classified them into "types": masturbation, nocturnal emissions, petting to climax, heterosexual intercourse, homosexual intercourse, and contact with animals. Kinsey's main research aim was to determine the incidence of each type of sexual activity in different subsamples of the male population. For example, he sought to determine whether masturbation varies with race, ethnicity, marital status, educational level, occupational class, rural-urban background, religion, and geographic location.

Kinsey's research method was to arrange to speak to groups such as Rotary clubs. He would use this opportunity to explain the purpose of his research emphasizing the safeguards he employed to ensure confidentiality. Structured interviews would then be scheduled with those who volunteered to participate. These interviews were analyzed statistically. The outcome of these analyses are summarized in his first book, *Sexual Behavior in the Human Male.*

Kinsey and his co-authors began their 800-page book by stating their aims:

For some time now there has been an increasing awareness among many people of the desirability of obtaining data about sex which would represent an accumulation of scientific fact completely divorced from questions about moral value and social custom. . . . Before it is possible to think scientifically on any of these [sexual] matters, more needs to be known about the actual behavior of people. . . .

. . . Human sexual behavior represents one of the least explored segments of biology, psychology and sociology. Scientifically more has been known about the sexual behavior of some farm and laboratory animals. . . .

KINSEY'S LONGEST INTERVIEW

Wardell Pomeroy, in his book *Dr. Kinsey and the Institute for Sex Research,* describes the longest sexual-history interview that he and Kinsey ever recorded. It was taken from a man who kept a lifetime record of his sexual behavior. According to Pomeroy:

> When we got the record after a long drive to take his history, it astounded even us, who had heard everything. This man had had homosexual relations with 600 preadolescent males, heterosexual relations with 200 preadolescent females, intercourse with countless adults of both sexes, with animals of many species, and besides had employed elaborate techniques of masturbation. He had set down a family tree going back to his grandparents, and of thirty-three family members he had sexual contacts with seventeen. His grandmother introduced him to sexual intercourse, and his first homosexual experience was with his father. If this

sounds like *Tobacco Road* or *God's Little Acre,* I will add that he was a college graduate who held a responsible government job. . . .

> At the time we saw him, this man was sixty-three years old, quiet, soft-spoken, self-effacing—a rather unobtrusive fellow. It took us seventeen hours to get his history. . . .

> At one point in his history taking he said he was able to masturbate to ejaculation in ten seconds from a flaccid start. Kinsey and I, knowing how long it took everyone else, expressed our disbelief, whereupon our subject calmly demonstrated it to us. . . . It was the only sexual demonstration among the 18,000 subjects who gave their histories.*

---

*Pomeroy, W. B. (1972). *Dr. Kinsey and the Institute for Sex Research.* London: Thomas Nelson and Sons. Pp. 122–123.

The present study, then, represents an attempt to accumulate an objectively determined body of fact about sex which strictly avoids social or moral interpretations of the facts.[1]

What followed was a review of previous sexual research and an explanation of their classification system. Next came a lengthy discourse on interviewing techniques in which the authors defended the validity of their "histories." The structured interview Kinsey used to collect data for the first book lasted several hours and included hundreds of standard questions covering everything from a person's background and religion to his sexual experiences with members of the same sex, opposite sex, and even with animals. Confidentiality was ensured by using codes in place of names, and the nine interviewers who worked on the project were carefully trained to avoid showing any emotion no matter what an interviewee might reveal. The interviewers must also have been highly persuasive because very few of the 12,000 men requested to participate refused to reveal details of their sex lives. (One person who could not be convinced to participate was a hotel manager who refused the research team permis-

sion to take histories "because I do not intend that anyone should have his mind undressed in my hotel.")

Kinsey never claimed that his interviewees were a random sample of the population; most came from the Midwest or East, and the majority were above average in education. Instead, Kinsey attempted to ensure broad coverage by interviewing all the members of the various groups he approached. He argued that this would ensure that his data were not contaminated by self-selection—that is, by people with potentially unusual histories electing not to participate.

The bulk of the first book was given over to presenting statistical summaries of the data collected from the interviews (see Table 9.1, for example). Many of Kinsey's findings were surprising, at least at the time. For example, people were engaging in considerably more sexual activity than had previously been acknowledged. Premarital, marital, and extramarital sex were all found to occur more frequently than anyone had guessed. The average male reported one to four orgasms per week (although orgasmic frequency gradually declined after age 30). Practices that were considered unusual,

TABLE 9.1   Kinsey presented his data in great detail as shown in this example that shows the relationship between petting to climax and religious activity for single males with less than a high school education.

Religious Group	Cases	Total Population				Active Population		
		Mean Frequency	Median Freq.	% of Total Outlet	Incid. %	Mean Freq.	Median Freq.
Age: Adol.–15								
Protestant, active	89	.02 ± .01	0.00	0.9	11.2	0.20	0.069
Protestant, inactive	422	.03 ± .01	0.00	0.9	13.5	0.20	0.060
Catholic, inactive	106	.03 ± .01	0.00	0.8	16.0	0.15	0.064
Age: 16–20								
Protestant, active	91	.03 ± .01	0.00	1.0	18.7	0.14	0.060
Protestant, inactive	431	.04 ± .01	0.00	1.3	21.6	0.20	0.063
Catholic, inactive	105	.05 ± .02	0.00	1.5	22.9	0.23	0.074
Age: 21–25								
Protestant, inactive	234	.04 ± .02	0.00	1.2	15.4	0.26	0.066
Catholic, inactive	60	.05 ± .03	0.00	1.7	23.3	0.23	0.075

Source: Adapted from Kinsey, Pomeroy, & Martin, *Sexual behavior in the human male*, p. 478.

even harmful, were found to be quite common. Masturbation and oral sex, for example, were reported by large numbers of males. Perhaps most unexpected was that one third of males admitted to having had homosexual experiences although only 4% declared themselves to be exclusively homosexual. The frequency of homosexual contacts was so much higher than the prevailing beliefs that critics cited this finding as ipso facto evidence that Kinsey's data were not valid.

Kinsey found that certain sexual practices were strongly related to education level. For example, males with only a high school education were much more likely than college-educated males to have experienced premarital sex. College graduates had fewer orgasms per week than did those who had not attended college. Masturbation, nocturnal emissions, and petting to climax were more common among college graduates than non–college graduates. (Kinsey and his co-authors hypothesized that intelligent males had more active imaginations, which produced a richer dream life and therefore more nocturnal emissions.) Premarital, extramarital, and homosexual outlets were all found to be more frequent among non–college graduates. Education also influenced marital relations. For example, professional men engaged in more foreplay, were more likely to be nude during sex, and were more experimental with positions than were working-class men.

Kinsey's second book, *Sexual Behavior in the Human Female* (published in 1953), followed largely in the path set by the first. However, female interviewees were asked not only about acts and numbers but also about their attitudes and motivations. The researchers found many important differences between men and women. Take, for example, the practice of masturbation. Most men experienced their first orgasm at age 13 or 14 by masturbation. In contrast, most women did not achieve an orgasm until age 20, and this was usually by sexual intercourse rather than masturbation. By age 20, 93% of males masturbated; the corresponding figure for females was only 33%. Kinsey also found that men had more sexual outlets and partners than women had. They also had more sexual dreams and were aroused by more stimuli. Unlike males, only 2% of females claimed to be exclusively homosexual.

TABLE 9.2   Summary of Kinsey's Main Findings

Behavior	Frequency	
	Female	Male
Premarital intercourse	50%	92%
Masturbation by age 20	33%	93%
Marital intercourse (frequency per week in couples below age 35)	2–3	2–3
Extramarital intercourse by age 40	26%	50%
Homosexual experience by age 45	20%	50%
Animal contacts	3.6%	8.0%

Source: Adapted from Kinsey, A. C., Pomeroy, W. B., & Martin, C. E. (1948). *Sexual behavior in the human male.* Philadelphia: Saunders; and Kinsey, A. C., Pomeroy, W. B., Martin, C. E., & Gebhard, P. H. (1953). *Sexual behavior in the human female.* Philadelphia: Saunders.

Kinsey found that younger married couples, in their 20s, had sex around two or three times per week. By the time they reached their 60s, the rate was two or three times per month. Curiously, when married couples were asked how often they had sex, women gave higher numbers than men. Kinsey attributed this difference to a tendency for women to define sexual activity differently from men. Men equated sex with orgasm whereas this was not always true for women. In fact, some married women did not have orgasms despite claiming frequent sexual activity. Among those females who were orgasmic, the frequency of orgasms reached their peak when they were in their 30s. The peak for men was at least 10 years earlier.

Education, age, religious beliefs, and the other factors that affected male sexual behavior were also found to affect females. Masturbation, for instance, was found to be more common among educated women while premarital sex was more common among the less educated. Later in life, female college graduates had more extramarital affairs than non–college graduates.

A summary of Kinsey's main findings appears in Table 9.2.

AFTERMATH

Today, when it is not uncommon to find psychologists interviewing people about their sexual behavior, it is difficult to imagine the furor caused when an Indiana professor published such an explicit survey of sexual practices. Religious leaders criticized what they perceived to be an excessive focus on the physical rather than the spiritual aspects of sex. They were also troubled by Kinsey's tolerant attitude toward what many believed to be sexual perversions. Consider, for example, Kinsey's views on sexual preference:

> Exclusive preferences and patterns of behavior, heterosexual and homosexual, come only with experience or as a result of social pressures which tend to force an individual into an exclusive pattern of one or the other sort. Psychologists and psychiatrists, reflecting the mores of the culture in which they have been raised, have spent a good deal of time trying to explain the origins of homosexual activity; but considering the physiology of sexual responses and the mammalian background of human behavior, it is not so difficult to explain why a human animal does a particular thing sexually. It is more difficult to explain why each and every individual is not involved in every type of sexual activity.[2]

Far from considering homosexuality to be a sickness, Kinsey saw it as one of the many possible sexual "outlets." These outlets, he argued, are not entirely fixed by biology but learned as part of the socialization process. Kinsey's view, which has many adherents today, was well ahead of its time. Not surprisingly, it won him few friends among conservative politicians and clergy.

CHANGING VIEWS ON HOMOSEXUALITY

The relationship between sexual behavior and biology is obvious. Irrespective of how he is raised, a male child with XY chromosomes develops testes and a penis. This does not mean, however, that this child will necessarily grow up to feel like a man, fall in love with a woman, and ejaculate during heterosexual intercourse. Some males will grow up to prefer other males as sexual objects; likewise, some females will grow up to prefer females.

Kinsey showed that homosexuality is not an "either-or" matter but one of degree. Many men, and a substantial percentage of women, have homosexual experiences, but only a small percentage of males or females grow up to be exclusively homosexual. Kinsey argued that homosexuality is at least partly a learned preference no different in kind from heterosexuality. If he were alive today, he would have no trouble accepting the frequently stated theory that boys who reach puberty early are more likely to become homosexual because they are mainly friends with other boys when their sexual urges begin to develop. Such boys might learn, through conditioning, to associate their sexual feelings with the affection they feel for their male friends. Kinsey would probably also accept the value of theories that attribute homosexual behavior to the effects of low male-hormone levels during gestation. However, he would be unlikely to accept that homosexuality is entirely biological or entire fortuitous; he was too good a biologist for that.

For many years, homosexuality was considered to be a mental disorder. However, in 1973 the American Psychiatric Association voted to remove homosexuality from the manual of mental disorders. This decision reflected the changing times as well as the views of most homosexuals, who do not consider themselves in need of treatment.

In addition to priests, politicians, and other self-appointed guardians of the public's morals, scientists, especially statisticians, also attacked Kinsey's research. Their criticisms centered on his research procedures which, they claimed, may have affected the validity of his findings. For example, because Kinsey thought it best to use language with which people were familiar, his interviewers did not stick to a precise wording when asking questions. Instead, they varied their wording to suit the person being interviewed. Critics argued that rephrasing questions in this way meant that different respondents may have actually answered different questions thus rendering comparisons among people difficult if not impossible.

Other details of Kinsey's method were subjected to similar close scrutiny. Critics noted that interviewers were instructed to assume that a respondent had engaged in a specific practice unless the person specifically denied it ("How old were you when you first . . . ?"). This assumption may have biased the results in the direction of finding more sexual activity than if interviewers were required to make the opposite assumption and form their questions accordingly ("Have you ever . . . ?"). In a similar vein, interviewers sometimes persisted in a line of questioning even after a person denied having engaged in a specific sexual behavior. It is possible that such aggressive interviewing tactics may have coerced some people into confessing to acts that never actually occurred.

Psychologists pointed out the strong probability that at least some of Kinsey's data were influenced by the average person's need to appear socially acceptable. Remember, the interviews were conducted in the early 1940s; for many respondents, this was the first time they had ever spoken to anyone about sex, and they may not have been entirely truthful about their private sexual behavior. (After all, who wants to be considered abnormal?) A possible example of the desire to appear normal was Kinsey's finding that lower-class males, who described masturbation as wrong, reported a lower frequency of masturbation than professional males.

SAMPLING AND INTERVIEWING

Surveys compile information about the attitudes and behaviors of a population by asking people questions. Because it is usually impossible to question everyone in a group (say, all male voters), surveys are ordinarily based on a subgroup called a sample. In general, larger samples produce more accurate results, but not always. For example, a poll conducted before the 1936 presidential election predicted that the Republican candidate, Alf Landon, would defeat the Democrat, Franklin Roosevelt. Although 2 million people were surveyed, the actual election result was just the opposite to the one predicted. Roosevelt won by a landslide. The problem was poor sampling. The survey sample consisted of telephone subscribers and automobile owners. But, in the middle of the Great Depression, only the wealthy had telephones and cars. Although they preferred the Republican candidate, the vast majority of the population, who did not own phones and cars, preferred Roosevelt. Interestingly, the correct outcome was predicted by George Gallup, whose very name would later become synonymous with opinion polls. Gallup surveyed only around 300,000 people, but his sample was constructed so that voters were polled in pro-

portion to their frequency in the population. Today, with advanced sampling techniques, a valid result can often be obtained with a sample of only 2,000.

Kinsey's sample did not represent the population as a whole. He did not attempt to obtain a random sample; he relied on volunteers. Nevertheless, the information he collected was probably the best available at the time. Indeed, some more recent surveys are probably less valid than Kinsey's. For example, Shere Hite, author of *The Hite Report* published in 1976, began by sending 100,000 questionnaires to members of the National Organization of Women, abortion rights groups, university women's centers, and to those who responded to advertisements placed in magazines such as *Bride*. Only around 3,000 questionnaires were returned, and these contained essay answers to open-ended questions such as "How do you masturbate? Please give a detailed description." The book was a best seller, and it did make interesting reading, but its underlying methodology is highly suspect. Despite the advances in statistics and polling, it is fair to say that no fully adequate survey of sexual behavior has yet been published.

Because they believed the practice to be unacceptable, it is possible that lower-class males concealed the real extent of their masturbation.

Kinsey's sampling strategy was also questioned. His data came from volunteers; thus, it is possible that those who refused to participate had different patterns of sexual behavior from those who agreed to take part in the research. The composition of Kinsey's sample was also criticized. College-educated subjects were overrepresented and so were midwesterners. Nonwhites were entirely excluded, and some population subsamples were very small. (Kinsey's finding that 50% of men who did not marry before age 35 had experienced homosexual orgasm was based on a subsample of only 200 people.) Critics argued, with some force,

that Kinsey's results could not be said to describe the sexual behavior of the entire U.S. population.

As if his social and scientific critics were not enough to contend with, Kinsey also encountered trouble from the federal government. To expand his research into all aspects of sexual behavior, he established an Institute of Sex Research library, which contained sexually explicit books, magazines, calendars, and films from all over the world. In 1950 the United States Customs Office challenged Kinsey's right to import these materials. Shortly thereafter, under pressure from a congressional inquiry, Kinsey's major patron, the Rockefeller Foundation, ceased supporting his research. Despite these setbacks, Kinsey persevered, working up to his death in 1956 (one year before the Customs Office case was settled in the Institute's favor).

In the decades since the publication of Kinsey's books, sexual behavior—and society's attitudes—have gone through remarkable changes. The inhibited 1950s gave rise to the permissive 1960s and 1970s, which in turn led to a backlash in the 1980s. The 1990s are likely to be years of consolidation. Society remains open to sex in the media, but the growing fear of sexually transmitted diseases ensures that the free-wheeling "sexual revolution" of the 1960s is unlikely to recur in the near future. Nevertheless, much of the legacy of the 1960s is still felt in the 1990s. Recent surveys show that puberty and sexual activity begin at younger ages than in Kinsey's day. Girls begin to menstruate at 13 rather than 16; boys lose their soprano voices at 12 rather than 17. Sex is more frequent in marriage than in Kinsey's day, and women have more orgasms. Yet, important differences between the sexual attitudes of males and females continue to exist decades after the publication of Kinsey's work. For example, when American students were asked about their problems in sexual functioning, women most often mentioned the following:[3]

1. Fear of pregnancy
2. Fear of rape
3. Fear of being used for sex alone
4. Fear of rejection if sex is resisted
5. Uncomfortable with masturbation
6. Insecurity about their looks or performance
7. Guilt feelings

Men, on the other hand, mainly listed complaints about women:

1. Women are too inhibited.
2. Men always have to be the aggressor.
3. Women are too modest, coy, passive, or aggressive.
4. Men are expected to know all about sex.

Kinsey's work was mainly aimed at gathering basic data about sexual behavior; nevertheless, he was concerned with the practical implications of his work. For example, he strongly believed that his findings demonstrated that sexual disorders are caused by faulty learning. That is, they result from the accidental association of sexual and nonsexual stimuli by classical and instrumental conditioning. Such conditioning could happen to anybody:

> To each individual, the significance of any particular type of sexual activity depends very largely upon his previous experience. Ultimately, certain activities may seem to him to be the only things that have value, that are right, that are socially acceptable; and all departures from his own particular pattern may seem to him to be enormous abnormalities. But the scientific data which are accumulating make it appear that, if circumstance had been propitious, most individuals might have become conditioned in any direction, even into activities which they now consider quite unacceptable. There is little evidence of the existence of such a thing as innate perversity, even among those individuals whose sexual activities society has been least inclined to accept. There is an abundance of evidence that most human sexual activities would become comprehensible to most individuals, if they could know the background of each other individual's behavior.[4]

Kinsey's formulation could be applied not only to sexual disorders such as those described by Krafft-Ebing but also to sexual "performance" dysfunctions such as impotence and premature ejaculation; that is, they too might be the result of faulty learning. If performance dysfunctions result from faulty learning, it logically follows that they can be "unlearned." This line of reasoning, which began with Kinsey, gained considerable credibility in the 1960s with the publication of the classic studies of William Masters and Virginia Johnson, whose work is described next.

THE MODERN ERA IN SEX RESEARCH

William H. Masters studied medicine at the University of Rochester, specializing in obstetrics and gynecology. His early research on hormones was enough to convince Washington University in St. Louis to allow him to set up a lab in 1954. Three years later, he was joined by a young research assistant, Virginia Johnson. For 7 years, Masters and Johnson worked together at Washington University supported by university funds and by external research grants. In 1964 they opened their own private clinic and research institute, the Reproductive Biology Research Foundation.

Masters and Johnson took the next logical step in sex research. In place of Kinsey's structured interviews and questionnaires, in which data are collected secondhand, they substituted direct observations of people engaging in sexual behavior under controlled laboratory conditions. Masters and Johnson were not the first to observe sexual behavior in the laboratory. John Watson, the founder of modern behaviorism, anticipated their work by some four decades. He studied the physiology of sex by attaching electrodes to couples and taking recordings as they engaged in intercourse. With the aid of his research assistant, Rosalie Rayner, Watson became an enthusiastic subject in his own research. Alas, Mrs. Watson was not amused, and Watson's academic career came to an abrupt end. Times change, however, and by the 1960s, Masters and Johnson could pursue their research with little real fear of repercussions. In the permissive atmosphere of the 1960s, they were free to experiment with new research techniques. For example, to measure the physiology of sexual responses in the laboratory, they constructed a clear plastic artificial penis through which the vagina could be filmed during sexual excitement. Initially, they used this device to study prostitutes, but because prostitutes rarely have orgasms, they switched to volunteers—males as well as females. Clearly, people who agreed to serve science in this way were not a random sample of the population, but they were not exactly rare, either. More than 700 males and females volunteered to be observed having sex. Using films and various physiological recording techniques, Masters and Johnson recorded more than 10,000 orgasms. In 1966 they published their findings in a book called *Human Sexual Response*. Four years later, Masters and Johnson published a second book, *Human Sexual Inadequacy*. Together, these two volumes heralded the dawning of the modern era in sexology and the birth of sex therapy.

CLASSIC STUDY 17
Human Sexual Response and *Human Sexual Inadequacy*

Human Sexual Response begins by acknowledging Kinsey's contribution to the "sociological study of sex" but highlights the lamentable lack of information on the "physiologic or psychological response to sexual stimulation." The authors set their task as answering two questions: "What physical reactions develop as the human male and female respond to effective stimulation?" and "Why do men and women behave as they do when responding to effective sexual stimulation?" Masters and Johnson argue that, until these questions are answered, it will not be possible to treat sexual dysfunction.

The authors then describe what they call the four phases of the sexual response cycle; they propose to use this four-phase cycle as a framework for further discussion. Interestingly, despite the many psychological and sociological differences between the sexes, the sexual response cycle turns out to be quite similar in both sexes:

1. *Excitement phase.* The excitement phase begins with petting and foreplay. It is marked by an increased heart rate and rapid breathing. The nipples become erect in women and in some men. Blood flows to the genitals making the penis erect and the clitoris swell. The lining of the vaginal walls becomes moist with lubricating fluid.

2. *Plateau phase.* The genitals continue to fill with blood, and muscle tension increases. The penis and testes enlarge, and the testes are pulled higher into the scrotum. The clitoris retracts under its hood and the tissues of the vagina swell. Subjective feelings of excitement increase.

3. *Orgasmic phase.* Muscles contract rhythmically causing the vaginal walls to contract and expand. Muscle contractions in the penis cause ejaculation to occur. For both sexes, the sensation of orgasm accompanies these muscle contractions.

4. *Resolution phase.* The body slowly returns to its unstimulated condition. For men there is a refractory period in which they cannot have another orgasm. This varies from minutes for some men to hours for others. The length of the refractory interval varies with age, the novelty of the partner, and other factors. Women may have multiple orgasms without a noticeable refractory period, but as in men, there is considerable individual variability.

The remainder of the book is devoted to a detailed examination of each of the four phases in both females and males. The authors make many contributions to our knowledge about the physiology of sex. For example, the "sex flush," a rash that first appears on the female chest during the excitement phase and appears related to the intensity of a woman's sexual tension, receives its first thorough treatment in *Human Sexual Response*. During the course of their investigations, Masters and Johnson also manage to shatter many popular myths about sexual performance and satisfaction. Take penis size, for example. Throughout the ages, men with small penises have worried that they would be unable to satisfy their sexual partners. By taking careful measurements, Masters and Johnson show that the size of a flaccid penis does not correlate well with the size of the same organ when erect. A full erection could double the size of a small penis whereas a larger flaccid organ may increase by only a small amount when erect. The result is that "the difference in average erective size increase between the smaller flaccid penis and the larger flaccid penis is not significant." Masters and Johnson also show that absolute penis length is irrelevant because the vagina is really only a "potential" space; it adjusts its size to accommodate the size of the penis.

Not only do they debunk penis size as a contributor to a male's sexual performance or a female's potential satisfaction, but Masters and Johnson also expose as false the Freudian distinction between clitoral and vaginal orgasms. Freud insisted that "clitoral" orgasms are second-best because they are produced by masturbation, a practice, you will recall, that he considered immature. "Vaginal" orgasms, he believed, are a sign that a woman has truly progressed to the genital stage of personality development. By showing that *all* female orgasms result from stimulation of the clitoris (in masturbation this stimulation is direct, during intercourse it is indirect), Masters and Johnson expose Freud's theory as a distinction without a real difference.

Their research also leads to some practical advice. For example, contrary to widely held belief, Masters and Johnson find that it is a mistake for the male to try to stimulate the clitoris during intercourse. In the plateau phase, the clitoris retracts making access difficult or even painful. Indirect stimulation through normal sexual movements is preferred by most women. In a similar vein, Masters and Johnson argue that the goal of simultaneous orgasm—as described in many works of erotic fiction—is not crucial to sexual satisfaction and can even be distracting if couples make this the main goal of lovemaking.

In *Human Sexual Response,* Masters and Johnson discuss some of the sexual performance inadequacies they observed in their laboratory; they also make a few suggestions about how such sexual dysfunctions may be treated. However, it is their second book, *Human Sexual Inadequacy,* that fully develops their ideas about "sex therapy." *Human Sexual Inadequacy* appeared in 1970; it described a treatment regimen for sexual dysfunction based on a study of more than 800 people with sexual problems. Although it was initially ignored by the medical community, the book was immediately taken up by psychologists who found Masters and Johnson's "behavioral" approach congenial. *Human Sexual Inadequacy* was also a hit with the general public, who made the book a best seller.

Masters and Johnson begin *Human Sexual Inadequacy* by dividing the sexual response system into two parts: biophysical and psychosocial. Biophysical problems (alcohol abuse or diseases such as diabetes, for example) can affect sexual performance, but these are relatively rare. In the majority of cases, sexual dysfunction has a psychological cause—people fail to perform adequately because they are afraid of sex or disgusted by it. Masters and Johnson identify eight major types of sexual dysfunction:

1. *Primary impotence.* A man has never been able to achieve an erection sufficient for intercourse with females or males. About 15% of the impotent men treated by Masters and Johnson fell into this category.

2. *Secondary impotence.* A man has been successful in obtaining erections in the past but is impotent now. Masters and Johnson found secondary impotence to be considerably more common than primary impotence.

3. *Premature ejaculation.* After secondary impotence, premature ejaculation was the second most common problem Masters and Johnson encountered in males. They defined premature ejaculation rather arbitrarily as ejaculation before the female is "ready" on more than half the occasions of sexual intercourse.

4. *Ejaculatory incompetence.* A male can have erections but cannot ejaculate in the vagina. This is a relatively rare condition.

5. *Dyspareunia.* Intercourse is painful.

6. *Primary orgasmic dysfunction.* A woman has never had an orgasm from intercourse or masturbation. This was the most common problem encountered among females.

7. *Situational orgasmic dysfunction.* A person can have orgasms only in certain situations (on vacation but not at home, for example).

8. *Vaginismus.* Around 8% of Masters and Johnson's female patients suffered from this condition, which involves contractions of the vagina that make penile insertion impossible.

Like Kinsey, who argued that sexual disorders such as the paraphilias result from faulty learning, Masters and Johnson believed that these eight performance disorders originate in unhealthy attitudes learned early in life. For example, a person may have been raised in an orthodox religious environment in which attitudes toward sexual enjoyment have changed little since biblical times. One woman suffering from vaginismus told Masters and Johnson that

> she was prohibited when bathing from looking at her own breasts either directly or from reflection in the mirror for fear that unhealthy sexual thoughts might be stimulated by visual examination of her own body. Discussion with a sibling of such subjects as menstruation, conception, contraception, or sexual functioning were taboo. . . . Mrs. A. entered marriage without a single word of advice. . . . The only direction offered by her religious advisor relative to sexual behavior was that coital connection was only to be endured if conception was desired.[5]

Such a strict upbringing, in which sexual enjoyment is taught to be dirty, can lead people to be disgusted by sex and to fear becoming sexually aroused.

Even those with "normal" upbringings can, through experience with partners who have sexual problems, develop performance dysfunctions of their own. For example, one of Masters and Johnson's patients traced his own performance dysfunction back to his wife's vaginismus.

According to Masters and Johnson, unhealthy attitudes set the stage for sexual problems, but attitudes alone are not sufficient to explain sexual dysfunction. Two other factors are necessary: a fear of failing at sex and a behavior they called "spectator-

ing." They believed that "fear of inadequacy is the greatest known deterrent to effective sexual functioning because it so completely distracts the fearful individual from his or her natural responsivity by blocking reception of sexual stimuli. . . ." Fear of inadequacy leads people to adopt the role of "spectator." Such people fail to fully immerse themselves in the sexual act. They prefer to be spectators so that they can keep a conscious watch out for any sign of inadequate performance.

In summary, then, attitudes learned early in life give rise to sexual dysfunctions that are maintained by a fear of failure and by the habit of adopting a spectator role. Clearly, there are important differences between vaginismus, primary impotence, and the other sexual disorders, but according to Masters and Johnson's formulation, they all share at least one common characteristic, anxiety. This anxiety, caused by doubts about their sexual ability, leads people to adopt the spectator role. "Spectatoring," in turn, causes males to be unable to perform and females to be unable to respond. A vicious cycle develops; anxiety leads to spectatoring, spectatoring results in poor performance, and poor performance produces more anxiety. Masters and Johnson acknowledge that factors other than anxiety—illness, ignorance about sex, poor marital communication—may also contribute to sexual inadequacy. But they considered these factors to be secondary to performance anxiety. According to Masters and Johnson, the main goal of sex therapy should be anxiety reduction.

MASTERS AND JOHNSON'S TREATMENT PROGRAM

Patients

Masters and Johnson's treatment program revolves around education, discussion, anxiety decrease, and "permission" to become sexually aroused. Although it is common to speak of a male's impotence or a female's orgasmic dysfunction, Masters and Johnson believe that most sexual problems arise out of the way in which partners interact—"regardless of the particular form of sexual inadequacy . . . , fears of sexual performance are of major concern to both partners in the marital bed." Because Masters and Johnson view sexual disorders as "relationship" problems that belong to couples rather than individuals, the marital unit is the focus of their therapy. (They do briefly refer to single patients in *Human Sexual Inadequacy* and also to surrogate partners, but few details are given.)

Therapists

Masters and Johnson stress the importance of having both a male and a female therapist. Although no specific educational backgrounds were deemed absolutely necessary, they believed that therapists should be unprejudiced, comfortable discussing sexual problems, and knowledgeable enough to provide factual information about sex when required.

Procedure

On arrival in St. Louis (couples came from all over North America), patients are introduced to their therapists, given an overview of the program, and encouraged to explore local restaurants and attractions. The idea is to have each couple look on therapy as a break from their routine, a chance to explore and deepen their relationship. The first step in the treatment program is a detailed case history, but before the history-taking stage even begins, couples are forbidden from attempting sexual intercourse until otherwise directed by the therapist. Histories are taken separately for the male, by the male therapist, and the female, by the female therapist. The idea is to explore each partner's specific attitudes uncontaminated by the other partner's presence. Patients are informed that nothing they say will be revealed to their partner without permission. This initial phase lasts for 2 days. In addition to the antecedents of the specific sexual complaint, the couple's general relationship is also explored. Coping mechanisms are discussed as well as fantasies, sexual practices, and each individual's "sexual value system." The latter is especially important because partners with very different sexual attitudes (it's dirty versus it's glorious, for example) may have to change their values before treatment could hope to succeed. Although possible physical illnesses or defects are investigated where appropriate, Masters and Johnson devote little attention to the possibility of psychiatric disturbance. They point out that sexual dysfunction does not necessarily imply any psychiatric abnormality. This is undoubtedly true, but the converse does not necessarily hold. We cannot assume that psychiatric problems are not present;

careful attention to possible emotional illnesses is an important part of modern sex therapy.

On the basis of the history elicited during the first 2 days, couples whose relationships are judged too precarious to survive treatment are discontinued. Every effort is made to terminate the treatment of such couples in a gentle manner that will "protect the marriage at current levels of psychosexual functioning." The remaining couples move into the second stage of treatment, which lasts another 10 to 12 days. First, couples are given the therapists' views on the source of their problems. Although the focus remains on the couple ("there is no such thing as an uninvolved partner" according to Masters and Johnson), the etiological importance of one partner's anxiety and spectatoring is explained. Information about sex is provided to those couples who need it. Therapy then settles down into a pattern. Couples meet with their therapists during the day and do "homework" on their own in their hotel room at night. Initially, homework involves practicing what Masters and Johnson called "sensate focus." Couples are required to engage in gradually increasing mutual erotic arousal without attempting sexual intercourse. Couples are instructed to undress and to give pleasure by touching one another's body. They begin by touching nongenital areas and later include the genitals and breasts. The idea is to permit one's partner to overcome his or her anxiety about sex, and give up the spectator role, by eliminating the performance pressure produced by sexual intercourse. Partners learn to be intimate, to communicate needs, and to give mutual pleasure, without any requirement for sexual performance. As therapy progresses, couples are instructed to give one another feedback and tell what activities they find sexually exciting. Therapists continue to offer guidance and information where required.

Once couples are comfortable with sensate focus, therapeutic instructions become more dependent on each couple's specific problem. Females suffering from orgasmic dysfunction are required to concentrate on their own pleasure. They are given some hints, but ultimately it is up to them to inform their partner about which techniques are most arousing. Arousal and pleasure are emphasized, not orgasms. When the female is able to get aroused through manual manipulation and other techniques, she is then asked to go further. She sits astride her partner, inserts his penis, and then moves in any way that she finds exciting. The female superior position as well as the emphasis on the female's satisfaction gives her control as well as responsibility for her own pleasure. Ultimately, the therapist tries to move the couple toward mutually satisfying intercourse.

Different techniques are used for different problems. For males suffering from premature ejaculation, Masters and Johnson recommend the "squeeze" technique. The female stimulates the male up to the point just before orgasm when, at a signal from the male, she squeezes his penis. This technique reduces excitement and prevents orgasm from taking place. The female then begins stimulating and again uses the squeeze technique to prevent the male from reaching the point of orgasm. Repetitions of this technique help the male to recognize the signs of impending orgasm and to gain self-control. In the next stage, the woman straddles the man and gradually builds up her level of pelvic movement. The male's urge to ejaculate is again repressed by the female dismounting and using the squeeze technique. The goal is to allow the male to put off ejaculation for a "reasonable" time period. What is reasonable in this context is defined by the individual couple.

A number of related techniques are used to treat other performance dysfunctions. Virtually all the therapeutic techniques give greater responsibility to the female than the male. Females are responsible for their own satisfaction as well as for helping the male to learn self-control. Moreover, the female-dominant position is recommended, at least initially, in the treatment of practically all performance disorders. Despite this emphasis on the female's therapeutic role, Masters and Johnson made it clear that no treatment could hope to work without the mutual understanding and cooperation of both partners.

Treatment Outcome

Masters and Johnson conducted an evaluation of treatment outcome. Their results are presented in two sets of statistics: outcome at the end of the 2-week treatment period and outcome after a follow-up conducted several years later at patients' homes or by telephone. Given that people came from all over the United States and Canada for treatment, this follow-up must have been an enormous task.

For the purposes of analysis, Masters and Johnson separated younger and older couples; they presented their outcome data in terms of failures. The initial outcome figures varied from no failures for vaginismus (29 cases) to 28% failures for primary and secondary impotence combined (245 cases). For premature ejaculation, there were only four failures in 186 cases. The failure rate for primary orgasmic dysfunction was 18%. For couples over age 50, who were analyzed separately, around 30% were classified as failures. Long-term follow-ups were conducted only on those couples who had a successful immediate outcome. Masters and Johnson reported very few reversals—the failure rate was only around 20%.

AFTERMATH

Human Sexual Response and *Human Sexual Inadequacy*, although widely read, had only a modest effect on scientific physiology. The reason was the lack of hard data: No actual physiological recordings are presented in either book nor are detailed physiological findings given. The sparsity of physiological data did not, however, keep the books from producing a dramatic effect on sex therapy. The apparent dramatic success of Masters and Johnson's approach to sexual dysfunction leads most psychologists to abandon the lingering Freudian idea that sexual disorders can only be treated as symbolic representations of some underlying psychological problem. Instead, creative energies were channeled into refining Masters and Johnson's treatment techniques. Their treatment program became the model for sex clinics established around the world.

As often happens in psychotherapy, initial enthusiasm soon gave way to caution and concern. Many psychologists were unable to replicate Masters and Johnson's favorable outcome figures. They found sex therapy to produce lasting effects on about 50% rather than 80% of patients. Part of the problem was the way Masters and Johnson presented their results. Although it's easy to be misled, they never actually claimed an 80% long-term "cure" rate. Their claim was that 80% of cases were *not failures*. It turns out that there is a big difference between not being a failure and being a complete success. Masters and Johnson classified partial successes as "not failures" while other researchers classified the same patients as "not successes." More recent, and more sophisticated, studies of sex therapy have shown that sex therapy is certainly not a miracle cure, but for those couples whose relationships are strong, it can often appreciably improve sexual functioning.

Changes to Masters and Johnson's treatment program were inevitable. Psychologists found, for example, that a single therapist worked as well as two and that weekly or twice-weekly office visits — combined with interpolated homework assignments — are as effective as a 2-week residential treatment program. For women who have never experienced orgasm, a graduated masturbation program has been introduced. Once the woman learns to experience orgasm by masturbation (in some cases using a vibrator), the male partner stimulates her, and when orgasm can be achieved, the couple moves to intercourse. Attempts have also been made to extend behavioral sex therapy well beyond sexual dysfunctions to various sexual disorders including fetishism and other paraphilias.

In recent years, psychologists have challenged the idea that all sexual dysfunctions are anxiety based. Some men, it has been shown, find danger sexually exciting. A man has even been known to perform sexually when being threatened for nonperformance by a knife-wielding woman! Although such observations clearly challenge Masters and Johnson's hypothesis that anxiety always affects performance, the implications for treatment have not yet been made clear. For now, it is fair to say that, although Masters and Johnson's therapeutic regimen has been modified, most changes are simply variations on the original program.

In the early days of sex therapy, critics complained that it focused too much on the physical aspects of sex. After all, there is more to love and affection than bedroom gymnastics. Over the years, however, it has become clear that overcoming sexual problems often — but not always — has beneficial spinoffs for other aspects of a couple's relationship. Thus, although it is not the primary aim, Masters and Johnson's treatment approach can have important psychological benefits far beyond the bedroom.

Masters and Johnson's legacy, a scientific approach to sexology and the development of modern sex therapy, has been widely praised, but no one has put it more graciously than Wardell Pomeroy, one of Kinsey's co-authors and his biographer:

> We observed directly more human sexual responses than any other scientist before Masters and Johnson. Later, the Saint Louis team showed that on some points we were simply wrong, and they recorded many observations we missed. Making their large body of observations under controlled laboratory conditions, they wove what they saw into a coherent pattern covering the entire cycle of female and male response, and that is the essence of their enormous achievement.[6]

Further Reading

Kinsey, A. C., Pomeroy, W. B., & Martin, C. E. (1948). *Sexual behavior in the human male*. Philadelphia: Saunders.

Kinsey, A. C., Pomeroy, W. B., Martin, C. E., & Gebhard, P. H. (1953). *Sexual behavior in the human female*. Philadelphia: Saunders.

Krafft-Ebing, R. von (1965). *Psychopathia sexualis: A medico-forensic study* (H. E. Wedeck, Trans.). New York: G. P. Putnam & Sons.

Masters, W. H., & Johnson, V. E. (1967). *Human sexual response*. Boston: Little, Brown.

Masters, W. H., & Johnson, V. E. (1970). *Human sexual inadequacy*. Boston: Little, Brown.

Notes

1. Kinsey, A. C., Pomeroy, W. B., & Martin, C. E. (1948). *Sexual behavior in the human male*. Philadelphia: Saunders. Pp. 3–5.

2. Kinsey, A. C., Pomeroy, W. B., Martin, C. E., & Gebhard, P. H. (1953). *Sexual behavior in the human female*. Philadelphia: Saunders. P. 451.

3. Tavris, C., & Offir, C. (1977). *The longest war: Sex differences in perspective*. New York: Harcourt, Brace, Jovanovich. P. 68.

4. Kinsey, A. C., Pomeroy, W. B., Martin, C. E. (1948). *Sexual behavior in the human male*. Philadelphia: Saunders. P. 678.

5. Masters, W. H., & Johnson, V. E. (1970). *Human sexual inadequacy*. Boston: Little, Brown. P. 254.

6. Pomeroy, W. B. (1972). *Dr. Kinsey and the Institute for Sex Research*. London: Thomas Nelson and Sons. P. 178.

PART IV

Psychological Treatment

The psychological treatment of emotional disorders, known today as psychotherapy, is as old as civilization itself. Dream interpretation, an important aspect of psychoanalysis, was widely practiced in biblical times. Similarly, the importance of having insight into one's motivations was well understood by the ancient Greeks, who inscribed the motto "know thyself" on the door of the Delphic Temple. Like modern therapists, the classical philosophers also took for granted that words have the power to change behavior. Compare, for example, the modern characterization of psychotherapy as the "talking cure" with Socrates' words: "The physician obtains the changes he wishes through drugs, the Sophists, instead, through the word."

Despite its ancient roots, psychological treatment remains a controversial subject. Some writers claim that psychotherapy is generally effective; others see large differences between different types of psychotherapy (some types work well, others not at all). A small, but influential, group of writers claim that psychotherapy is nothing more than a placebo, a "sugar pill" that only works because people think it does.

The origins and effectiveness of psychological therapy are the subject of the next two chapters. Somatic therapies — drugs, electric shocks — are not covered here as they are primarily the province of psychiatrists rather than psychologists. Chapter 10 describes a classic collection of case studies that marked an important turning point in the development of modern psychological treatment. Chapter 11 is concerned with evaluating traditional psychotherapy and the development of behavioral alternatives. Because psychotherapy is at least partly an art, establishing its efficacy is no easy task. For example, a particular psychological treatment may claim to give people greater insight into their behavior. But because psychotherapy is a highly individualized verbal art, it is often difficult to specify just what the treatment involves — to isolate its "active" ingredients. Matters are complicated further by the lack of any reliable measure of what the treatment is trying to achieve. How do we go about measuring insight? And, if we cannot measure it, how can we know whether insight is achieved? The same questions may be asked about "self-fulfillment," "self-actualization," or any of the personality traits that psychotherapy is meant to affect. These measurement problems, and other aspects of psychotherapy, are discussed in detail in Chapters 10 and 11.

CHAPTER 10

Minister to a Mind Diseased

The history of psychological treatment has always been more interesting to historians than to practitioners. There are probably two reasons for this: Clinicians tend to be practical people, and most historical information is of little day-to-day use. (Not even the most committed historian would claim that a sound knowledge of biblical dream interpretation makes it any easier to help a patient overcome a debilitating depression.) A second reason for avoiding medical history is that it is so unpleasant. According to physician and essayist Lewis Thomas:

> For century after century, all the way to the remote millennia of its origins, medicine got along by sheer guesswork and the crudest sort of empiricism. It is hard to conceive of a less scientific enterprise among human endeavors.[1]

It is certainly true that, prior to the 19th century, psychological medicine was pretty much a hit-and-miss affair. Weird theories (abnormal behavior is caused by venturing out in the light of a full moon), and even stranger treatments (cupping, bleeding, purging) were accepted as if they had some basis in fact. Anything that could be dreamed up was given a try; it did not seem to matter that practically all treatments were demonstrably worthless and that some treatments were worse than the conditions they were designed to cure. The main reason that bizarre and useless treatments continued to be used for so long was that clinicians felt compelled to do *something*. The common belief was that untreated patients inevitably deteriorated.

The perceived need to treat every patient, combined with the absence of any scientific rationale on which such treatment could be based, inevitably led to gross empiricism ("let's try it and see"). Add in a lack of interest in history, and it is no surprise that

Canst thou not minister to a mind diseas'd,
Pluck from the memory a rooted sorrow
Raze out the written troubles of the brain,
And with some sweet oblivious antidote
Cleanse the stuff'd bosom of that perilous stuff
Which weighs upon the heart?

—William Shakespeare

each generation rediscovers the treatments of the past. Shock therapy (both psychological and physical), catharsis (exorcising disturbing emotions or troublesome demons), soothing manipulations (music, dance, massage, drugs), reassurance (counseling, love, unconditional positive regard), insight (dream analysis), and relearning (inculcating new habits and ways of relating) have all made periodic reappearances in the history of psychological treatment. Although modern psychotherapy continues to use techniques familiar to previous generations of therapists, there is a difference. Unlike the therapies of the past, all current brands of psychotherapy purport to be "scientific." The development of psychotherapy is usually portrayed as a series of discoveries each forming the theoretical basis for a new treatment. At best this is an idealized version of history; at worst it is a gross distortion. Today's psychotherapy derives from a variety of sources—literary and religious as well as scientific. More important, the most influential publications in the development of the field were not experimental investigations but case studies. Perhaps the most important and far-reaching in their effects were the case studies contained in *Studies on Hysteria* by Josef Breuer and Sigmund Freud. The background and influence of this classic work are described in this chapter.

ORIGINS OF PSYCHOTHERAPY

The First 1,800 Years

Writing in the first century, the Roman doctor Soranus outlined his approach to caring for the mentally ill. Rooms should be kept free from disturbing noises, he suggested, and therapeutic personnel must learn to be accepting and sympathetic. As they improve, patients should be encouraged to speak in group meetings and to engage in role playing—comedy if they are depressed, drama if manic. It is remarkable that, despite the advances in scientific medicine over the centuries, when it comes to caring for the mentally ill, little has changed. Soranus' principles continue to form the basis of most hospital treatment. Other "modern" therapeutic techniques, such as dream interpretation, music therapy, group therapy, suggestion, and even some forms of behavior modification were also well known in the classical world.

This does not mean that the ancients did not have any specialized treatment techniques of their own. One that enjoyed a long run of popularity was known as *incubation*. Patients, whether physically or mentally ill, were first subjected to ritual cleansing and then given a prescribed diet. On a specially selected night, with the aid of hypnotic drugs, they were put to sleep in a holy temple. While music played, they were visited by the God Asclepias, who could appear in a variety of different forms, as an animal, as a human, or even as an ephemeral spirit. In patients' dreams, Asclepias often touched the sick part of their bodies. Upon awakening, each patient's dream would be decoded by a special priest. In addition, group discussion sessions were held in which patients explored the symbolic nature of their dreams under the guidance of a priest. After several such experiences, patients began to "understand" the symbolic meaning of their illness and their symptoms would supposedly disappear. Although incubation is no longer practiced, it has many striking parallels with modern psychotherapy. For example, the ancient healers manipulated patients into changing their behavior by a combination of physical setting, social expectations, suggestion, and drugs. The modern therapist also uses social expectations (the various diplomas on the wall, for example), suggestion, and sometimes drugs to induce people to behave in certain ways. Similarly, group discussions guided by an authoritative leader, dream interpretation, and an emphasis on understanding the causes of one's behavior remain important elements of some types of psychotherapy.

The sophistication of the Greeks and Romans is usually contrasted with the brutality of the Middle Ages, a supposedly benighted period in which all the learning of the classical world was forgotten. While medieval brutality was certainly not uncommon, it is worthwhile noting that many psychotherapeutic services survived the Fall of Rome. Throughout the Middle Ages, for example, monasteries continued to care for the sick and the elderly. Their treatments were often strange—swinging the mentally ill in baskets suspended from the ceiling, for example—but it is not true to state, as many psychology textbooks do, that the mentally ill were simply ignored or burned as witches. Indeed, it is not at all clear that those persecuted as witches were actually mentally ill. Many were political opponents of the then current regime, others simply disbelievers in the religious orthodoxies of the day. Of course, some "witches" may have been mentally ill, but wholesale burnings were never the general mental-health policy of any medieval town or country nor were such incidents especially common in the Middle Ages. In fact, the majority of witch burnings took place during the supposedly enlightened Renaissance, and a few particularly notorious incidents occurred as recently as the 17th century in America. We have little reason to feel superior to our medieval ancestors—or to non-Western nations for that matter. While Europe was in the grip of the Dark Ages, the Moslem world continued to apply the classical prescription for emotional illness: humane care in peaceful surroundings. The Moslems believed that the mentally ill were specially loved by God, who chose them to reveal his divine message. As a consequence, the Moslems worshipped as saints people whom we would consider to be mentally ill.

By the 16th century, most doctors eschewed exorcisms and the trappings of witchcraft advocating instead a "scientific" approach to the treatment of the mentally ill. Alas, because there was very little scientific knowledge available at the time, there was not much that could be done. The seriously disturbed were warehoused in special hospitals, first in Spain and its colonies, later in other countries. These hospitals varied in their treatment philosophies, but it is fair to say that many, if not most, were unpleasant, violent, degrading, and unhealthy. Dr. Thomas Munro, superintendent of St. Mary of Bethleham Hospital in London, summarized his treatment program as follows:

> Patients are ordered to be bled about the latter end of May, or the beginning of June, according to the weather, and after they have been bled they take vomits once a week for a certain number of weeks; after that we purge the patients. This has been the practice for years; it was handed down to me by my father, and I do not know any better practice.[2]

Popular usage shortened the name of Munro's hospital from St. Mary of Bethleham to Bedlam, a word that eventually became synonymous with confusion. Confused it most certainly was, and also degrading. Bedlam regularly put its patients on exhibition charging the public a few cents to view the show. These exhibitions continued right through to the 18th century attracting around 100,000 visitors per year.

In areas without suitable hospitals, the mentally ill were placed in the care of boardinghouse proprietors who looked after their charges for a fixed weekly fee. These private facilities ranged from comfortable "gentleman's lodgings" (with room for a servant) at one extreme to the home run by a Mr. Spencer of Wiltshire, England, at the other. Spencer kept his lodgers in small compartments overlooking a dunghill and pigpen. The lodgers' cells had bare earth floors and no light or ventilation except when the doors were opened. Patients spent most of their time chained to a wall or lying in boxes filled with straw (see Figure 10.1). There is no doubt that these were dreadful conditions, but they should be kept in historical context. The 1700s were hard times for the poor, whether mentally ill or not. Most French peasants and many European immigrants to England lived squalid lives in conditions scarcely more comfortable than those provided by Mr. Spencer. When local priests complained about the conditions in boardinghouses, mentally ill patients were simply set loose with nowhere to go. In a haunting premonition of the present situation in some of our largest cities, they became vagrants who simply wandered the cities and countryside. The British Parliament was so troubled by these homeless and helpless people that it passed a vagrancy act which permitted judges to detain "Persons of little or no Estates, who, by Lunacy, or otherwise, are furiously Mad."

During the 17th and 18th centuries, there were sporadic attempts to bring more humane treatment to the mentally ill; some were more successful than others. For example, in 1751 a public appeal raised the funds to establish a second London hospital, St. Luke's, which was designed to serve as an alternative to Bedlam. Wards for the mentally ill were also added to general hospitals in several European cities (an idea that was rediscovered 200 years later). Independent inspectors were hired to police the standards of private, boardinghouse asylums, which were also required to have qualified medical staff. Influential writers such as Daniel Defoe, Jonathan Swift, and many others campaigned to improve the treatment of the mentally ill, especially in private facilities. As a result of their efforts, numerous new hospitals and clinics were opened. But no matter how many places were made available, there seemed no way to keep up with demand. By the end of the 18th century, public mental hospitals

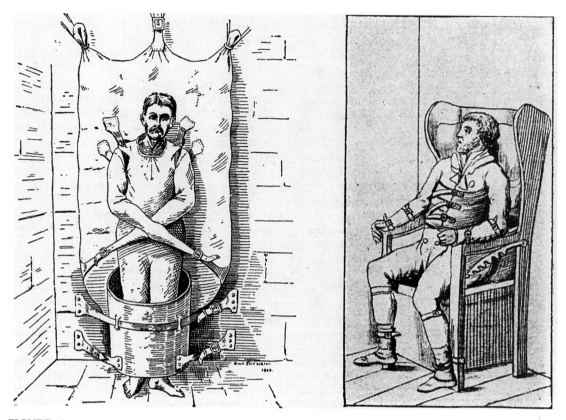

FIGURE 10.1 Patients were routinely kept in restraints.

were bursting at the seams. Crowd control was more common than humane treatment; brutality once again replaced compassion. Fortunately, reform was just around the corner.

Reform and Reaction

In 1788 Vincenzo Chiarugi was appointed superintendent of a new hospital for the mentally ill in Florence. He arrived to find an overcrowded institution in which patients spent their days chained to walls receiving only minimal custodial care. Chiarugi removed these restraints, instituted humane regimes for care, and provided all patients with opportunities for work and recreation. The results were dramatic: fewer violent episodes, healthier behavior, and a more harmonious relationship among pa-

tients and staff. Chiarugi never received much credit for his reforms because, at the same time, a much more famous doctor, Philippe Pinel, was making influential changes in France.

Born in 1748 and educated at the medical school in Montpellier, Pinel later moved to Paris. In 1793 he became superintendent of the Bicêtre—a dungeonlike institution for male criminals, mentally retarded patients, and the mentally ill. Two years before Pinel arrived at the Bicêtre, a former mental patient named Jean-Baptiste Pussin had been made custodian of Ward 7, the home of incurable mental patients. Pussin set about instituting a number of Chiarugi's reforms including releasing inmates from their chains. He retained straitjackets but used them only when violence threatened. Pussin also ensured that the staff treated patients with respect.

FIGURE 10.2 Pinel liberating the patients at the Salpêtrière. In this fictional episode painted 80 years after the event, Pussin is probably the figure in the apron standing to the left of Pinel.

The result was outstanding: Patients were much better behaved than previously, and despite the minimal use of restraints, violence was well contained. Ward 7 became a relatively peaceful, if not exactly pleasant, backwater. Pinel was greatly impressed. After 2 years at the Bicêtre, when he left to take charge of the Salpêtrière (a large Paris hospital for prostitutes and insane women), Pinel arranged for Pussin to be transferred as well. At that time, in the Salpêtrière, as in the old Ward 7, mentally ill patients spent most of their time in chains. Pussin instituted the same humane policies that were so successful at the Bicêtre. Once again, patients responded. Violence, and even much nonviolent psychotic behavior, disappeared. Largely because of a famous painting done decades after the event, Pinel is usually given credit for freeing mental patients from their chains (see Figure 10.2). The honor really belongs to Pussin and, perhaps, to the French Revolution, which emphasized freedom and the rights of every individual and helped establish a receptive social climate for these important reforms.

Pinel may not have been entirely responsible for freeing patients from their chains, but he did make two important contributions to psychological treatment. First, unlike many doctors of his time, Pinel distinguished between *organic* and *nonorganic* mental illnesses. Organic illnesses have a physiological basis whereas nonorganic illnesses have psychological causes. Pinel not only coined the term *functional* to describe nonorganic conditions, but he also insisted that the majority of mental illnesses are functional. Pinel's second major contribution to psychopathology was his treatment program. In his influential writings, he portrayed mental illness as a loss of self-control. Patients, Pinel argued, allow their instinctual urges to get the best of them. His treatment required several steps. First, doctors subdued patients by staring at them until the poor patients were totally under the doctor's domination. This was followed by kindness, gentleness, and persuasive discussions during which patients were confronted with their irrational behavior. Pinel realized that patients' private beliefs were an important contributor to their behavior, and he had no qualms about using deceptive methods to try to change them. For example, Pinel administered a vomit-inducing drug to a patient who believed that he had a snake in his stomach and then concealed a snake in the patient's vomit to make him think that the snake had been purged.

Pinel's humane approach to treatment was anchored in the legacy of the French Revolution. He believed that all people deserved to be treated with dignity and that the state owed a duty of care to its citizens. In England, new, humane treatment methods were also being developed, but these were grounded in religion rather than politics. The most important figure in late-18th-century English treatment was the Quaker philanthropist William Tuke, who established the York Retreat in England. Tuke, an ultra-religious wholesale coffee and tea merchant, and his descendants, dedicated the York Retreat to the "moral-religious treatment of the mentally ill." Their approach gradually came to be known as *moral treatment.*

The term "moral" as used then was closer in meaning to what we would now call "psychological" than to morality or even ethics. The basic idea was that mental illness could not have any permanent effect on the immortal soul (which was by definition perfect), so it must represent a brain disturbance caused by physical or, more often, psychological factors. These latter factors included: an unhappy childhood, faulty education, sudden emotional shocks, lustful thoughts, sexy novels, too much sleep, too little sleep, momentous events such as war and natural catastrophes, political upheavals, revolutions, urban crowding, rural loneliness, economic downturns, and just about every other vicissitude of life. It is worth noting that if modern psychologists were asked to list the causes

of emotional distress, they probably would produce a similar, if not identical, list.

According to the proponents of moral treatment, psychological disturbance results from a loss of balance between reason and the emotions. Treatment was dedicated to restoring the balance by making the emotions subservient to the intellect and thereby giving patients what they lack most: a sense of self-control. At the everyday level, moral treatment involved kindness, comfort, calmness, and heavy doses of the Protestant ethic. Plenty of manual work, organized recreation (such as concerts, poetry readings), and the inculcation of healthy habits were seen as paramount along with humane sympathy and removal from the normal environment. Of course, there were still some violent patients; when necessary, straitjackets — but not chains — were used to restrain them. These restraints were removed as soon as possible, however.

Moral treatment soon spread to many of the better hospitals and asylums but, because moral treatment was heavily labor-intensive, only a small number of patients could be accommodated at any one time. The high cost effectively limited moral treatment to those who could afford to pay for quality care. The poor were sent to workhouses or prison. According to the reports of the time, moral treatment cured somewhere between 50% and 90% of patients. These figures, which are much higher than those claimed by modern hospitals, were viewed with considerable suspicion even then. However, there were few alternatives, especially for the middle class. Moral treatment's apparent success led to increasingly greater numbers of hospital admissions, which, ironically, eventually rendered moral treatment impossible. When the numbers became too large for treatment, custodial care inevitably took over.

The first half of the 19th century saw an explosion of mental hospitals throughout the world. In the United States, Dorothea Dix was successful in establishing asylums in every state, and by the start of the Civil War, there were no fewer than 48 mental hospitals. These were established with the best of humanitarian intentions; the mentally ill were sick people who deserved medical care in a therapeutic environment. It is ironic to note that, today, exactly the same sentiments have been used to argue for the *removal* of patients from mental hospitals.

Despite the success of Dorothea Dix and others, mid-19th-century asylums were severely overcrowded. Hospitals were being used to house not only the mentally ill but also vagrants, runaways, and the mentally retarded. The crowded conditions made treatment difficult, and as a consequence, "cures" became increasingly rare. The pioneers of moral treatment had passed away, and their optimism — their belief that most mental illnesses could be cured — had perished with them. It was replaced with a deep and profound pessimism. Benedict Morel's claim that the mentally ill always degenerate (see Chapter 2) became accepted wisdom. By the latter half of the century, most doctors had rejected Pinel's functional explanations of mental illness focusing instead on organic causes. Instead of traumatic life experiences, such as the death of a loved one or a natural catastrophe, doctors began to blame mental illness on heredity and disease. They had good reason. By the 19th century, organic etiologies were discovered for alcoholic psychosis, senile dementia, and the general paralysis caused by advanced syphilis. Because most, if not all, psychological treatments were useless against these disorders, doctors put their efforts into diagnosis. Indeed, accurate diagnosis became such an obsession that more time was spent verifying diagnoses by autopsy than on actually treating patients when they were alive. Pioneers such as Emil Kraepelin (whose Classic Study is described in Chapter 2) adapted the classification methods used in botany and other branches of biology to psychopathology. Their efforts helped make accurate diagnosis almost the sole purpose of psychological medicine.

In the course of little more than a century, several basic underlying beliefs about psychopathology had changed dramatically. The widely held view that psychological disturbances have physical causes was replaced by the concept of functional disorders, which was itself replaced by a return to somatic hypotheses. Optimism about treatment, and about the perfectibility of human beings, was replaced by Morel's pessimistic "degeneracy" notion. But by far the biggest change in outlook still lay ahead.

Mesmerism Redux

To understand the development of modern psychotherapy, it is necessary to become reacquainted with Franz Anton Mesmer, who was introduced in the opening pages of this book. As you will recall, Mesmer, who was born in 1734, was an industrious but roaming scholar who shifted from divinity to philosophy, to law, and finally to medicine. After graduation, he married a wealthy widow and settled down to a life filled with culture, social engagements, and only the occasional patient. After a decade of this pleasant existence, when Mesmer was about 40, he came across Father Maximilian Hell, the Royal Astronomer and a proponent of "magnetic" cures. Father Hell cured patients by holding magnets to their bodies. Mesmer was intrigued by the coincidence; some years earlier, he himself had submitted a thesis to the University of Austria called "The Influence of the Planets on the Human Body." In it he had tried to prove that the planets influence people through a special fluid called "animal magnetism," which had curative properties. Mesmer decided to try out his theory on one of his patients, Fräulein Osterlin. Fräulein Osterlin, a classic hysteric, had recurrent bouts of fever, convulsions, earaches, vomiting, breathlessness, paralysis, and just about every other problem known to medicine. Mesmer was sure that his patient's symptoms waxed and waned with the movement of the planets; he was also certain that a little magnetism would help. So, he borrowed some magnets from Father Hell. When Fräulein Osterlin was in a particularly bad phase of her illness, Mesmer applied magnets to her feet and hung a heart-shaped magnet from a chain around her neck. Immediately, she felt an intense pain shoot up her legs and into her breasts. After a few minutes she felt the pain leaving her body. For the rest of the day, at least, she was free of symptoms.

Mesmer was triumphant. With this case, he claimed to have shown not only that magnets could cure but also that his speculations about animal magnetism and planetary influences were correct. He soon had patients eating magnetized food, drinking magnetized water, wearing magnetized clothes, and living in magnetized homes. Using the *baquet* (see the Introduction), Mesmer magnetized as many objects as possible. Everything worked. Magnetized clothing cured illness as well as real magnets did. Resurrecting his thesis, Mesmer sought publicity for his theories. Much to his chagrin, instead of fame, his efforts led to his expulsion from the Viennese medical community.

Mesmer's next stop was Paris where the public avidly adopted both his theories and his ministrations. Dismissed as a fraud by scientists and by orthodox doctors, Mesmer became something of a folk hero to everyone else. As the money poured in, he refined his methods. Dispensing with the *baquet*, he began to rely solely on the force of his personality. He found that he could cure people merely by staring into their eyes or touching them lightly with his fingertips. Mesmer had some vague idea that his cures depended on the relationship he established with patients, but he stuck to his theory that magnetic fluid was the medium by which this relationship operated. Thus, although he came close, he never realized that his effectiveness depended on the power of suggestion which he exerted over his patients. Mesmer left Paris when the famous Royal Commission concluded that he was little more than a faith healer, curing patients who were not physically ill but only "mentally disturbed." Mesmer eventually wound up in Switzerland where he died in obscurity. But *mesmerism* lived on. It was used as a form of surgical anesthesia as well as a general cure-all.

Early in 1841, an English doctor, James Braid, witnessed a demonstration of mesmerism at a local neighborhood séance (not an uncommon event at the time). He was particularly impressed by the hypnotic subject's inability to raise his eyelids. Braid concluded that physiological fatigue, induced by intense staring, had temporarily weakened the person's eye muscles to the point where he could not raise his eyelids. To test this theory, Braid had his wife stare at his shiny metal lancet case until her eyes felt tired. To his surprise, not only did her eyelids become too heavy to lift but she also fell into a trance. He tried the procedure on others with the same result. Braid concluded that all that was necessary to produce a trance was to have subjects stare at a bright object; animal magnetism had nothing to do with it. Braid called his trance-inducing process *hypnotism,* from the Greek word *hypnos,* which means "sleep."

By the end of the year, Braid's paper on hypnosis had appeared in the *British Medical Journal* where it produced quite a stir. Instead of mesmerism's mystical trappings, Braid required only that patients stare at a bright object for 3 minutes after which they fell into a "cataleptic" state. Patients in this state sat rigidly and would remember nothing when later

awakened. Braid reported hypnosis' curative effects on rheumatism, paralysis, headache, epilepsy, heart disease, deafness, and visual problems. Although he denied that magnetic fluids played any role, Braid offered no explanation for hypnosis' effects. He did note, however, that hypnosis seemed to make patients docile and "most anxious to comply with every proper request or supposed wish of others." Although this statement implied that suggestibility plays a role in hypnotic cures, Braid did not press the point. Instead, he offered to lecture doctors on his technique, but his offer was firmly declined by the British Medical Association most of whose members viewed hypnosis with considerable suspicion. In Paris, however, Braid's ideas were actively pursued by such luminaries as Jean Charcot.

Charcot first came to the Salpêtrière hospital as a medical intern. The hospital, which had been founded in 1656, had been home to a conglomeration of syphilitic prostitutes, epileptics, and mentally disturbed females since its inception. Taking advantage of this raw material, Charcot set about systematically describing his patients' symptoms and experimenting with different treatments. As noted in the Introduction, he became interested in hypnosis when he realized how easily hypnotized patients could be made to develop hysterical symptoms. Charcot set himself the task of discovering the scientific basis for hypnotism and establishing hypnosis as a recognized neurological tool. He was so successful that in 1880 the French Academy of Medicine reversed its earlier decision decrying mesmerism and accepted hypnosis as a legitimate form of therapy.

Charcot's work, which set the stage for much of modern neurology, became famous among doctors and also among the public at large. He wrote numerous articles for the popular press and gave regular public demonstrations at the Salpêtrière. The latter were always scheduled for Tuesday mornings. Dressed in a frock coat, Charcot would appear on a footlit stage where his flowing hair, low voice, and commanding presence were displayed to best effect. The upper classes of Paris sat amazed as he put his women patients into trances and had them assume odd postures including the *arc de cercle* in which the patient was so rigid that her body formed an arc resting at both ends on her head and heels. Predictably, Charcot's theatrics, not to mention his popularity, created a certain amount of resentment among his medical colleagues. Rumors that he exaggerated the power of hypnosis and that his patients were carefully coached for their performances spread through the medical community. These rumors barely made a dent in Charcot's great international prestige. Nevertheless, the great master did feel the need to defend himself. He denied coaching patients. Hysteria, he claimed, was not a matter of coaching; it was a neurological illness that resulted from some physical trauma to the brain. This brain damage caused *both* hysterical symptoms and a susceptibility to hypnosis. It followed, to Charcot at least, that only hysterics could be hypnotized.

Charcot's claim that only hysterics can be hypnotized was specifically attacked by a former Salpêtrière student named Hippolyte Bernheim. Bernheim, a professor of medicine famous for his publications on typhoid fever, had left academia for private practice in 1871. He specialized in hypnosis and soon found himself successfully treating all sorts of ailments — skin rashes, ulcers, chronic pain, headaches, insomnia, and many others — by suggestion. Bernheim would hypnotize patients and "suggest" that when they awoke their symptoms would be gone. Charcot's claims to the contrary, Bernheim claimed that practically anyone (90% of people was his figure) could be hypnotized. All that was required was that a person be open to suggestion. Indeed, according to Bernheim: "There is no such thing as hypnotism; it is all just suggestion."

Bernheim and Charcot — not to mention their respective students — argued for decades. In the end, Bernheim's views prevailed. Hypnosis came to be seen as a method of influencing people through suggestion. Because patients were often unaware that they were being influenced, hypnotism was believed to operate "unconsciously." This latter view was developed further by Pierre Janet, a doctor who worked at the Salpêtrière and who later became professor of experimental psychology at the Collège de France. Under hypnosis, Janet's patients were able to recall events and feelings that they were unable to remember in their normal state. Janet believed that such memories and feelings, although unconscious, were nevertheless able to influence conscious behavior. Despite their theoretical advances, and their extensive clinical work, Janet, Charcot, and Bernheim all failed to develop their observations into a coherent system of psychological treatment; their

approach remained largely ad hoc. It is unlikely that their work would even be remembered today had it not been for Sigmund Freud.

Beyond Hypnotic Suggestion

As described in Chapter 3, the young Sigmund Freud was a research-oriented physician whose interests mainly concerned physical diseases of the nervous system. This all began to change in the early 1880s when Freud met Josef Breuer. Breuer was a respected Viennese internist with a large private practice and a distinguished reputation for his scientific papers. Although Breuer was a senior physician and Freud only a relative beginner, the two became close friends. It was only natural that Breuer would tell his friend about his most fascinating case, a hysteric woman known as Anna O. whom he had treated from 1880 to 1882. At first Breuer relied on Bernheim's technique: He hypnotized his patient and told her that when she awoke her symptoms would be gone. Anna O. did not respond well. However, like Janet before him, Breuer noticed that hypnosis prompted her to talk about her symptoms and her past. Under hypnosis she relived the trauma of her father's death (for which she wrongly felt responsible), and her symptoms eventually disappeared. Breuer concluded that hypnotic suggestion alone is not always sufficient to cure hysteria; patients must also recall traumatic memories and express the associated emotions. Breuer called the release of pent-up emotions *catharsis,* from the Greek word meaning "to purge" or "to purify."

A few years later, Freud used a travel grant to spend a year in Paris studying with Charcot. He tried to interest the French master in Breuer's cathartic treatment technique but without much success. Freud eventually dropped the subject concentrating instead on Charcot's hypnotic approach to hysteria. On his return to Vienna in 1886, Freud went to work establishing a neurological practice specializing in hysteria. Like his contemporaries, he treated his patients with a combination of rest, baths, massage, electric currents and hypnosis. At the same time, Freud became increasingly interested in the therapeutic value of hypnotic suggestion and translated two of Hippolyte Bernheim's books into German. In 1889 Freud again journeyed to France, this time to study directly with Bernheim. As a direct result of this experience, Freud became convinced that suggestion was the active ingredient of hypnosis. Back in Austria, Freud applied Bernheim's hypnotic-suggestion technique to a wide variety of hysterical patients. Like most clinicians, Freud hypnotized patients and, while they were under hypnosis, suggested that their symptoms would disappear once they awoke. However, following Breuer, Freud also used hypnosis as part of the cathartic method — to help patients express their pent-up emotions.

Breuer and Freud frequently discussed their patients as well as their ideas about the origin and cure of hysteria. Eventually, their ideas coalesced into a theory: Hysterical symptoms, at least in some patients, are the physical manifestation of unexpressed emotions. Although Breuer and Freud did not entirely agree on every detail, they decided to publish their theory in the form of a two-part journal paper called *On the Psychological Mechanisms of Hysteria*. Breuer and Freud indicated the tentative nature of their ideas by giving their paper the modest subtitle *Preliminary Communication*. Although the authors considered their work preliminary, it was widely and warmly reviewed. Within a year after its publication in 1893, the paper was translated into several foreign languages. Ironically, the only countries that seemed uninterested in their work were their native Germany and Austria where their paper was almost totally ignored. Undeterred by their colleagues' disdain and encouraged by the response of foreign doctors, Breuer and Freud decided to illustrate their theory with case studies. The result, 2 years later, was the publication of their classic work, *Studies on Hysteria*.

CLASSIC STUDY 18
Studies on Hysteria

In the preface to *Studies on Hysteria*, Breuer and Freud describe their aim as the description of a new method of examining, treating, and understanding hysteria. They note that patient histories are included for illustrative purposes but that some case materials had to be omitted to protect social sensibilities and patients' privacy. Much of the omitted material was sexual. Somewhat unusually, the preface ends by stating that the authors did not always agree "in their interpretations." We now know that

this was Breuer's first attempt to distance himself from Freud's radical idea that hysteria has sexual origins. Some years later, Breuer's reservations led to the end of their collaboration and their friendship.

On the Psychological Mechanisms of Hysteria

The first part of Breuer and Freud's book was a reprint of the "preliminary communication," *On the Psychological Mechanisms of Hysteria*. In 17 pages, Breuer and Freud attempted to develop a theory of hysteria based on the role of "repressed" childhood traumas. According to their theory, the details of the trauma are too disturbing to be admitted into consciousness so they are actively kept unconscious. But the incident (along with its associated emotions) is not forgotten. Instead, it acts like a festering "foreign body" producing hysterical symptoms for years after the traumatic event.

Sometimes the connection between a hysterical symptom and its precipitating event is quite clear. For example:

> A highly intelligent man was present while his brother had an ankylosing hip-joint extended under an anaesthetic. At the instant at which the hip joint gave way with a crack, he felt a violent pain in his own hip-joint, which persisted for nearly a year.[3]

More commonly, there is only a "symbolic" relationship between the precipitating cause and the hysterical symptom. (An example is the patient who, disgusted at some early event in her life, develops the hysterical symptom of vomiting.) Whether symptoms are direct representations of traumatic events or symbolic derivatives of early traumas, the authors claimed that both types can be eliminated provided the original trauma can be recalled. This is, in fact, the underlying rationale for treatment by catharsis:

> *Each individual hysterical symptom immediately and permanently disappeared when we had succeeded in bringing clearly to light the memory of the event by which it was provoked and in arousing its accompanying affect, and when the patient had described that event in the greatest possible detail and had put the affect into words* [Breuer and Freud's italics].

Because the authors used hypnosis to help patients recall traumatic events and express the accompanying emotions, they were aware that

FIGURE 10.3 Bertha Pappenheim (1859–1936). As Anna O. she was immortalized in Breuer and Freud's book, *Studies on Hysteria*.

suggestions and expectations may be playing a role. Specifically, they note the possibility that "the patient expects to be relieved of his sufferings by this procedure, and it is this expectation, and not the verbal utterance, which is the operative factor." However, Breuer and Freud dismiss this idea because they were able to remove some hysterical symptoms by having patients recall the details of their trauma without any use of hypnotic suggestion. In a crucial break with previous practice, Breuer and Freud began to use hypnosis not as a cure in itself but simply as a means of uncovering unconscious memories.

The remainder of the first part of the book was given over to a comparison of their views with those of Charcot, Janet, and the other leading neurologists of the time.

Anna O.

The second part of *Studies on Hysteria* consisted of five case histories, the first by Breuer and the remaining four by Freud. Breuer's case was the famous Anna O., who was actually Bertha Pappenheim, introduced in our Chapter 3.

Breuer first met Fräulein Anna O. in 1880 when she was just 21. He found her remarkably intelligent (she spoke five languages), generous, and kind with no previous history of mental disorder. Despite her age, Anna was sexually innocent; she claimed to have never even been attracted by a man.

Her parents were wealthy orthodox Jews who restricted their daughter's life to home and family. As an escape from her monotonous existence, Anna developed an active fantasy life and spent much of her time daydreaming.

Anna's illness seems to have begun when her father, of whom she was "passionately" fond, fell ill with tuberculosis. Anna spent all her waking hours nursing her father, neglecting her own health. She lost weight, developed a persistent cough, and soon had to be put to bed herself. In parallel with her father's condition, Anna's health continued to deteriorate. In addition to sleeping for a good part of the day, she developed a paralysis of the eye muscles (her eyes became "crossed"), her neck became paralyzed, she had frequent headaches and visual disturbances, and her legs and arms became numb. Anna's personality also changed. Sometimes she was depressed and anxious; at other times, she became violently excited. While in the latter state, she would tear off her clothes, throw objects around the room, and complain that she was going mad. After some months of this, Anna began to lose the power of speech. First, she simply left isolated words out of sentences, but after a while her syntax and grammar deteriorated to the point that she was virtually unable to communicate. It was at this point that Breuer first came to believe that Anna's symptoms were symbolic: "And now for the first time the psychical mechanism of the disorder became clear. . . . she had felt very much offended over something and had determined not to speak about it." Anna eventually began speaking again, but only in English — much to the confusion of her German-speaking nurses and relatives.

Anna's father eventually died of his illness in April 1881. This event induced a profound depression in Anna and a refusal to recognize anyone other than Breuer. She also had "fits" that mimicked epileptic seizures and severe anxiety attacks during which it appeared she might harm herself. For her safety, she was transferred from her third-floor bedroom to a one-story country house. At this stage of her illness, Breuer began to note the symbolic connections between Anna's symptoms and the trauma of her father's illness and death. For example, a year after her father's death, Anna began to misrecognize colors. The specific colors she failed to recognize were those of a dressing gown she had made for her father while he lay ill.

In the country, Anna experienced frequent "absences," in which she became lost in daydreams. In the evenings, Breuer would visit her and, under hypnosis, have her describe the daydreams she had had during the day. These daydreams often contained symbols of horror and death. Nevertheless, Anna invariably felt better after talking about them. (She called her conversations with Breuer the "talking cure.") Slowly, over many months, some of Anna's symptoms began to diminish and disappear. Breuer concluded that reliving events during hypnosis was the curative factor:

> — that in the case of this patient the hysterical phenomena disappeared as soon as the event which had given rise to them was reproduced in her hypnosis — made it possible to arrive at a therapeutic technical procedure. . . . Each individual symptom in this complicated case was taken separately in hand; all the occasions on which it appeared were described in reverse order, starting before the time when the patient had become bedridden and going back to the event which had led to its first appearance. When this had been described the symptom was permanently removed.
>
> In this way her paralytic contractures and anaesthesias, disorders of vision and hearing of every sort, neuralgias, coughing, tremors, etc., and finally her disturbances of speech were "talked away."

Breuer described his procedure as follows:

> I would visit her . . . and hypnotize her. (Very simple methods for doing this were arrived at empirically.) I would next ask her to concentrate her thoughts on the symptom we were treating at the moment and tell me all the occasions on which it appeared. . . .
>
> Thus we were able to trace back all of her disturbances of vision to . . . more or less clearly determining causes. For instance, on one occasion, when she was sitting by her father's bedside with tears in her eyes, he suddenly asked her what time it was. She could not see clearly; she made a great effort, and brought her watch near to her eyes. The face of the watch now seemed very big — thus accounting for her [visual symptoms].

Ultimately, the technique revealed what Breuer believed to be the root cause of Anna's hysterical illness:

> In July 1880, while he was in the country, her father fell seriously ill of a sub-pleural abscess. Anna shared the duty of nursing him with her mother.

FREUD VERSUS BREUER

Freud knew that Breuer purposely omitted important data from Anna O.'s case history. Many years after the publication of *Studies on Hysteria*, Freud revealed his suspicions in a letter to his friend Stefan Zweig:

> What really happened with Breuer's patient I was able to guess later on, long after the break in our relations, when I suddenly remembered something Breuer had once told me in another context before we had begun to collaborate and which he never repeated. On the evening of the day when all her symptoms had been disposed of, he was summoned to the patient again, found her confused and writhing in abdominal cramps. Asked what was wrong with her, she replied: "Now Dr. Breuer's child is coming!"
>
> At this moment he held in his hand the key ... but he let it drop. With all his great intellec-

tual gifts there was nothing Faustian in his nature. Seized by conventional horror he took flight.*

The "key," according to Freud, was the sexual nature of all neuroses. Breuer could not accept this and, in any event, would never have embarrassed his patient or his wife with this revelation. Breuer's "conventional horror" eventually led him to abandon any connection with Freud or psychoanalysis.

---

*Quoted in Freud, E., Freud, L., & Grubrich-Simitis, I. (1976). *Sigmund Freud: His life in pictures and words* (C. Trollope, Trans.). Brisbane: University of Queensland Press. P. 139

She once woke up during the night in great anxiety about the patient, who was in a high fever. . . . Her mother had gone away for a short time and Anna was sitting at the bedside with her right arm over the back of her chair. She fell into a waking dream and saw a black snake coming towards the sick man . . . to bite him. (It is most likely that there were in fact snakes in the field behind the house and that these had previously given the girl a fright. . . .) She tried to keep the snake off, but it was as though she were paralysed. Her right arm, over the back of the chair, had gone to sleep and had become anaesthetic . . . ; and when she looked at it the fingers turned into little snakes with death's heads (the nails). . . . When the snake vanished, in her terror she tried to pray. But language failed her: she could find no tongue in which to speak, till at last she thought of some children's verses in English and then found herself able to think and pray in that language.

According to Breuer, this revelation marked the crucial breakthrough. Once Anna's hysterical symptoms were traced back (either directly or symbolically) to the traumatic events surrounding her father's illness, Anna began speaking German again and most of her symptoms disappeared. She soon left on a long vacation from which she returned completely cured. Breuer ends his case description

at this point, but we now know from other sources that he omitted one final episode.

To understand this omission, it is important to note the effect Anna's case had on Breuer's personal life. Neither Breuer, nor anyone else, had ever before seen anything quite like Anna's ability to remove symptoms by reliving traumatic experiences. Quite understandably, Breuer was fascinated by this strange and puzzling young woman. He spent as much time as he could with Anna, sometimes neglecting his own family. Breuer's wife, resentful of this intrusion into her life, grew jealous and angry. Although Anna never so much as mentioned sex at any time during her treatment, Breuer feared that his wife's jealousy could be professionally embarrassing. So, immediately following Anna's description of her "snake" dream and the disappearance of her remaining symptoms, Breuer abruptly terminated treatment and went home. A few hours later, he was called back to Anna's bedside and found her in great distress. She complained of abdominal cramps and seemed to be in the labor preceding childbirth. The birth, of course, was entirely imaginary; it was, in fact, yet another hysterical symptom. But this one was special. Even Breuer, the prudish Victorian, could not help but recognize Anna's sexual feelings toward him. At one point, she even claimed that it was his baby she was having. Breuer eventually calmed Anna down with hypnosis and fled home in terror. Almost immediately, he and his wife left for a second honeymoon in Venice. Anna went on to lead a normal life and became a leader in the women's movement—a "suffragette."

Four Freudian Case Studies

Although Anna O. was Breuer's patient, not Freud's, her case marks the beginning of psychoanalysis. Indeed, the four remaining case studies contained in the second part of *Studies on Hysteria* served only to elaborate and extend the hypotheses generated by the treatment of Anna O. As already noted, all four cases were treated and written up by Freud. The first concerned a 40-year-old woman called Emmy von N. who suffered from a variety of hysterical complaints including pains and paralyses. Freud used hypnosis both to make suggestions ("your pain will disappear when you awake") and to reveal unconscious memories, which he eliminated using Breuer's cathartic technique.

Freud's second case, Lucy R., suffered from a chronic nasal infection and depression that Freud traced back to her unrequited love for a former employer. In his description of this case, Freud presented a clear formulation of the etiology of hysteria. The process begins with a traumatic experience, which stirs up intense emotions. These events and their associated emotions are incompatible with the "dominant mass of ideas constituting the ego." That is, the person finds them disagreeable, frightening, embarrassing, or all three. As a form of self-protection, the traumatic ideas, memories, and feelings are *intentionally* repressed from consciousness. (As psychoanalysis evolved, Freud came to believe that repression need not always be intentional, but at this stage he had not yet considered any other possibility.) The *psychic tension* associated with repressed material cannot be discharged in the normal way—by having a good cry, for example—because the repressed material is not available to consciousness. Instead, psychic tension (which Freud saw as real, not metaphorical, physical energy), is expressed in the form of hysterical symptoms. All that remains conscious is a symbolic representation of the original trauma. For example, Lucy R. claimed to smell "burnt pudding," which Freud interpreted as a substitute for the smell of her

employer's cigar during the traumatic movement when he rejected her. The notion that "trapped" energy is expressed as physical symptoms led naturally to the concept of *symptom substitution*. That is, as one hysterical symptom is removed—say, by hypnotic suggestion—another will take its place. This is inevitable, according to Freud, because the psychic energy associated with the repressed trauma remains unexpressed. The only way to eliminate hysterical symptoms entirely is to bring the traumatic event into consciousness and express the associated emotions thereby releasing the trapped psychic tension.

Freud's third case, Katherina, is probably the shortest psychoanalytic treatment ever described. Katherina worked in a hotel at which Freud was a guest. She sought his advice on the chronic anxiety she had felt for over 2 years. After just a few conversations, Freud uncovered Katherina's repressed memory of her father's sexual advances toward her many years earlier. Her anxiety mimicked the fear she felt years before. Freud's final case concerned Elizabeth von R., a 24-year-old woman whose hysterical symptoms left her unable to walk without assistance. She also had various pains and skin sensitivities. In her case, the various hysterical symptoms had developed over many years, sometimes in response to memories of traumatic events rather than to the events themselves. Freud went to great lengths to emphasize that hysterical symptoms can develop years after an event. To illustrate this, he briefly described another patient, Rosalia H.:

> Fräulein Rosalia H., aged twenty-three, had for some years been undergoing training as a singer. She had a good voice, but she complained that in certain parts of its compass it was not under her control. She had a feeling of choking and constriction in her throat so that her voice sounded tight. For this reason her teacher had not yet been able to consent to her appearing as a singer in public. Although this defect affected only her middle register, it could not be attributed to a defect in the organ itself. At times the disturbance was completely absent, and her teacher expressed great satisfaction; at other times, if she was the least bit agitated, and sometimes without apparent cause, the constricted feeling would reappear. . . .
>
> In the course of the hypnotic analysis which I carried out with the girl, I learned the following facts about her history. . . . She lost her parents early in life and was taken to live with an aunt

who herself had numerous children. In consequence of this she became involved in a most unhappy family life. Her aunt's husband, who was a manifestly pathological person, brutally ill-treated his wife and children. He wounded their feeling more particularly by the way in which he showed an open sexual preference for the servants and nursemaids in the house. . . . After her aunt's death Rosalia became the protector of the multitude of children who were . . . oppressed by their father. She took her duties seriously and fought through all the conflicts into which her position led her, though it required a great effort to suppress the hatred and contempt she felt for her uncle. It was at this time that the feeling of constriction in her throat started. Every time she had to keep back a reply, or forced herself to remain quiet in the face of some outrageous accusation, she felt a scratching in her throat, a sense of constriction, a loss of voice. . . . She used often to hurry off to her singing lesson while she still had the constriction in her throat that used to be left over after violent scenes at home. Consequently a connection was firmly established between her singing and her hysterical paraesthesia—

I did my best to get rid of this "retention hysteria" by getting her to reproduce all her agitating experiences. . . . I made her abuse her uncle, lecture him, tell him the unvarnished truth, and so on.

One day the patient came for her session with a new symptom, scarcely twenty-four hours old. She complained of a disagreeable pricking sensation in the tips of her fingers, which, she said, had been coming on every few hours since the day before and compelled her to make a peculiar kind of twitching movement with her fingers.

Freud assumed that such a new symptom must have been the result of some recent trauma. He hypnotized his patient and sought the cause of this new symptom:

To my astonishment, the patient produced a whole number of scenes without any hesitation and in chronological order, beginning with her early childhood. They seemed to have in common her having had some injury done to her, against which she had not been able to defend herself, and which might have made her fingers jerk. There were such scenes, for instance, as of having had to hold out her hand at school and being struck on it with a ruler by her teacher. . . . [In another scene] her bad uncle, who was suffering from rheumatism, had asked her to massage his

back and she did not dare refuse. He was lying in bed at the time, and suddenly threw off the bed-clothes, sprang up and tried to catch hold of her and throw her down.

Freud related Rosalia's tingling fingers to the feelings she received when massaging her uncle as well as to the punishment meted out to her by her teachers. This case, and other similar cases, convinced Freud that repressed sexual guilt was almost always the root cause of hysteria.

Theory and Practice

The last two parts of *Studies on Hysteria* consisted of six chapters by Breuer in which he elaborated his theory about the etiology of hysteria and a section on treatment by Freud. Breuer's theory was based largely on the existence of so-called *hypnoid* states produced by undischarged psychic energy. The hypnoid state is an altered state of consciousness in which part of the mind is split off from the rest. Breuer called such states hypnoid because he believed they are similar to the state of consciousness produced by hypnosis; patients have no conscious memory for their behavior during hypnoid states. Breuer believed that hysteria results when a person in a hypnoid state undergoes a traumatic experience. The contents of the trauma are not available to the rest of the personality (although there may be unconscious symbolic links), and symptoms remain mysterious until their symbolic meaning is determined through hypnosis.

Freud had little faith in the notion of hypnoid states. As far as he was concerned, they really did not explain much. After all, saying that someone is hysterical because they experienced a trauma while in a hypnoid state simply leaves open the question of why they fell into such a state in the first place. In the fourth part of *Studies on Hysteria*, Freud gives his own views on treatment and etiology.

As already mentioned, Freud believed that hysteria and other neuroses are almost always caused by sexual conflicts. Originally, he believed that these conflicts arise from some traumatic sexual experience. He soon realized, however, that many of the sexual episodes related to him by his patients never actually occurred. As a consequence, Freud modified his theory. Sexual fantasies, he believed, can also trouble people sufficiently to cause hysterical symptoms even though they had no actual traumatic sexual experience. Freud noted that patients often *resisted* revealing or even admitting to sexual fantasies; they *repressed* such information as a way of *defending* themselves from the anxiety such revelations cause. These three concepts—resistance, repression, and defense—became important cornerstones in the further evolution of what Freud began to refer to as "psychoanalysis." The therapist's job, according to Freud, is to facilitate catharsis by breaking down defenses and resistances and helping patients to recognize and express their repressed sexual conflicts.

Freud's detailed case studies reflect the evolution of his thinking about the etiology and treatment of hysteria. Initially, he used hypnosis in the same way as his French teachers. He would hypnotize patients and suggest that, when they "awake," their symptoms would disappear. Unfortunately, such cures were temporary—new symptoms soon reappeared. Hoping for a more permanent cure, Freud augmented hypnosis with Breuer's cathartic method. At first, as in the case of Emmy von N., he used hypnosis as a method of helping patients retrieve and verbalize traumatic memories. This method was partly successful, but some patients just could not be hypnotized. One such patient was Elizabeth von R. To help Elizabeth recall traumatic experiences, Freud developed a method he called "concentration":

> The idea occurred to me of resorting to the idea of applying pressure to the head . . . [and] instructing the patient to report to me faithfully whatever appeared before her inner eye or passed through her memory at the moment of pressure. She remained silent for a long time and then, on my insistence . . . she had thought of an evening on which a young man had seen her home from a party, of the conversation that had taken place between them and of the feelings with which she had returned home to her father's sick bed.
>
> This first mention of the young man opened up a new view of ideas the contents of which I now gradually extracted. It was a question here of a secret, for she had initiated no one, apart from a common friend, into her relations with the young man and the hopes attached to them.

Freud's concentration technique—in which the patient lay back on a couch with eyes closed while Freud sat alongside with his hand to the patient's forehead—appeared successful until one day an uncharacteristically quiet Elizabeth remarked that she was not sure what he wanted to hear. This remark served to help Freud realize that suggestibility is not so much the result of hypnosis as of the relationship between patient and therapist; a patient need not be hypnotized to be suggestible. He decided to be totally nondirective and allow patients to produce their thoughts without interference. Eventually, this nondirective approach led to the development of the "free-association" technique in which patients produce whatever comes into their mind no matter how irrelevant or nonsensical.

Freud claimed to have accidentally discovered the free-association technique, but as an avid classical scholar, there is at least one precedent with which he probably was familiar. In Aristophanes' play, *The Clouds*, Socrates invites a troubled individual to lie on a couch and say anything that comes to mind. The "patient" begins to talk of "putting the moon in his pocket." By diligent probing, Socrates finds that the patient wishes to halt the progression of days to the new moon in order to avoid paying the debt that falls due on the first of the new month. Clearly, Freud's technique, using free association to uncover the symbolic meaning of behavior, was anticipated centuries earlier.

No matter where Freud got the idea, he certainly put free association to good use. However, he did not see it as a panacea for all psychological problems. Freud ends *Studies on Hysteria* by providing readers with an interesting insight into what he believed are the limits of psychotherapy:

> When I have promised my patients help or improvement by means of cathartic treatment I have often been faced by this objection: "Why, you tell me yourself that my illness is probably connected with my circumstances and the events of my life. You cannot alter these in any way. How do you propose to help me, then?" And I have been able to make this reply: "No doubt fate would find it easier than I do to relieve you of your illness. But you will be able to convince yourself that much will be gained if we succeed in *transforming your hysterical misery into common unhappiness* [italics added]. With a mental life that has been restored to health you will be better armed against that unhappiness."

AFTERMATH

In the decades following the publication of *Studies on Hysteria*, Freud continued to refine psycho-

BERTHA PAPPENHEIM: GERMAN FEMINIST

Historians have always been interested in what happened to Bertha Pappenheim whose hysterical disorder could legitimately be said to have given birth to the entire field of psychoanalysis. Ironically, the case widely seen as a great treatment success was actually a failure.

After her hysterical pregnancy, Bertha had to be hospitalized for 3 months in a Swiss sanitorium. Hospital records show that her hysterical symptoms were not cured (as implied by Breuer in his case history) but remained severe and debilitating problems. She was treated with morphine during her hospitalization, and for some years after her discharge she remained a confirmed drug addict. It took more than 6 years for Bertha to shed her habit and also overcome the remnants of her hysterical symptoms.

In 1880 Bertha published a book of children's stories, and in 1899 she published a German translation of Mary Wollstonecraft's feminist tract, *A Vindication of the Rights of Women.* The same year, Bertha published a play called *Women's Rights,* which became a well-known statement of European feminism. A few years later, Bertha became director of an orphanage for girls. She also became an active campaigner against the white slave trade in which young females were sold into prostitution. Over the years, she became well known in many fields of social work helping to establish homes for girls and women.

Although, as a Jew, Bertha was harassed by the Nazis, she stayed in Germany working for social welfare causes throughout the 1930s. Twenty years after her death in 1936, the German government issued a postage stamp in her honor.

Although she was described as attractive, it is interesting to note that Bertha never had a sexual relationship nor would she allow any of the girls in her care, even those who were clearly psychologically distressed, to receive psychotherapy. It would seem that, despite her preeminent place in the origin of the field, Anna O. did not believe in the value of psychoanalysis.

analysis. He published case studies as well as observations from everyday life in which he showed how free associations, slips of the tongue, dream fragments, and neurotic symptoms can be traced back to the past and understood in the light of personality dynamics. Over time, psychoanalysis developed a set of principles and procedures that are too complicated to be more than summarized here. Briefly, hypnosis was completely replaced with the free-association technique, which was soon augmented by dream analysis. Freud felt that the *manifest*, or obvious, content of dreams often masks a *latent* content to which it is symbolically connected. By careful dream analysis, unconscious conflicts that the patient resists revealing through free association may be uncovered. Over time, Freud also became increasingly occupied with the analysis of the transference relationship. Freud believed that patients transfer their habitual modes of interpersonal behavior (love as well as hate) to the patient-therapist relationship. Thus, by analyzing the transference relationship, patients can come to understand and eventually change the way they react to other people. Ultimately, unraveling the transference relationship became the single most important aspect of psychoanalysis. Freud offered patients *interpretations* of their transference that connected present behaviors toward him with unconscious personality dynamics. These interpretations were designed to help patients gain insight into their behavior. Insight, in turn, was thought to release the psychic energy patients previously spent avoiding insight by repression and other defense mechanisms. By *working through* the same conflicts in many contexts, the patient allegedly gained increasing insight and ultimately abandoned neurotic symptoms.

While Freud devoted himself to seeing patients, developing his theory of personality (see Chapter 3), and refining psychoanalysis, his German and

Austrian medical colleagues almost totally ignored him. As already noted, because of the Victorian morality of the time, Freud lost Breuer as a collaborator; he was also shunned by most European academics, who found his "obsession" with sexual matters distasteful at best and perhaps even a sign of depravity. Despite these adversities, Freud continued to work on his own gradually attracting a group of young doctors to work with him. His fame, minimal at home, began to spread abroad. In 1909, for example, he was awarded an honorary degree from Clark University in Worcester, Massachusetts, where he gave a series of lectures. Freud later described what this moment meant to him:

> At that time I was only fifty-three. I felt young and healthy, and my short visit to the new world encouraged my self-respect in every way. In Europe I felt as though I were despised; but over there I found myself received by the foremost men as an equal. As I stepped on to the platform at Worcester to deliver my *Five Lectures on Psycho-analysis* it seemed like the realization of some incredible daydream; psycho-analysis was no longer a product of delusion, it had become a valuable part of reality.[4]

Freud's most creative period was the two decades following the publication of *Studies on Hysteria*. After 1920 he was content to simply refine his earlier ideas. In 1938 Freud was driven out of Austria by the Nazis. He fled to England where he died a year later, at age 83.

Psychoanalysis did not stagnate with Freud's death. Neo-Freudians extended and in some ways transformed psychoanalysis in ways never anticipated by Freud. Other forms of psychotherapy—humanistic, existential, gestalt, primal scream, rational-emotive, and others—have also appeared (and in some cases, disappeared). In the years since Freud's death, behavior modification (which is covered in the next chapter) has also developed into a major treatment approach. Its roots are considerably different from psychoanalysis although perhaps not quite as different as was once thought. Clearly, the idea of a "talking cure" has come a long way since Anna O. first used the phrase. Yet, despite their many differences, it is fair to say that much of modern psychotherapy can be traced back to that fateful day when Breuer decided to ask Anna how she felt rather than to follow normal hypnotic practice and just tell her to feel better.

Further Reading

Breuer, J., & Freud, S. (1956). *Studies on Hysteria* (J. Strachey & A. Strachey, Trans.). London: Hogarth Press. (Original work published 1895.)

Freud, S. (1955). Lines of advance in psychoanalytic therapy. In *The complete works of Sigmund Freud* (J. Strachey, Trans.). London: Hogarth Press. (Original work published 1918.)

Notes

1. Thomas, L. (1979). Medical lessons from history. In L. Thomas (Ed.), *The Medusa and the snail*. New York: Viking Press. P. 131.
2. Jones, K. (1972). *A history of the mental health services*. London: Routledge & Kegan Paul. P. 16.
3. Unless otherwise noted, quotations are from: Breuer, J., & Freud, S. (1956). *Studies on hysteria* (J. Strachey & A. Strachey, Trans.). London: Hogarth Press. (Original work published 1895.)
4. Quoted in: Freud, E., Freud, L., & Grubrich-Simitis, I. (1976). *Sigmund Freud: His life in pictures and words* (C. Trollope, Trans.). Brisbane: University of Queensland Press. P. 188.

CHAPTER 11

Does Psychotherapy Work?

From the mid-1950s to the 1990s, the number of Americans who have ever sought psychotherapy increased from less than 10% to more than 30% of the population. Each year, 16 million Americans receive psychotherapy from around 170,000 therapists; similar large numbers are treated in other countries. Before World War II, psychotherapy was mainly the province of the medical profession, but increasing demand over the past 50 years has far outstripped the production of psychiatrists; most psychotherapy today is performed by clinical psychologists, social workers, and psychiatric nurses. Given its widespread acceptance, it would be logical to assume that psychotherapy is an effective treatment for psychological disorders. Yet, even after decades of research, opinions remain mixed. As will be shown in this chapter, whether or not psychotherapy is judged effective depends on what we mean by "psychotherapy" and what we mean by "effective."

Apt words have power to suage
The tumors of a troubled mind

—John Milton

PSYCHOTHERAPY: THE FIRST 50 YEARS

In the previous chapter, the modern era in psychotherapy was shown to have begun with the publication of Breuer and Freud's book, *Studies on Hysteria*, in 1895. Although Breuer soon gave up on catharsis, Freud made it his exclusive treatment technique. Every day, in his private practice, he applied the cathartic method to a vast array of patients. His therapeutic observations (the sexual nature of hysteria, for example) led him to develop his theory of personality structure (id, ego, and superego) and his ideas about the stages of psychosexual development (oral, anal, phallic, and genital). Most important for the future development of psychotherapy, Freud

FIGURE 11.1 Psychoanalysis was derived mainly from Freud's observations of patients. Freud preferred to sit at the head of the couch, out of sight of his patients. "I cannot bear being gazed at for 8 hours a day," he once said.

used his observations to continually refine his therapeutic procedures.

Freud's habit was to ask patients to lie back on a couch and let their thoughts run free (see Figure 11.1). Frequently he found that his patients told about their dreams. Freud believed that these dreams were connected in some way to his patients' symptoms. To find out how, he began to study dreams, including his own. In addition, he used dreams as a starting point for free association, again practicing first on himself. In this way, Freud's clinical observations led him to develop the new therapeutic technique of dream analysis. Later, Freud used his clinical observations to devise other ways of helping patients get around their defenses and express their repressed emotions. Most important, the analysis of the "transference" relationship, an essential part of psychoanalysis, developed out of Freud's experience with patients.

Freud was a prolific and gifted writer. In the first years of the 20th century, his books and papers appeared with astonishing rapidity. *The Interpretation of Dreams, The Psychopathology of Everyday Life, Three Essays on the Theory of Sexuality,* and the *Analysis of a Phobia in a Five-Year-Old Child* (which was discussed in detail in Chapter 3) were particularly important because they made Freud famous internationally. Eventually, even the insular and hostile Viennese academic community could no longer simply ignore him. In 1902 he was awarded a "titular" (honorary) professorship at the University of Vienna Medical School. Around the same time, Freud formed a group of like-minded people who met each Wednesday evening in his home to discuss and explore psychoanalysis. Beginning with only four members, this informal study group grew so that, by 1910, meetings could no longer be squeezed into Freud's apartment and a formal venue was acquired. Also, in that same year, the International Psychoanalytical Association as well as the first psychoanalytic journal were founded to accommodate the increasing interest in Freud's ideas.

Despite these developments, psychoanalysis might have remained an obscure movement had it not been for Eugen Bleuler. Bleuler, whose work on schizophrenia was described in Chapter 5, was one of Europe's leading academic physicians. Curious about the new developments in Austria, Bleuler sent one of his students, Carl Jung, to visit Freud in Vienna. Jung returned to Switzerland an enthusiastic devotee of psychoanalysis. He convinced Bleuler to use Freud's techniques with his patients, thus giving psychoanalysis the respectability it would otherwise have lacked. Freud's visit to the United States in 1909 brought him a large number of American and Canadian followers. By the end of 1910, it became clear that Freud had founded an international "school" of psychological thought.

World War I was a difficult period for Freud, as his sons were serving at the front (one was a prisoner of war) and both money and patients were scarce. However, after the war, Freud and his followers were in great demand to treat the returning soldiers whose "war neuroses" did not respond to the treatments available at the time. The willingness of psychoanalysts to treat these patients gave their profession added respectability, especially among those in the government responsible for veterans' affairs. As a result, for the first time, it became possible to make a living as a psychoanalyst.

In the postwar years, Freud's fame and influence continued to bring new members into the psychoanalytic community. Unfortunately, intellectual movements that depend heavily on one person's personality are often hostile toward new ideas. As a result, they become conservative and resistant to change. Psychoanalysis was no exception. One by one, Freud's followers broke away from their master to pursue their own variations on the original psychoanalytic theme. The first to go was Alfred Adler, one of Freud's favorites and a former president of the Vienna Psychoanalytical Society. Adler's *individual psychology* was based on his theory of "organ inferiority" (hysterical symptoms, he thought, occur in "vulnerable" organs that vary from person to person). Adler gained many adherents and developed his own distinctive therapeutic style, but his

approach never seriously challenged orthodox psychoanalysis.

The next important disciple to go was Jung, who split with Freud in 1914 to pursue his semimystical *analytical psychology*, which included concepts such as the "racial unconscious." Jung attracted considerable attention from organized religion, nationalistic German politicians, and poets as well as psychologists, and Jungian psychology continues to have numerous adherents even today. Otto Rank and Ludwig Binswanger left next in quick succession. The first focused on the importance of "birth trauma"; the second was one of the founders of the school known today as *existential therapy*.

Despite these defections, Freud persevered, continuing to see patients and to write books and articles on various aspects of psychology, philosophy and literature. Despite a serious cancer of the jaw that required repeated operations, he continued to be productive throughout the 1920s receiving awards and recognition from around the world. Unfortunately, the peace that should have accompanied Freud's old age was shattered by Hitler's Nazis, who persecuted him and his family. In one especially horrifying night, they burned his books in a giant bonfire. At the time, Freud commented ironically that this book burning was evidence for how far humanity had progressed. In the Middle Ages, he said, it would have been he rather than his books that were set alight. Despite this brave front, Freud realized that he had no future in Austria. With the help of friends, he eventually moved to England where he died in 1939.

Like the First World War, World War II produced an enormous demand for psychotherapy. Soldiers returned from the front "shell-shocked" and in need of treatment. There were insufficient psychiatrists to meet the need, and psychologists moved in to fill the gap. Fueled by government scholarships and fellowships, the number of clinical psychologists and psychiatrists expanded rapidly in the postwar years. By 1950 psychotherapy was a thriving industry not only in America but in Europe as well. Considerable government and private resources were being spent on training therapists and treating patients. The amount of money involved grew so large that it was only a matter of time before someone asked whether these funds were being well spent. There were a few hints in the 1930s and

1940s that psychotherapy might not be as effective a treatment as its proponents claimed, but it was not until 1952 that the question of psychotherapeutic effectiveness was tackled head on. The person responsible was a psychologist at the University of London, Hans J. Eysenck.

HANS JURGEN EYSENCK: REBEL WITH A CAUSE

Hans Jurgen Eysenck was born in Germany in 1916, right in the middle of World War I (see Figure 11.2). He grew up during the bleak postwar years when weak governments and the harsh reparations Germany was forced to pay to the allied victors produced economic chaos. Hyperinflation (a wheelbarrow full of money was required to buy a loaf of bread) followed by mass unemployment produced the inevitable social tensions—crime, despondency, fear, and anger. All told, it was not an ideal time to be a child.

Eysenck's family was somewhat unusual. His father, Eduard Eysenck, was an actor and a popular cabaret performer. His mother was the German movie actress Helga Molander. The family was nominally Roman Catholic, but they did not practice any religion. At the age of 8, Hans appeared in one of his mother's films. He played his own mother's son in a tear-jerker about the effects of divorce on a family. Ironically, Eysenck's own parents were divorced when he was just a child. Eysenck's mother married Max Glass, a Jewish film writer, producer, and director. The couple was devoted to music, theater, films, and fine art. They associated with the most cultured people of Weimar Germany and had little time for young Hans, whom they left to be brought up by his maternal grandmother in Berlin. Even when his mother lived nearby, Hans rarely got to see her, and he hardly benefited from her relative wealth. For example, Hans's mother would not pay for him to attend a junior tennis championship even though he was a promising player. Although he was an excellent student, Hans was a willful youth who was sometimes rather difficult for his grandmother to control. Fortunately, he learned to channel his prodigious energies into schoolwork and sports. As already mentioned, he was a keen tennis player (which he has remained throughout his life), a boxer, and all-around sportsman.

FIGURE 11.2 Hans Jurgen Eysenck (1916–).

The 1930s were miserable years for Germany. The social strains produced by the poor economy had resulted in Hitler's rise to power. Hitler's Nazis glorified Germany's authoritarian traditions especially its romantic warrior legends. Young Eysenck rejected such mysticism and the related claims of Aryan racial superiority. Although his father had joined the Nazi party, Hans resisted his father's attempts to help his son through his party connections. He also refused his father's wish that he join the Hitler Youth. Instead, he resisted nazism at school and in sports. Ultimately, Hitler's regime became too much and Hans Eysenck became a political exile. At the age of 18, he voluntarily left Berlin for France where his mother and her Jewish husband had fled some years before. His grandmother, who could not be convinced to leave, eventually perished in a concentration camp. Many years later, Eysenck discovered that this devout Catholic woman was probably born Jewish.

Eysenck spent only a short time in Paris before migrating to London. There, a series of accidents led him to psychology. He wanted to be a physicist, but the University of London would not admit him to study physics claiming that he did not have the proper prerequisites. He chose to study psychology instead because it was the closest he could get to "real" science. Eysenck studied psychology at University College, which was home to one of the two main psychology departments in England at the time. The other department, at Cambridge University, specialized in experimental psychology. In contrast, the University College approach to psychology was mainly statistical. Its statistical methods were derived from the 19th-century work of Francis Galton, who set out to measure individual abilities and invented the correlation coefficient along the way. As the mathematics grew more sophisticated, the measurement of individual differences became known as psychometrics. Its main exponent during Eysenck's student days was his mentor, University College professor Cyril Burt. Under Burt's guidance, Eysenck became a leading proponent of the psychometric approach to psychology.

Although he was able to complete both an undergraduate degree and a Ph.D., the British government still classified Eysenck as an "enemy alien," and he only narrowly avoided being interned for the duration of the war. Despite his self-imposed political exile, Eysenck was considered a security risk and was consequently prohibited from joining the army to fight the Nazis. His alien status also made it difficult for him to find work. He considered it a stroke of good fortune when he finally gained employment as a psychologist at the Mill Hill Emergency Hospital. After the war, he moved to the newly formed Institute of Psychiatry located at the University of London's Maudsley Hospital. The director of the Institute, Aubrey Lewis, was an Australian psychiatrist with a considerable respect for experimental psychology. Lewis agreed to establish the first course in clinical psychology in the United Kingdom at the Institute and sent Eysenck to the United States to investigate how the profession of clinical psychology had developed there. Eysenck was not particularly impressed with what he found. American clinical psychologists were little more than assistants to psychiatrists; their role was mainly confined to testing. Eysenck wanted clinical psychologists to be independent professionals who could provide therapy and other psychological services without working directly under the supervision of psychiatrists. Not surprisingly, Eysenck and Lewis, the psychiatrist, fell out over this issue but

Eysenck eventually prevailed. Indeed, the clinical psychology course he established at the Institute of Psychiatry became the model for all other clinical courses in the United Kingdom and the British Commonwealth.

Curiously, Eysenck was not himself a practicing clinician. His devotion was to scientific psychology, especially the psychometric approach to personality. Over the years, he used both statistical and experimental techniques to define such personality dimensions as extroversion-introversion and to give these constructs a theoretical basis grounded not only in psychology but also in genetics and biochemistry. In addition to research, Eysenck has had an enormously influential teaching career. At one point in the early 1990s, one third of all psychology professors in the United Kingdom were Eysenck's former doctoral students. He has also influenced many nonpsychologists through his popular writings. *Uses and Abuses of Psychology,* a book he wrote in just 2 weeks in 1953, has been reprinted 20 times. It was followed by books with similarly alliterative titles (*Sense and Nonsense in Psychology, Fact and Fiction in Psychology*), which together with his other popular books (*Know Your Own IQ,* for example) have sold millions of copies.

As he makes clear in the title of his autobiography, *Rebel with a Cause,* Eysenck enjoys being a controversial character. Perhaps as a consequence, he has never feared to champion unpopular causes when he felt the data warranted it. For example, Eysenck has examined (and has claimed to have found) a relationship between IQ and race. For this he was jeered by audiences and, in some cases, treated as a pariah. He has also been criticized for writing a book that questioned the link between smoking and cancer while serving as a consultant to the Tobacco Research Council. This criticism has not dampened Eysenck's attraction to unpopular causes. For example, he is almost alone among his peers in having something positive to say about astrology. Despite his iconoclastic tendencies, Eysenck's work has remained influential among the scientific community. He is the most frequently cited psychologist in the United Kingdom, and in the worldwide psychological literature, only Sigmund Freud is cited more often than Hans Eysenck.

Eysenck's reputation for attacking cherished beliefs began early in his career, when he was still in his 30s. The source of the controversy was his classic study of the effects of psychotherapy.

CLASSIC STUDY 19
The Effects of Psychotherapy

In the 1940s, the American Psychological Association formed a committee to advise universities on how best to train clinical psychologists. The committee believed that there was an important social need for psychotherapy (which remember, was mainly psychoanalytic at the time). The committee's report recommended that all clinical psychologists be trained as psychotherapy providers. Eysenck took exception to this recommendation largely on the grounds that it put the horse before the cart. He argued that, before all clinical psychologists are forced to learn how to do it, psychotherapy should first be shown to be an effective treatment. In typical fashion, Eysenck decided to let "the data" resolve the issue. His review of the available literature appeared in a brief article titled "The Effects Of Psychotherapy: An Evaluation." The article, which was published in the *Journal of Consulting and Clinical Psychology* in 1952, sparked a debate that has lasted 40 years.

EXAMINING PSYCHOTHERAPY OUTCOME

Eysenck began his article by pointing out that evaluating the effectiveness of psychotherapy is a difficult task. In the past, practitioners had taken the "easy" approach; they simply counted the number of patients who improved after treatment. Finding that most patients improved, they concluded that their treatment must have worked. One problem with such naive reasoning is the phenomenon known as "spontaneous remission." Put simply, some patients get better without any treatment at all. Depressive episodes are a good example; left untreated, most depressions will lift after running a fairly typical course. We know, of course, that not all spontaneous remissions are really "spontaneous." Patients who do not receive psychotherapy still confide in friends, take vacations, and help themselves in other ways. Still, the existence of patients who

improve without formal psychotherapy makes therapy outcome figures exceedingly difficult to interpret. How do we know that a successful outcome is really the result of the therapy? Is it possible that the patient would have improved spontaneously, without treatment? The only way to answer these questions is to perform a controlled experiment. As described in the Introduction, such an experiment requires at least two groups: one that receives the treatment of interest and a group of control subjects, similar in all respects to the first group, who do not receive the treatment. A particular treatment is considered effective only if more treated than control patients improve. Unfortunately, in 1952 no controlled experiments on psychotherapy outcome had yet been conducted, so Eysenck looked for some other way to estimate the number of patients who improve without treatment.

Fortunately, some relevant data had been collected independently by Carney Landis and P. G. Denker in the 1930s and 1940s. Neither Landis nor Denker studied individual patients; instead, they gathered their data from public and private records. Landis, for example, studied the amelioration rate for neurotics in state hospitals. Because neither "amelioration" nor "neurotic" had any universally agreed-upon definition at the time, Landis was forced to rely on expert medical opinion. If a doctor said that a patient fell into the category of "neurotic," then the patient was neurotic. If a doctor said that a patient was "improved," then the patient was considered to have improved.

Landis found that, when discharged from hospitals, 68% of neurotic patients were described as "recovered" or at least "much improved." He admitted that there were some problems with using this figure to estimate the spontaneous remission rate. In addition to the subjective nature of doctors' judgments, which has already been mentioned, hospitalized neurotics were not strictly comparable to outpatient psychotherapy patients. Hospitalized patients were likely to be more seriously disturbed than outpatients receiving psychotherapy, and they mainly came from lower-class socioeconomic backgrounds. Moreover, even the most primitive state hospitals still provided some form of therapy, so it was not really accurate to say that inpatients received no treatment. Nevertheless, it was possible to argue that the figure of 68% represented a reasonable criterion by which to judge psychotherapeutic effectiveness. That is, to be considered effective, psychotherapy must produce a recovery rate greater than 68%.

In contrast to Landis, Denker examined the records of 500 "neurotic" patients who had filed disability insurance claims with the Equitable Life Insurance Company. Although they were out of work at least 3 months, Denker's patients were neither hospitalized nor treated by mental-health professionals. Their care was provided by general practitioners who prescribed sedatives and offered reassurance but no psychotherapy. Defining recovery as a return to work with little or no remaining difficulty, Denker found that 45% of his sample had recovered after 1 year. After 2 years, 72% had recovered. After 5 years, Denker reported that 90% of patients had recovered. There were obvious differences between Denker's subjects and Landis's patients. Denker's were from middle and high socioeconomic classes and relatively well-off; Landis's were mainly people from low socioeconomic classes who were involuntarily committed to state mental hospitals. Yet the recovery rates reported by Landis and Denker were remarkably similar. Reassured by this similarity and taking what he described as a conservative approach, Eysenck estimated that approximately two thirds of neurotic patients eventually recover without psychotherapy. He took this figure as the benchmark for psychotherapy to beat; psychotherapy could be considered an effective treatment only if *more* than two thirds of treated patients improved.

RECOVERY AFTER PSYCHOTHERAPY

Having established a criterion for success, Eysenck turned to the outcome data. Searching the literature, he found 24 psychotherapy outcome studies emanating from a variety of hospitals and mental-health professionals. These studies provided follow-up data on over 7,000 patients who were classified by their doctors as "cured," "much improved," "improved" or "not improved." As already noted, these terms were subjective and rarely defined; thus, it would be foolish to assume that all doctors and therapists meant the same thing when they said that a patient was "cured" or "much improved." Nevertheless, after removing studies that he considered

methodologically inadequate, making a few "informed" corrections to some of the sloppier data, and focusing only on neurotic cases, Eysenck found the results of the various follow-up studies to be generally unimpressive.

Forty-four percent of psychoanalytic patients were described as either cured or much improved. For eclectically treated patients (a category that included everything except classical psychoanalysis), the corresponding figure was 64%. Both of these figures were below the required 66%. One might conclude from this dismal result that being psychoanalyzed actually led to a worse outcome than receiving no treatment at all, but this would be overstating the case. Eysenck had classified all psychoanalytic patients who discontinued treatment as "not improved." While it is undoubtedly true that some patients dropped out of treatment because they were not making progress, there may have been many other reasons for prematurely terminating therapy: relocation to another city, financial problems, car accidents, and so on. It is entirely possible, therefore, that at least some of those who left psychoanalysis early would have been helped by their treatment. Admitting this possibility, Eysenck recalculated his results omitting those patients who discontinued therapy prematurely. This time he found that 64% of psychoanalytic patients were cured or much improved, the same percentage that improved with eclectic psychotherapy. These research results are summarized in Table 11.1. Eysenck concluded that the data

fail to prove that psychotherapy, Freudian or otherwise, facilitates the recovery of neurotic patients. They [the data] show that roughly two-thirds of a group of neurotic patients will recover or improve to a marked extent within about two years of the onset of their illness, whether they are treated by means of psychotherapy or not. This figure appears to be remarkably stable from one investigation to another, regardless of type of patient treated, standard of recovery employed, or method of therapy used. From the point of view of the neurotic, these figures are encouraging; from the point of view of the psychotherapist, they can hardly be called very favorable to his claims.[1]

Eysenck concluded his article by noting some of the methodological shortcomings of "actuarial" research (studying records rather than patients) and

TABLE 11.1   Summary of Psychotherapy Outcome Studies (following
Eysenck, 1952)

	Cured; Much Improved; Improved	Slightly Improved; Not Improved; Left Treatment	% Cured; Much Improved; Improved
Psychoanalytic treatment	335	425	64%*
Eclectic treatment	4,661	2,632	64%

*Omitting those that left treatment.

calling for carefully controlled research into the effects of psychotherapy. Nevertheless, he felt compelled to emphasize that it was up to those who believed in psychotherapy to demonstrate its value. Because this had not yet been done, Eysenck wrote that "it seems premature to insist on the inclusion of [psychotherapy] training in . . . the curriculum of the clinical psychologist."

AFTERMATH

Not surprisingly, given its conclusion, Eysenck's five-page article created quite a stir. Academics committed to the teaching of psychotherapy were not pleased to learn that they were engaged in a futile enterprise. They mounted a critical counterattack arguing that the data used by Eysenck were inadequate because he had lumped together patients with different types and degrees of disturbance. He was also criticized for relying on the subjective opinion of many different doctors who may have used quite different criteria for judging whether a patient had improved. Critics also noted that the treatments were not carefully described and that there was no way to be sure that the hospitalized neurotics and the worker's compensation subjects did not receive any psychotherapy. (If these patients did receive therapy, then they did not really recover spontaneously and Eysenck's estimate of the "spontaneous recovery" rate was too high.) Finally, critics pointed out that Eysenck used his subjective judgment to assign outcomes to cases when the data were unclear.

These criticisms were entirely accurate, but their force was somewhat diminished because Eysenck was not only aware of them, but he also discussed them all in his paper. More important, not one critic

claimed that the evidence available in 1952 showed psychotherapy to be an effective treatment. The major difference between Eysenck and his critics seemed to come mainly from preexisting biases. Psychotherapists wished to consider psychotherapy effective unless it could be shown otherwise while Eysenck argued for the reverse—that psychotherapy should be assumed to be ineffective until it could be proven differently. From a scientific point of view, Eysenck's position was far easier to justify. It is customary in both psychology and medicine to begin by assuming that no difference exists between treatment and control groups and then wait for the evidence to prove us wrong. Assuming the reverse—that psychotherapy is effective—puts researchers in the impossible position of having to prove a negative proposition (known in psychological research as a "null hypothesis"). It is like having to show that the Loch Ness monster does not exist. Simply failing to find it is not sufficient because it is always possible that we looked in the wrong place. Similarly, a failure to find evidence that psychotherapy is effective can never prove that it doesn't work; we may have used the wrong patients, poor therapists, or inappropriate measures of therapeutic success. Because researchers can collect data forever and never prove that psychotherapy, or any other treatment, is completely ineffective, Eysenck was correct to require those who claim that psychotherapy works to prove their case.

In the years following the publication of Eysenck's paper, several researchers have taken up his challenge; so, in 1960, Eysenck decided to have a second look at the literature. This time he was able to examine studies that used control groups. For example, there was the famous Cambridge-Sommerville study named after the two Boston suburbs in which it was conducted. Six hundred and fifty boys, whose disadvantaged backgrounds predisposed them to delinquency, were subjected to an elaborate series of delinquency-prevention interventions, including psychotherapy, over an 8-year period. To ensure that appropriate conclusions could be drawn, half the boys received some form of individual psychotherapy while the other half did not. Those boys who received therapy were very pleased with their treatment; they felt confident that their psychotherapy had produced substantial benefits. Their therapists agreed. Yet, despite the positive evaluation of both the boys and their therapists, an analysis of official records revealed that there were actually *more* reported incidents of delinquency among boys treated with psychotherapy than among untreated boys. Clearly, this study failed to demonstrate the effectiveness of psychotherapy (at least for preventing delinquency). More important, it highlighted a serious problem for psychotherapy researchers: the choice of outcome measure. If the investigators had been content to rely on the boys' self-reports and the reports of their therapists, they would have concluded that psychotherapy was indeed an effective treatment. However, the investigators realized that patients may report benefits simply to please their therapists or to justify the time they have devoted to psychotherapy. They also knew that therapists can also be biased; they may exaggerate the benefits of psychotherapy to sustain their professional reputations and self-esteem. The Cambridge-Sommerville study was one of the first psychotherapy outcome studies to demonstrate the unreliability of subjective reports and the crucial importance of obtaining objective outcome measures.

Eysenck also reviewed a study of 150 outpatients conducted by the notorious LSD guru of the 1960s, Timothy Leary, and his colleagues. Because of the high demand for psychotherapy services, some of the patients seeking help from their clinic had to wait for 7 or more months before seeing a therapist. The investigators reasoned that those on the waiting list could serve as an appropriate control group for those who received treatment. They administered the MMPI personality test (see Chapter 1) to both treatment and waiting-list control patients at the outset of the study and then again around 7 months later. The researchers found almost no difference between the treatment and the waiting-list control group. According to MMPI scores, at least,

psychotherapy was no more effective in producing change than being placed on a waiting list. Following this early study, the use of waiting-list controls became common in psychotherapy outcome research although the approach was not without its critics. Some clinical psychologists worried about the ethics of making people wait a long time for treatment; others argued that members of the waiting list do not really constitute an untreated control group because they may seek out other forms of help while they wait. Some patients may receive counseling from priests and ministers; others may obtain alternative types of guidance. We cannot really be sure that the improvement shown by those on the waiting list is really spontaneous; it could be the result of these alternative "therapies." Nevertheless, the results of Leary's study were hardly positive for psychotherapy. At best, the data suggested that formal psychotherapy is no better than the counseling offered by nonprofessionals.

In 1960 Eysenck did find a few studies that purported to show that traditional psychotherapy is effective, but the overall preponderance of evidence was still, in Eysenck's eyes, negative. Eysenck once again threw down the gauntlet to psychotherapy researchers in unambiguous terms:

> They must define clearly what is meant by neurotic disorder and what is meant by cure; they must put forward methods of testing the effects of treatment which are not dependent on the subjective evaluation of the therapist, and they must demonstrate that their methods give results that are clearly superior to any alternative methods.[2]

Eysenck reviewed the field a third time in 1966, this time in a book titled *The Effects of Psychotherapy*. His summary of the research on psychotherapy was even more pessimistic than previously:

> The writer must admit to being somewhat surprised at the uniformly negative results issuing from all this work. In advancing his rather challenging conclusion in the 1952 report, the main motive was stimulating better and more worthwhile research in this important and somewhat neglected field; there was an underlying belief that while results to date had not disproved the null hypothesis, improved methods of research would undoubtedly do so. Such a belief does not seem to be tenable any longer in this easy optimistic form, and it rather seems that psychologists and psychiatrists will have to acknowledge the fact that current psychotherapeutic procedures have not

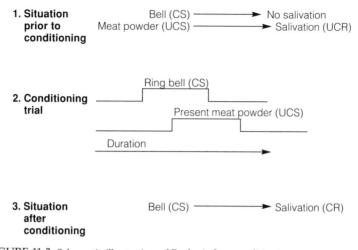

FIGURE 11.3 Schematic illustration of Pavlov's first conditioning experiments. Before conditioning, the meat powder (Pavlov couldn't afford real meat) elicits salivation but the bell does not. After repeated pairings, the salivation response becomes conditioned to the bell.

lived up to the hopes which greeted their emergence fifty years ago.[3]

Eysenck's pessimism was reserved for traditional forms of insight-based psychotherapy. He was optimistic about the future of treatment based on "learning theory," which he believed held great promise for becoming a truly psychological (as opposed to a quasi-medical) form of therapy. Indeed, from the 1960s on, Eysenck has been an active proponent of what is known as "behavior therapy.[4]

ORIGINS OF BEHAVIOR THERAPY

Although precursors of behavior therapy may be found in the writings of Hippocrates, modern behavior therapy really begins with the work of Ivan Pavlov early in the 20th century. Pavlov, who won the Nobel Prize twice, is justifiably famous for his demonstration that a previously neutral "stimulus" such as the sound of a bell can, through repeated pairings with another stimulus, come to elicit certain specific behaviors. For example, dogs naturally salivate when shown meat. In learning theory terms, salivation at the sight of meat is known as an unconditioned response, or UCR. Pavlov repeatedly paired the sound of a bell (the conditioned

stimulus, or CS) with the sight of meat (the unconditioned stimulus, or UCS) and showed that a dog will learn to salivate to the sound of the bell even when the meat is no longer present (see Figure 11.3). At this point, the dog's salivary "response" is said to be "conditioned" to the bell "stimulus." Conditioning works with just about any neutral stimulus even an unpleasant one. For example, applying an electric shock to a dog's leg will produce a reflex—the leg will be withdrawn. Pairing a bell with the shock will result in the withdrawal reflex becoming "conditioned" to the bell even when no shock is present. Although not specifically targeted, the emotional signs of fear produced by the shock become conditioned as well. Thus, every time the bell rings, the dog barks and begins to breathe heavily.

Pavlov found that, although they were not used in training, stimuli similar to the one used in the original conditioning (other bells, tones, buzzers) also elicit the newly conditioned response; this phenomenon is known as "generalization." The strength of the response produced by a new stimulus is a function of its similarity to the conditioned stimulus used in the original conditioning. In the present examples, the more similar a new sound is to the original bell, the more salivation or fear it will produce. Of course, conditioned responses do not

↑ Standing on a ledge outside an upper-story window.

↑ Climbing a steep mountain.

↑ Walking on a ridge with a clear drop to earth.

↑ Sitting in a ski lift as it goes up a mountain.

↑ Riding a cable car up a hill.

↑ Driving across a high bridge.

↑ Looking out the window of the top floor of an apartment building.

FIGURE 11.4 A sample anxiety hierarchy for a patient who fears heights.

last forever. After repeated presentations of the conditioned stimulus (the bell in our examples) without the presence of food or electric shock, the salivation or the fear response eventually "extinguishes" (disappears).

In the 1920s, there were numerous attempts to apply Pavlovian conditioning principles to the understanding and amelioration of behavior problems. John Watson's case of Little Albert is probably the most famous. As noted in Chapter 3, Watson and his assistant, Rosalie Rayner, claimed to have produced a phobia toward rats by repeatedly startling a baby with a loud noise while he played with a previously unfeared laboratory rat. Although the evidence they presented for their claim was equivocal at best, and although all attempts to replicate their results have been unsuccessful, Watson and Rayner's paper stirred the imagination of psychologists who were seeking an alternative to psychoanalysis based on the psychological principles of learning.

One of Watson's students, Mary Cover Jones, took the then unknown field of behavior therapy a giant step forward when she used conditioning to "cure" a child called Peter of his fear of rabbits. Her technique was to use conditioning to replace Peter's typical reaction to rabbits, fear and crying, with a new set of conditioned responses — smiling, reaching, and happy curiosity. Because Peter's favorite dessert, ice cream, elicited just such positive behaviors, Jones decided to pair the dessert with the rabbit. A caged rabbit was placed on a distant table and left there as Peter happily ate his dessert. On successive occasions, the cage was moved gradually closer until Peter no longer showed signs of fear. Jones claimed to have replaced Peter's fear of rabbits with acceptance and even fondness using condition-

ing — one of the first demonstrations of what behavior therapy could accomplish.

The idea that fears can be eliminated through conditioning was carried further in the 1950s by Joseph Wolpe, a South African psychiatrist, who gave up psychoanalysis to work on learning-based psychotherapy. Viewing "neurotic" symptoms as learned habits that can be unlearned given the proper training, Wolpe developed a technique he called "desensitization through reciprocal inhibition," or simply "desensitization." The main idea behind Wolpe's technique is that it is impossible to be anxious and relaxed at the same time. The two states are incompatible (they "reciprocally inhibit" one another). It follows, then, that fears can be eliminated by teaching people to relax in anxiety-provoking situations.

Wolpe began by first teaching people to relax. He did this using a technique that required patients to concentrate on the elimination of muscle tension. Once the relaxation technique was perfected, patients (or "clients" as they are often called by behavior therapists) were instructed to relax and imagine themselves in a hierarchically graded series of anxiety-producing situations. Figure 11.4 shows an example of such a hierarchy. As soon as a patient could imagine a situation without anxiety, the therapist moved up to the next one on the hierarchy. When the patient could calmly imagine all of the graded situations without anxiety (and with undisturbed relaxation), patients found that they could also face the real-life feared situation without fear. The desensitization that took place in therapy had generalized to situations outside the clinic. When, for one reason or another, patients were unable to imagine the situations in the anxiety hierarchy, Wolpe physically placed them in the various disturbing

THE ETHICS OF AVERSIVE THERAPY

Conditioning techniques are not only useful for helping people overcome their anxiety but also may be used to *produce* anxiety where none previously existed. For example, alcoholic patients may be given their favorite drink followed by a nauseating drug. The idea is that repeated pairings of the drink and the drug will result in the drink, alone, producing nausea. Once this happens, the person will avoid the drink. This type of behavior modification is known as aversion therapy because it makes use of an unpleasant stimulus. Although the conditioning principles involved are no different from those applying to any other type of conditioning, aversion therapy has always been controversial. Books and movies, such as *A Clockwork Orange,* have portrayed aversive conditioning as a form of brainwashing. People are shown being involuntarily subjected to such "behavior modification" not for their own benefit but for the purposes of some malevolent state. Although most psychologists would not dream of treating anyone against their will, these portrayals have had the effect of making clinicians wary of aversive conditioning and reserving it as a last resort to be used only when all else has failed.

Treatments based on B. F. Skinner's operant conditioning have been also caricatured as "coercive." Operant conditioning is based on the principle of "reinforcement," which states that any behavior followed by a reward will tend to be repeated. Because the cessation of pain is rewarding (we learn to perform behaviors that reduce or eliminate pain), aversive stimuli may also be used in operant conditioning. Indeed, using the strategic application of aversive stimuli, and a gradual approach, people can be taught many new behaviors. For example, autistic children, who often avoid eye contact with other people, have been taught to attend to teachers using a painful stimulus. Specifically, they have been exposed to electric shock devices and given painful shocks until they make the required attentive response (eye contact or some reasonable approximation). Because the electric current is switched off when the child makes eye contact, the appropriate behavior comes to be associated with the cessation of pain and is thereby reinforced.

No one likes to inflict pain; for this reason, many psychologists avoid using aversive stimuli in their treatment. Yet there is often no other method to obtain the desired results. Ultimately it comes down to a judgment of cost and benefit. If the autistic child is going to be better off being exposed to aversive stimuli than being allowed to remain unresponsive, and if there is no less "costly" alternative, then the treatment is justified. Otherwise, it is not.

situations. It should be obvious that this *in vivo* ("in life") desensitization and systematic desensitization in general, is conceptually identical to the conditioning procedure used by Mary Cover Jones.

Although Wolpe was a psychiatrist, systematic desensitization found a large following among psychologists. Much of the credit goes to his colleague, Arnold Lazarus, who was a prolific writer, a tireless speaker, and an effective proponent of their views. Wolpe and Lazarus also had the good fortune to be speaking and writing at just the right time. Through the efforts of Eysenck and others, postwar clinical psychology had developed into an independent profession no longer subservient to psychiatry.

What better way to assert one's independence than to develop treatments based on psychological principles and psychological research. Moreover, from the very beginning, behavior therapists saw themselves as scientists as well as practitioners. For example, in *Behavior Therapy,* one of the first textbooks in the field, Aubrey Yates wrote that *"the most important role which the clinical psychologist can fulfill at this time is that of fundamental research worker* [Yates's italics]."[5] Behavior therapists were not only helping clients, according to Yates, but they also were advancing psychology by pursuing applied research on how symptoms are learned and how learning theory can be used to eliminate them.

Despite their dedication to research, the initial outcome reports on the effectiveness of behavior therapy were almost entirely anecdotal. Wolpe, for example, reported extraordinarily high success rates for desensitization based solely on his clinical assessment of his own patients. Psychologists, trained to be skeptical about uncontrolled clinical observations, were not satisfied with such subjective evidence for behavior therapy's effectiveness. They also were not impressed with the poor methodology used in most psychotherapy outcome research. Like Eysenck, they abhorred the vaguely specified patient groups ("neurotic," for example), the poorly constructed control groups, and the highly subjective outcome measures (clinical impressions) that characterized psychotherapy research. By the 1960s, practically all psychologists admitted that psychotherapy research required a new, more rigorous methodology. Thus, the time was just right for Gordon Paul's landmark outcome study, which is described next.

CLASSIC STUDY 20
Insight Versus Desensitization

Gordon Paul began working as a musician when he was 13. In his late teens and early 20s, music took him far from his native Iowa, across the continental United States, Hawaii, and Canada. For 4 years, he was a musician with the navy, but in 1958, he returned to Iowa to study psychology and mathematics. After receiving his B.A. from the University of Iowa, Paul moved to the University of Illinois where he received his Ph.D. in clinical psychology in 1964. He spent the next 15 years at Illinois where he rose to be professor of psychology. He also maintained a clinical private practice and consulted widely. In 1980 Paul moved to the University of Houston where he became Cullen distinguished professor of psychology.

Paul has won many awards and honors including the Creative Talent Award of the American Institutes of Research. He is a fellow of the American Psychological Association and has been president of the Association's Division of Clinical Psychology (who awarded him its Distinguished Scientific Contribution Award). He has been principal investiga-

tor on research grants totaling more than $4 million. Although Paul is the author of more than 120 articles and books, his most influential publication was one of his first, *Insight vs. Desensitization in Psychotherapy.* This book, which was published in 1966, described work begun while Paul was still a graduate student at Illinois.

The aim of the research described in *Insight vs. Desensitization in Psychotherapy* was to determine which was "better": traditional, insight-oriented psychotherapy or the behavior therapy technique of systematic desensitization. This is a laudable goal but, as we have already seen, one fraught with difficulties. How do we choose patients? How do we choose therapists? How do we define success? How can we be sure that any improvement is not the result of spontaneous remission or some other factor not specific to the therapies? Paul's answers to these and other questions set a new standard for rigorous psychotherapy outcome research.

METHODOLOGICAL ISSUES

Choosing Patients

One of the most serious criticisms made about previous psychotherapy outcome studies was the heterogeneous nature of the patient groups. Describing a group of people as "neurotic" really tells us very little about them. Their problems may differ in type; some may suffer from phobias, others from obsessions, and still others from depression. Their problems may also differ in degree: Some patients who have a phobia of spiders, for example, may simply avoid contact with a spider when they see one; others may refuse to leave their house lest they encounter the feared insect. Because of these differences among patients, it is entirely possible that psychotherapy may help some patients but not others. Indeed, some patients might even be harmed by psychotherapy. Researchers who find that the *average* improvement of the patient group is no different from the controls might wrongly conclude that psychotherapy is ineffective when in reality it helps some patients but not others. The way around this problem is to keep all patients as similar as possible. Only then will researchers be able to tell whether psychotherapy is effective for their patients' particular problems. This is the approach taken by Paul, whose patients were all University of

NONSPECIFIC FACTORS IN PSYCHOTHERAPY

Although the various schools of psychotherapy each have their own theoretical rationale, there is little doubt that they share much in common. These commonalities fall into three categories:

1. *Expectations of help.* All types of psychotherapy offer hope to people in need. People seek therapy when they are suffering. Patients can be depressed or anxious (or both); they often lack self-esteem and see the future as bleak. Therapy, any therapy, offers hope that their situation will get better. Often the expectation of improvement alone can help people improve. This is the basis of the placebo effect. Placebos work because people believe in them; because patients expect to get better, they often do.

2. *Explanations.* Psychotherapy offers patients a rationale for their problems. Behavior thera-

pists teach their patients to view their symptoms as learned habits; psychoanalysts teach theirs to look for the symbolic meanings behind their problems. These explanations give patients a way to explain their often bewildering behavior. Such explanations, while not always correct, may still serve to reduce anxiety because they permit patients to believe that their problems are not mysterious, but understood by scientists who also know how to help them.

3. *An empathic relationship.* Most therapies involve a relationship with a warm and caring person. This relationship alone, irrespective of whatever therapy is practiced, can give patients the reassurance they need to help themselves.

Illinois students who had a fear of public speaking. While it is true that these were not "real" patients recruited from clinic waiting lists, they were all seriously troubled by their "stage fright," which not only interfered with their university life but could also affect their future careers.

Paul's students were recruited from a required course in public speaking. Before the research began, each student enrolled in the course completed a battery of psychological tests designed to measure his or her anxiety about public speaking and anxiety in a number of related interpersonal situations. In addition, the students gave a test speech to the class. Immediately before this speech, researchers recorded each student's pulse rate and degree of palm sweating (both physiological reflections of anxiety). While making their speech, students were observed by specially trained judges who noted such signs of anxiety as facial tics, hand tremors, stammering, and so on. Using the psychological tests, the physiological measures, and the observations of public-speaking performance, Paul identified a group of students who were highly anxious about public speaking and motivated to change. These students were randomly assigned to the various experimental conditions described next.

Treatments and Controls

There were four main conditions in Paul's study: three treatment conditions and a control group. Students assigned to the first treatment condition received insight-oriented psychotherapy. Although this therapy could not be equated with traditional psychoanalysis, it was similar in one important respect: Therapists attempted to provide their patients with an explanation of their fear of public speaking. The therapy usually involved an exploration of the patient's past, and the insight provided usually referred to unconscious motives and conflicts.

Students in the desensitization condition received a formalized version of Wolpe's systematic desensitization treatment in which they were taught to relax and required to imagine a graded sequence of anxiety-provoking scenes concerned with public speaking.

The third treatment group was called the "attention-placebo" group. Placebos are inert substances commonly used to assess the effectiveness of a drug. In drug research, patients are randomly assigned to either the treatment group, which receives the real drug, or the control group, which receives a

Improvement shown by the attention-placebo group > No-treatment control = Nonspecific effects of therapy
Improvement shown by the insight therapy group > Attention-placebo = Specific effects of insight therapy
Improvement shown by the desensitization group > Attention-placebo = Specific effects of desensitization
Improvement shown by the desensitization group < > Insight = Relative effectiveness of therapies

FIGURE 11.5 Logic of Paul's experimental design.

placebo disguised to look like the real drug. Because the patients in the two conditions are treated identically and because they (and often their doctors) do not know whether they are receiving the placebo or the drug, any differences between the two groups cannot be the result of suggestion, expectation, or differential treatment—differences can only be the result of the drug. Extending the concept of placebo to include "inert" psychological treatments, Paul devised a plausible, but artificial, psychological treatment. He gave students what they thought was a "tranquilizer" but was really a placebo and then had them practice detecting a specific sound in a noisy tape. Students in the placebo group were told that this "therapy" would improve their tolerance for stress and thereby help to relieve their public-speaking anxiety.

Paul's purpose in including the attention-placebo group (the name is appropriate because students received "attention" as well as a placebo) was to control for the "nonspecific" factors that are present in any type of psychotherapy, insight or behavioral. These nonspecific factors include a therapeutic relationship with a caring and attentive person, an expectation that treatment will help, and perhaps most important of all, heightened suggestibility. As Mesmer showed so many years ago, many medical problems can be helped by suggestions from a person who is perceived to be caring and knowledgeable. According to Paul, insight and behavioral therapy can only claim to have their own specific ameliorative effects if students in these treatment conditions show a greater improvement than those in the attention-placebo condition.

The fourth group in Paul's study was a no-treatment control group. These students completed the psychological test battery and performed the test speech, but they were not given any treatment. Because they continued participating in their public-speaking class, these students did practice public speaking and were therefore expected to show some reduction in anxiety. However, because they did not receive any type of therapy or placebo, their gains were expected to be modest.

The inclusion of a no-treatment control group permitted Paul to make a number of relative comparisons. Specifically, a greater improvement in the attention-placebo group than in the no-treatment control group would demonstrate the therapeutic effectiveness of the nonspecific therapy factors present in the placebo condition but not in the control group. Similarly, a greater improvement in either of the therapy groups than in the attention-placebo group would reflect the specific effects of the therapy. Finally, a comparison of the two groups would show which therapy is more effective. These comparisons are illustrated schematically in Figure 11.5.

Choosing Therapists

Psychotherapy is an intense interpersonal encounter in which the therapist's personality plays an important role. As already noted, talking with a caring, empathic therapist can help patients to improve irrespective of the particular therapeutic technique used. If, by chance, the most caring, or most skillful, therapists were all found in one treatment condition, that treatment would be given an unfair

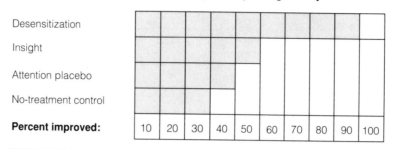

FIGURE 11.6 Results of Paul's study.

advantage which could bias the outcome. To avoid this possibility, Paul used the same five therapists in all three treatment conditions. Because students in all conditions were treated by the same therapists, any differences in outcome could not be attributed to differences in the therapists' personalities or skills.

Ideally, from a research point of view, therapists should be equally adept at administering all treatments and they should not have a strong preference for one treatment which they could, perhaps inadvertently, communicate to the students. Unfortunately, completely unbiased therapists do not exist. Paul's five therapists were all highly qualified and were all trained to be experts in administering each of the three treatments, but they were not unbiased. Like most therapists at the time, they were originally trained in, and preferred, insight-oriented therapy. This bias should be kept in mind when reviewing the results, which are presented next.

INSIGHT VERSUS DESENSITIZATION

At the conclusion of therapy, students again completed the battery of psychological tests. They also gave a second test speech to their class. Because the same physiological and behavioral measures recorded at the time of the first speech were recorded again for the second, the most straightforward way to measure therapeutic effectiveness was to compare the results obtained on the two occasions. If a treatment was effective, we would expect to find fewer overt indications of stress and less subjective anxiety at the time of the second test speech than at the time of the first.

Paul compared scores on the various objective and subjective anxiety measures taken on the two speaking occasions and found that students in all conditions, including the no-treatment control group, showed fewer signs of anxiety during their second speech than they did during their first. This finding was not unexpected. Practice (this was, after all, their second speech) and various factors not specific to any particular treatment—expectations for improvement, suggestibility, and so on—were expected to produce some positive change. As already noted, a therapy can be considered effective only if it leads to greater improvement than that produced by practice and nonspecific factors alone. And this is precisely what Paul found. Anxiety reduction was not equal in magnitude in the four conditions, as shown in Figure 11.6. The most marked improvement was shown by students who underwent desensitization. The insight group was next followed closely by the attention-placebo group. The no-treatment control group showed the smallest level of improvement.

An examination of the findings of the psychological tests administered at the outset and the conclusion of therapy largely corroborated the physiological and behavioral observations recorded during the two speeches. According to the psychological tests, the desensitization group showed the largest reduction in anxiety, but this time it was the attention-placebo group that came in second place followed by insight therapy and the no-treatment controls. Assuming that the placebo treatment (detecting signals in noise) really had no direct effect on public-speaking anxiety, it is notable that students in this condition showed around half the rate of improvement of those who received desensitization (see Figure 11.6). Put another way, half the improvement recorded for the desensitization group (and almost all the improvement shown by the insight therapy group) may not have been the result of the therapy itself but of such nonspecific factors as faith in the treatment and an expectancy on the part of the students that they would improve. The substantial effect of the placebo on anxiety reduction clearly demonstrated the crucial importance of controlling for nonspecific factors in psychotherapy outcome research.

In addition to the various measures already described, Paul asked both students and therapists to supply ratings of their (or their patients') improvement. These ratings are similar to the global outcome ratings used in previous psychotherapy outcome research. Paul found no differences in self-ratings among students in the three treatment groups. All students reported that they improved to the same degree regardless of the treatment they received. The discrepancy between students' self-ratings of improvement and the other measures of speech anxiety illustrated dramatically the dangers of relying on subjective reports to evaluate psychotherapy outcome. Like the researchers in the Cambridge-Sommerville study, Paul found little relationship between what subjects reported and more objective evaluations of therapeutic outcome.

In contrast to the students' self-ratings, the therapists' ratings were more in line with the other measures. Despite their professional bias toward insight therapy, therapists rated students in the desensitization condition as most improved. Although they had not used the technique prior to the study, several therapists said that in the future they would recommend desensitization to their patients. It is important to note that this favorable evaluation was confined to desensitization's effects on public-speaking anxiety. The therapists still believed that insight therapy leads to better functioning in other areas of life because it deals with underlying causes. Several therapists feared that "symptom substitution" (the appearance of a new problem) might occur in students treated only with desensitization because this treatment deals only with the symptom of public-speaking anxiety and leaves its underlying cause unresolved.

Examining his data, Paul could find no basis for this fear. The students in the desensitization group had not developed new problems. He concluded that his study had demonstrated the value of behavior therapy:

> The results of the study clearly demonstrate the superiority of treatment based on a "learning" model (modified systematic desensitization) over treatment based on the traditional "disease" model (insight-oriented psychotherapy) in the alleviation of maladaptive anxiety. Desensitization therapy produced a consistently greater reduction in the cognitive, physiological and motoric aspects of stress-engendered anxiety.[6]

While Paul's research showed the superiority of learning-based treatments, at least for public-speaking anxiety, it was even more important as an example of how careful psychotherapy research should be conducted. It demonstrated the critical importance of controlling for nonspecific factors while demonstrating once again the folly of relying on subjective global self-evaluations to gauge psychotherapeutic effectiveness.

AFTERMATH

As might be expected, Paul's study generated considerable interest. Although it was widely regarded as a landmark study, it was not without its detractors. The placebo group came in for particularly close scrutiny. Critics pointed out that drug research is usually conducted "double-blind": Neither doctors nor patients know who is receiving the real drug. In psychotherapy research, it is nearly impossible for psychotherapists to be "blind." Because they cannot help knowing when they are delivering a placebo, therapists may communicate their doubts to their patients thereby reducing their faith in the treatment. Following this logic, critics claimed that Paul's attention-placebo group was not an adequate control for the nonspecific effects of psychotherapy. It is important to be clear about the implications of this criticism. If the therapists lacked conviction, the nonspecific effects of the placebo would have been diminished. On the other hand, if the therapists could have been given more faith in the placebo, it would have been even more effective. Indeed, if we could invent a placebo treatment that did have the complete confidence of therapists, some writers claim that we might find that psychotherapy, at least the insight variety, has no specific effects whatsoever — that it is nothing but a placebo.

PLACEBOS

Virtually any type of therapy, no matter how strange, can produce positive results. Mesmer was effective with his animal magnetism and, according to *Time* magazine, at least one California therapist has cured patients using "past-lives" therapy. The magazine reported the case of a writer who had trouble finishing her books and articles. During treatment by a past-lives therapist, she had a vision of herself in the 17th century on trial as a witch. In this past life, she tried to avoid conviction by hiding an incriminating diary. Now, in her present life, she continued to "hide the book" by never finishing her work. Once this was revealed, her writer's block disappeared.

The idea behind past-lives therapy is an extension of the psychoanalytic notion that present-day problems have their origin in the past. But, instead of the problem originating in childhood, past-lives therapists look for the causes of emotional problems in previous lives when their patients were Roman guards, citizens of Atlantis, or even residents of Mars.

Time quoted an expert's evaluation of past-lives therapy as follows: "Suckers are born every minute and customers can be found for anything." While no doubt true, this does not mean that people who believe in past-lives therapy or animal magnetism or any other placebo are not helped. Placebos can be very effective as Paul's research showed.

In recent years, placebo control groups have come in for criticism from those who question the ethics of purposely exposing patients to an ineffective treatment. As a result, the placebo group has lost some of its appeal. Nevertheless, it remains the best way to ensure that a treatment has specific effects above and beyond those present in any form of "therapy."

Paul's failure to find much difference between insight therapy and the placebo lends some support to this possibility. However, his comparison of desensitization and insight therapy suggests that the behavioral approach does have its own specific effects. Paul's therapists believed in both treatments—perhaps they even favored insight therapy—yet desensitization produced clearly superior results. This superiority seems attributable only to the specific effects of desensitization.

Insight-oriented therapists were critical because Paul's students underwent only five sessions of psychotherapy. Insight therapy, they argued, requires considerably longer to work. Although this may be true, it seems hardly an argument in favor of insight therapy. Even if we concede the possibility that a longer course of insight-oriented psychotherapy might have produced as good an outcome as desensitization, desensitization would still be preferable because it is more efficient. Why spend the time and money for insight therapy if a shorter course of desensitization is just as effective? Insight-oriented therapists answer this question with the same concern voiced by Paul's therapists—the fear of symptom substitution. They claim that only insight-oriented psychotherapy, which attacks the underlying psychological cause of public-speaking anxiety, will ensure that a new symptom does not develop to take the old one's place. Paul addressed this criticism directly in a follow-up study conducted 2 years after the conclusion of his psychotherapy study. He retested the students and found that those who received systematic desensitization maintained their initial gains; they still showed less public-speaking anxiety than those in the other conditions. More important, he found no evidence for symptom substitution. On the contrary, students who received desensitization seemed to have generalized their anxiety reduction well beyond public speaking. They belonged to more clubs, went out more socially, and generally were less anxious than students who were in the other conditions.

Added to his original results, Paul's follow-up confirmed Eysenck's optimistic evaluation of learning-based therapy. Desensitization was shown to be more effective than insight-based treatment for public-speaking anxiety. This does not mean, however, that learning-based treatments are always superior. As psychologist Allen Bergin pointed out at the time, the question of whether one type of psychotherapy is more "effective" is too broad. It is like asking whether "surgery" is more effective than medical treatment. Clearly, this is a silly question. No one expects a tonsillectomy to help someone with a rash. It only makes sense to ask whether a particular operation is effective for a specific condition. The same is true for psychotherapy. Bergin urged researchers to focus on specific questions such as "*What* treatment, by *whom*, is most effective for *this* individual with *that* specific problem, and under *which* set of circumstances?"

With Paul's study as an example, psychotherapy research became increasingly sophisticated, but few researchers took up Bergin's specific advice. For example, in 1980, almost 30 years after Eysenck's first paper, psychologist Mary Lee Smith and her colleagues published a review of 475 psychotherapy outcome studies that lumped together not only heterogeneous patient groups but also different types of therapy and outcome measures. Using statistical techniques, Smith and her co-workers reported that "the evidence overwhelmingly supports the efficacy of psychotherapy." They found that the average psychotherapy patient ends up better off than 80% of those patients who were assigned to control groups. This means, of course, that 20% of control-group patients do better than the average psychotherapy patient. Nevertheless, Smith and her colleagues concluded that "psychotherapy benefits people of all ages as reliably as schooling educates them, medicine cures them or business turns a profit."

Interestingly, Smith could not find any advantage for one type of treatment over another nor did it seem to matter how long treatment lasted or how well trained the therapists were. If a new therapist is as good as an experienced one and one therapy is as good as another, one cannot help suspecting that Smith has demonstrated the powerful nonspecific effects of psychotherapy rather than the effectiveness of psychotherapy itself. At least this was the view of many writers, including Eysenck. To add to the debate, in 1983 Leslie Prioleau and her colleagues reevaluated the literature reviewed earlier by Smith and her co-workers looking only at studies with placebo control groups and excluding studies of behavior therapy that they believed to be fundamentally "different" from traditional, insight-based therapy. They found only 32 methodologically acceptable studies. These showed that traditional nonbehavioral psychotherapy was no more effective than a placebo. The researchers concluded that

> thirty years after Eysenck . . . first raised the issue of the effectiveness of psychotherapy . . . and after about 500 outcome studies have been reviewed — we are still not aware of a single convincing demonstration that the benefits of psychotherapy exceed those of placebos for real patients.[7]

Theirs is unlikely to be the end of the matter, however. The journal that published their article followed it with 23 commentaries by leading experts on psychotherapy research. The majority disagreed with the conclusion that traditional psychotherapy is no more effective than a placebo; all called for more research. As this is precisely the same call issued by Eysenck in 1952, it seems fitting to let him have the last word (at least for now):

> Psychoanalysts and psychotherapists generally assert that their methods cure psychoneurotic disorders. . . . Clearly, therefore, it is on them that the onus of proof must rest. They must define clearly and unambiguously what is meant by neurotic disorder and what is meant by cure; they must put forward methods of testing the effects of treatment which are not dependent on the subjective evaluation of the therapist; and they must demonstrate that their methods give results which are clearly superior to any alternative methods, such as those of behaviour therapy, or of spontaneous remission. . . . Until [these things] have all been done I find it very difficult to see how any doubt can be thrown on my conclusion that published research has failed to support the claims made [for the effectiveness of psychotherapy].[8]

Further Reading

Eysenck, H. J. (1952). The effects of psychotherapy: An evaluation. *Journal of Consulting and Clinical Psychology, 16,* 319–324.

Eysenck, H. J. (1990). *Rebel with a cause.* London: W. H. Allen.

Paul, G. L. (1966). *Insight vs. Desensitization in psychotherapy.* Stanford, CA: Stanford University Press.

Notes

1. Eysenck, H. J. (1952). The effects of psychotherapy: An evaluation. *Journal of Consulting and Clinical Psychology, 16,* 321.

2. Eysenck, H. J. (1960). The effects of psychotherapy. In H. J. Eysenck (Ed.), *Handbook of abnormal psychology.* London: Pitman. P. 100.

3. Eysenck, H. J. (1966). *The effects of psychotherapy.* New York: International Science Press. P. 40.

4. Readers may also encounter the term *behavior modification* used to refer to learning-based treatments. For the present exposition, the terms may be considered interchangeable.

5. Yates, A. J. (1970). *Behavior therapy.* New York: Wiley. P. 12.

6. Paul, G. L. (1966). *Insight vs. desensitization in psychotherapy.* Stanford, CA: Stanford University Press. P. 71.

7. Prioleau, L., Murdock, M., & Brody, N. (1983). An analysis of psychotherapy versus placebo studies. *Behavioral and Brain Sciences, 6,* 284.

8. Eysenck, H. J. (1966). The outcome problem in psychotherapy: A reply. In A. P. Goldstein & S. J. Dean (Eds.), *The investigation of psychotherapy.* New York: Wiley. P. 158.

REFERENCES

Adams, P. R., & Adams, J. R. (1984). Mount Saint Helen's ashfall: Evidence for a disaster stress reaction. *American Psychologist, 39,* 252–260.

Allderidge, P. (1979). Hospitals, madhouses, and asylums: Cycles in the care of the insane. *British Journal of Psychiatry, 134,* 321–334.

American Psychiatric Association (1987). *Diagnostic and statistical manual of mental disorders* (3rd ed.-rev.). Washington, DC: American Psychiatric Association.

Barlow, D. H. (1986). Causes of sexual dysfunction: The role of anxiety and cognitive interference. *Journal of Consulting and Clinical Psychology, 54,* 140–148.

Baron-Cohen, S. (1988). The autistic child's "theory of mind": A case of specific developmental delay. *Journal of Child Psychology and Psychiatry, 30,* 285–287.

Basedow, H. (1925). *The Australian Aboriginal.* Adelaide: F. W. Fleece.

Beck, A. T. (1973). *The diagnosis and management of depression.* Philadelphia: University of Pennsylvania Press.

Beck, A. T., Ward, C. H., Mendelson, M., Mock, J., & Erbaugh, J. (1961). An inventory for measuring depression. *Archives of General Psychiatry, 4,* 561–571.

Becker, R. E., Heimberg, R. G., & Bellack, A. S. (1987). *Social skills training for depression.* Elmsford, NY: Pergamon Press.

Beers, C. (1908). *A mind that found itself.* New York: Longmans, Green.

Bettelheim, B. (1967). *The empty fortress.* New York: Free Press.

Bleuler, E. (1950). *Dementia praecox or the group of schizophrenias* (J. Zinkin, Trans.). New York: International Universities Press.

Bliss, J., Cohen, D. J., & Freedman, D. X. (1980). Sensory experiences of Gilles de la Tourette Syndrome. *Archives of General Psychiatry, 37,* 1343–1347.

Bowlby, J. (1951). *Maternal care and mental health.* Geneva: World Health Organization.

Bowlby, J. (1984). *Attachment* (new ed.) Harmondsworth: Penguin.

Breuer, J., & Freud, S. (1956). *Studies on hysteria* (J. Strachey & A. Strachey, Trans.). London: Hogarth Press. (Original work published 1895)

Brill, A. A. (1939). In memorium: Eugen Bleuler. *American Journal of Psychiatry, 96,* 513–516.

Brown, R. (1965). *Social psychology.* New York: Free Press.

Bruch, H. (1978). *The golden cage: The enigma of anorexia nervosa.* Cambridge, MA: Harvard University Press.

Cannon, W. B. (1927). The James-Lange theory of emotion. *American Journal of Psychology, 39,* 106–124.

Cannon, W. B. (1939). *The wisdom of the body.* New York: Norton.

Cannon, W. B. (1942). Voodoo death. *American Anthropologist, 44,* 169–181.

Christenson, C. (1968). Alfred Kinsey. In D. C. Sills (Ed.), *International encyclopedia of the social sciences* (Vol. 8, pp. 389–390). New York: Macmillan.

Cleckley, H. (1968). Psychopathic personality. In D. C. Sills (Ed.), *International encyclopedia of the social sciences* (Vol. 13, pp. 113–120). New York: Macmillan.

Cleckley, H. M. (1976). *The mask of sanity.* St. Louis: C. V. Mosby.

Coe, C. L., Rosenberg, L. T., Fischer, M., & Levine, S. (1987). Psychological factors capable of preventing the inhibition of antibody responses in separated infant monkeys. *Child Development, 58*(6), 1420–1430.

Cohen, D. (1977). *Psychologists on psychology.* London: Routledge & Kegan Paul.

Cohen, D. (1978). Referential communication deficit in schizophrenia. In S. Schwartz (Ed.), *Language and cognition in schizophrenia* (pp. 1–34). Hillsdale, NJ: Erlbaum.

Cohen, R. A. (1975). Manic-depressive illness. In A. M. Freedman, H. I. Kaplan, & B. J. Sadock (Eds.), *Comprehensive textbook of psychiatry* (Vol. 2, pp. 1012–1024). Baltimore: Williams and Wilkins.

Coleman, J. C., Butcher, J. N., & Carson, R. C. (1980). *Abnormal psychology and modern life* (6th ed.). Glenview, IL: Scott, Foresman.

Custance, J. (1952). *Wisdom, madness and folly.* New York: Farrar, Straus and Cudahay.

Da Costa, J. (1864). *Medical diagnosis with specific reference to practical medicine.* Philadelphia: Lippincott.

Darwin, C. (1965). *The expression of emotion in man and animals.* Chicago: University of Chicago Press.

Dawes, R. (1988). *Rational choice in an uncertain world.* Orlando, FL: Harcourt, Brace, Jovanovich.

Drinker, C. K. (1945). Walter Bradford Cannon. *Science, 102,* 470–472.

Eaton, W. W. (1986). *The sociology of mental disorders* (2nd ed.). New York: Praeger.

Eberhardy, F. W. (1967). The view from the "couch." *Journal of Child Psychology and Psychiatry, 8,* 257–263.

Eisenberg, J. (1981). In memoriam. *American Journal of Psychiatry, 138,* 1122–1125.

Ellenberger, H. (1954). The life and work of Hermann Rorschach (1884–1922). *Bulletin of the Menninger Clinic, 18,* 173–219.

Eysenck, H. J. (1952). The effects of psychotherapy: An evaluation. *Journal of Consulting and Clinical Psychology, 16,* 319–324.

Eysenck, H. J. (1960). The effects of psychotherapy. In H. J. Eysenck (Ed.), *Handbook of abnormal psychology* (pp. 697–725). London: Pitman.

Eysenck, H. J. (1966). *The effects of psychotherapy.* New York: International Science Press.

Eysenck, H. J. (1966). The outcome problem in psychotherapy: A reply. In A. P. Goldstein & S. J. Dean (Eds.), *The investigation of psychotherapy* (p. 158). New York: Wiley.

Eysenck, H. J. (1990). *Rebel with a cause.* London: W. H. Allen.

Eysenck, H. J., Arnold, W., & Meili, R. (1972). *Encyclopedia of psychology.* New York: Herder & Herder.

Faris, R. E. L., & Dunham, H. W. (1939). *Mental disorders in urban areas.* Chicago: University of Chicago Press.

Fleischman, P. R. (1973). Psychiatric diagnosis. *Science, 180,* 356.

Freud, E., Freud, L., & Grubrich-Simitis, I. (1978). *Sigmund Freud: His life in pictures and words* (C. Trollope, Trans.). Brisbane: University of Queensland Press.

Freud, S. (1909). Analysis of a phobia in a five-year-old boy. In E. Jones (Ed.) (1959), *Sigmund Freud: Collected papers* (Vol. 3, pp. 149–295). New York: Basic Books.

Freud, S. (1955). Lines of advance in psychoanalytic therapy. In *The complete psychological works of Sigmund Freud* (J. Strachey, Trans.). London: Hogarth Press. (Original work published 1918.)

Friedhoff, A. J., & Chase, T. N. (Eds.) (1982). *Gilles de la Tourette Syndrome.* New York: Raven Press.

Friedman, H. S., Thoreson, C. E., Gill, J. J., Ulmer, D., Powell, L. H., Price, V. A., Brown, B., Thompson, L., Rabin, D. D., Breall, W. S., Bourg, E., Levy, R., & Dixon, T. (1986). Alteration of type A behavior and its effect on cardiac recurrences in post myocardial infarction patients: Summary results of the recurrent coronary prevention project. *American Heart Journal, 112,* 653–665.

Frith, U. (1989). *Autism: Explaining the enigma.* Oxford: Pergamon.

Garber, J., & Seligman, M. E. P. (Eds.) (1980). *Human helplessness: Theory and applications.* New York: Academic Press.

Garfinkel, P. E., & Garner, D. M. (1982). *Anorexia nervosa: A multidimensional perspective.* New York: Brunner/Mazel.

Gibson, H. B. (1981). *Eysenck: The man and his work.* London: Dufour.

Gleitman, H. (1981). *Psychology.* New York: Norton.

Goetz, C. J., & Klawans, H. L. (1982). Gilles de la Tourette on Tourette Syndrome. In A. J. Friedhoff & T. N. Chase (Eds.), *Gilles de la Tourette Syndrome* (pp. 1–17). New York: Raven Press.

Goldberg, L. R. (1970). Man versus model of man: A rationale, plus some evidence, for a method of improving on clinical inferences. *Psychological Bulletin, 73,* 423–432.

Goldstein, M. J., Baker, B. L., & Jamison, K. R. (1986). *Abnormal psychology: Experiences, origins and interventions* (2nd ed.). Boston: Little, Brown.

Gottesman, I. I., & Shields, J. (1972). *Schizophrenia and genetics: A twin study vantage point.* New York: Academic Press.

Gray, J. (1971). *The psychology of fear and stress.* London: Weidenfield and Nicholson.

Gregory, M. (1939). *Psychotherapy scientific and religious.* London: Macmillan.

Gull, W. W. (1874). Anorexia nervosa. *Transactions of the Clinical Society of London, 7,* 22–27.

Hackett, T. P., Rosenbaum, J. F., & Chasem, N. H. (1985). Cardiovascular disorders. In H. I. Kaplan & B. J. Sadock (Eds.), *Comprehensive textbook of psychiatry* (Vol. II, 4th ed., pp. 1148–1158). Baltimore: Williams and Wilkins.

Hare, R. D. (1970). *Psychopathy: Theory and research.* New York: Wiley.

Hare, R. D. (1972). Psychopathy. In H. J. Eysenck, W. Arnold, & R. Meili, (Eds.), *Encyclopedia of psychology* (Vol. 3, pp. 71–75). New York: Herder and Herder.

Hearnshaw, L. S. (1987). *The shaping of modern psychology.* London: Routledge & Kegan Paul.

Hollingshead, A. B., & Redlich, F. C. (1958). *Social class and mental illness: A community study.* New York: Wiley.

Holmes, T. H., & Rahe, R. H. (1967). The Social Readjustment Rating Scale. *Journal of Psychosomatic Research, 11,* 213–218.

Howells, J. G., & Osborn, M. L. (1984). *A reference companion to the history of abnormal psychology.* Westport, CT: Greenwood Press.

Jones, K. (1972). *A history of the mental health services.* London: Routledge & Kegal Paul.

Kahn, E. (1945). Emil Kraepelin. *American Journal of Psychiatry, 113,* 289–294.

Kanner, L. (1943). Autistic disturbances of affective contact. *Nervous Child, 2,* 217–250.

Kanner, L. (1972). *Child psychiatry.* Springfield, IL: Charles C. Thomas.

Kaplan, H. I. (1985). Psychological factors affecting physical conditions (psychosomatic disorders). In H. I. Kaplan & B. J. Sadock (Eds.), *Comprehensive textbook of psychiatry* (Vol. II, 4th ed., pp. 1106–1120). Baltimore: Williams and Wilkins.

Kaplan, H. I. (1985). History of psychosomatic medicine. In H. I. Kaplan & B. J. Sadock (Eds.), *Comprehensive textbook of psychiatry* (Vol. II, 4th ed.). Baltimore: Williams and Wilkins.

Kety, S. S., Rosenthal, D., Wender, P. H., & Schulsinger, F. (1968). The types and prevalence of mental illness in the biological and adoptive families of adopted schizophrenics. In D. Rosenthal & S. S. Kety (Eds.), *The transmission of schizophrenia*. New York: Pergamon Press.

Kinsey, A. C., Pomeroy, W. B., & Martin, C. E. (1948). *Sexual behavior in the human male*. Philadelphia: Saunders.

Kinsey, A. C., Pomeroy, W. B., Martin, C. E., & Gebhard, P. H. (1953). *Sexual behavior in the human female*. Philadelphia: Saunders.

Kraepelin, E. (1919). *Dementia praecox and paraphrenia* (R. M. Barclay, Trans.). Edinburgh: E. & S. Livingstone.

Kraepelin, E. (1919). *One hundred years of psychiatry*. London: Peter Owen.

Krafft-Ebing, R. von. (1965). *Psychopathia sexualis: A medico-forensic study* (H. E. Wedeck, Trans.). New York: G. P. Putnam and Sons.

Langmeier, J., & Matejcek, Z. (1975). *Psychological deprivation in childhood* (3rd ed.). Brisbane: University of Queensland Press.

Lippert, W. W., & Senter, R. J. (1966). Electrodermal responses in the sociopath. *Psychonomic Science, 4,* 25–26.

Lykken, D. T. (1981). *A tremor in the blood: Uses and abuses of the lie detector*. New York: McGraw-Hill.

Lykken, D. T. (1984). Psychopathic personality. In R. J. Corsini (Ed.), *Encyclopedia of psychology* (Vol. 3, pp. 165–167). New York: Wiley.

Maas, H. S. (1963). *The young adult adjustment of twenty wartime residential nursery children*. New York: Child Welfare League of America.

Madsen, K. B. (1988). *A history of psychology in metascientific perspective*. Amsterdam: North-Holland.

Mailer, N. (1979). *The executioner's song*. Boston: Little, Brown.

Malmo, R. B. (1986). Obituary. Hans Hugo Seyle (1907–1982). *American Psychologist, 41,* 92–93.

Maranon, G. (1924). Contribution à l'eacutetude de l'action emotive de l'adrenaline [The precise action of adrenaline on the emotions]. *Revue Franccidillaise d'endicrinologie, 2,* 301–325.

Masters, W. H., & Johnson, V. E. (1967). *Human sexual response*. Boston: Little, Brown.

Masters, W. H., & Johnson, V. E. (1970). *Human sexual inadequacy*. Boston: Little, Brown.

Mathews, K. A. (1988). Coronary heart disease and type A behaviors. *Psychological Bulletin, 104,* 373–380.

Mednick, S. A. (1966). A longitudinal study of children with a high risk for schizophrenia. *Mental Hygiene, 50,* 522–535.

Mednick, S. A., Parnas, J., & Schulsinger, F. (1987). The Copenhagen high-risk project, 1962–1986. *Schizophrenia Bulletin, 13,* 485–495.

Mednick, S. A., Venables, P. H., Schulsinger, F., Dalasi, C., & Van Dusen, K. (1984). A controlled study of primary prevention: The Mauritius project. In N. F. Watt, E. J. Anthony, L. C. Wynne, & J. E. Rolf (Eds.), *Children at risk for schizophrenia: A longitudinal perspective*. Cambridge, UK: Cambridge University Press.

Meehl, P. E. (1954). *Clinical versus statistical prediction*. Minneapolis: University of Minnesota Press.

Meehl, P. E. (1986). Causes and effects of my disturbing little book. *Journal of Personality Assessment, 50,* 370–375.

Money, J., & Musaph, H. (1977). *Handbook of sexology*. Amsterdam: Elsevier/North Holland.

Murray, T. J. (1982). Dr. Samuel Johnson's abnormal movements. In A. J. Friedhoff & T. N. Chase (Eds.), *Gilles de la Tourette Syndrome* (pp. 25–30). New York: Raven Press.

Neale, J. M., & Oltmanns, T. F. (1980). *Schizophrenia*. New York: Wiley.

Oltmanns, T. F., Neale, J. M., & Davison, G. C. (1991). *Case studies in abnormal psychology* (3rd ed.). New York: Wiley.

Page, J. D. (1975). *Psychopathology: The science of understanding deviance* (2nd ed.). Chicago: Aldine.

Paul, G. L. (1966). *Insight vs. desensitization in psychotherapy*. Stanford, CA: Stanford University Press.

People. (1977, October 3). *Time,* p. 53.

Peterson, D. (1982). *A mad people's history of madness*. Pittsburgh: University of Pittsburgh Press.

Pirke, K. M., & Ploog, D. (Eds.) (1984). *The psychobiology of anorexia nervosa*. Berlin: Springer-Verlag.

Pomeroy, W. B. (1972). *Dr. Kinsey and the Institute for Sex Research*. London: Thomas Nelson and Sons.

Prichard, J. C. (1837). *Treatise on insanity and other disorders affecting the mind*. Philadelphia: Haswell, Barrington & Haswell.

Prioleau, L., Murdock, M., & Brody, N. (1983). An analysis of psychotherapy versus placebo studies. *Behavioral and Brain Sciences, 6,* 284.

Rachman, S. (1971). *Effects of psychotherapy*. Oxford: Pergamon.

Ribble, M. A. (1943). *The rights of infants*. New York: Columbia University Press.

Rimland, B. (1964). *Infantile autism: The syndrome and its implications for a neural theory of behavior.* New York: Appleton-Century-Crofts.

Robak, A. A. (1961). *History of psychology and psychiatry.* New York: Citadel Press.

Robins, L. N. (1966). *Deviant children grow up.* Baltimore: Williams and Wilkins.

Rochester, S., & Martin, J. R. (1979). *Crazy talk: A study of the discourse of schizophrenic speakers.* New York: Plenum.

Rorschach, H. (1942). Psychodiagnostics (P. Lemkau & B. Kroneberg, Trans.). New York: Grune and Stratton. (Original work published 1921)

Rosenhan, D. L. (1973). On being sane in insane places. *Science, 179,* 250–258.

Rosenhan, D., & Seligman, M. E. P. (1984). *Abnormal psychology.* New York: Norton.

Rosenman, R. H. (1986). Current and past history of Type A behavior pattern. In T. H. Schmidt, T. M. Dembroski, & C. Blümchen (Eds.), *Biological and psychological factors in cardiovascular disease* (pp. 15–40). Berlin: Springer-Verlag.

Rosenman, R. H., Brand, R. J., Jenkins, C. D., Friedman, R., Straus, R., & Wurm, M. (1975). Coronary heart disease in the Western Collaborative Group study. *Journal of the American Medical Association, 233,* 872–877.

Rosenthal, D., & Kety, S. (Eds.) (1968). *The transmission of schizophrenia.* Oxford: Pergamon.

Roth, M., & Kroll, J. (1986). *The reality of mental illness.* Cambridge, UK: Cambridge University Press.

Rutter, M. (1972). *Maternal deprivation.* Harmondsworth: Penguin.

Rutter, M. (Ed.) (1988). *Studies of psychosocial risk: The power of longitudinal data.* Cambridge, UK: Cambridge University Press.

Sarton, G. A. L. (1954). *Galen of Pergamon.* Lawrence: University of Kansas Press.

Schachter, S., & Latané, B. (1964). Crime, cognition and the autonomic nervous system. In D. Levine (Ed.), *Nebraska symposium on motivation* (Vol. 12, pp. 221–273). Lincoln: University of Nebraska Press.

Schachter, S., & Singer, J. (1962). Cognitive, social and psychological determinants of emotional state. *Psychological Review, 69,* 379–399.

Schmauk, F. (1970). Punishment, arousal and avoidance learning in sociopaths. *Journal of Abnormal Psychology, 76,* 443–453.

Schneidman, E. S. (1975). Suicide. In A. M. Freedman, H. Kaplan, & B. J. Sadock (Eds.), *Comprehensive textbook of psychiatry* (Vol. II, 4th ed., pp. 1774–1785). Baltimore: Williams and Wilkins.

Schopler, E., Chess, S., & Eisenberg, L. (1981). Our memorial to Leo Kanner. *Journal of Autism and Developmental Disorders, 11,* 257–269.

Schopler, E., & Mesibov, G. B. (1987). *Neurobiological issues in autism.* New York: Plenum Press.

Schulsinger, F. (1972). Psychopathy: Heredity and environment. *International Journal of Mental Health, 1,* 190–206.

Schulsinger, F. (1977). Psychopathy, heredity and environment. In S. A. Mednick & K. O. Christiansen (Eds.), *Biosocial bases of criminal behavior* (pp. 109–126). New York: Gardner Press.

Schwartz, S., & Griffin, T. (1986). *Medical thinking: The psychology of medical judgement and decision making.* New York: Springer.

Schwartz, S., & Johnson, J. H. (1985). *Psychopathology of childhood* (2nd ed.). New York: Pergamon Press.

Seligman, M. E. P. (1975). *Helplessness: On depression, development and death.* San Francisco: W. H. Freeman.

Seligman, M. E. P., Abramson, L. V., Semmel, A., & Von Baeyer, C. (1979). Depressive attributional style. *Journal of Abnormal Psychology, 88,* 242–247.

Selye, H. (1936). A syndrome produced by diverse noxious agents. *Nature, 138,* 32.

Selye, H. (1950). *The physiology and pathology of exposure to stress: A treatise on the concept of the general adaptation syndrome and the diseases of adaptation.* Montreal: Acta.

Selye, H. (1956). *The stress of life.* New York: McGraw-Hill.

Selye, H. (1983). Introduction. In C. L. Cooper (Ed.), *Stress research issues for the eighties* (pp. 1–8). Ann Arbor, MI: University Microfilms International.

Shapiro, A. K., Shapiro, E. S., Bruun, R. D., & Sweet, R. D. (Eds.) (1978). *Gilles de la Tourette Syndrome.* New York: Raven Press.

Spitz, R. (1945). Hospitalism: An inquiry into the genesis of psychiatric conditions in early childhood. *Psychoanalytic Study of the Child, 1,* 53–74.

Spitz, R. (1946). Hospitalism: A follow-up report. *Psychoanalytic Study of the Child, 2,* 113–117.

Spitz, R. (1965). *The first year of life.* New York: International Universities Press.

Tavris, C., & Offir, C. (1977). *The longest war: Sex differences in perspective.* New York: Harcourt, Brace, Jovanovich.

Taylor, S. E. (1990). Health psychology: The science and the field. *American Psychologist, 45,* 40–50.

Thomas, L. (1979). *The Medusa and the snail.* New York: Viking Press.

Tversky, A., & Kahneman, D. (1983). Extensional versus intuitive reasoning: The conjunction fallacy in probability judgment. *Psychological Bulletin, 90,* 293–315.

Watson, J. B. (1950). *Behaviorism.* New York: Norton.

Watson, J. B., & Rayner, R. (1920). Conditioned emotional reactions. *Journal of Experimental Psychology, 3,* 1–14.

Watt, N. F., Anthony, E. J., Wynne, L. C., & Rolf, J. E. (Eds.) (1984). *Children at risk for schizophrenia: A longi-*

tudinal perspective. Cambridge, UK: Cambridge University Press.

Wehr, T. A., & Rosenthal, N. E. (1989). Seasonality and affective illness. *American Journal of Psychiatry, 146,* 829–839.

Weiss, J. M. (1977). Psychological and behavioral influences on gastrointestinal lesions in animal models. In J. D. Maser & M. E. P. Seligman (Eds.), *Psychopathology: Experimental models* (pp. 232–269). San Francisco: W. H. Freeman.

Wing, L. (1976). *Early childhood autism* (2nd ed.). Oxford: Pergamon Press.

Witkin, H. S., Mednick, S. A., Schulsinger, F., Bakkeström, E., Christiansen, K. O., Goodenough, D. R., Hirschhorn, K., Lundsteen, C., Owen, D. R., Philip, J., Rubin, D. B., & Stocking, M. (1976). XYY and XXY men: Criminality and aggression. *Science, 193,* 547–555.

Wolfgang, M. E. (1968). Cesare Lombroso. In D. C. Sills (Ed.), *International encyclopedia of the social sciences* (Vol. 9, pp. 471–472). New York: Macmillan.

Yates, A. J. (1970). *Behavior therapy.* New York: Wiley.

Zusne, L. (1975). *Names in the history of psychology: A biographical sourcebook.* New York: Wiley.

CREDITS

Text

Page 69 Excerpts from *The Collected Papers of Sigmund Freud*, Volume 3. Authorized translation under the supervision of Alix and James Strachey, published by Basic Books Inc. by arrangement with Hogarth Press Ltd. and the Insitute of Psycho-Analysis, London. Reprinted by permission of Basic Books, a division of HarperCollins, Publishers.

Page 168 "Stanley" from *The Mask of Sanity* by Hervey M. Cleckley, reprinted by permission of Mrs. Emily S. Cleckley.

Photographs

Page 2 © The Mansell Collection Limited.

Pages 7, 22, 67, 108, 113, 133 © The Bettmann Archive.

Pages 24, 48, 65, 74, 213 © The Granger Collection.

Pages 31, 76 From *Psychology*, 2nd ed., by H. Gleitman. W. W. Norton & Co.

Page 34 Courtesy Dr. Paul Meehl.

Page 56 Courtesy Dr. David Rosenhan.

Page 70 From *Sigmund Freud: Collected Papers.* Translated by James Strachey. Published by arrangement with Hogarth Press Ltd. and The Institute of Psycho-Analysis, London. Reprinted by permission of Basic Books, Inc., Publishers, New York.

Page 80 From *The First Year of Life,* R. Spitz, 1965, International Universities Press.

Page 85 Courtesy of The Alan Mason Cheney Medical Archives of The Johns Hopkins Medical Institutions.

Page 89 From *Autism: Explaining the Enigma* by Eta Frith, Basil Blackwell Ltd.

Page 90 Courtesy Sandra Irvine.

Page 91 From *Nadia: A Case of Extraordinary Drawing Ability in an Autistic Child* by L. Selfe, 1977, Academic Press, Inc.

Page 100 From *Gilles de la Tourette Syndrome* by A. J. Shapiro, 1978, Raven Press. (Courtesy A. Lucas)

Page 116 From *Abnormal Psychology: Experiences, Origins, and Interventions,* 2nd ed. by Michael J. Goldstein, et al. Copyright © 1986 by Michael J. Goldstein, Bruce L. Baker, and Kay R. Jamison. Reprinted by permission of HarperCollins Publishers.

Pages 121, 123 Reprinted with permission from *The Transmission of Schizophrenia* by D. Rosenthal and S. Kety. Copyright © 1968 Pergamon Press PLC.

Page 125 From *Children at Risk for Schizophrenia* by N. F. Watt et al. by permission of Cambridge University Press, England.

Page 129 From *Manic Depressive Illness* by E. A. Wolpert, 1977, International Universities Press.

Pages 135, 187, 222 © AP/Wide World Photos.

Pages 138, 206, 207 From *Pictorial History of Psychology and Psychiatry* by A. A. Roback and T. Kierman, by permission of Philosophical Library.

Page 153 From *The Physiology and Pathology of Exposure to Stress* by H. Selye, Acta Press.

Page 154 From *Psychopathology: Experimental Models*, by Martin E. P. Seligman and Jack D. Maser. Copyright © 1977 by Martin E. P. Seligman and Jack Maser. Reprinted by permission of W. H. Freeman and Company.

Page 156 From *American Psychologist, 39,* 257, P. R. Adams and G. R. Adams. Copyright 1984 by the American Psychological Association. Reprinted by permission.

Page 167 Courtesy Mrs. Emily S. Cleckley.

Page 176 From *Abnormal Psychology,* 3d ed., by G. C. Davison and J. Neale. Copyright © 1982 G. C. Davison and J. Neale. Reprinted by permission of John Wiley & Sons, Inc.

Page 180 © Mary Evans Picture Library.

Page 181 © Mary Evans/Sigmund Freud Copyrights/ Sulloway.

Page 224 Courtesy Dr. Hans Eysenck.

Tables

Page 28 Adapted from H. Rorschach, *Psychodiagnostics,* Grune and Stratton.

Page 42 From *Abnormal Psychology and Modern Life,* 6 ed. by James C. Coleman, James N. Butcher, and Robert C. Carson. Copyright © 1980, 1976 by Scott, Foresman and Company. Reprinted by permission of HarperCollins Publishers.

Pages 53, 54, 94, 97, 101, 115, 128, 130, 166 *Diagnostic and Statistical Manual of Mental Disorders,* Third Edition-Revised, Washington, DC, American Psychiatric Association, 1967.

Page 157 Adapted from T. H. Holmes and R. H. Rahe, The social readjustment rating scale, *Journal of Psychosomatic Research, 11.*

Page 190 Adapted from A. C. Kinsey et al., *Sexual Behavior in the Human Male,* W. B. Saunders Company.

Page 191 Adapted from A. C. Kinsey et al., *Sexual Behavior in the Human Female,* W. B. Saunders Company.

Page 228 Adapted from H. Eysenck, The effects of psychotherapy, *The Journal of Consulting and Clinical Psychology, 16.*

NAME INDEX

SUBJECT INDEX